The Minutemen

THE
MINUTEMEN

J. Harry Jones, Jr.

1968   DOUBLEDAY & COMPANY, INC., GARDEN CITY, NEW YORK

Library of Congress Catalog Card Number 68–17786
Copyright © 1968 by J. Harry Jones, Jr.
All Rights Reserved
Printed in the United States of America
First Edition

To Jo

PROLOGUE

On display in the front of the basement meeting room of the town hall in little Shiloh, Illinois, were several hand grenades and small arms, an impressive array of M-1 rifles, an automatic M-4 rifle, two Browning automatic rifles, a Browning submachine gun, a 20 mm. antitank gun, a 75 mm. recoilless rifle and a 60 mm. mortar.

Nearly two dozen persons from Missouri, Indiana and other parts of Illinois had driven to Shiloh that crisp autumn afternoon of October 21, 1961, a Saturday, and parked their cars and pick-up trucks near the community's new town hall. They then proceeded to the stairwell that led to the hall's basement where they caught their first glimpse of the weapons display. Few were astonished at what they saw, for they had traveled to Shiloh to learn how to fight a guerrilla war after the Communists, either by invasion or internal subversion, take over the United States.

In charge of the meeting were Robert Bolivar DePugh, a deceptively ordinary appearing man in his late thirties, president of a little veterinary drug firm in Norborne, Missouri, and Rich Lauchli, a big, friendly mechanic and gun buff from nearby Collinsville, Illinois.

Soon the visitors were seated and ready for their lecture on guerrilla warfare.

It is difficult to estimate how much anyone learned about the subject, or about the attack for which they were preparing, because the meeting suffered from a variety of distractions. The newsmen who were in the audience were, certainly, a diverting influence. But the deputy sheriffs, local township supervisor and police magistrate who eventually made their presence known created the most problems. They, in fact, broke up the meeting before its scheduled conclusion by arresting Lauchli on a charge of possession of illegal weapons.

"Arms Seizure Jolts a Group" was one of the headlines the incident prompted, once the Associated Press had taken notice of Shiloh's visitors.

Some of the group went home that evening. But about a dozen—

including DePugh, his wife and Lauchli—remained in the area overnight.

The fields in that part of southern Illinois were cold and damp the following morning and fog hung close to the ground. Those who had remained Saturday night gathered before dawn at Lauchli's Collinsville home. They dressed themselves in camouflage suits or Army fatigues, donned battle helmets, slung M-1 rifles over their shoulders and boarded an open truck and jeep that were waiting for them outside.

Of the twelve men and one woman in the group that morning, all but the DePughs and Lauchli managed to keep themselves anonymous. In revealing his identity to newsmen, DePugh said he was national coordinator of something called "The Minutemen." And Lauchli said he was regional coordinator of the same organization, for Illinois and eastern Missouri.

The truck and jeep took them to a farm outside Collinsville where DePugh and Lauchli put the others through their paces in a strenuous two-hour field exercise in guerrilla warfare. They dashed from tree to bush to a narrow ravine, then up a hill in an advance on an imaginary enemy outpost. They maneuvered themselves across a field behind cover of smoke screens laid down by smoke grenades. They were shown how to ford a stream and conceal themselves by intelligent use of the terrain. With others watching dutifully, Lauchli, who had brought with him a 60 mm. mortar and 57 mm. recoilless rifle, lobbed several dummy mortar shells from atop a hill. Somehow no one suffered even a scratch. By nine o'clock in the morning they were through and the reporters who had been invited along had themselves yet another story.

Something new had appeared on the American political scene. Perhaps it was significant. The newsmen, at that point, really couldn't tell. But it was unusual. The "Minutemen"! It seemed wild. It was a new slant on anti-Communism. Weapons on display. One man arrested. And then guerrilla warfare field maneuvers in fog-shrouded southern Illinois.

"We don't want to influence anyone politically and we're not radicals," this soft-spoken Missourian, DePugh, had told them. "We're just loyal American citizens who are tired of being pushed around by the Communists and who want to do something to stem the tide of their advance. We hope that we never have to use the weapons but we're afraid the time will come when we will be forced to stand up and fight."

Calm, articulate, pleasant appearing. Odd ideas, certainly. But entirely quotable under the circumstances.

"But how big is your organization?" someone apparently asked. "Have you been doing things like this for long?"

Exercises similar to the one held at Shiloh already had been held secretly in San Antonio, Omaha, Philadelphia, Columbus, Kansas City, and Newark, DePugh told them. As for membership in the Minutemen—why, about 25,000, said the national coordinator.

Who was to disprove him at that point? And so his claims were quoted. Some readers scoffed. Some wondered. Some probably believed. A few years later DePugh was to acknowledge that at that time the Minutemen did not have even 600 members—and that, probably, was an exaggeration too. But who knew this in 1961?

It had been an ingeniously simple but eminently successful publicity stunt. Before that weekend, most Americans had known the Minutemen only as something in their American history textbooks, a group of patriots who had distinguished themselves near the start of the Revolutionary War against the British.

By the following Monday morning, newspaper readers across the country knew them as a mysterious organization of the twentieth century, a group whose self-proclaimed leader claimed for it a large national following.

Not only had the wire services nibbled DePugh's bait, but *Time* and *Newsweek* also were intrigued. *Newsweek*, in a cover story about the Far Right the following December, introduced the new organization with ". . . on the fringe of lunacy, the gun-toting Minutemen, arming against a Russian invasion."

Indeed, to many they did seem on the fringe of lunacy. Who in his right mind, many laughed, could actually think this country was in danger of invasion by the Russians, the Chinese or anyone else? But DePugh's timing—whether intentional or not—had been excellent. The John Birch Society, of which he was a member at the time, had been criticized into prominence early that same year and other similarly alarmed organizations were forming or reviving at the radical or ultra-conservative extreme of the political spectrum. By fall of 1961, the new Far Right had become the subject of wide discussion nationally. *Newsweek's* cover story was but one indication of the new concern.

There were many reasons for this, not all of which I can even pretend to understand. Some seem obvious. We had not really felt secure since losing exclusive control of nuclear weapons. The Korean War had been a disquieting experience for we were used to vanquishing all our foes in war. It was difficult for even the most eloquent of partisan apologists to explain away very convincingly how so many nations—especially China—had been allowed to fall under Communist rule after our glorious World War II victories. We had been so all-powerful then, and everyone else had been on their knees trying to recover from the devastation of the war. Had this growth of Communism all around us been the result of inevitable fate? Honest miscalculations by our leaders? Or could it be, some began to whisper, that some of our leaders had been guilty of treason?

By 1961, John F. Kennedy, a young, relatively inexperienced, liberal Democrat, had won the presidency by a perilously narrow margin to replace the older, more comfortable Republican in the White House. The Berlin wall went up that year. The Bay of Pigs invasion had failed miserably. We were becoming more jittery over the prospects of nuclear war than we had been in several years—remember all the bomb-shelter talk at that time?

McCarthyism was not dead. It had simply lain dormant for a few years, waiting. The fall of Cuba to Castro and the Cuban revolutionary's subsequent confirmation of the fact that he was indeed a Communist had a devastating effect on many who already were leaning toward the right. So many people had said Castro was not a Communist, and now it was clear he was. How many others were there like him, abroad and inside the United States? And Cuba was so close to home. Just ninety miles from our sacred shores. Whatever happened to the Monroe Doctrine? Where will this all end?

Simultaneously, the civil rights movement was tugging more and more on the consciences and prejudices of the nation. Every time a Communist tried to involve himself in it, there was someone else ready to insist this was proof that the entire struggle for equal rights for Negroes was being run by Moscow. It was so much easier calling yourself anti-Communist than racially prejudiced. To those who saw conspiracies all about them, this theory fit well inside the over-all far-right movement. Frustrations were on the rise. And many sought an outlet with easy answers. The Far Right had plenty of those.

As the Far Right grew, it was only natural that strong opposition would build quickly to fight it. And it was just as natural, as public officials began their attacks against this new political force, that some would mention the vigilante Minutemen as one of their foes. President Kennedy alluded indirectly to them in a speech in Los Angeles less than a month after the Shiloh affair. Before the end of that year the governors of California and Illinois and Senator Jacob Javits of New York also had taken public notice of this new little organization that boasted of so many secret members and had received so much recent publicity. Some critics, eager to discredit conservatism in general, were happy to have the Minutemen around to attack, just as many conservativies more recently have welcomed bearded, long-haired draft-card burners and pot-smoking hippies as useful in shaming liberalism.

As the '6os progressed, the Minutemen organization grew and slowly changed its complexion. Guerrilla-warfare field exercises began to be downgraded, for it was hard to convince many persons that an actual invasion from an external power was imminent. The emphasis shifted to the threat of an internal take-over of the country by the "Communist-Socialist" conspiracy. The defense against this lay not quite as much in learning how to ford streams and ambush foreign troops as it did in espionage, the gathering of intelligence against Americans they suspected of being Communists (e.g., many, many liberals), propaganda and the caching of weapons and ammunition, sometimes in defiance of federal laws.

As a result, the Minuteman, when he occasionally would be heard from publicly, was found not so often darting about a field in a camouflage suit as hiding machine guns or explosives, harassing liberals with anonymous mail or middle-of-the-night telephone calls, talking, if not actually plotting, violence up to and including possible assassinations at sometime in the unspecified future, training himself in a variety of bizarre skills in anticipation of the day when he would be needed and lamenting the decline and fall of the United States, once the great Land of the Free.

Slowly, as investigations of the Minutemen were made in various parts of the country, it became clear that this was no huge, grotesque practical joke. Violence. This was the catalyst. Violence that was not yet to be used. But violence that was to be taught for eventual use. Pamphlets on how to make booby traps were circulated by the Minutemen leaders to their members, with diagrams. "The Use of Ammonium Nitrate in High Explosives" was the title of another of the organization's pamphlets. ("Ammonium nitrate is a common fertilizer used on farms throughout the United States and most foreign countries. It is readily available from farm agencies, general stores, fertilizer companies, etc. in most farming communities," said this pamphlet. "Most people know that ammonium nitrate can be used as the basis for various high explosive mixtures. . . .") Instructions were even sent out on how to make a silencer for your pistol.

A Minutemen bulletin turned up in New Jersey instructing members on their weapons and ammunition caches: "Wrap, seal and bury or hide all other of your firearms remembering to put at least 100 rounds of ammunition away with each gun. Keep the .22 out and use it for target practice. In the event of a wholesale gun roundup, surrender it to the confiscating parties. UNDER NO CIRCUMSTANCES TRY ANY DOORSTEP HEROICS BY SHOOTING IT OUT WITH THOSE WHO COME FOR YOUR WEAPON! Most likely the National Guard will be the unlucky ones selected for the gun roundup. DON'T SHOOT NATIONAL GUARDSMEN. Many of them are already in our organization and many others are fully sympathetic with our position. . . ."

Such rhetoric also has included the preaching of revolution, most often called "counterrevolution" by the Minutemen leadership, for the "revolution" is of Communist origin and is under way now in the United States, in fact it is very nearly over. So say the Minutemen. So believe many of them. Thus, they store up bazookas, machine guns, mortars, dynamite, silencers, even homemade "nerve gas."

It is not the size of the Minutemen that sets them apart from the bulk of other organizations that crowd the Far Right. They are by no means so numerous that you should start wondering whether your next-door neighbor is a secret member with an arsenal of weapons buried in his back yard. He could be, but the odds are against it. Probably a thousand, and possibly several thousand persons now belong to the Minutemen organization across the country, either in small teams or as individuals, some zealously active, others more cautiously preparing themselves for The Day—The Day when the Minutemen slogan "Words Won't Win—Action Will" is to be applied against someone, in some way.

What most distinguishes the Minutemen from their ideological allies is the urgency of their belief that a Communist takeover from within the United States is so imminent, coupled with their preparations—through training and the acquisition of weapons of war—to defend the country from this threat.

Of significance in considering this organization is the fact that many thousands of persons who are not members, and never would be members, of the Minutemen support or at least sympathize with their goals. "Who knows, we may need the Minutemen around here one of these days," is a comment I have heard more than a few times the last several years from persons I otherwise had regarded simply as strong, rational conservatives.

Negro riots in the cities the last three years, and especially in 1967, prompted even stronger sentiments from some white conservatives as well as the non-ideological who simply were afraid. "The Minutemen don't look so goofy now, do they?" was not untypical of these observations as Negro snipers were making reputations for themselves from ghetto rooftops. Fortunately no Minutemen—as far as is known at this writing—took to the rooftops in retaliation during the 1967 riots or following the assassination of Dr. Martin Luther King in April, 1968. DePugh, in fact, said he did not want Minutemen mixing in any of the race riots. "If we do, we'll be blamed for starting them," he said, not without wisdom, scapegoats being greatly in demand at the time.

Unquestionably these riots did improve the Minutemen's image with a segment of the general public, at least at first blush. Especially when some tried to claim that the Communists were behind all the riots. But a calmer view may also have produced a new kind of backlash against DePugh's organization, with the white Minutemen and the black rioters cast into similar disrepute—the Negro rioters for the violence they perpetrated, the Minutemen for the violence they have been threatening for so long.

The July, 1967, issue of *Esquire* magazine, which was devoted to the subject of violence in America, reflected this in a two-page picture layout. Rich Lauchli and two of his friends were pictured opposite Charles Kenyatta and two of his armed pals in the Mau Maus of Harlem, with appropriate quotes from each. Said Kenyatta: ". . . Poor white people and poor black people are going to join together. I know some of these Minutemen. I've worked out on the rifle range with them."

And in June, 1967, after several members of the all-Negro RAM

(Revolutionary Action Movement) were arrested in Queens and accused of plotting the assassinations of several Negro civil rights leaders they apparently regarded as too moderate, the New York *Times* quoted James Farmer, former national director of CORE, as saying, "this shows that we are really equal now. You've got your Minutemen and we've got our RAM."

To many Americans, the Minutemen have been simply laughable. It is true that in years past they have provided the country some justified chuckles. By 1968, however, they are a grim, sick joke at best.

Many of the persons I have met within the organization are generally likable, sincere in their ultraconservatism and passionately convinced they are on the right track. I somehow have been unable to summon up a feeling of hatred for any of them individually, despite the fact that I abhor the course they have set for themselves. Hatred, per se, is not one of my favorite emotions, however. Some readers probably will conclude I have treated the Minutemen too gently at times in these pages. DePugh, for instance, may be behind bars as this is read. He is a fugitive in hiding as this book goes into print. Even if he is imprisoned, I doubt whether I will experience any feeling of personal pleasure over it. Subsequent events or revelations, of course, could prove me naïve in feeling this way.

I also recognize the danger that the contents of this book could inspire some persons to join the Minutemen, for I have tried to present their viewpoint fully, and often in their own words. There will be those in the Far Right, I am certain, who will choose to believe only those portions devoted to direct quotations from Minutemen interviews and literature and will regard all else as lies, lies, lies. This is why, I assume, DePugh was willing to devote considerable time in interviews with me. If you do join up as a result of this, I can only hope you will be careful with your rifle, nitroglycerine, flame thrower, poison gas or whatever else you arm yourself with, and don't harm anyone else—or yourself—with it.

As for the rest of the readers, I hope you will at least cease laughing at the Minutemen, even at times when they seem hell-bent on making themselves appear silly. Instead, I hope you will try to understand them, the appeal they have to some Americans and, perhaps most important, what we can learn about ourselves and our nation by studying them. There is, after all, a little of the violent activist in many of us. In a large sense we are a violent nation by tradition and instinct. Those who have been identified publicly as Minutemen have seemed to come from almost every walk of life—mechanics, businessmen, milkmen, policemen, truck drivers, students, cab drivers, and even some professional men. Too often in public pronouncements by officials and in news-media prose the use of such words as "fanatics," "oddballs," "kooks" or "psychotics" in describing the Minutemen has led the public to oversimplify its conclusions about them.

The Minutemen offer attractions to a variety of tastes. The strong anti-Communist and ultraconservative ranks provide the organization with its recruits, naturally, but other characteristics and personality traits also play an important part in leading men and women into the Minutemen. Gun buffs are attracted, and America has lots of gun buffs. Anyone with a fascination for weapons will find kindred souls in the Minutemen. Persons who enjoy intrigue for its own sake are susceptible, spying and counterspying being so much in vogue in contemporary fiction. Where else, without sending in box tops to a cereal company, can someone obtain his very own secret code number and mail drop and then be asked to keep suspected Communists in his city under surveillance?

"All too many are superficially good people," former Attorney General Stanley Mosk of California said in an anti-Minutemen speech in 1964, "the man next door, the fellow at the next desk in your office. Each was trapped into membership through different motivation. Some have a genuine belief that armed Communists are around the corner. Some merely like uniforms and martial music. Some prefer military drilling to dull handball at the YMCA. Some are eager joiners, and chose these groups just as their fathers donned white sheets and rode with the Ku Klux Klan back in the 1920s. Some crave the excitement and satisfaction derived from participation in a secret conspiracy. However innocent their motivation, once these individuals join with a group, they take on the group coloration, all of its conspiratorial qualities."

Still others are genuinely unstable persons unable to fit into society and who can find an identity and perhaps a purpose in the Minutemen obtainable nowhere else. Being unstable, they are more inclined to err, land in trouble and become known publicly. It therefore has been this group rather than the man-next-door members by whom the Minutemen most often are judged. Thus so much laughter, and too little serious regard for the social and political implications of the Minutemen, or the danger they pose the nation, individually and as a philosophy of activism.

An understanding of DePugh is essential to fathoming the Minutemen, but other individuals who have joined the organization and some of those who have defected from it provide valuable perspectives not obtainable from its founder. Weaving in and out of the history of the Minutemen of the 1960s has been as unusual a cast of characters as one could hope to meet.

There is, for instance, Troy Houghton, the thirty-five-year-old West Coast coordinator of the Minutemen, whom the California attorney general accused of disseminating "what he claimed to be intelligence reports of the massing of Chinese troops below the border in Northern Mexico poised for a military strike at this nation." (Houghton emphatically denies having done this, yet tells equally amazing stories about himself. He claims to have posed as an Army colonel during "Operation Desert Strike" in 1964, inspecting troops with the help of a borrowed jeep and his own Minuteman driver.)

Another is Jerry Brooks, a thirty-eight-year-old enigma who emerged from the fringe of the East St. Louis underworld to spy on Communists for the Minutemen, then spy on Minutemen for the FBI and U. S. Treasury Department.

Cindy Melville and Mary Tollerton, two attractive young Missouri women, who combined secretarial work for the Minutemen with involvements of dark intrigue, are two more. Mary, who likes to read Ayn Rand and says she became active with the Minutemen "for kicks," once spent a week secluded in a small house in Richmond, Missouri, school-marming two younger girls in anti-Communism and the art of espionage. The young girls later chose to interpret this as part of their "kidnaping" by DePugh. Cindy, who was DePugh's confidential secretary and chief cryptographer for three years, drove the two girls to Richmond for their schooling. Later, because of her activity as something of an unofficial chauffeur and bodyguard for DePugh, she landed in brief—now resolved—trouble with federal authorities.

Walter Patrick Peyson, an ex-Marine from Chicago, is another. After tangling with military intelligence in the Marines for sending right-wing literature anonymously to Marine Corps officers, he became DePugh's top side-kick, founded his own little organization,

"Onward Christian Soldiers," and eventually wound up in all sorts of trouble over some submachine guns federal agents dug up beside a cemetery in rural Missouri.

The insights these and others have offered often have been inadvertent rather than intentional. Sometimes as important as the facts they have related or the incidents in which they have been involved are the lies they have told me and others. What someone wants others to believe, whether true or not, can be revealing. But to call some of them liars is not, in their terms of reference, necessarily to defame them. Lies can be integral to good security, to effective espionage, to the gathering of important intelligence data about the "enemy." A dedicated Minuteman can rationalize his way to thinking of lying as simply another act of loyalty to the framers of our Constitution, perhaps the least outrageous of a long series of "patriotic" acts he believes he may have to perform before he has done his best to keep the nation safe from the Communist conspiracy.

Sometimes the lies have been simply mischief. As I was interviewing Jerry Brooks in an East St. Louis motel room shortly before Christmas, 1966, I happened to ask him about a note I had been told he had written to Mary Tollerton after he had defected from the Minutemen.

"Did you write Mary Tollerton a note saying you'd photographed Minutemen records?" I asked.

"That's correct."

"Did you photograph any records?"

"I did."

"What records did you photograph?"

"The membership files. I was a photographer."

"Did you turn them over to anybody?"

"I did."

"Who?"

"The Communists."

With this, Brooks bounded from his chair in the motel room and stomped around in a circle, laughing uncontrollably, the veins in his neck protruding grotesquely.

"Which Communist did you turn it over to?" I asked him once he had dropped back into his chair.

"Gus Hall," and he cackled another laugh, immensely pleased with himself.

"Oh, come on."

"You wanta bet?"

"How many Minutemen's names did you turn over to him?"

"Oh, I guess it'd be about a thousand membership cards."

"Did you give it to anybody else?"

"No."

This line of questioning continued awhile, although I hardly believed him. In earlier interviews, however, he had told several far wilder stories which, when checked out, either had some basis in fact, or were actually true. He persisted in this story about Gus Hall even after I told him I would be in New York soon and would try to verify it with Hall.

Once I had switched off my tape recorder and was preparing to drive Brooks back to his home, he confided:

"Say, what I told you about sending those records to Gus Hall—forget it. I just told you that so you could play the tape back to DePugh. It'll shake him up. He won't know what to think. Will you play it back to him? It'll reeeeeal-ly shake him up."

It took me nearly three years after first hearing about the Minutemen to regard them as important enough to study in any real depth, although I was a reporter for the Kansas City *Star* then, as now, and the Minutemen's national headquarters were well within our circulation area. Initially I had viewed them as simply a minuscule bunch of crackpots with a windy leader. I decided to look again in the summer of 1964.

Lee Harvey Oswald had reminded us tragically the previous November of what impact just one man with a rifle and telescopic sight can have on world history—whether part of a conspiracy or not. Soon after President Kennedy's assassination, a Texas Congressman was proclaiming in Washington that he and nineteen of his colleagues had been openly threatened by the Minutemen in the March 15, 1963, issue of "On Target," the Minutemen's newsletter. "Cross hairs are on the back of your necks," they had been warned, because they had voted against the House Committee on Un-American Activities.

Soon came the great "extremism" debates at San Francisco's Cow Palace in the summer of 1964, followed by a majority of delegates to the national convention of one of the nation's two major political parties voting against condemning the John Birch Society. That vote

—much more than Goldwater's nomination—belatedly awakened me
to the growth and power of the far right ideology. Robert Welch,
leader of the Birchers, was firmly on record as having accused former
President Eisenhower of being "a conscious agent of the Communist
conspiracy" and was continuing to push the sale of the book in which
he had made the accusation. Yet Eisenhower's own party would not
vote repudiation of Welch's society.

I was now convinced that I had ignored the Minutemen too long.
DePugh had been a member of the Birch society in the early years
of the Minutemen, leaving it formally three months before the GOP
convention. More importantly, DePugh had carried the basic doctrines
of the Far Right one step further along the ideological spectrum—
to what he apparently felt was their logical conclusion. After the
Birchers and their allies have cried "Treason!" long enough at Americans with whom they disagree, is it so fantastic that heartier or less
stable souls in their midst would cry, "Kill the traitors?" Or at least,
"Prepare to kill the traitors—sometime in the future?" Treason,
after all, is a capital crime.

Who these "traitors" are and when they should be killed, of course,
is never quite explained—not consistently anyway. Tomorrow? Next
month? If DePugh is imprisoned? If Robert Kennedy had become President? Many years from now? Probably never? It is left to the imagination of everyone, including the individual members of the Minutemen. Is the "enemy" some college professor who teaches evolution?
All the civil rights leaders? Everyone who belongs to the Anti-Defamation League or Americans for Democratic Action? DePugh may not
necessarily have said so, or even thought so, but he took few precautions against letting into his organization persons who are inclined toward such thoughts or prejudices, and who have the capability for such violent action. The man whom DePugh had designated
"chaplain" of the Minutemen told me in late 1966, after he said he
had traveled around meeting about a thousand midwestern Minutemen, that he regarded ten percent of the membership too "trigger
happy" for his liking. And one reason a Korean War combat veteran
quit his $115-a-week job with DePugh, he later testified in federal
court, was that "I refused to train a bunch of nuts and kooks into
becoming assassins."

While feeding his followers' minds with dark suspicions about
their "enemies" inside the United States, DePugh has disseminated to

them detailed instructions on how to make and hide various weapons of war. A "nerve gas" projectile he says he has fashioned for firing from an ordinary shotgun can kill everyone in a theater of ordinary size, he claims. He has offered these in the context of eventual political activism, call it "counterrevolution"—as he likes to—or what. And he has aimed it at persons who, by their membership in the Minutemen, are potential activists.

Each month, as the "On Target" newsletter of the Minutemen has arrived in the mail to subscribers across the country, it has provided a visual reminder of the nature of the Minutemen which no amount of patriotic euphemisms can erase. Decorating "On Target's" masthead have been the cross hairs of a telescopic sight in the "O" of "On." And beneath it is the warning: "We guarantee that all law suits filed against this newsletter will be settled out of court."

"Does that mean you're going to shoot me if I sue you?" I asked DePugh one day.

"Oh," he laughed, "I don't suppose so. . . ."

And he added, ". . . but we've never been sued."

And he smiled.

Minutemen often are "asked" by their leadership whether, in order to win the war against Communism, they are not morally justified in using the Communists' own tactics against them. Those tactics, it is also made clear to them, are unspeakably cruel and unconscionable. "Fellow patriots," the Minutemen message seems to say, "anything goes." The end justifies the means.

It was also in 1964 that the federal investigative agencies stepped up their visible interest in the Minutemen. A great deal more has been revealed about them as federal and local law enforcement agencies have tried to stop Minutemen from breaking (or to catch them breaking) the law in the pursuit of their goals, DePugh among them.

The Minutemen, of course, regard this as persecution because of their political beliefs, part of a left-wing conspiracy to do them in. Had they not been so vocal about using violent methods in support of their political convictions, it seems reasonable to assume that the federal investigators would have paid no more attention to them than they have the Birchers, and would not have looked for or discovered the various law violations of which some have been accused. To call this political persecution seems, from the available evidence, extremely speculative. The Minutemen are lucky, in fact, not to have been officially branded subversive.

Twenty Minutemen were arrested in New York in October, 1966, and the astonishing amount of weapons and ammunition confiscated in the raids caused many persons to wonder how much more was buried around the country. Less than a month later, new and at times surprising details about the secrecy-shrouded Minutemen in Missouri and California were revealed in the six-day trial of DePugh and two other Minutemen in a federal court in Kansas City on charges of violating federal firearms laws. The two events, less than a month apart, expanded the over-all public awareness of the Minutemen and, in effect, exposed them as an organization meriting closer, more serious attention.

In the meantime, DePugh had organized a political party all his own —the Patriotic Party—without even a pretense at disassociating it from its parent Minutemen organization. It hopes to run a presidential candidate all its own by 1972. For 1968, it endorsed George Wallace.

Certainly there will be more learned about the Minutemen in the future, as new leaks develop in their ranks, as more Minutemen caches of weapons and ammunition are discovered buried here and there around the country, as trials of Minutemen already charged with crimes are held, as investigations now under way are concluded and as new investigations are launched. But from what I now know about this bizarre organization, I fear that they are rushing toward an inevitable catastrophe that, at best, will be self-destructive and, at worst, harmful to the entire country. Unless, of course, they fade into obscurity. At times in the late months of 1967 I had the feeling that the Minutemen were beginning to fall apart at the seams organizationally. Internal strife seemed more prevalent than ever before. The events of early 1968, with DePugh moving to "Minutemen Underground Headquarters" while FBI "wanted" posters bearing his pictures and fingerprints began to appear on post office walls over the country, made the organization's future all the more uncertain. Yet even if the Minutemen organization should dry up and disappear soon, few of those who now belong to it, unfortunately, will alter their basic beliefs quickly. Many will find or form a new group of similar peculiarities. Minutemen thinking, if not the organization itself, promises to be with us for a while yet. Perhaps a long time.

BOOK ONE

The Formative Years

CHAPTER 1

JOIN THE MINUTEMEN

. . . As a chemist and businessman, Bob DePugh is respected by his colleagues in both fields. As a patriotic American, he has been branded as a fanatic and extremist. . . .

> From the back cover of *Blueprint for Victory* (1966) by Robert B. DePugh.

Our nation has reached a point of no return—a point beyond which the American people can no longer defend their freedom by the traditional means of politics and public opinion. . . .

> Opening paragraph of *Blueprint for Victory*.

Now in his mid-40s, Robert DePugh has developed a slight paunch on his 5-foot, 11½-inch frame that pushes his weight above 200. His coal-black hair has receded a goodly distance, giving his thin, expressive eyebrows and brown eyes a more commanding position on his face for reflecting the subtleties of his many moods.

In public, when before the television cameras or among persons who do not share his views, he is usually calm, personable and almost matter-of-fact about the great questions of the day. Although seldom reluctant to express views that many would feel are extreme, he does not do so in the overbearing, dogmatic way characteristic of many persons on the Far Right or Far Left. He even tends toward graciousness in discussions of his beliefs if his adversary will conduct himself in a similar fashion, although his repeated references to himself and his followers as "patriots" to the implied exclusion of all others can at times become irritating. In interviews, even with hostile newsmen, he usually is friendly and relaxed, quite able to laugh at himself if necessary.

Talking about his six children, he once volunteered with good humor that although his oldest children shared his political beliefs he had not yet taken his then eighteen-month-old daughter, Roxanne, onto the rifle range to give her target practice.

Before his own followers, DePugh attempts to be folksy and inspirational, but tends more to the cornball. Taping a message for regional Patriotic Party meetings from a cabin in the Colorado Rockies in 1967, he wistfully reported:

"An hour ago, I wandered away from the tape recorder and I stood looking out of the window. It's raining and I stood listening to the rain, looking at the drops of water standing on the pine tree needles, watching the clouds drift down through the valley, admiring the rocky cliffs and the mountains beyond. . . . It leaves me with a feeling of sadness, and I find the question going through my mind—who will save America? Who will save this great land? Who will save our freedom?"

In the same speech, while answering this question, he sounded more the demagogue: "Oftentimes we are kidded—and in the conservative movement, we kid ourselves—about the little old ladies in tennis shoes. Well, if this country is saved, I think that the little old ladies in tennis shoes will take a good part in saving it. . . . If this nation is saved, it must be saved by the backbone of this nation, by the working people, by the students, by the middle class businessman, by those who are willing to sacrifice, by those who are willing to work, by the *little* people of this country. . . ."

He can also be peevish, a mood that projects especially poorly for him because of the slightly whiny, nasal Missouri twang in his voice.

"I'm not asking you to believe it," he pouted at a Birch society heckler on a radio call-in program. "I couldn't care *less*, my friend, whether you believe it or not. It couldn't interest me in the *slightest* whether you believe it or not."

During his trial on federal firearms law violations in November, 1966, a friend whispered to me to watch DePugh's face as the next witness entered the courtroom. It would be the first time, the friend said, that DePugh would know that the witness was not a friend and follower, but an agent for the Alcohol and Tobacco Tax Unit of the U. S. Treasury Department.

DePugh was unbelievably cool. When the man he had known as Jim Wilson identified himself as Jim Moore of Omaha and gave his true occupation, a faint smile crossed DePugh's face. After Moore had testified against him and started to walk out of the courtroom, the smile broadened and remained until he was gone. Later DePugh confirmed that before the trial he had offered the federal agent the job of Nebraska State Chairman of the Patriotic Party.

DePugh's smile suggested to me his admiration for Moore's demonstrated abilities at infiltration and a certain self-satisfaction that the government was on record as having bothered to plant a man in his organization. It helped reinforce his long-held contention that the government was actively plotting his destruction in devious as well as bare-handed ways. He long had claimed government infiltrators existed in the Minutemen. Here was proof. He had little reason, really, to be shocked by the revelation.

In some ways, too, this had been part of the "game" DePugh has often seemed to be playing with his adversaries. When asked about an accusation of Jerry Brooks that the Minutemen had sent Brooks on a $99 bus tour of the country in 1962 to assassinate "Communists," arming him with three vials of strychnine, DePugh smiled and said that like all good lies, this had an element of truth in it.

The $99 bus trip for Brooks, he said, had been designed as part of a psychological warfare campaign. Brooks was to visit persons viewed as Communists by the Minutemen and use his nearly photographic memory to note little peculiarities inside their offices, as DePugh described it.

"Then we were going to wait quite a little while," he said, "so they would no longer associate it with his visit and then write to them in such a manner they would think for sure that recently someone had been in their office. You know, like for example, we were going to write Elizabeth Gurley Flynn (American Communist Party Chairman when she died in 1964) and tell her, 'Why don't you wash the windows in your office? They're so dirty we can hardly see through our telescopic lens.'"

"No strychnine?"

"No strychnine. No," he laughed, "but I thought it was worth the $99 for the fun we'd have had out of it."

He also likes to shock his listeners or interviewers. I have not talked with him at length yet without his quite calmly and unexpectedly volunteering some incidental tidbit designed to alarm or chill me. While discussing the relative likelihood of nuclear or bacteriological warfare being used against the United States, DePugh, who regarded the latter as a more logical prospect, wrinkled his brow and with seeming seriousness said, "Do you realize that I could kill everyone in the United States except myself if I wanted to?"

"Oh? How?"

He explained he could do this with a virus developed in his own Biolab Corporation laboratory, a veterinary drug firm he heads in Norborne, Missouri. After immunizing himself against it, he said, he could spread the virus throughout the country simply by coughing on enough outbound passengers at Kansas City's Municipal Air Terminal. In two weeks, DePugh said, everyone else in the nation would be dead.

Two and a half years after I had reported this in a series of articles, DePugh, recalling without visible rancor how the series had "hurt" the Minutemen, volunteered:

". . . For example, one thing I've chuckled about lots of times was when I was talking about how easy it would be to start a national epidemic by going down to the airport and spreading disease germs on the floor so they could be tracked onto the aircraft and carried all over the United States in a short span of time. I think you wrote it up something to the effect that I had said I'd go down to the airport and cough on people. . . . I don't think I put it in just that way."

As I recall still, my original version was correct, for I can remember having the mental picture of DePugh standing at various airline gates coughing on passengers. Still, perhaps his memory is better than mine. DePugh is equally sporting over this. After we had discussed his complaint over this detail, he obligingly commented, "Okay, maybe I did."

DePugh was born in Independence, Missouri, April, 1923, nine months before Nikolai Lenin died and the same year that Adolph Hitler wrote *Mein Kampf* in a jail cell. Another Independence resident, Harry S Truman, was Eastern District Judge of the Jackson County Court that year—a county embracing both Independence and Kansas City, Missouri—and Warren G. Harding was in his final months as President of the United States. The convictions of Sacco and Vanzetti were still being fought in the East and the Ku Klux Klan was very, very big in the country, Missouri included.

DePugh's father, Ralph DePugh, was a deputy sheriff in Jackson County for many years. The job was part of a cutthroat political patronage system, and while he received plaudits for his work in the

sheriff's office, he was also a precinct captain for the dominant Democratic machine in the county, led by the famed Boss Tom Pendergast of Kansas City.

"In my Dad's precinct," DePugh recalled, "the other side just didn't have a chance. He knew all the gimmicks. . . . He felt that this is politics, this is the way it's run, they'll do it to me, I'll do it to them a little bit better, you know?"

Growing up in such a political atmosphere taught DePugh to take "a pretty cynical attitude toward the democratic process," he said, adding: "The majority of people who vote today are people who have a very superficial idea of what's going on in the country, and they vote as they are persuaded to vote through the mass media and the political machines."

The 1941 edition of *The Gleam*, the yearbook of William Chrisman High School in Independence, provides a fleeting but objective view of DePugh the year he was graduated. On page twenty, second from left, bottom row, is a picture of a bright-looking lad with his black hair combed sideways across his head in the fashion of the day, a faint smile on his face. Pictured neatly attired in his ROTC uniform, as were many others in his class of 261 students, the youth is identified as: "Bolivar DePugh, Cadet Second Lieutenant Company F, Wild Life Conservation Club Secretary, Radio Club, Phenomena."

"Phenomena" was not a prophecy. As DePugh recalls, it was the name of a program his physics class put on one day, demonstrating various marvels of science. His project was to bounce artificial lightning bolts across the room with an ultra-high voltage generator.

DePugh started using his first name, Robert, after he began selling encyclopedias following World War II. His middle name, Bolivar, was given him by his father after Simón Bolívar, known as the "George Washington of South America," the man who led revolutions in five South American countries against Spanish domination in the early part of the nineteenth century.

Elsewhere in the yearbook, it is revealed that Bolivar DePugh had been one of four boys in his class sent to Warrensburg, Missouri, to represent the school in examinations in the field of physics. A Mr. Page, his instructor, picked the four boys because of their interest and high grades in that subject.

The ROTC training Bolivar DePugh excelled in was "truly preparing better citizens and leaders for the world of tomorrow," the

yearbook states, but later conceded, "On account of the late start, the rifle team did not make many achievements."

The sixteen members of the Wild Life Conservation Club—Bolivar DePugh, Secretary—concerned itself with "the urgent need for wildlife and forest conservation." One of the boys' projects that year, the book reveals, was banding Independence's trees against cankerworm infestation.

"In high school," DePugh recalls, "I didn't have any particular interests. I never went to a football game while I was in high school. I was pretty interested in ROTC and stayed the extra year."

"Why?"

"Oh, I'm not real sure. Originally, I think it was because I'd rather take ROTC than gym. I wasn't at all interested in physical sports."

"How were the grades?"

"Oh, average or a little above. I was pretty much of an introvert. I didn't mix too well. It seemed a lot more people knew me than I knew them. I wasn't popular. I didn't have a great many friends. I was interested in amateur radio and had my own license and my own station and I spent most of my time working on my different pieces of electronic equipment and chatting with other ham operators around over the world. . . ."

One of the other William Chrisman graduates of the class of '41 was Alex Petrovic, who was elected to Harry Truman's old job, Eastern District Judge of the Jackson County Court, in 1966. In a general way, Petrovic confirmed DePugh's self-appraisal in high school. Since DePugh has become prominent, old classmates have thought back reflecting on how they remembered him back when.

"I remember him as a loner in high school," Petrovic recalled. "He was a little hard to communicate with. He wasn't in any of the 'groups' . . . You never took Bolivar seriously about anything. You'd see him at school and you'd say, 'Well, there goes old Bolivar.' That was the name we knew him by."

DePugh was graduated in tense times, with Europe falling to Hitler and Pearl Harbor only seven months away. " 'Three cheers for the red, white and blue' is a sentiment echoed in every part of our country because America is a democratic nation," began the 1941 *Gleam*. ". . . The future of democracy will be what the students of today, as citizens of tomorrow, make it. . . ."

But when the United States entered the war later that year, Bolivar

DePugh was not imbued with patriotic fervor. "I wasn't in favor of World War II. I wasn't in favor of our involvement," he said.

"Do you still feel that way?"

"Yes, I think so. I think that if we had not gotten into it in the way we did, that certainly Russia would be no threat, Communism would be no threat to the world today, and you'd probably have the Japanese and the Germans fighting among themselves the way you have the Chinese-Russia split."

"Where would Europe be, though?"

"Well, I don't believe that German Fascism was quite the threat that international Communism is. . . . Of course, it's a hard thing to say what would have happened the other way, so maybe it would have turned out even worse. I don't know. But at the time I wasn't particularly in favor of it."

He credits his maternal grandmother, now deceased, with providing him with his youthful insights into the Communist threat. "When I was in high school," he said, "I was perhaps more politically aware than most high school students. My father, of course, was in politics . . . and my grandmother was quite a politically aware person as far as world politics were concerned.

"As World War II developed on the horizon, it was of no surprise at all to any member of our family because there was a lot of discussion about the war that I overheard four or five years before Pearl Harbor. And my grandmother, looking back, was an astute woman. She recognized the twin dangers of Fascism and Communism and I think she foresaw the outcome of the war and what would happen if and when Germany were defeated, what would happen if we stayed out of it and Germany had defeated the Soviet bloc. Her feeling was that we should stay out and let the Communists and the Fascists fight each other down to the point that it could very easily develop into a long stalemate that would dissipate both systems to a point where they would no longer be a real threat to this country.

"At the same time, she foresaw that we would go into this war on the side of the Soviets. She was very much concerned with the degree of ultraliberal penetration into our own political system, so I used to have some long talks with her.

"While I was in high school I got one of the early editions of *Mein Kampf* and I read it pretty carefully and in fact I read it two or three times, and I also read *Das Kapital, The Collected Works of*

Lenin and the so-called fundamental text on Communism. Of course, all this was purely academic as far as I was concerned."

It seemed a little odd to me as he spoke that DePugh would have made a point of telling me he had read *Mein Kampf* two or three times. It was possible he was simply being candid, of course, but why had he not simply mentioned reading the book, among others, without such emphasis? DePugh had grown accustomed to being branded a Fascist by some of his more severe critics. Was he hoping I would do just this and thus attract more Fascist-minded individuals into the Minutemen? I did not know. He continued:

"To me there's always been a great deal similar between Fascism and Socialism. You have your national socialism and international socialism and both of them, of course, are a dictatorial form of government that I disagree with. . . . Respect for the individual, to me, is one of the most important things in my political philosophy. And I realize that neither Fascism nor Communism has respect for the individual."

Taken out of the context of the rest of his philosophy, this seemed entirely palatable. I found it hard to equate, however, with such writings of DePugh's as: "One important thing for conservatives to remember is this—the tactics of resistance warfare are neither good nor evil. Only the 'cause' is good or bad" (*Blueprint for Victory*).

DePugh enrolled at the University of Missouri that fall, eying electrical engineering with particular interest. He enlisted in the Army in 1942 and was sent to the University of Colorado where, he said, he studied radar as a civilian.

"There were a lot of practical considerations," he explained. "I knew that if I enlisted at that time, I could go get that schooling, which was at that time a consuming interest to me, and I figured there was no better training that I could get in this field at this time. So that certainly was a strong consideration."

"Did you feel as patriotic as you do today, when you enlisted in 1942?"

"No, I don't believe so. And, of course, my patriotism today is a kind of funny patriotism. I mean, I don't go into ecstacy exactly at the sound of the national anthem, although it does represent to me an ideal, a dream of freedom, of self-determination for the people. But if I lived in some other country and was trying to protect a system of government that offered maximum freedom to the individual,

I'd feel the same way toward any other country. And of course, as our own government, I feel, has abdicated the responsibilities for the freedom of the individual, I feel less and less patriotism toward the government of the United States. . . . I'm patriotic toward the original concept of the United States as a constitutional republic."

DePugh met and married his wife while in Colorado. He began active duty with the Army in August, 1943, first at Camp Murphy in Florida, and then Fort Monroe, Virginia, where he was a student and researcher, he recalls, working on radar-jamming equipment.

"I got into a fight (argument) with a couple of civilian instructors there," he said. "They were quite outspoken, so far as being pro-Communist, not just merely pro-Allies, and I knew if anyone walked up to these people and said, 'How about handing me the plans for the microwave radar?' that they'd have had no compunction about doing it at all. If the man was a Communist, they'd say, 'Welcome to it!'

"I'm not saying that they did," he added. "I don't know that they did. But I complained about it pretty bitterly and was very surprised to find that I was the one that was called on the carpet instead of them, as an agitator and troublemaker."

Later, when the late Senator Joseph McCarthy was trying to expose Communists in the Army Radar School, DePugh said, he wondered why McCarthy was being criticized so much for saying things he knew were true.

Twenty-two years after DePugh's discharge from the Army, the reason for that discharge was made a matter of public record in U. S. District Court in Kansas City in a motion by the government to have DePugh examined by a psychiatrist to determine whether he was mentally able to stand trial. The government said he had been discharged on August 31, 1944, for "medical" reasons after a board of medical examiners had concluded he was unfit for military service because he suffered from "psychoneurosis, mixed type, severe, manifested by anxiety and depressive features and schizoid personality."

"Soldier is unable to perform duty due to anxiety, nervousness and mental depression," the report said. "This condition is chronic and for three years has been attended with vague auditory hallucinations and mild ideas of reference."

A more detailed report by an Army psychiatrist described the young pfc. as having been restless during interview, fidgeting with his fingers, his fingernails closely bitten, admitting to frequent daydreaming and suicidal thoughts. "Patient has had vague hallucinatory experiences for the past three years. In a crowd he seems to hear someone call, 'DePugh,' but can't identify the caller. . . . There is a paranoid trend to his thinking. He believes he is superior to most of the instructors at the radar school except that they may know a little more than he does in their specialty. . . . Intelligence: average normal. . . . Insight: lacking. . . . Diagnosis: psychoneurosis, mixed type, severe, anxiety and depressive features, schizoid personality and incipient schizophrenia. . . ."

Judge Elmo B. Hunter granted the motion and a court-appointed psychiatrist reported, after examining DePugh, that he could stand trial. As the judge put it at the start of DePugh's trial in 1966:

". . . We got back the report concerning Mr. DePugh. It showed that in every respect he was ready for trial, he was fully competent, able, knowledgeable, could advise with his counsel and assist in his defense and that there was nothing wrong with him in any respect mentally. . . ."

DePugh says that the psychiatric report in his service jacket was news to him, that he had thought his discharge had been for ordinary medical reasons. His psychiatric examination in 1944 lasted only ten minutes, he said, and was a routine examination given everyone being discharged for medical reasons at that time. The medical doctors, he said, already had decided he would be discharged for physical reasons because of a systemic strep infection that had caused him to lose forty pounds in the Army hospital.

"By that time the war in Europe was about all over," he said (incorrectly, in that VE Day did not occur until eight months after his discharge). "I guess they figured it was going to take months and months for me to get back on my feet and they might as well go on and discharge me. I guess this (psychiatric) report was strictly an aftermath. I didn't take it seriously at the time."

DePugh said he remembered the psychiatrist, a major, had been busy with other matters at the time of his talk with him.

"They were running through there like cars off an assembly line," he said, "and he only had about ten or fifteen minutes for each one of us, and I was tired, I was discouraged, I was sick, I was disgusted. I didn't give a hoot about anything, and when he asked me such questions as, 'Do you think you know more about this than your instructors?' I said, 'Yeah, some of them at least.' And so I guess he thought I had delusions of grandeur. I knew I was getting out. I didn't give a damn what he put down there. That was the way I felt about it at the time. I hardly remember it. And of course, I never knew anything about it."

Out of the Army, DePugh enrolled at Kansas State University in January, 1946, and attended there a year and a half. While there, he earned no degree, but founded something called the Society for the Advancement of Canine Genetics which came to publish a periodical titled *The Journal of Canine Genetics.*

Between 1947 and 1954, DePugh held several jobs, a majority in sales. At one point he started an advertising agency in St. Joseph, Missouri. He recalls having had to discipline himself greatly in this period of life because he had not been used to talking with people as much and in such a manner as these jobs demanded.

His father was still active in county politics and ran unsuccessfully for sheriff in 1948's Democratic primary. Robert DePugh filed for the U. S. House of Representatives from Missouri's Fourth Congressional District in the Democratic primary of 1952, but not as a serious candidate, both he and his father say. He had filed with the intention of withdrawing in time to have his name left off the ballot as part of a time-honored, faction endorsement-swapping tradition in Jackson County Democratic politics. His father recalled that young Robert had failed to withdraw in time, however, and finished fourth in a field of five with 1774 votes against the victor's 30,000.

He started the Biolab Corporation in 1953. Its principal product was "Fidomin," a dog food supplement containing vitamins and minerals. But within two years Biolab had folded, due to "differences of opinion" with other officers in the corporation, as he explained it.

Through the late '40s and the first several years of the '50s, DePugh was not especially preoccupied with political or ideological matters, as he describes it.

"The division of Europe after the war hurt as far as I was concerned," he recalled. "I thought it was a gross miscarriage of justice. Nobody ever asked the people of Lithuania or Estonia or Poland what they wanted to do. I had sort of a feeling of regret, but there was nothing I could do about it. I didn't necessarily blame it on treason. It was very, very poor politics. I thought our government had let those people down. . . . I felt somebody should do something, but who was to do what, I had no idea."

As he discussed the events of the late '40s and early '50s, I had the impression that DePugh had been no more and no less concerned with world affairs than the bulk of the apathetic public. I had to draw him out too much on the issues of those days and his comments were limited in scope. On more current topics, he can and does talk at length.

In the final days of his first attempt to make a success of Biolab—in March, 1955, specifically—a peculiar incident occurred in Atchison, Kansas, in the northeast part of the state. A bank official there had grown suspicious of a new account that was made out in the name of C. L. Tipton. A man identifying himself as Tipton had opened the account with a small deposit and soon afterward had made more deposits with checks made out to him by persons with the names of Glen Archer (drawn on a Kansas City bank), William Wyatt (drawn on a St. Joseph, Missouri, bank) and Robert Bolivar DePugh (drawn on an Independence bank). And the man who said he was Tipton began writing checks on his new account in Atchison.

The bank official called in the city's chief of police and one day when "Tipton" appeared at the bank, the police chief stopped him and asked him a few questions. It did not take many for the man to admit that his real name was Robert Bolivar DePugh and that Wyatt and Archer were as nonexistent as Tipton.

Recalling the incident later, DePugh said that the bank official's suspicious had been raised by two of DePugh's business partners in the Biolab Corporation with whom he was having numerous disagreements at the time.

DePugh signed a statement for the police on April 4 admitting he had opened up accounts in three banks under assumed names in order to keep checks he had written on his own account in Independence from bouncing—a practice usually known as "check kiting."

"I have been working for seven years to build up a laboratory and I have put everything into it, and so has my wife and my kids," DePugh told the chief of police. "There have been times when, really, they have gone to school shabby, in hopes I could make the company succeed, and my wife works too, to try to help the thing along. . . ."

He told of a man who owed him $1500 and two other men who had written him bad checks, all at a critical time when he was counting on the debt to be paid and the checks to be good so as to balance his Independence account. He had opened up the false accounts and had written checks against them as a delaying step until he could balance his Independence account, he said.

"I thought it was going to be a one-time thing," he said in his statement. "I thought I would have the money and put it in the bank, but it didn't come. . . . I didn't think it would catch up with me when I started, as this fellow told me he would pay the money. I tried everything before I wrote the checks and actually, when I started this, I was kind of half mad at the world or I wouldn't have done it. . . ."

DePugh offered to make restitution but was arraigned three days later on charges of forgery and issuing worthless checks in Atchison. He was released on $2000 bond. He did pay back the money, as promised, and in about a year the charges were dropped.

DePugh went to Topeka, Kansas, after Biolab's collapse, obtained a job as manager of the professional-products division of the Hill Packing Company, selling prescription-type foods for animals to veterinarians. He also enrolled at Washburn University in Topeka, where he studied from September, 1956, until February, 1957.

Although he has described himself as a "scientist by education," DePugh did not earn a Bachelor of Science degree. He insists that he has never pretended otherwise. However, more than one writer somehow fell under the impression in 1961 that DePugh had a degree from Washburn.

DePugh and his wife, still living in Independence at the time, started up Biolab in 1959, using a one-story building at 613 East Alton Avenue, Independence, as their place of business. Their major product at first was Enzodime tablets, designed to keep old dogs healthy and alive longer. It is still one of Biolab's major products.

"We've sold twenty to thirty million of them," DePugh said. "My wife and I used to bottle those pills on the kitchen table."

Efforts to succeed in business through the '50s and the added burden of his Minutemen activities in the '60s has left DePugh with little time for recreation or hobbies.

Although an outspoken foe of further firearms-control laws, an advocate of weaker laws in this area and, he claimed, possessor of a lifetime membership in the National Rifle Association,* DePugh does not classify himself as much of a hunter.

"I just like to get out in the wide open spaces," he explains. ". . . I used to do some duck hunting, but lots and lots of times we'd go up there (to a duck blind) and I'd set my gun in the corner and fix breakfast for the bunch and just sit and take in the morning mists off the lake."

He is far more interested in target practice with rifles and pistols, often keeping his eye sharp at a target range on the banks of the Missouri River near Norborne.

"I've been a target shooter for a long time," he said. "My Dad . . . was rated as one of the world's best marksmen. . . . The first time I ever shot in a pistol match, I wasn't more than nine or ten years old."

He did not even own a firearm through the 1950s, DePugh said, and his efforts to oppose a proposed Search and Seizure Law introduced in 1959 in the Missouri Legislature were motivated solely on ideological grounds. The bill would have given law-enforcement officers wider latitude in this ticklish area. DePugh purchased space for an advertisement in the Kansas City *Star* to protest the bill, charging that it violated the constitutional rights of private citizens, which, indeed, it may well have.

"History proves," his ad declared ". . . that tyranny is the inevitable consequence when people forfeit their individual freedom."

He printed up petitions, he said, started them in circulation, held a meeting at a downtown Kansas City hotel and even managed to be a guest on a late-night radio call-in program to discuss the issue.

"I thought it smacked of police-state tactics," DePugh said, "and . . . I've always been very, very opposed to anything even remotely approaching police-state tactics, dictatorial governmental tactics."

The bill did not pass, although it is not certain that DePugh can claim credit for this fact. The episode, however, provided him with valuable experience for his later activities in the business of championing a cause.

In late 1960, as the Minutemen idea was taking shape, DePugh moved his family, home and business to Norborne, Missouri, seventy

---

* The NRA disputes this claim. A spokesman in Washington said that DePugh applied for a lifetime membership in 1959 but failed to submit endorsements for himself, as required, and therefore never became a member. He did pay $100 for a lifetime subscription to the NRA's magazine, however, the spokesman said.

miles northeast of Kansas City, although he kept the building at 613 East Alton for his use in Independence. A quiet little town with nearly a thousand inhabitants, Norborne was entirely unprepared to become the dateline on news stories all over the country, as has happened since the DePughs moved there. The DePughs experienced understandable difficulty trying to blend into the small town's routine of daily life. His wife and children did eventually win acceptance there, but the Minutemen chieftain exerted less effort and, according to the townspeople with whom I chatted, has yet to be particularly accepted in Norborne.

Driving into the town from the west, past sign after sign advertising "Funk's Hybrid," "Sweet Lassy Feed," and "Pioneer Feed," one is struck immediately by the high percentage of homes that have been painted white. If there is some monotony to this pattern, it is compensated for by the over-all freshness the effect achieves.

Norborne is charmingly relaxed and its tolerant attitude toward DePugh and his Minutemen reflects this well. The weekly Norborne *Democrat-Leader*, its newspaper, has studiously ignored DePugh in his role as leader of the Minutemen except for occasional second-hand reports of what the metropolitan newspapers have written about him now and then. Dorsey Hill, the editor, explained this practice by his desire to help the DePugh children and DePugh's brother and sister-in-law as they have tried to fit themselves into Norborne's way of life. His weekly, Hill added, is designed to report on what the big city papers ignore in Norborne—which includes just about everything except DePugh and an occasional fatal traffic accident in or near the town. The biggest news anyone in the DePugh family had made in the recent past, when I talked with Hill, was Chris DePugh's selection as Homecoming Queen at Norborne's high school in the fall of 1966. That was front-page news.

Norborne civic boosters, hoping to lure new industry into their town, had formed the Norborne Development Company in the late 1950s and notified the state industrial commission that it was ready to offer certain financial inducements to firms that might want to relocate there. The first to apply was Robert DePugh's Biolab Corporation, which DePugh runs and in which he and his wife are the major stockholders. The development company loaned him $7500 to relocate in Norborne under the impression that Biolab would employ Norborne citizens. There also was the feeling, one leader in that company told me, that Biolab appeared to have a good growth potential. At first DePugh did hire several Norborne residents, but as the Minutemen idea grew in his mind, he began to devote less attention to Biolab and before long was employing no one outside his own family in the old one-story plant in downtown Norborne. Out-of-towners also could be seen about Norborne doing work of some sort for DePugh, although the citizens were not quite sure what. These, as it turned out, were visiting Minutemen from various parts of the country, helping fold, print, and mail Minutemen literature or working on Minutemen files.

But if the civic leaders in the development company are disappointed over this turn of events—and all of the publicity DePugh has brought Norborne—they seem to have no intention of voicing it publicly. One of its leaders was quick to point out to me that DePugh had paid off nearly all of the loan and fully expected him to continue paying on it as long as necessary. He acknowledged that on business trips to other areas, he is frequently joshed about being from the home of the Minutemen, but that this is always done in good humor.

The closest I came to receiving what seemed like a representative view of DePugh and his family in Norborne was in their neat, well-stocked little public library which serves once a week also as the meeting place of the Norborne city council. Three middle-aged women were chatting there when I arrived and upon learning my interest, quickly began praising the DePugh children. They like to read books, the ladies said proudly, were bright youngsters, well-liked about town, well-behaved. Chris in particular had charmed them and they laughed over the day she had gone to the library looking for a good book she could read and report on in one of her high school classes. When the librarian had suggested *The Good Earth*, they said, Chris had replied she most certainly would not read that because of Pearl Buck's political leanings.

"They're *very* patriotic," one of the women said of the children with a smile, using the description more in Minutemen terms than her own, it seemed.

There has been no move to run DePugh out of town, nor has there been any visible effort by the community to warm up to the Minutemen leader. When I asked the three women in the library whether many Norborne citizens had joined the Minutemen since DePugh's arrival, they promptly said No, but then began a cryptic conversation among themselves about one unnamed "suspect" in town whom they seemed to view with more amusement than alarm.

DePugh was described by several Norbornites with whom I talked as usually aloof to others, seldom speaking to anyone on the street unless spoken to first. Mrs. DePugh, on the other hand, was generally praised as a quiet, unassuming woman who minded her own business and devoted her time almost exclusively to the children and work at Biolab.

DePugh's two-story frame house at 408 South Pine blends harmoniously into the Norborne residential area during the daylight hours but, according to one neighbor, is a subject of some mystery at night. Many lights burn in it from dusk to dawn, she reported, while all the homes around it are usually darkened by ten o'clock in the evening. When I asked Mrs. DePugh about this, she laughed heartily and explained that her children simply have never learned to turn out lights before they go to bed. There was nothing sinister about it, she assured me.

"Most everybody here has lived here all their lives," DePugh said, describing his relationship with his new home town, "or is related to somebody. So the very fact that we moved in here from the big city set us apart. It takes you a long time to be accepted by a small town community. Now, my brother, who came up here to work with me, he's become a deacon in the church, his wife is secretary of the PTA and they're in a dozen different things in a small town community, but that's just because they have the time and the inclination to get involved.

"Bill (his brother) and I sort of agreed between ourselves that he could help the cause best by just taking as much of the Biolab load on his shoulders as he could, freeing me of the time and responsibility."*

DePugh likes to describe his children as his best public-relations agents—which the townspeople confirm. Ralph, his oldest son, married a Norborne girl before joining the Marines and going to Vietnam. Chris, who is his oldest daughter, is a nurse's aid at the hospital in nearby Waverly on weekends "and they think the world of her." This is understandable. A cute, lively redhead, Chris displayed a strong devotion to her father's cause on our one meeting. The children at

* William DePugh did this until early 1968, when he decided to enter a Baptist seminary with the intention of becoming a minister.

school seldom speak to her about the Minutemen, she said, and if they did, it appeared to me, Chris would have been able to handle just about any comment with ease. Some of the boys at school at times have been unkind to her brother John, one year younger, with such remarks as, "Is your father still out of jail?"

But John would seem to be no pantywaist about such matters either. In the summer of 1965, as police converged on the DePugh home shortly after midnight with a warrant for his father's arrest, John stood guard behind the front screen door with a loaded rifle in his hand, allowing them entry only after they had shown him their warrant.

A year earlier, Ralph's agreement with his father's cause came to light when he was arrested by Independence police in the middle of the night for violating a city ordinance regulating the posting of handbills. Just as Robert DePugh had gone about Independence sticking up campaign posters for his father when he ran for sheriff in 1948, young Ralph had posted numerous "Wanted for Murder" handbills in Independence denouncing Nikita Khrushchev, "alias the Hangman of the Ukraine, alias the Butcher of Budapest," and signed at the bottom, "Minutemen." By placing some of the handbills under the windshield wipers of parked cars and on utility poles, Ralph had violated an ordinance, however.

"They argue with their teachers," DePugh said proudly of his children. "If John has something out of one of his textbooks he doesn't agree with, why, he tells his teacher, why, they're trying to brainwash him and he's not going to stand for it. But it's all good-natured."

Mrs. Ramona Van DePugh—"Van" to her husband—works energetically on Minutemen affairs when she has time. Her trip to Shiloh in 1961 may have been more for publicity purposes than training in guerrilla warfare, but she has performed many more thankless jobs since then to advance her husband's cause. She expressed genuine embarrassment over having had her photograph printed in numerous newspapers with an M-1 rifle slung over her shoulder during the Shiloh exercises, but DePugh laughingly reported that she was miffed at news reports at the time describing her as having had to stop and rest occasionally during the early morning maneuvers. This wasn't so, DePugh said. Some of the male Minutemen had had a hard time keeping up with her. As he told this, Mrs. DePugh smiled her agreement.

Being the family of the national coordinator of the Minutemen naturally has had other disadvantages. The accidental death of "Dusk," the family's big Irish wolfhound, is but one example of this. DePugh, it seems was trying to develop a lethal nerve gas in his Biolab laboratory in Norborne one day when—but to let DePugh tell it (and I have only his word for it):

"When I was first experimenting with it, I had a dog that was an Irish wolfhound, weighed 180 pounds. This dog was the kids' pet and a great big old lovable hound. Everybody in Norborne thought that this dog was just the cat's whiskers. Kids rode it like a pony.

"The first batch of nerve gas I ever made—of course it's a liquid, not a gas—I figured what I thought would be a minimum lethal dose, a minimum effective dose for this dog. I just wanted to see if I had the thing right, you know. And I figured the minimum effective dose and then I cut that by ten, and I put it on this dog's nose, and the dog walked six steps and dropped dead."

CHAPTER 2

JOIN THE MINUTEMEN

. . . The American people are moving inexorably toward a time of total control and frustration such as must have been felt by the people of Budapest and East Germany when they finally staged their suicidal revolts. Therefore, the objectives of the Minutemen are to . . . prepare for the day when Americans will once again fight in the streets for their lives and their liberty. We feel there is overwhelming evidence to prove that this day must come. . . .

> From a pamphlet, "A Short History of the Minutemen," to prospective members—1961.

. . . OUR NATION IS IN IMMEDIATE DANGER. It is possible that within a very few years, perhaps even within months, our nation could be conquered and enslaved by the Communists. . . .

> From a pamphlet, "To Prospective Members of the Minutemen" —1961.

. . . The hopes of millions of Americans that the Communist tide could be stopped with ballots instead of bullets have turned to dust. . . .

> Opening sentence in "On Target," the Minutemen newsletter, upon the defeat of Barry Goldwater—November 4, 1964.

The varied versions of how the Minutemen came into being, how their expansion began, how their philosophy and techniques have changed in six years, how large the organization has become and who has led it (if not DePugh), deserve attention before the events from 1961 to the present can best be understood. One must also consider the vague possibilities of whether—as some observers believe—DePugh may be a patriot-for-profit rather than a dedicated anti-Communist. Or —as a few others have whispered—possibly a Communist in disguise.

"It could never happen again in a million years," DePugh marveled in 1964 as he recited the "official" version of how the Minutemen

came into being—the same version contained in a 5½-by-8½-inch booklet titled "Minutemen—America's Last Line of Defense Against Communism."

According to this tale, the organization sprang from a chance re-
mark by a duck hunter in June, 1960, as he and nine other sportsmen,
DePugh among them, were building a duck blind somewhere in
Missouri.

"Well," the duck hunter is supposed to have quipped, "if the
Russians invade us, we can come up here and fight on as a guerrilla
band."

One of the other hunters in the group, who had had Special Forces
training, was then prompted to respond, so the story continues, that
it might not hurt Americans to know a little more about defending
themselves if "this war" ever degenerates to a last-ditch stand. "Slowly,"
the booklet continued, "the joke turned into a serious project."

In an interview in mid-December, 1966, DePugh offered a more
plausible, though unverified story of the Minutemen's orgin.

DePugh said he had become a devotee of Fidel Castro after reading
an article by the Cuban revolutionary in the February, 1958, issue of
Coronet magazine titled "Why We Fight."

Two of DePugh's friends also had become strong admirers of Castro,
DePugh said, and even went to Havana intending to join him in
the hills to fight Batista.

"But they found that if you wanted to contact Castro," he said,
"you went through the Left Wing instead of through the general people. So they came back quite disillusioned."

Aware now that Castro was a Communist, his two friends—whom
DePugh refuses to identify, for he says one of them helped found
the Minutemen—began talking with DePugh and others in Independence about the problem.

"They'd come in and we'd talk until two or three in the morning
about the situation," DePugh said, "and we began to ask around and
we found several other people in Independence who were a little more
savvy than we were—they had been anti-Communists for a long time,
and we began getting a little literature from them, and we began to
get John Birch literature and quite a little bit from the Reserve Officers
Association. For the first time, we were introduced to the reports on
the hearings of the House Committee on Un-American Activities and
the Senate Internal Security Subcommittee, and the DAR (Daughters

of the American Revolution) put out a little material that was pretty good, and the Institute of Economic Freedom, I believe it is.

"So we decided that we would sort of take about six months and kind of unravel the situation and study it, and then we really went into it in seriousness. We tried to find out everything we could. We subscribed to a lot of different magazines and newspapers, both left and right, everything from *American Opinion* on the right to *The Worker* and *National Guardian* and *People's World* on the left."

Some in this group did belong to a duck-hunting club and did discuss such matters while sitting around in the duck blind, he said, but if someone joked about fighting as a guerrilla band from the duck blind, "that certainly didn't mark the beginning of the organization."

The question naturally arises—who were these other nine men? The answer, according to DePugh, is that the seven who are still alive (two died of natural causes, he explained) are now members of the Minutemen's National Council, sometimes called the "Executive Council," a group of men to whom he has been answerable on major decisions as national Minutemen coordinator.

While this may be so, available evidence indicates that DePugh has always been the Minutemen's sole leader. At this writing, investigations of the Minutemen by federal and some state agencies have not turned up even one of these council members as such, if they exist. Investigators, infiltrators, and defectors have plagued the Minutemen consistently, at least the last four years. And while some of the defectors have left with the impression there is someone over DePugh, none have offered concrete evidence to this effect, nor has DePugh himself.

In an interview in 1964, DePugh told me that eight of the ten founders had sold their homes and fanned out over the country to spread the membership and influence of the Minutemen over a wide base. Their identities, naturally, would have to remain secret.

A couple of years later, he supplied occupations for each of the council members (an electrical engineer, a fireman, a minor official in the Mormon church, etc.) and the states in which they lived (Texas, California, New Jersey, etc.), yet when I asked him to do it again a month later, he changed several of the occupations and states. It became a wearisome game after a while, so DePugh decided to liven it up a bit.

"I'll tell you something maybe you don't know," he said. "I testified under oath before the Grand Jury there wasn't any council."

"Why are you telling me this?" I asked.

"Well," he grinned, "just to mystify you a little bit further."

"Why are you so secretive about this council? Just because (Robert) Welch has a council, do you feel you have to have one?"

"Maybe we have," said DePugh.

"It doesn't sound like you're in contact with them very often."

"Well, maybe I'm not."

Then he seemed to tire of the game.

"This is one of the things I have absolutely got to keep my adversaries guessing about," he said. "As long as they don't know, as long as they can conjecture, they can think, they can plan, they can speculate, they can snoop. This is one thing that is very important for me to keep 'em guessing on."

Just as there are more than one version of the Minutemen's origin, there have been minor inconsistencies in the stories of how the group began to grow. His most recent, containing the most details, went like this:

DePugh and some of his friends had been visiting the Kansas City public library two and three times a week looking for books on guerrilla warfare. A woman employed at the library began to notice this unusual interest by DePugh and the fact that he frequently arrived there with different men on different visits. This woman, DePugh said, was a member of another organization that also was interested in guerrilla warfare.

Shortly after he had moved his home to Norborne, he said, he received a telephone call from a man whom he refuses to identify.

"You don't know me," the man said, "but I belong to an organization very much like your own. We've been kinda watching you fellows and we think that you've got the right idea but you've still got a lot to learn. Maybe we can help you out a little bit."

DePugh relates that it was arranged for him to meet this man at eleven o'clock the following night at the junction of two highways in northeast Kansas. He kept the appointment and was led to a darkened farmhouse, he said. In front of the farmhouse he saw several men "getting their gear together." Inside he found several more "plotting their night's work."

The men took DePugh with them on a twelve- to fourteen-mile

hike that led them beneath a moonless sky to a railroad trestle which they pretended to mine.

"The whole thing was done absolutely in pitch-black darkness with virtually no noise," DePugh recalled admiringly, "and how in the world they ever got there and back, and found their way, I couldn't hardly tell you. But I realized they were a long way ahead of me in know-how of military operations. I later concluded they were made up mostly of reserve military officers. Most all of the original literature we put out as Minutemen literature of political indoctrination came from them."

For a time in the first months of 1961, DePugh said, these men used the Minutemen as their "front." The Minutemen put advertisements in the newspapers, he said, trying to recruit members, and the trestle raiders contacted some of the persons who replied to them.

"It's my impression now," he added, "that they figured, well, here's a bunch of boobs that didn't know any better and were all going to get themselves killed early in the game anyway, so they would just let us do their recruiting for them. But it didn't work out that way, because we just grew too fast and began running into other groups, and because we were the one group advertising openly, they could get in touch with us where they couldn't with others.

"We became more or less a system of communications between these other groups and, I didn't know it then, but found that the chain of command develops along lines of communications. So since we were the chain of communications, we just almost automatically developed into the chain of command."

The numerous inconsistencies noted so far in the birth and infancy of the Minutemen and in the reality or fiction of the Minutemen's council leadership may suggest that DePugh is none too reliable a source of information about his organization. To be caught in as many self-contradictions as he has in the last several years would probably bother most persons, but it does not seem to trouble DePugh. When caught, he quite calmly explains that deception is part of being a Minuteman. A lie is not a lie, it is a deliberate subterfuge and anyone, he seems to suggest, should understand that he is entirely justified in this practice. While he may not wish to mislead a newsman interviewing him or the American public at large, he says any public pronouncement by him will quickly reach the enemy. And he wishes to keep the enemy guessing, wondering, off balance.

His juggling of membership figures to suit his needs and mood is the most obvious example of this. His first public pronouncement, in 1961, placed the Minutemen's size at 25,000. Later, he admitted it had been only 300, 400 or "less than 600" at that time. In 1964 he told me: "When somebody says we have no more than 2000 members, I'm happy. When someone else says we have 35,000, I'm happy too. The very fact that people question this is an advantage."

Later he began publicly explaining there were different types of members in the Minutemen—"secure" or hard-core members, "regular" members, and "associate" members, and he offered vastly inflated figures for all three. More recently—early in 1968—he told members in a bulletin that the Minutemen were "several thousand" strong.

If a guess is in order—and it probably is not, for I could be disproved tomorrow—it would not amaze me to learn that there are as many as 1000 to 2000 active Minutemen in the country today. It would surprise me if there are many more than that. Many more undoubtedly have written letters of inquiry or applied for membership in the last six or seven years, but most of them, it seems logical to assume, later departed.

Between 200 and 300 names of persons believed to be Minutemen were confiscated, for instance, when twenty members were arrested in New York state in late 1966, but how many of these were active in the organization was not revealed, even after a ten-month investigation by the New York attorney general's office—probably because it did not know.

The California attorney general estimated from 100 to 600 members in his state in 1964.

DePugh has described New York and California as his two strongest states in terms of members.

To all this, consider one more statistic: J. Edgar Hoover estimated the entire national membership in early 1968 at less than 500.

Two theories—neither of which I happen to subscribe to—have come up about DePugh, and perhaps it is wise to wait no longer in examining them. One is that DePugh is a confidence man out for money; the other, that he is a Communist.

I find no evidence to indicate he is either. Both theories have arisen quite naturally, however, because of the secretiveness of the

Minutemen and the world of suspicions and countersuspicions in which they exist.

DePugh insists he has no financial angel, that his largest single contribution has been $500 and that he has received such a lump sum no more than four or five times.

Members' dues have been more or less on a pay-as-you-can basis with a minimum of $2 preferred each month, a maximum of $10 suggested. Recently both have been increased slightly. But DePugh adds that his members are not good at paying dues.

There have been other sources of income from members, of course. For a time—and perhaps still—there was a $5 fee involved in joining the Minutemen. Some Minutemen literature and some books were sold to members from the national headquarters. His *Blueprint for Victory*, sells for $1. DePugh said he was still offering members for "less than" $5 what in 1961 was dubbed the "Minute Mask," a protective plastic covering to protect Minutemen against toxic or nerve gases.

"All it is," DePugh explained, "is sort of a plastic tent that you throw over your entire body and tuck in under you and breathe through a long plastic tube that's filled with chemical neutralizers and a filter. It's a real simple thing, really. It has the obvious handicap that you can't move around. You've just got to get in there and wait for the danger to blow itself over."

And there are donations. From all over the country. How much, it is impossible to say. A sixteen-year-old girl who worked briefly for the Minutemen in 1965 claimed afterward that she had seen a total of about $200 in small amounts arrive in just one day's mail at the Independence Minutemen office.

Suspicions about Minutemen money matters naturally arise because of such letters as this, sent to members in late 1961, before the organization really had begun to accumulate many followers:

". . . The fact that our members have been making monthly financial donations may be a possible source of trouble. In the past we have insisted that these contributions be made with cash. Any checks or money orders which I have received are still in my possession and so far as I know most of the other members of the Executive Council have not cashed any checks or money orders which have been sent to them.

"This insistence upon cash has not been due to any desire to avoid a financial accounting or to receive money which could be traced to us. As many of you realize, nearly all banks nowadays keep a photographic record of all checks which they handle. If we did receive checks from our members and cashed them it might at some future time be possible for an enemy to obtain from the bank records a list of the names of a sizable percentage of our members.

"This handling of money implies a certain degree of control and a certain degree of leadership. For tax purposes some type of tax records have to be kept. And someone has to file an income tax report covering these records. The only way we can see that this can be done is for the individual group leaders such as myself to treat their participation in the Minutemen as a business and file a Schedule C Form in addition to their personal income tax report. In these records it will only be necessary to show the source of this money as coming from membership dues and nothing else need be given except the member's number. If we incorporated, as some members have suggested, the various records and legal documents required would be much more revealing to a potential enemy."

Money for weapons and ammunition apparently is not a large part of the Minutemen budget, for individual members are told to acquire their own weaponry. Judging by the size and content of the caches of weapons found hidden by Minutemen over the country—in California, Colorado, Missouri and New York alone—it would seem that considerable expenses were involved.

When one looks at the over-all Minutemen operation, it appears highly possible that outside of the money spent by individual members for weapons, it really is not a high-cost organization. Postage stamps and paper cost something, naturally, but the Minutemen's mailings are not so extensive as to put those items down as a major expense.

One big organizational expense in evidence is paying lawyers' and bail bondsmen's fees for DePugh and others who have run afoul of the law.

DePugh has missed no opportunity to make pitches for funds to pay his legal expenses. He claimed—and an independent source confirms—that at a rally of 125 conservatives in Kansas City in August, 1965, and through personal follow-up fund-raising efforts the following day among Kansas City ultraconservatives, $1700 was raised for his defense against a kidnaping charge that was pending against him at the time.

A year later a letter went out to members stating that Robert DePugh was among Minutemen in jail for want of enough money to make bond. DePugh actually had not spent any time in jail, having made bond immediately upon each of his arrests.

"Convince me you're not a con man," I asked DePugh early in 1967 (without belligerence).

He began by starting to list his creditors, suggesting first I call a man to whom he owed $7000 on a long-term lease purchase agreement he had with him on a Biolab pill machine. The man was contacted and confirmed this.

"The Internal Revenue Service's fraud squad is on me right now," he said, "not that I've made money off the Minutemen, but because they are claiming that for five years I have been taking money out of Biolab and used it to support the Minutemen organization."

"How much?"

"That is something I've spent $2900 so far on accountants to argue with them over," he said. "It's a sizable amount."

He said that a few of his own members have accused him of dipping into Minutemen coffers and "it's practically impossible to convince anybody by simply quoting figures."

To all appearances, DePugh has not profited financially from his Minutemen efforts. If anything, they may have hurt him. He recently moved from a home on which he was paying $50-a-month rent to 408 South Pine in Norborne for which he and his wife paid $5000. His rent for the building in which Biolab is located in Norborne is only $75 a month, he added. Considering the lower property values in a rural town such as Norborne, a look at these structures lends credibility to DePugh's figures.

The building at 613 East Alton Avenue in Independence that first served Biolab, then the Minutemen and finally the Patriotic Party as well, is run-down inside and out.

DePugh seems to have devoted far more time to the Minutemen than he has to Biolab and presumably could have helped build up the company's business had he spent all his time on it. Its net worth in 1964, he said, was $350,000. More recently, he said, it was down to around $200,000.

The closest DePugh comes to high living is when he travels, and he travels frequently, flying often. After he lands, chances are good he will be found in a respectable hotel.

"My time is more valuable to me than the money," he explains. "The difference between plane and train fare is negligible compared to the time involved. When I'm driving I stay pretty economically, but . . . I try to combine Biolab business with Minutemen business and I try to talk with distributors and customers, and it's just good business to try to put on a reasonable front for the Biolab Corporation when I'm doing business. It's also one of the things Internal Revenue doesn't worry too much about."

I am unable to sit down with anyone and flatly prove that DePugh is not a con man. It is just a feeling, based on available evidence. Most con men do not take the risks he has. And considering the amount of attention paid him the last few years by the federal investigative agencies, I'm inclined to think they would have pinned him to the wall by now if the Minutemen had been simply a money-making scheme for the national coordinator.

As for the other theory . . .

"You know," DePugh said in 1964, "there are some people who even think I'm a Communist."

Already, in the April 1, 1963, issue of the Minutemen's "On Target," the possibility had been raised. It read:

"If several different men were asked to name the leaders of the more important 'anti-Communist organizations' in America we would certainly expect a wide difference of opinions. Many people would probably include some, or all the following: Robert Welch, Bill Hargis, Fred Schwartz, G. L. K. Smith, W. Cleon Skousen, Dean Manion, Dan Smoot, Frank McGehee, P. A. del Valle, Ed Walker, Frank C. Hanighen, (George) Lincoln Rockwell, Ned Dupes, M. G. Lowman and Bob DePugh.

"The Communists have done a masterful job of infiltrating the fields of education, religion, government, communications, entertainment, labor, law and the news media. Why should they ignore the field of anti-Communism? The most logical reason for assuming that one or more of the above mentioned individuals is a Communist is the simple fact that if it were not true it would mean that the Communists would not be running true to form. They would be missing too good a bet. . . . We should (not) be blind to the actions of other people just because they label themselves anti-Communists . . .

"We would offer the following suggestions by which others can judge the real merit of either individuals or organizations that label themselves anti-Communists:

"1. Ignore most of what they say.

"2. Ignore most of what they do.

"3. Analyze very carefully the RESULTS of what they say and do.

"No matter how consistently a person talks against Communism, his efforts will be worthless if he ignores the most salient points of a conspiracy against freedom. If that person causes others to be misdirected in their thinking then he is helping Communism, not hurting it. If an organization spends its members' time, energy and money on projects that do not contribute directly to the ultimate victory over the enemy then it is helping Communism, not hurting it. . . ."

Asked about this unusual article from his own publication, DePugh said that he later had abandoned his original plans of exposing Communism in the right wing because it is so difficult to prove. "But there are some right-wing organizations that I very greatly suspect," he added.

"That issue of 'On Target' could have made some people think you were a Communist," I suggested.

"There's always these people," he replied, "who figure, well, the Minutemen could be an awfully good means of identifying those Americans who would be inclined to jump for their guns and start shooting Communists. It's an interesting possibility."

Suddenly I felt he was back playing games—if he had ever stopped. Did he actually want me to start wondering? Or did he think I already was?

"When a person asks me to my face, it's a difficult thing to convince him otherwise, if they really get to believing it," DePugh said. "If a person just has a little doubt, I point out two facts to him. I begin by pointing out that there's nobody except me who knows whether I'm a Communist or a patriot or a patriot-for-profit, you know. I'm the only one who knows for sure. But there are certain clues that I think I would look for in another person. Now, it also could be argued that if I'm clever enough to look for them in another person, I'm clever enough to plant them in my own environment.

"But a person has a very, very strong tendency to pass his own beliefs on to his own children. I can't imagine Herbert Aptheker trying to instill a fervor and patriotic feeling in Bettina in order to plant her into a right-wing organization. It would be a very difficult thing to do with your own kid. And anyone who knows my kids knows that they're all strong, young patriots.

"The other thing, if you are in the Minutemen a long while and you do your work well, you are going to come out a trained, dangerous individual. Trained in the skills of underground warfare and dangerous to anyone that is opposed to the patriotic ideas of the organization. Now, if I was really a Communist, I'd have to look at this thing from the point of view of what we would gain and what we would lose. We would gain the names of several thousands of people, but in doing so, we would inadvertently create several thousand people who would know all our tricks, who would be 100 times as dangerous to the Communist cause after they went through this thing than they would before.

"In other words, from a cold-blooded point of view . . . they might set up an organization like the John Birch Society or something like that to lead people down a continual program of frustration to a point where, after studying this and that and listening to this and that, they'd throw up their hands and say this is too much for me. I can imagine that. I can't imagine they'd ever set up a militant underground organization that would train many thousands of skilled, dedicated fighters merely to get a bunch of people who would, without this training, be relatively innocuous."

Then he addressed himself to the question of whether he could be a Communist out to discredit the right wing with the Minutemen.

"Rich Lauchli," DePugh said, referring to the former Minutemen regional coordinator, "one time told me that to my face. He said, 'Hell, nobody could get in as much trouble as you do unless they did it deliberately.'"

Lauchli, in fact, had recently offered me a similar theory in an interview at his home in Collinsville, Illinois. Lauchli, however, had been in as much trouble with the law as DePugh, a fact that DePugh said he had pointed out to him.

"We decided it was about a draw," he smiled.

Lloyd Pullen, an ex-Marine from Long Beach, California, who was in the Minutemen briefly, thought somewhat along the same lines as Lauchli.

"I kind of think they want bad publicity," he told me. "I kind of think sometimes that maybe the Minutemen were started to get all these kooks together and get all these nuts in one pile and then make anyone else figure, 'Jeez, I'll never join a militant guerrilla group or right-wing organization.' They make the whole right wing look like a bunch of nuts, like the Nazi party. You know, they're not right. They're so far right they're left. . . . All they want to do is go out and shoot up the public, shoot up the left-wingers, shoot up the guy that's sitting in the middle; if he doesn't take a stand, shoot him."

But DePugh faces up to such thoughts with forbearance.

"From a plus and minus point of view," he said, "I don't think I've hurt the right wing that much."

Perhaps, if DePugh had not come along, the Communists would have created a Minutemen organization in an effort to discredit their opposition. But DePugh has made it unnecessary for them to try such a strategy.

Harry and Bonaro Overstreet suggested in *The Strange Tactics of Extremism* (W. W. Norton & Co., 1964) that the Birch society is serving the cause of Communism in several ways, including the creation of "confusion by its loose and irresponsible resort to derogatory labels" and by "labeling as Communist-inspired or Communist-controlled a host of indigenous American efforts to solve pressing social and economic problems," thus "acting as a brake upon social ingenuity at the very time when we most need to find American ways of coping with colossal forces of change." The same observation, it would seem, fits DePugh and the Minutemen.

As one looks over the rash of literature and the abundance of interviews DePugh has granted over the years, a definite change in Minutemen thinking—perhaps more accurately described as DePugh thinking—can be discerned. The organization, in fact, has gone through at least five perceptible stages of development.

Concern over nuclear attack against the United States pops out as the first real Minutemen fear. One reason DePugh moved his home and business from Independence, which abuts Kansas City, to Norborne, seventy miles northeast of the big target city, was his fear in late 1961. (In 1964, he denied having said this. In 1966, he of nuclear attack, he told Steve Underwood, another *Star* reporter, acknowledged having said and meant it. Tricky man to interview,

DePugh.) He and his brother built two bomb shelters in Norborne after moving there in 1960.

But the fear of nuclear attack was only short-lived, soon to be replaced by fear of alien troops hitting America's beaches or dropping out of the skies. To combat this new menace, the antidote of guerrilla warfare was offered. A little "Join the Minutemen" pamphlet in 1961 observed:

"It is easy to see why most Americans have shied away from the government's civil-defense program. It is the American tradition to stand up and fight. It is not in keeping with this tradition to ask Americans to dig holes to hide in or to abandon their homes and flee helter-skelter to nowhere.

". . . The bomb shelters which we are building are not merely holes to hide in. Each one is being well camouflaged, stocked and fortified to serve as a 'center of resistance' for a future underground army."

Soon, another shift took place. Since an armed invasion by a foreign power, after all, seemed most unlikely, guerrilla warfare training became only one of numerous Minutemen projects aimed more at internal rather than external Communists. A pamphlet titled "To Prospective Members of the Minutemen" observed:

". . . Sabotage, espionage, infiltration, escape and evasion, clandestine fabrication of supplies, counterfeiting enemy documents, recruiting, training, communications and propaganda are other phases of underground activity. An effective Minuteman must have a working knowledge of all these tactics as well as the military tactics more commonly associated with guerrilla activity. . . ."

Not that the acquisition and hiding of weapons was to be overlooked. The same pamphlet advised:

"Each member will be expected to buy his own gun, ammunition and other equipment. This can be as little as thirty dollars or as much as several hundred depending on what you can afford and how fancy you want to get. . . ."

The twenty-page Minutemen booklet, later off the presses, advised:

"We need radio repairmen and operators, mechanics, truck drivers to act as couriers, waitresses to act as 'message drops,' businessmen, students to train as intelligence and espionage agents; typists to help carry our heavy load of correspondence; salesmen to help recruit others to the cause, housewives that will share the chores of baby-sitting thus freeing some other housewife for other work, farmers to provide space for rifle ranges and training areas. We need weapons instructors, photographers, first-aid instructors, pilots and many others. Who do you know that will help?"

Minutemen were encouraged individually or in small groups to place certain suspected leftists under surveillance and write reports on their activities. Some were put to work in public libraries reading and preparing reports on various books and periodicals deemed of importance to the organization. Most continued their target practice, either secretly or openly at established target ranges where the members naturally would not identify themselves as Minutemen. Some obviously devoted considerable time to acquiring various weapons and hiding them. Enough instructions were sent out to them that it can be assumed some members also busied themselves making weapons. Recruiting was stressed and individual Minutemen were urged to take elaborate steps to bring new, safe members into the organization in manners most tedious and time-consuming. Some members devoted their energies to checking out the loyalty of new members, although it is clear now that not enough of this work was accomplished satisfactorily, infiltrations and defections being what they are in the Minutemen.

The emphasis all along was on individual or small group activity. Except for a few large training exercises at which members were identified by numbers to one another, a Minutemen "meeting," in the usual sense of the word, consisted of no more than a half dozen persons getting together at one time. Working together in larger numbers entailed too many risks of discovery.

Discipline from national headquarters has always been minimal. Secrecy was stressed so emphatically that few Minutemen knew more than a handful of others by name or by sight. One former regional coordinator complained to me that his authority over his group was at times undercut by national headquarters which sometimes dealt directly with the members instead of going through him. The result has been that the individual member, if he wishes, is relatively free to go off and pursue what he regards as a Minutemen objective in any way he pleases without much risk of discovery or censure as long as he isn't stopped by authorities and his deeds made a matter of public knowledge.

There are many advantages to this system as well as disadvantages.

When the twenty men in New York were charged with conspiracy to commit arson in connection with Minutemen activity, evidence connecting them with DePugh and Norborne, Missouri, was uncovered by authorities, yet DePugh was not indicted or charged. Presumably, no conclusive evidence was found indicating that he personally had even known of the alleged plans to burn any left-wing study camps that were named as the New Yorkers' targets. DePugh stated afterward that if these men had planned to burn the camps, they had done so without the knowledge of anyone outside their bands.

The fourth discernible shift in emphasis—direct political action through the Patriotic Party—may well have been a subterfuge in that its stated goal of running a presidential candidate successfully in 1972 is so absurd as to suggest another motive for its formation. The most obvious motive was to give DePugh and a few others of like mind an additional platform from which to express their views. Another may well have been to create a new recruiting ground for the Minutemen organization.

The fifth change, involving reorganization of the Minutemen into "resistance networks" in 1967, added a new sense of urgency to all that their members did and thought. A new militancy was discernible. The Day seemed, somehow, closer at hand. Minutemen rhetoric became even more irresponsible than before.

The shift in Minutemen thinking from the fear of an external Communist threat to jitters over Communists inside the United States was the most important of the changes, and the most natural one. As the 1960s progressed, national and world developments made this shift quite easy. As frustrations over Vietnam, the New Left, civil rights and "Black Power," the vice-presidency of Hubert Humphrey (one of the Minutemen's prime bogeymen), the apparent growth in influence of Robert Kennedy (a Bogeyman Supreme to their way of thinking) and the inglorious defeat of Goldwater in 1964, DePugh found many new arguments with which to confront the public.

The Minutemen's fundamental appeal is, after all, to the strong conservative who wakes up one morning, reads one more disturbing headline and finally declares, "I'm so mad I'd like to go out and start shooting." He doesn't start shooting at anyone, thank goodness, but he has other outlets available to him. One of them: Join the Minutemen.

There have been plenty of disturbing headlines for such persons to read. Every day something new from Vietnam, usually disheartening. Someone on the New Left at a university has burned his draft card, publicly embraced Maoism, or made a speech declaring the virtues of words better left on bathroom walls. The Supreme Court says it is all right for Communists to teach in the public schools in New York. The school-prayer decision still sticks in the throats of many. Stokley Carmichael offers a new thought on "Black Power" then shows up in Havana. Another chiseler is exposed in the Poverty program. Taxes increase. Action and reaction. A new thrust by the left—a fresh scream by the right. Dr. Martin Luther King wants to march on Cicero, Illinois—out come the swastikas and a fresh crop of Northern red-necks. A white man shoots Dr. King. Negroes riot. Troops respond.

And looming bigger and bigger is the federal government, to some trying to solve the great problems of the day since no one else will do it; to others a power-hungry bureaucracy, seeking to meddle, interfere and eventually control our every movement.

At one point in a long interview in January, 1967, as DePugh sat at a desk in his small office at 613 East Alton in Independence and twirled a throat lozenge on the desk top with his fingers, the conversation turned to the techniques he had used for six years to inspire his followers to prepare for possibly violent political action someday. I was especially interested in the menacing nature of many of his public utterances and writings.

"Your purpose seems to be to frighten people, to frighten the government, from going too far to the left," I suggested, somewhat naïvely.

"No," DePugh said, "the purpose is to provoke the government into taking harsh and repressive measures against the general population so people will be turned against the government."

"You're trying to provoke a catastrophe."

"Well, I suppose maybe you're right," he said.

"Is this desirable? Is this patriotic?"

"It's all whether you believe the ultimate outcome is going to be good or bad," DePugh said. "Certainly, as I've tried to point out, violence itself is not necessarily bad."

"Why do you want to provoke the government into taking repressive actions against the general population?"

"Well, because according to our theory, the Communist-Socialist

clique is taking over the country according to a very skillfully pro-
grammed timetable. They do this in such a slow and insidious manner
that the conditions become gradually more restrictive. They gradually
gain greater power. They build the bureaucracy and the bureaucratic
control in such a subtle manner that the day never comes—if they
have their way, according to their strategy of protracted conflict—
that there's never a day that the people say, 'Well, yesterday we
could tolerate this, today we cannot.' We want to make the opposition speed up their timetable to the point where people will
realize the threat."

"And what are they supposed to do when they realize it?"

"Well, they can revolt by one means or another."

"The goal, then, is a revolution?"

"The goal is a counterrevolution. There's already been a revolution,
a non-violent revolution in which the original constitutional republic
of the United States has been superseded by an alien, socialist
ideology."

This was not a casual conversation between us. My tape recorder
was spinning in full view of DePugh as he talked in this manner.
He knew a book was being written about the Minutemen. He had
written essentially the same ideas to the members of his organization.
Those who have chosen to belong to the Minutemen know this is
representative of his thinking, and to a lesser or greater extent, most
I have met endorse it.

DePugh's "provocation" idea is part of his oft-stated theory of
underground warfare. It is to be applied after "the principle of deliberate delay" has been followed to its conclusion: a principle which,
simply stated, means "don't do anything rash yet, boys—we aren't
ready yet."

An inadvertent application of the "principle of provocation" might
be attributed to the Minutemen in their ability to have attracted
activity against it by the FBI. As a result, DePugh has cried harassment
by the FBI repeatedly, and seems to think many persons believe him.

"How many conservative organizations do you hear defending the
FBI any more?" he asked me.

"Most of them," I replied, "except for the Minutemen."

But he disagreed. Because of its activity against the Minutemen,
he assured me, the FBI had alienated large numbers of his ideological
allies.

Asked for examples of acts of provocation he had in mind, and what type of "repressive" steps by the government he thought would prompt a "counterrevolution," DePugh was evasive by design.

The sabotaging of several pieces of government property over the country, he said, would provoke federal agents into stopping, searching and questioning hundreds of persons, and no matter how polite federal agents usually try to be, few can avoid creating bitterness in those questioned. This seemed a questionable theory to me in that most of the federal agents I have met seem entirely capable of tactfully obtaining information. DePugh, however, thought differently.

"The Minutemen have their own strategy of provocation planned," DePugh added, "and it does not include what I've mentioned. . . . It probably won't begin for a long time. It depends on what happens."

Openly acknowledging the several changes in the Minutemen approach that have occurred so far this decade, DePugh said his current tack had come about "by an interplay of ideas, of forces, an evolution of thought."

"Certainly six years ago," he said, "if someone had talked to me about the principle of provocation, I wouldn't have known what he was talking about."

"Are you so sure of your analysis of the 'enemy' that you can take it upon yourself to inspire others to take action?" I asked.

"Of course, that's a question I've asked myself many a time," DePugh said. "And believe me, I don't take it lightly. People can always ask themselves—and it's always a valid question—are you so sure of your beliefs that you're justified in taking this action or that action? And I think I would be bordering on egomania if I said that I was. No, to tell the truth I am wrought with grave doubts. . . . After studying all the material that I can find—and I do have, whether anyone wants to believe it or not, perhaps far greater sources of information than the average voter—and after trying to carefully analyze all of the material available, and having thought long and hard on it, I evolved my thinking from one thing into another, often with misgivings, and sometimes I backtrack."

From all this, DePugh has developed a following with a definable philosophy or, if "philosophy" is too ostentatious a word to describe it, at least a point of view. Individual Minutemen naturally share this viewpoint with varying degrees of intensity, for not all joined the organization for reasons of pure, intense patriotism, political conservatism, or fear of an imminent takeover or invasion by the Communists. But all were taught this viewpoint, once they joined.

Communism, to a good Minuteman, is an aggressive, consummate evil, representing world slavery and at work twenty-four hours of each day inside the United States seeking (or already having assumed) control. Differences may exist between Communism and Socialism, Socialism and liberalism and even liberalism and anticonservative moderation, but the differences are small and unimportant to many of them.

DePugh at times has sugar-coated the Minutemen image for public consumption by likening it, for instance, to a life-insurance policy (". . . Whether we need it or not, it's just a good, safe, sane policy to have it available"), but members are taught to have a more desperate view of the world and the need for such insurance. A Minutemen training pamphlet, for instance, relates that recruits should enter the organization convinced:

". . . That the Communists can and will win with the tactics they are now using, whereas our government cannot possibly win by the tactics they are now using . . . that the Communists already have such complete control over the American news media and political processes that it is impossible to change our own government's policies by the customary means of politics and public opinion . . . that a life-and-death conflict is raging right now between the forces of freedom and advocates of world slavery, the chief weapons of which are espionage, subversion, propaganda and psycho-political warfare . . . that our government is not using these weapons effectively . . . that if the American people expect to be saved from slavery they are going to have to do so themselves . . . that the Minutemen are the most experienced, most dedicated and best disciplined organization that is involved in this fight at the grass-roots level. . . ."

CHAPTER 3

JOIN THE MINUTEMEN

Join the Minutemen. An organization of loyal Americans dedicated to the preservation of both national and individual freedom. Help put real strength into civilian defense. Pledge yourself and your rifle to a free America. For full details, write, 'Minutemen,' 613 East Alton, Independence, Missouri!

Ad placed in the Kansas City *Star* classified section August 13, 1961.

The little ad reprinted above was run in several newspapers off and on in the summer of 1961, squeezed usually between notices for lonely-hearts clubs and massage parlors in the classified sections. It was the Minutemen's initial bid for public recognition, and a weak one at that. The ads presumably prompted some inquiries to 613 East Alton, but most persons who noticed one of them undoubtedly viewed it only as a source of curiosity and possibly mild amusement.

A minuscule organization, no matter what its cause, needs publicity if it is to get off the ground. And to obtain publicity with any impact, the organization needs a gimmick.

On October 15, 1961—one week before the events in Shiloh, Illinois—Denver, Colorado, newspaper readers were alerted to the existence of DePugh and the Minutemen by virtue of the fact that the Denver press somehow had learned that an unusual meeting of fourteen persons was being held at the Denver Hilton. There, they found, the obscure head of a small veterinary drug firm in Norborne, Missouri, felt the need for guerrilla warfare squads in the Midwest. This proved a sufficient novelty that the meeting was reported, none too reverently and without alarm.

But it was all talk. Anyone could talk. No impact.

The Shiloh meeting was something else. Weapons! An arrest! And field maneuvers! With that, DePugh could talk and newsmen listened, and wrote. The gimmick had been found.

Yet DePugh claimed he had sought no publicity at Shiloh.

"Once newspaper reporters and other people learned of the meeting," he wrote members afterward, "I had to make a spur-of-the-moment decision. Perhaps it was right and perhaps it was wrong but at the time it seemed best to give a true statement regarding the purposes and actions of our organization and something of our plans rather than have the news media report rumors and suppositions. . . ."

But others in the Minutemen disagree.

"It was for publicity," Troy Houghton, West Coast coordinator of the Minutemen, assured me, although he had been in California at the time.

"Bob told the press," said Rich Lauchli, who should know. "It wasn't intended to be a secret meeting. We didn't care. Anybody could come. I made the arrangements to use the Shiloh community hall. There was lots of press there, and we had twenty-three members there.

"There were six or eight people who I had brought in and the rest Bob had brought in," Lauchli said. "Bob brought several along from Norborne and Independence. There were two from Indianapolis, but they took one look at the proceedings, threw their hands up and went back home right now. As soon as they saw all those newspaper people, they said, 'To hell with this.'"

The large assortment of weapons he had put on display for the meeting had been selected, Lauchli said, "for their ability to stir the imagination, which (and he chuckled) they certainly did."

Slightly irked at DePugh's apparent duplicity on this point, I eventually quoted Lauchli and Houghton to him and marveled at the skill with which he had grabbed so many headlines that weekend. DePugh smiled the smile of someone uncertain of whether to accept an apparent compliment, and he let it drop.

I was not present at Shiloh that weekend, so have had to rely on the several different news accounts of what happened and Lauchli's and DePugh's memories. Peter W. Salsich, writing for *The Nation*, reported that it was the arsenal that had caused the furor among officials and that they had spent several hours in confused deliberation before deciding what to do—arrest Lauchli and haul away four of the weapons. But Lauchli remembers that the township supervisor was pushed into signing a complaint against him by some unidentified Communist "agitators" who had shown up mysteriously at the meeting and then disappeared from it with equal furtiveness.

"What we didn't know," Lauchli said, "was that the Commies, the real Reds, the genuine article, they had been calling up the sheriff's office and agitating and working from the time they found out that we were going to be in there. These real Commies had been working in there in a telephone campaign to disrupt us. Of course, we didn't know this. In fact we were kind of naïve about it because we should have realized that they would do a thing like that, and they had been lying, spreading lies, saying we were going to shoot in the hall and all kinds of crazy things like that."

In his letter to members later, DePugh reported: "The circumstances of the Shiloh seminar were such as to strongly indicate that someone was purposely trying to break this meeting up. I had a little impromptu debate with the 'Justice of Peace' that seemed to be the instigator of the trouble. He certainly talked the Communist line. . . ."*

Lauchli was arraigned and released immediately on $1000 bond. The charges were later dismissed when the weapons were found to be legal, but the four confiscated weapons, Lauchli said, were never returned. He blamed this on a reporter for the St. Louis *Globe-Democrat*, who he said asked the officials about the weapons so often that they were afraid to return them to him. Not that he acted very upset over this. "Frankly," he said, "we've always had more guns than we knew what to do with."

Lauchli was surprised and pleased at the reaction to his and DePugh's weekend venture.

"I sat here every night for three months at this kitchen table," he said, "pounding the typewriter, answering letters. I daresay I must have had well over a bushel of letters to answer. I'd write eight to ten letters a night for three months, and out of the whole works, we had one or two at the most that were against us. And I mean it came from politicians, college professors, there was no limit. It was a complete cross section of the country, and they were tremendously behind us."

---

* The St. Louis *Post-Dispatch* offered a little more detail to this incident, reporting the following exchange between DePugh and the police magistrate:
DEPUGH: Are you a Communist?
MAGISTRATE: No, are you?
(No reply)
MAGISTRATE: I answered your question, you answer mine.
DEPUGH: I solemnly swear before Almighty God that I am not a Communist.

Muscular and thickset, a little overweight, Troy Houghton, at thirty-four years of age, cut a commanding figure in the land of southern California palm trees, sun, surf and smog with his heavy head of dark, flat-topped hair, horn-rimmed glasses and demeanor of intense purpose. Aggressive and frequently articulate, the Minutemen's West Coast coordinator is sometimes inclined to outbursts of temper, acts of mischief, a wide, indefatigable range of suspicions and a certain inability to please law-enforcement officers, as his long and somewhat bizarre police record illustrates.

Houghton lived in a tidy, one-story home in San Diego with his pretty, dark-haired, dark-eyed wife, the former Bettie Jones of southern Iowa farm upbringing, and their three little boys, all of whom appeared on our one encounter to be delightfully bright and active youngsters.

Troy and Bettie Houghton were married in 1954 while he was a service-station attendant and she an art student in Los Angeles.

Soon Troy was on his way to the Panamint Mountains on the west edge of Death Valley, intending to prospect for uranium. His newlywed wife accompanied him and became "head cook and bottle-washer," as she good-naturedly describes her role. Their interest turned to tungsten soon after their arrival in the mountains. At the time, Bettie Houghton later related, the government was paying a good price for tungsten, but by the time they had mined a sizable amount and were ready to sell, the price had dropped to unprofitable depths. Their many months in the wilderness had gone almost for naught. They earned enough, she said, to pay for their bread and butter, but little more.

The Houghtons moved back to Los Angeles in 1956 and Troy did some part-time work with a UCLA geologist before leaving again for the mountains with Bettie, this time to mine for silver and lead. A flash flood from a cloudburst washed out their camp, destroying much of their equipment. This time the Houghtons abandoned the mining business for good.

The experience, Bettie Houghton said, strengthened their marriage and enabled her to bear up under the even greater adversities that befell them later after Troy had become interested in the need, as he puts it, "to establish an underground army ahead of the Communist take-over."

"Even in the desert," Bettie Houghton said, "Troy was interested in what was going on politically. We'd pack up and drive fifty or sixty miles just to vote."

In 1961, after they had settled in San Diego, Bettie said, the newspapers, not Troy, informed Bettie of the nature of Troy's new interest—guerrilla warfare and the Minutemen.

"I thought, 'Oh my God, what is this thing?'" she recalled. "But Troy would tell me what was wrong in the country, and gradually I swung over. After meeting others in the organization—it made a lot of difference."

She describes herself as always having believed in "the basic fundamentals" politically—"America first, last and always, although I'm not a real flag-waver. This is the greatest country in the world and I want it to stay that way. I can see why Russia wants this country."

If one were to guess blindly in what area of the nation the Minutemen were strongest, most persons familiar with our regional peculiarities probably would name Southern California quickly, even if they had never heard of Houghton or his followers' activities. It seems best to leave it to the nation's sociologists, psychologists, meteorologists and perhaps even the metaphysicians to explain what it is about this area that seems to attract and spawn so many persons of unusual persuasions. Suffice it to say that Southern California has, indeed, proven fertile soil for all sorts of political, religious and personal organizations and cults, including the Minutemen.

At first blush in late October, 1961, it appeared that someone else was leader of the California Minutemen, however. DePugh, still basking in the limelight he had gained in Shiloh, Illinois, was telephoned by the San Diego *Tribune* while he was in Norborne. He told the newspaper he intended to visit San Diego in November to meet with California guerrilla leaders.

"I've been in contact with William F. Colley for months," the newspaper quoted DePugh as saying. "We communicate by code number so that names are protected, but that's the man in San Diego."

It is quite difficult to understand why the San Diego newspaper would have printed this if it were not so, but DePugh now insists he never said such a thing. Troy Houghton was always his man in California, he says, not Colley.

Since I wasn't in California at that time either, I have been presented with a somewhat confused picture of exactly what was the relationship in 1961 between Colley and DePugh, Colley and Houghton, and Houghton and DePugh.

Colley, a free-lance photographer from San Diego, had formed a tiny group calling itself the Loyal Order of Mountain Men sometime in 1961. Rather than guerrilla warfare, Colley was later to explain, his group specialized in survival, search and rescue work.

The Nation carried an article about Colley and his Mountain Men in its November 11 issue and *Time* had mentioned Colley, not Houghton, in its November 3 Minutemen report.

Time, reporting on the California Minutemen contingent, had written of one of their bivouacs in the Anza Desert State Park where for two days the small group "lived on cactus wrens, roast coyote, baked alligator lizard, boiled hairless caterpillar ('The hairy kind is poisonous') and mesquite-bean coffee." *Time* said they scaled cliffs and tossed Molotov cocktails made from ten-ounce beer cans filled with gasoline and stuffed with kerosene rags. The magazine quoted Colley as having said that California's 2900 Minutemen had buried medicine, supplies and 10,000 rounds of ammunition up and down the state, adding:

"We hope we never have to use that gear up there in the mountains. But it's not hurting us to put it there. And if we ever do need it, we'll be better off than those folks buried under radioactive ash in their concrete coffins."

Hans Engh's article in *The Nation* included other Colley quotes: "We prefer to keep our meeting places secret to avoid such things as calls from dumb nuts who want to go and fight Castro. . . . We don't want anyone to get the idea that we are a group of panic-button pushers or gun-toting ex-servicemen."

November was barely underway when California began to grow increasingly aware of the presence of Minutemen in their midst. This was partly because of Colley and Houghton, but they had help from Governor Edmund (Pat) Brown, the liberal Democrat who was defeated for re-election in 1966 by Ronald Reagan.

Responding to the news that some Southern Californians had said publicly they would defend their bomb shelters against invading urban dwellers in the event of a nuclear attack, Governor Brown told 2500 UCLA students that "any move toward anarchy" would be met successfully by the National Guard. Straying somewhat afield, and using some as yet unverified statistics, the governor told his audience:

"The movement has gained considerable headway. Not since the heyday of the 'America First' movement—before World War II—has there been such an upsurge of negative sentiment. We hear reports that there are twenty-three guerrilla bands with 2400 among their number in California who wish to be their own civil defenders, carry their own arms and choose their own hiding places in the event of nuclear war. . . ."

Somehow—either when answering questions by reporters afterward or inadvertently—the name of the Minutemen became equated that weekend with the guerrilla bands Governor Brown had mentioned.

The Minutemen most certainly interpreted it that way publicly, for one of the first things a fledgling organization needs, if it is to achieve any significance in the public eye, is an important, newsworthy foe. Governor Brown so qualified.

The Minutemen stayed in the news in California for the next two weeks, but not entirely as they had hoped.

Colley, the Mountain Men leader, and Houghton, who at that time was going by the name of Don Alderman, entered into something of a public squabble over who the real Minutemen leader of California was. As Colley was denouncing "Alderman" as not even being a member of the Minutemen, "Alderman" was announcing a large Minutemen meeting scheduled at a spot in the wilderness near Fresno for the weekend of November 4 and 5.

On the fifth—one day after he had denounced "Alderman" (Houghton)—the Los Angeles *Times* quoted Colley as saying: "I was way out of line when I made that statement last night. I thought I was speaking for the Minutemen because I thought I was a member. But I found out I am not."

I later asked Houghton why Colley had bowed out so gracefully at this point. Houghton raised his right hand, formed it into a fist, shook it menacingly in front of my face and smiled.

A day later DePugh told the *Times* by long-distance telephone that he would arrive in Los Angeles the following evening to coordinate "divisive elements" within the organization, the *Times* reported. There was no cause for controversy between Houghton and Colley over leadership, he said, because the national organization promoted a policy by which more than one group can exist in the same city without knowledge of other Minutemen groups also in operation there.

Alderman (Houghton) was next to be heard from, telling the Fresno *Bee* that Colley was "an adventure photographer and with twelve other adventurers heard about our organization and asked if they could become members. They attended one of our meetings but definitely never became members. I think he started the publicity about the organization in order to sell some of his films."

Of himself, Alderman (Houghton) said he formerly had been "helping to fight Communism" in Central America with "certain chemical knowledge I passed on." (He later told me he had helped overthrow the Communist government of Guatemala in 1953 and 1954.)

Houghton and Colley had provided DePugh with considerable advance fanfare prior to DePugh's arrival in Los Angeles November 7 and his press conference on November 10, at the Statler-Hilton, with Houghton by his side and Colley apparently forgotten.

"The third World War has already started, gentlemen," DePugh proclaimed, "and if we don't win it, we're going to lose it—there's no middle ground. We're risking our lives by what we're doing. But no matter what happens to this country, we're going to crawl out of this hole as a well-knit combat outfit."

To the delight of photographers, DePugh demonstrated a "Minute Mask" by putting the plastic bag over himself and was promptly photographed wearing it. Alderman (Houghton) was shown nearby watching.

Within twenty-four hours, DePugh had reason to regreat such prominent news coverage.

Suddenly both Colley and Houghton were exposed as having failed to register as convicted sex offenders, as required of persons in California who had been convicted of certain crimes.

"I was still out there calling on my veterinary trade," DePugh was to recall several years later, "and here, all of a sudden, all of this big smear hit the papers about Troy Houghton . . . and I thought, boy-oh-boy-oh-boy, I'm absolutely ruined. My business is ruined. Not another vet is going to buy another pill from me, and when I get back to Missouri, the council's going to chop my head off. I didn't know what to do. It was at a time when we were doing our best to put on a strong front, you know, to show an image of a nationwide organization. . . ."

The available evidence indicates that a great deal too much has been said about Houghton's sex life in the last several years. I am not going to presume to judge the man in this light—it's a bit too personal for my own tastes.

Too many versions of an "indecent exposure" incident in 1957 exist to waste time exploring them all. He and his wife say he had been sun bathing in the nude when seen by two young girls riding horseback in a remote part of a national forest. The police report on the case indicates a slightly less innocent set of circumstances. Whatever the case, the charge of failing to register as a "sex offender" in California was brought against him too soon after he had appeared with DePugh at a well-covered press conference to qualify as a coincidence in timing. No matter whether Houghton was a Minuteman or Communist, this—the evidence available to me indicates—was perhaps legally correct, but a below-the-belt blow at him and his organization. Discrediting the Minutemen with such methods side-steps the weightier issues raised by the Minutemen movement.

Several years later, Houghton provided me with a copy of an article in *The Valley News* of El Cajon, California, dated November 13, 1961. It had quoted a police official in San Diego as saying he believed the threat posed by the Minutemen never had amounted to much and was now non-existent. And:

"We accomplished our purpose in arresting the man who called himself Don Alderman. We never did think the Minutemen amounted to anything—we were never impressed with it and we now have accomplished our purpose, which was to discredit the organization."

Later in the article, Arlo E. Smith, Deputy State Attorney General in California, was quoted as saying he felt it unfortunate that Alderman (Houghton) had been arrested at that time because it may have blocked a phase of his investigation into "his activities in connection with the possession and securing of automatic weapons."

A few days later, a banner headline across the front page of the San Francisco *Sunday Chronicle* on November 12, 1961, proclaimed: "Guerrilla Boss Orders State Unit to Disband," and the accompanying story, under the by-line of George Draper, began:

"California's machine-gunning guerrillas were ordered disbanded yesterday by Robert B. DePugh, national commander of the super-patriotic Minutemen organization.

"DePugh, a drawling Missouri pill salesman, snapped out his demobilization order from his Los Angeles hotel room after the arrest of the Minutemen's California coordinator for failure to register as a sex offender. . . ."

Said DePugh recently, when reviewing this traumatic episode in the Minutemen history: "I never asked him to disband. . . . One of the newpaper reporters out there, I forget what his name was, he was on the San Francisco *Chronicle*, just put that in the paper, but I didn't say it."

"What did you say?"

"I don't remember that I said anything. I wish I could think of this fellow's name. He was a real sarcastic individual. He used to call me up there at the hotel about every evening and read me the next morning's headlines and gloat and laugh and try to prod me into making some kind of statement, you know. . . . I never told him I had asked Troy to disband or anything of the sort."

Draper's response to this, when I asked him about it, was: "There were several conversations, as I recall, both when he was in Missouri and in L.A. Really all I can remember about them was that DePugh was evasive and that I had to push him a little in order to get any satisfactory response to questions. In general, I would say, the conversations ended being acrimonious. . . . His position was not misrepresented. . . ."

Who has the best memory? Draper or DePugh? I'll vote for Draper. DePugh had apparently forgotten that in 1964, while I was conducting another interview with him, he had told me that he had not actually told Houghton to disband, but had told the newspapers that he had done so, for the good of the organization's image.

The Los Angeles press next quoted DePugh, as the Minutemen leader was recoiling from the image-smashing, that he had never heard of Houghton until mid-October when Houghton had written him, asking to affiliate his group with the "national organization."

More recently, Houghton offered me a different version of their original alliance in 1961. Houghton said he had formed his Minutemen organization at about the same time that DePugh had started his, coincidentally with the same name and same basic objectives. Houghton learned of DePugh's group through one of his own members who lived in the Midwest, Houghton said.

By the time of the training exercise at Shiloh, Illinois, other small guerrilla warfare groups had joined forces with DePugh's Minutemen too, Houghton said, including ones from Vermont, Virginia, Nebraska, Florida, the Deep South, Washington or Oregon and Illinois.

Fresh on the heels of the revelations about Colley's and Houghton's pasts came an announcement from the California attorney general's office to the effect that it had investigated and found untrue a report that the Minutemen had planned to assassinate Governor Brown and Attorney General Stanley Mosk in case of war.

Deputy Attorney General Smith added that the investigation also had disclosed that the Minutemen "do have weapons and gunpowder and we have information that they possess automatic weapons. But we have concluded tentatively that there are no large caches of these weapons and gunpowder," Smith continued, "but small ones, individually owned. . . .

"Our investigation stems from reports of reckless statements allegedly made by leaders of the Minutemen to the effect that they had a liquidation list of state officers, including the governor and attorney general, but our investigation showed there was no substance to this report."

Presumably aware by now that Governor Brown should not have thrown out the 2400 membership figure so loosely—however he may have meant it to sound—the attorney general's office also said that the Minutemen in California numbered only between fifty and one hundred at that time.

Representative John F. Shelley (D-Calif.) did not miss the opportunity on November 17 to tell the University of San Francisco alumni at a meeting that such groups as the John Birch Society and Minutemen were as dangerous to freedom as the Communists, and on December 4, the chief of staff of the California National Guard Reserve said he would ask for additional funds from the state. One reason: To counter the secret Minutemen guerrilla organization.

Through the rest of November and much of December, 1961, many an editorial writer across the country took time to pen a few thoughts about the Minutemen, and if any were favorable, I have yet to find them. The Kansas City *Star*, had been quick to react on October 24 with such thoughts as: ". . . The whole idea of the Minutemen could be laughed off as ridiculous if it did not reflect what may be rather widespread hostility or contempt for the government of the United States. We don't believe the people of this country are ready to confuse anarchy with patriotism . . ." and ". . . The Minutemen reflects a psychosis of the times. . . ."

The San Francisco *Chronicle* observed on November 16 that the idea that a few thousand riflemen could save the U.S. from its enemies was "so preposterous as to approach the incomprehensible." The San Francisco *News* likened them to flag-pole sitters and marathon dancers of the 1920s and '30s and called them "little pimples on the face of an era." The Los Angeles *Times* called them "a ragged band of comic-book guerrillas." The Chicago *Sun-Times* called them "nuts," and quite logically asked, "Who is to say that tomorrow they will not declare war on some legitimate group of Americans with whom they happen to disagree?" The Milwaukee *Journal* called them "a lunatic fringe group."

President Kennedy, while in Los Angeles in November, lashed out at the Far Right in a speech that included an apparent reference to the Minutemen: ". . . Devote more energy to organizing the free and friendly nations . . . and less energy to organizing armed bands of civilian guerrillas that are more likely to supply local vigilantes than national vigilance."

DePugh was quick to respond to this apparent attack with an open letter to the President on Minutemen stationery, assuring the President that his organization was not trying to raise a private army "or take any other action which is in conflict with the principles of our constitutional republic."

Maybe the letter pacified the President, but others remained upset. Governor Otto Kerner of Illinois ordered an investigation of the Minutemen in his state on December 5. On December 19, Walter and Victor Reuther stepped into the picture.

The president of the United Auto Workers of America, and his brother, the director of the international affairs department of the U.A.W., submitted a lengthy document to then Attorney General Robert F. Kennedy concerning possible administration policies and programs to combat the "Radical Right." It has since become known, especially in ultraconservative circles, as the "Reuther Memorandum" —and when these two words are spoken by the right, they are spoken with harsh contempt. The right wing, somehow having discovered the existence of the document, has been using it ever since as "proof" of an elaborate conspiracy to destroy various of their organizations through innumerable regulatory powers of the federal government and the occasional help of local authorities.

It undoubtedly delighted DePugh, however, for it tended to upgrade the status of the Minutemen substantially. After discussing the extent of the problem of the "Radical Right" at considerable length and naming numerous larger, better-known organizations on which it frowned, the Reuthers presented a five-point program under the heading: "Action on the Problem." One of those five points read as follows:

"The Administration should take steps to end the Minutemen. . . . Free speech is the essence of democracy, but armed bands are not the exercise of free speech. There is no warrant for permitting groups to organize into military cadres for the purpose of taking the law into their own hands.

"It is not known whether the Minutemen will grow or whether they will fade out of the picture. They do, however, represent a dangerous precedent in our democracy. Consideration should be given to the question whether they are presently violating any federal laws and, if not, to the federal government calling a conference of States where the Minutemen exist to see what action could be taken under state laws. There is, of course, the additional possibility, as indicated earlier, that the Minutemen might fall within the terms of the Attorney General's list of subversive organizations."

Although numerous other, larger right-wing groups are mentioned in this document and at greater length, only the Minutemen rated a section devoted to it alone under the heading of "action."

In the following years, with each indictment against him by a grand jury, DePugh has pointed to the Reuther Memorandum as having been somehow behind it, whether the grand jury was state or federal. DePugh once even described the memorandum as Walter Reuther's "ultimatum" to Robert Kennedy.

Victor Reuther, in a letter replying to queries about this memorandum, wrote me that he and his brother had submitted it in response to a request from Attorney General Kennedy. In reply to the question of why they had singled out the Minutemen as they had, Reuther wrote:

"We did not single out the Minutemen for attention. It was a very minor part of the memorandum which dealt with extremist groups on both sides of the political spectrum ranging from the Birch society to the Communist Party. We made passing reference to the

Minutemen because we believed it illustrated an important problem for democratic government: how to protect free speech without countenancing the threat of armed rebellion. We used the Minutemen to illustrate our belief that all the words of the Birch society could not hurt the country, but that free speech did not require tolerance of caches of military equipment. . . ."

"Why were we singled out?" DePugh asked an audience in 1965. "Because the Minutemen represent what the Communists fear the most—that the Communists' own methods might be used against them."

Elaborating on this in an interview more recently, DePugh speculated: "They recognized that this was a new element in the opposition, that although it was small, it was a major deviation from the prior anti-Communist movement, the first time anybody ever picked up a gun and said, 'Look, I've got a gun to fight Communism.'"

Before the end of 1961, it was evident, however, that the Minutemen were intended as more than just an organization of men with guns to fight Communism in guerrilla warfare fashion one day. DePugh had told the San Diego *Tribune* in October that part of his group's objective was to form a nationwide spy network to discover subversives. And in mid-December, he outlined to Steve Underwood of the Kansas City *Star* some of the other, broader goals of the Minutemen.

He told Underwood of the secrecy involved in Minutemen membership, with band leaders not knowing the identities of other band leaders, for instance. He told of how he kept vital organization documents chemically treated and in a nitrogen-filled metal cabinet so they would burst into flames if exposed to the air. He told of code numbers and code names used by members (DePugh was No. 551) and of mail drops and the necessity to wrap letters in an opaque material before putting them in envelopes for mailing.

He also spoke of plans to distribute a booklet to members on how to make munitions in their homes—which he did, indeed, follow up on later, although in pamphlet rather than booklet form. Until the point when the government no longer represents the people as a true constitutional form of government, DePugh also said in this interview, the Minutemen would conduct themselves in a completely lawful manner. They would not, however, turn in their legally owned weapons or comply with a national registration law for firearms, he said.

He also told of what at that time was becoming the Minutemen's "biggest project," although it did not remain so long. This was to study textbooks being offered in schools to ferret out what material they felt was Communist-tinted. Wives of Minutemen, he said, were already at work on this and in six months he hoped to have Parent-Teacher Associations recommend or condemn certain textbooks to school boards. In a year, he added, they hoped to take legal action against certain books and in two years, legal actions against those responsible for the books. To illustrate his point about the books, he compared a current fifth grade text with one that was fifty years old. The current book devoted only four pages to the American Revolution, he said, while the old one spent thirty-five pages "in small type" on this subject. The Minutemen leader said he had tried these two books on a fifth grader who read both versions. The child was unimpressed with the current book, but after reading the longer version said, "Gee, it makes me feel good I'm an American."

DePugh also told Underwood that by 1963, he hoped there would be one million Minutemen active in the United States.

Back in California, Senator Jacob Javits, (R-N.Y.), in a speech late in 1961 before the San Francisco Bay Area Republican Alliance, mentioned the Minutemen by naming them and the Birch society as two of the extremist movements he felt "feed on our national frustrations and undermine our national purpose of freedom."

"At a time in our history when confidence in our institutions was never more necessary to meet the challenge of the Communists," he said, "the radicals of the right tend to confuse and divide us by adopting much the same methods as do the radicals of the extreme left. . . ."

It had been an exciting year for DePugh. His fledgling organization had been indirectly criticized by the President of the United States and ordered investigated by two governors—Brown and Kerner. The brothers Reuther had advised the U. S. Attorney General that his group should be eliminated and Senator Javits had warned California Republicans that the Minutemen were undermining our freedom. The Minutemen were off to a fast start.

CHAPTER 4

JOIN THE MINUTEMEN
(Or at least the Counter-Insurgency Council.)

. . . The true guerrilla is never beaten. He will never negotiate away his freedom. He will never compromise his ideals. He will never surrender.

History offers many examples of far larger and better equipped armies that were finally defeated by guerrillas. They can fight on for years, even generations. Guerrilla bands can fight in the cities, country, forests, swamps, deserts or mountains. They are everywhere and yet nowhere. They strike without warning and vanish without a trace. They take away with them the arms, food and ammunition they will need to fight again another day.

The guerrilla is a grim fighter and a terrible foe. His strength is in his heart—in his love for his country—in his hatred of the enemy. His chief weapons are stealth, cunning, endurance and most of all, an intense belief in the righteousness of his own cause.

He will fight to the death with a fury that makes his enemies cower before him.

From "Principles of Guerrilla Warfare," copyright 1961, Robert B. DePugh—a booklet.

The Minutemen slowly began to pick up new members in the early 1960s, but it also lost a few. Sometimes those who left were simply disenchanted with the whole Minutemen idea. Others departed because they wished to go it alone in their quest for "freedom" and preparedness against Communism. And some severed their ties because of internal disputes—an inevitable problem in any group as odd as this.

Rich Lauchli, who had been resident host at the eye-opening southern Illinois Minutemen gathering in October, 1961, was one of the first to openly break with the organization. Since he fairly well left the stage on which this drama is set before the end of 1962, it seems that a closer look at Lauchli is now in order.

Back in his high school days, young Lauchli showed early signs of being eventually good Minutemen material. He demonstrated this in manual-training class when he told his teacher a mischievous lie. He told him his project for shop class would be the construction of a power lawn mower.

"We all had to have a project," the forty-year-old Lauchli chuckled over the incident more than two decades later. "You know how it is in high school. And hell, it didn't look any more like a power mower than you. My shop teacher was kind of a funny old coot, I guess you might say, although I shouldn't be disrespectful to him, he was nice enough. But anyhow, he woke up one day to the fact that this wasn't any power lawn mower."

No, it was a homemade automatic submachine gun.

"It shot all right," he recalled, "but I used a piece of old barrel which was oversized and the bullets used to come out sideways and everything else."

Lauchli was reprimanded by the school principal, but not so harshly that he seems to have learned much from the experience. This can be documented by his subsequent record of convictions in federal courts, the most important of which resulted in a sentence of four concurrent two-and-one-half-year terms in federal prison—which he began serving on March 13, 1967, at Terre Haute, Indiana. For Lauchli's preoccupation with machine guns and a wide variety of other weapons of war has grown since his high school days, reaching the point in 1964 that he was able to acquire and rework an arsenal of weapons so large that he sold them for $17,000 to a man who said he was a general from a Latin American country.

His initial reluctance toward the idea of an interview about himself and the Minutemen lasted about thirty seconds before, without any particular persuasion, he was saying, "Well, come on inside," and soon, "Would you like a beer?"

A sign beside the highway that passes two blocks from his home in Collinsville, near St. Louis, reads simply, "Machine Shop. LOXCO. Welding," with an arrow pointing northward. (Originally, LOXCO was to stand for Lauchli Ordnance Experimental Company.) On a hillside within shouting distance of his home are his machine shop and the home of his parents. Inside the shop Lauchli can do anything from make machine guns (that no longer fire bullets sideways) to repairing farmers' plows and producing special parts for racing cars.

A big, friendly, garrulous teddy bear of a man, an ex-paratrooper, apparently happily married, the father of a teen-age girl, Lauchli talked freely about himself, his problems with the federal government, his days as a regional coordinator for the Minutemen and the present organization of guerrilla warfare trainees he founded in 1962—the little Counter-Insurgency Council.

He quickly tired of seeing his interviewer scribbling notes in longhand at his kitchen table, suggested lending me his typewriter and, when a tape recorder was suggested, he readily agreed to its use. For various intangible reasons, I received the impression as he talked that, for the most part anyway, Lauchli was telling the truth.

A native of St. Louis, Missouri, Lauchli moved with his family to Collinsville in 1943 to become in less than twoscore years its most widely known citizen. Once out of high school in 1945, he joined the Army and made, as he remembers, seventeen jumps as a member of the 82nd Airborne Division before his discharge in October, 1946. He was also a gunnery instructor on automatic weapons while in the Army. He returned to Collinsville and began work as a machinist with a special interest in guns but an apparently limited knowledge of the laws pertaining to them. By 1955 he stood accused of manufacturing machine guns without a federal license, was fined $100 in federal court and given a suspended sentence.

Two years later, the Collinsville machinist and nine other men became sufficiently alarmed over the prospects of impending armed conflict in the United States against a foreign enemy that they formed the Internal Security Force, a guerrilla warfare group designed, he said, primarily for their own self-defense in southern Illinois. This organization lasted only about three years, he said, but long enough for Lauchli to land in more trouble with the federal government, this time on a more serious charge.

As he tells it, he was buying scrap metal from the government at the Madison proving grounds in Indiana, hauling it away by truck. A friend who was helping him happened to notice a number of World War II bazookas lying in a building, unused, perhaps forgotten by the Army. His friend, who owned an airplane and was a member of the Internal Security Force, suggested that some night they ought to fly there and sneak the bazookas over a fence to a spot where they later could haul them away with the scrap metal Lauchli was purchasing.

His friend never quite got around to acting on this idea, Lauchli said, so one night Lauchli and another friend drove there by truck and stole away with four of the surplus bazookas. A month later they returned, cut through the fence and took the nineteen remaining weapons.

"It was the wrong thing to do," he now concedes, "I mean, I can't deny that. I mean, you can say you were buying all this scrap and so forth and so on, which is true, but when you get right down to it, it was stealing just the same, and it wasn't the right thing to do."

It did not take the FBI long to find out who had taken the weapons, he said. He was fined $500 this time and given two years probation.

Following the dissolution of the Internal Security Force in 1960, Lauchli started looking around for another similar organization to join. He investigated several small ones that came to his attention but nothing really appealed to him until he read a "Join the Minutemen" ad in a St. Louis newspaper in the summer of 1961. He answered the ad, received a reply from DePugh personally, and joined. He was assigned the secret Minutemen number of 579, as he remembered it, and in July or August, No. 551 stopped off to see him in Collinsville.

"I was very impressed," Lauchli said. "Bob's a great talker. Later I went to Independence for a gun show at the armory there. Bob and his brother and I stood under a tree near the armory until four o'clock in the morning just picking each other apart, you know, getting to know each other. In late August, I got all of Illinois and part of Missouri, with the informal title of coordinator."

He went to a secret Minutemen seminar in Omaha in mid-September and played host a month later to the Shiloh meeting and two-hour field exercise the following day. Several other field maneuvers were held following that, but all in southern Missouri. Lauchli said he went on three or four before quitting the Minutemen in October, 1962.

"We used private property and we used government property," he said. ". . . We took live ammunition on occasion, but it wasn't shooting indiscriminately here and and there and so forth. For example, now, we might be running a patrol and we'd pick out some point on a cliff, maybe a rock sticking out or something like that, and we'd say 'Lay the fire down there,' just to make some noise and get the people in the proper state of mind, you know."

Explosives, Lauchli said, also were used on these training maneuvers.

"We've done everything from make homemade grenades and so forth. I mean, people had to be acquainted with what was to be expected out of them and so forth. But it was strictly training. We used to make up the more exotic stuff like platter charges, and earmuff charges, shape charges, this sort of thing, and we'd run 'em off, strictly to show the people how. . . ."

"This was training for what purpose?"

"Well, here you have to become sort of indefinite," he replied. "Because none of us know. You could wake up tomorrow and you would say, 'Well, this is The Day,' like apparently these people up in the East did (referring to the New York Minutemen who had recently been arrested on charges of conspiring to commit arson). I mean, they woke up and said, 'Well, hell, we've taken all we're going to and we're going to do something about it.' (He was speculating here, of course, having no personal knowledge of the New York case.) This is one of the things from where I differed from the national Minutemen office. I felt that everybody had to do what they thought was right in their own way, and that our purpose was limited to teaching them how such things could be done at their own discretion. I figured they had to live with themselves. They had to make their own decisions."

"What if you trained some guy who decided the next day to go off and start shooting people?"

"Well, this is certainly a hazard, there's no question about it. And this again was where I differed from the national organization. At the time I was coordinator, we had something like sixty people in my sphere of influence, which by that time was the southern half of Illinois and a 100 mile radius of St. Louis. We had about sixty people and I tried to contact each one. This was the early part of 1962. And I found people that were sincere, and tops all around, to plain *nuts*, I mean, people that shouldn't have been running around on the street, and these people were all in the organization.

"So this kind of bothered me. I mean, I'll tell you, to give you some idea of these people, I had one guy, for instance, that says, 'Where's the guns? I want the guns,' and I said, 'What the hell you want the guns for?' and he says, 'Man, I want to go out and kill a bunch of them Communists.' I said, 'Well, how do you know they're Communists?" and he says, 'Well, they're Communists all right.'"

This particular Minuteman, Lauchli continued, had been raised in Texas but could not make a living there. His uncle, who lived near Collinsville, took him in and, because he was a good member of the painters' union, talked the union officials into letting his nephew work as a painter.

"Now, the uncle dies," Lauchli said, "and the union figured, well, we know this guy from nobody, I mean, he's an out-of-towner, and so forth, so they wouldn't give him any more permits, they took his livelihood away from him. And, of course, he figured right away that anybody that does this must be a Communist, so he was going to wipe out everybody. I mean, this is only one. I could go on with a half dozen of them like this."

Of the sixty Minutemen in his area of responsibility in 1962, Lauchli classified only a few as "nuts" but about a third of the total as "unstable." He said he wrote DePugh recommending they be dropped from the organization but "as long as they'd make some sign that maybe they'd put a buck into the kitty, they were retained. . . . This was something I resented."

Through most of 1962, Lauchli said, he slowly grew more and more disenchanted with DePugh personally. This was, he explained, primarily because he could not believe anything DePugh said.

DePugh would telephone him, Lauchli related, and tell him he needed, for example, fourteen Minutemen to attend a meeting in Independence on May 28. Lauchli would call as many members as was necessary to find fourteen who could be free to make the trip on that day. Then DePugh would send out a form letter to each member telling them of the meeting, he said, but saying it was to be held on May 21.

"This made it look to me and I'm sure the rest of the world that I didn't know what the hell I was doing," he said. "There was always this problem. Bob would say this thing is such and such a way and you'd find out it wasn't such and such. . . . Anything and everything, it didn't make the slightest difference what it was, there were always these God-dern lies. No, Bob, no matter what else he done, if he could have stayed away from the lies I think we could have got together. I thought, 'I've got to have these people's faith. If they don't believe what I tell them, I'm in bad shape.'"

Lauchli said he decided to make the final break with DePugh while he and a few other Minutemen in his region were on a particularly unpleasant field exercise in southern Missouri. All of them felt the same way as he did about DePugh, he said, but had not discussed it among themselves.

"It rained solid, just poured, for two days," he recalled, "and everyone was getting wet and miserable and, you know, mad at the world anyway, and we got a little fire built trying to get halfway dry and warm and so forth, and the general dissatisfaction started pouring out. So we finally came to the conclusion, why the hell don't we start our own organization and get away from the other. . . . I sent in a formal resignation and we formed the Counter-Insurgency Council."

The CIC has only twenty-four members, Lauchli said, "and it's going to stay that way, too." Its members all live in the St. Louis area and are known personally to Lauchli. He is extremely apprehensive —as experience has taught him—about the possibility of infiltrators.

The CIC has maintained liaison with DePugh and the Minutemen, Lauchli said, and "we get along fine with him, but I still get that baloney he always gives."*

"I'm 100 percent in agreement with Bob's objectives," Lauchli added. "I think that guerrilla warfare—and I think this is well proven today —is something that every one of us has to consider. Now, I don't say the way we go about it is the best way, in fact, I'm sure it's not. But I do say it's the only way open to us. I think this should be a government function . . . organized at a state level and the federal government should cooperate with it . . . but they're not going to do it, no matter what they say. They (the government) are afraid of the *people*, possibly with good reason."

Lauchli talked quite humbly about his own role in such an organization, stressing that he does not think he has the right or the capability to decide for others when it is time for his group to strike out at the enemy. It has to be up to the individual member, he said.

"Does DePugh think he's going to make the decision for all his people?"

"I don't know," Lauchli replied. "I'll say this—he considers that a lot more leading from the national office to the rest of the country (is necessary) than I would. In my organization, there's no president,

* "We're still friendly," was the way DePugh put it. "We exchange information and do each other a favor when something arises."

no leader. We work together. I'm just another one of the people. There's no one at the top."

Lauchli said he believes there is a national council of Minutemen, as DePugh has claimed, basing this opinion on the fact, he said, that DePugh asked him to become a member of the council in 1962. Lauchli said he declined the offer. He also has gained the impression, he said, that DePugh is answerable to some person or group over him in the Minutemen organization, but stressed this was only an impression.

"For instance, where does the money· come from for the operation of the Minutemen?" he asked. "I mean, I know these people don't put enough money in to finance an operation like he's running. You couldn't buy the paper that he prints with the money that organization is donated. Somebody's got to be heading it up."

This opinion was predicated on Lauchli's further belief that the Minutemen is an organization of only 200 or 300 persons with perhaps twice that many who contribute money to it.

"You take the people that have written a letter, then I don't think this 25,000 that he talks about is a bit too high," he added. ". . . I think this figure is the one Bob takes. Anybody that agrees with the way he thinks, why, he's a gooooood member. But this is just an opinion. I don't have any access to the records."

Believers that the principles of guerrilla warfare will someday have to be used in this country to defend us against the Communists number far beyond even the mythical membership of the Minutemen, Lauchli believes.

"There's people all over who believe in these principles," he elaborated, "and if they've given it any thought—and a lot of them have—they have something put away. I'll give you an example and so forth and so on. Back in 1956, eight or ten years ago, there was imported into this country a very light submachine gun. I mean, it looked nice, it had a good reputation, although truly in my own experience it was not much, but it had a good reputation and they weren't deactivated to the point that they couldn't be reworked and so forth and so on. I don't know how many were brought in, but there must have been several thousand.

"They've completely disappeared off the market. They aren't available whatsoever anywhere. Now, where are these weapons?"

And his voice turned to a near-whisper.

"They're put away for The Day.

"These people," he continued, "are all prepared for The Day. And I say this—I say that what the individual is doing today in this country is the greatest deterrent to Communism in this country that's ever happened, because Communism can't come into this country unless the people let it, and they'll only let it if they don't have the tools to stop it, and I'm telling you, this is an armed camp! There's millions, actually millions of weapons put away for The Day, and I'm not talking about hunting guns and so forth. I mean people have *put stuff away!*"

Lauchli believes this has happened because the people do not trust the government to protect them from Communism any longer. They are additionally shaken up by so much talk about firearms-control legislation, he said.

"You can't stop weapons," he said. "Today we think in terms of rifles and pistols, but we're on the verge of something so much greater, breakthroughs in chemistry and so forth that are going to let the average man in the street get a weapon that'll knock out the whole city of St. Louis."

As an example, Lauchli said, in 1963 a man he declined to identify offered to trade him enough nerve gas to knock out the entire metropolitan St. Louis area of 2,000,000 persons in exchange for just $50 worth of more conventional weapons.

At another point in the interview, a question was put to Lauchli concerning the mystery of who is on the National Council that Lauchli believes exists.

"Not knowing who's on the council," I asked, "you don't know if they're leftists or rightists."

"That's right. That's right," Lauchli replied with enthusiasm. "And don't think this hasn't crossed everybody's mind, either. I mean, you're not the first one to come up with this idea. I mean, there's a possibility that Bob DePugh himself is an *agent provocateur* and he'd be a very good one if he were. What better way to discredit guerrilla warfare in this country than the manner in which he's gone through."

"You really think so?"

"I got an open mind on the thing. I think it's a possibility."

"What has he done to discredit it?"

"Well," said Lauchli, "guerrilla warfare in this country today is considered bad. Say 'guerrilla warfare' and you're saying Bob DePugh. He's

'Mr. Guerrilla Warfare' himself in this country today. Now, I don't say that Bob *is*. I just say I got an open mind to it."

"You're more or less inclined to think he's sincere, I take it?"

"I don't know that I'd say that. Like I said before, I've lost so much faith in Bob. I don't believe anything he says. So I couldn't say I believe he's sincere. I felt that he was sincere at the time that I joined the organization, but I can't say I feel he's sincere today. . . ."

"You think there's any possibility he's in it just for the money?"

Lauchli laughed heartily at this and replied, "No."

"Why do you laugh?"

"Well, there's no money there. He's dedicated. There's no two ways about that. The only question lies in which side is he dedicated to. He's giving his life. His life is ruined. He's ruining it for a cause. The only question is which cause? Anybody that's gone through what Bob has, and I've gone through on some scale myself, you understand, there's no money in the world that could compensate for that."

Although apparently out of the Minutemen after October, 1962, Lauchli did not stay out of trouble with the federal government. A federal grand jury in Springfield, Illinois, indicted him in September, 1964, on charges of manufacturing and transferring illegal firearms, conspiracy, and interstate transportation of firearms by a convicted felon. This had been in connection with a wildly improbable set of circumstances triggered by a man who represented himself to Lauchli as a general from a Latin American country and said he wanted to buy a large supply of weapons and ammunition from him. The "general," Lauchli discovered much too late, was an agent of the Treasury Department's Alcohol and Tobacco Tax Unit (ATTU).

The agent never told Lauchli what country he was from, but Lauchli said the inference was that it was either Cuba or Chile, and that he was an anti-Communist.

"I made it definitely understood," Lauchli said, "that I wouldn't even be interested in talking to him unless he were anti-Communist and this he very definitely did."

"Did he prove that he was an anti-Communist?"

"How do you prove it?" Lauchli laughed.

"You were sure you weren't selling this to some Communist?"

"It sure could be. . . ."

"But you felt you were selling to an anti-Communist?"

"That's right. . . . You couldn't have a man come to you and say, 'I can prove to you without any doubt that I'm anti-Communist.' I mean, I don't know what your philosophy is. Like I told you, I'm not even sure about Bob DePugh. So you don't have any way. . . . But I had in my mind that what I was doing was right. . . . Here's the thing—would the Communists be coming to me for this?"

"If you've got 'em to sell."

"I don't think so. I don't think so. For instance, I know the personal pilot of Raul Castro, who was with Raul Castro in Cuba. And I know who supplied Raul Castro's weapons. The Russians did, by submarine."

Testimony at Lauchli's trial in Springfield, Illinois, in October, 1965, brought out that Russian submariners may not have been the only suppliers of weapons to Castro. Another, according to the testimony, was Rich Lauchli.

Thomas Moseley, a Chicago bus driver who did part-time work as an undercover agent for the ATTU and other federal investigative agencies, testified that as he and "General Joe Camillo," actually the ATTU agent, were collaborating with Lauchli over the purchase of numerous weapons, Lauchli tried to impress "the General" that he was no amateur as an arms supplier. Moseley quoted Lauchli as saying:

"Well, I've supplied in the past guns to Castro, I've supplied guns to (the) anti-Castro movement, I've been supplying guns to the Minutemen and indirectly to the John Birch Society."

Moseley later elaborated slightly, but significantly, on the alleged Lauchli-Castro connection, saying Lauchli had said he had supplied weapons to Castro "when Castro made his bid for power" and that "since then he has supplied anti-Castro movements, various movements."

Lauchli's was a lively trial, not without its humor (to most everyone but Lauchli, his family and friends). The ATTU and their bus-driving compatriot did a masterful job of leading Lauchli into a provable law violation, although not in such a manner that the defense of entrapment by the government was sufficient to save him.

In March, 1964, Lauchli had received a shipment from Provo, Utah, of parts from 1537 Thompson submachine guns, 110 Browning .30-caliber machine guns and four Browning .50-caliber machine guns. Judson Doyle, an ATTU agent, visited Lauchli at his home and asked him to surrender them but Lauchli, who had paid $2500 for this shipment, refused, insisting he had done nothing in violation of the law.

Moseley, the bus driver, meanwhile had been in contact with a young Cicero, Illinois, man, and had ordered a large number of Thompson submachine guns from him. The man said he had a source for such weapons and would have that source drive up to Chicago and meet with him. The source, it developed, was Lauchli, who did drive to Chicago with forty-six of the unassembled weapons and met Moseley. No sale resulted, however.

Soon Moseley and "General Camillo" were knocking on Lauchli's door at Collinsville. They agreed to pay Lauchli $150 per submachine gun. Lauchli accepted the offer since he would have received only $90 per weapon by dealing through the middleman in Cicero. The ATTU agent, whose real name was Fortino Gutierrez, and Moseley met with Lauchli seven or eight more times, it was testified, as negotiations over the weaponry continued.

In the initial dealings with the Collinsville machinist, Lauchli agreed to furnish them submachine guns without barrels. When pressed, he told them they could order the barrels from a man in Kalispell, Montana, but Moseley and "the General" later claimed they could not telephone the Montanan.

"They said they had tried to contact this man out there and they couldn't do it," Lauchli testified, "and actually, they impressed me as a couple of rummies. They claimed they couldn't make a telephone call or anything. . . ."

Lauchli's use of the word "rummies" to describe Moseley and "the General" was grabbed by Leon G. Scroggins, the assistant U.S. district attorney, and used repeatedly thereafter. In cross-examination:

"I believe . . . you referred to Mr. Moseley and Mr. Gutierrez as impressing you as being a couple of rummies?"

"The next morning they did," said Lauchli.

"How do you define a rummy?" Scroggins asked.

"Someone who can't do the simplest thing."

"Is that the ordinary use of the word rummy?"

"I wouldn't know. That's my connotation of it."

"Does it denote simple-mindedness?"

"Yes, sir."

"Being easily led?"

"No, not necessarily."

"Just not too bright?"

"In this case, yes."

"You sold two people, who weren't too bright, 102 Thompson submachine guns?"

During their negotiations for the purchase of the guns, Moseley and "the General" were given a tour of the interior of Lauchli's machine shop. Moseley described it from the witness stand in detail, ending his discourse with the observation that it contained: ". . . Just about anything you wanted if you wanted to start your own private revolution."

"Object to the witness' characterization of what . . ." began the defense attorney, and the jury was told to disregard the remark.

After making a few individual purchases from Lauchli, "the General" and Moseley began to press him for the big order that would bring him $17,000. Lauchli protested that the submachine guns were not ready yet, but Moseley insisted "the General" needed them immediately and his "group" would finish what work remained to be done on them. A truck, he said, was already on the way to Collinsville to pick up the merchandise.

The truck arrived the morning of May 19, 1964, driven by an investigator for the ATTU named Joe Scott.

"He's colored," testified Moseley, "and Lauchli said, 'Who's that guy out there? I don't trust those kind of people.' I said, 'Well, he's all right, Rich. I've known the man for ten years. He's worked with me before. I trust him. He's all right.' "

They loaded the submachine guns onto the truck along with various other weapons and warlike devices (smoke grenades, a flame thrower, flares, etc.) and Lauchli asked for the money. "The General" disappointed Lauchli with the news that they would have to go to a bank at Clinton, Illinois, north of Collinsville, to obtain the $17,000 and it was arranged that they would all meet later at the water tower in Wapella, Illinois, near Clinton. Lauchli was growing suspicious by this time, but not nearly suspicious enough.

"Rich said, well, to go along, he'd have to wait awhile before he could leave," said Moseley. "He had to get—as he described it—his 'muscle man,' and he said he was going down to the house, put through a call for his 'muscle man.' "

This, it later developed, was a locksmith and friend of Lauchli named Donald Sturgis, who Lauchli said was innocently involved in the whole affair—not so innocently, however, that Lauchli failed to arm Sturgis with his wife's semi-automatic rifle. Lauchli, in turn, armed himself with an automatic "grease gun" plus an automatic pistol holstered to his belt.

Eventually they all reached what was called the Butterworth farm, which Moseley told Lauchli belonged to some of his relatives.

Lauchli and Sturgis, weapons at the ready, inspected several farm structures in the vicinity to make certain no one was hiding inside. They failed to enter only the farmhouse where, it so happened, two more ATTU agents were, indeed, hiding.

Before completing the transfer of weapons, "the General" insisted that Lauchli demonstrate that the submachine guns worked. Against his better judgment, Lauchli agreed to test-fire some of the weapons inside the barn. He stationed Sturgis about 100 feet from the barn with his semi-automatic rifle and proceeded to assemble seven submachine guns and try to fire them. Only one of the seven worked. Five of the others fired only one, two or three rounds at once. Lauchli later was to explain to me that this was because of the weak springs he had had to put in the weapons in order to meet "the General's" early deadline. Of the more than 100 submachine guns sold "the General," only six were found to function perfectly.

Lauchli worked in the heat of the hot May afternoon for about an hour with the weapons and might have continued longer except for the unexpected appearance of a light airplane over the deserted farm.

". . . And this plane flew over," testified Moseley. "With that, this Don Sturgis hollered out, 'There is a plane coming in, Rich, shall I bring it down?' and with that he motioned, made a motion with his gun toward this low-flying airplane some 150, 200 feet off the ground. Rich said, 'No,' he said, 'Give them a pass this time.'"

The plane, which later was identified to have been an innocent private pilot curious over the activity on the ground, prompted Lauchli to end his work with the submachine guns and insist upon his money. He was handed the $17,000 in a metal box, and was so worried by then that he neglected even to count it.

As Lauchli and Sturgis headed away from the point of exchange on a country road, they noticed a car pull out from the first farmhouse they passed and begin following them.

"I said to Don, 'I don't like the looks of what's going on here.'" Lauchli related to me later, "and then when we get to the second house, here was a car coming down from there. Well, you had to be pretty dense to think something wasn't going on by that time."

The cars were unmarked, Lauchli said, and he and his friend could not be certain whether they were government agents or a group of men after the $17,000.

Soon three more cars were also following them down the country road. The chase reached speeds up to 95 m.p.h. before it was over.

"Truthfully, now, I'm going to lay it right down for you," Lauchli said. "If we'd wanted to be rotten about it, we had the material there that we could have stopped any kind of force that they could have put out at us. We had the weapons. We had a submachine gun. We had a high-powered rifle. We had the equipment to stop them if we were so inclined. But I'm not built that way."

After about ten miles, with the police and government cars honking fiercely much of the way, Lauchli said he stopped and he and his friend climbed from the car without their weapons.

"There was this one guy with a sawed-off shotgun," Lauchli recalled. " 'Get 'em up, higher, higher, higher,' and, man, pretty soon you're on your toes. They were a nervous bunch of people, I'll tell you, boy. They all had their hammers back on their revolvers. I mean, if we'd have said, 'Boo,' I mean, we'd have had a thousand holes in us right now. . . . These guys were really expecting us to put up a fight."

Lauchli took the stand in his own defense and was, in fact, the only defense witness to testify. He admitted most of the events offered by the government as having taken place, but insisted he did not feel he had been in violation of the law "willfully and knowingly." His attorney also argued that the government had entrapped Lauchli.

Lauchli identified himself as belonging to the Kankakee Gun Club and the American Ordnance Association, which he said was somehow connected with or blessed by the U.S. government. He said he was president of the Cahokia Gun Collectors, a southern Illinois group, and was a former member of the National Rifle Association.

One of Lauchli's main points was that he bought submachine guns and other weapons to sell as curios and museum pieces. He said he advertised openly in *Shotgun News, Shooting Times* and *Gun and Ammo* magazines, a fact which the government later was to observe showed intent to transfer parts across state lines although Lauchli was a convicted felon.

Robert B. Oxtoby, the defense counsel, argued in his closing statement that Lauchli had operated so openly that it should be clear he was obviously not a man of evil intent.

"There is no evidence here that the defendant at any time ever sold weapons or arms to the underworld," Oxtoby argued. ". . . He probably shouldn't be enticed into selling them to a foreign country on some type of insurrection of the Communist faction of the government. But that wasn't his idea. Keep in mind that was the government's idea, that he should do that.

"If it had been somebody else that had come to him and ensnared and entrapped him, we couldn't have the defense of entrapment. But if the general had, in fact, been a general, and if his friend had been a compatriot and an agent from the foreign country, then the defense wouldn't exist. But it so turns out, the general and his pal were agents of the United States government, embarked upon the course to get the defendant to commit a crime, if, in fact, he did commit a crime."

Scroggins' final argument dealt with the entrapment issue too.

"I told you," the assistant D.A. said, "you were going to hear about the enticement. I was enticed. I was sitting down in my little old machine shop in Collinsville, Illinois, minding my own business, of course, I had this hobby, (Lauchli had called his interest in weapons a hobby) but I was sitting down in my machine shop and here come the agents. But before that, I was paying a social visit to a friend of mine in Cicero, Illinois. . . . Was it social by nature? Yes, it was a social visit. Well, I took up a truckload of weapons, but frequently, when I visit friends, I take a truckload of weapons along with me. . . ."

Judge Omer Poos explained the law regarding entrapment to the jury before it began deliberating.

". . . The defense of unlawful entrapment is not established if the defendant was either engaged in similar crimes, or was ready and willing to violate the law," he said, "and the law enforcement officers or their agents merely afforded him the opportunity of committing the crime. Under these circumstances entrapment is lawful rather than unlawful, even though the law officers may have used a ruse or otherwise concealed their identity."

The jury's verdict—guilty.

The government, incidentally, recovered its $17,000.

A month after being charged with that crime, the indomitable Lauchli happened to read an editorial by Karl L. Monroe, editor of the Collinsville *Herald*, recalling Lauchli's Minutemen activities in 1961 in and around Shiloh. The editorial was in connection with the editor's opposition to the John Birch Society and its type of thinking. It prompted Lauchli to write a letter to the editor, objecting to "the inference Rich Lauchli is a thing of the past."

To prove this very valid point, Lauchli informed Monroe that in July of that year he had conducted a seminar on weapons and explosives on a farm two miles from Collinsville, offering classes on high-power rifle fire, combat pistol shooting, the bazooka and rocketry. Several types of explosives were detonated, he wrote the editor, for demonstration purposes.

Later in the year he tried to start a drive to solicit money in Collinsville for an armored car that he said the Counter-Insurgency Council would loan to police departments in the area around Collinsville and St. Louis for use during riots or to dislodge fugitives who had barricaded themselves against capture. The subscription drive failed, however.

When I talked with Lauchli in December, 1967, he was still concerned about "The Day." When I asked him what sort of development on the national or international scene might provoke him or the Minutemen into overt action, Lauchli replied earnestly:

"There's nothing you can say at this time, because this is something you have to live with. Say you hate some guy in an extreme way. You hate a neighbor, say. You hate his guts. How do you say, 'Well, Thursday I'm going to go kill him?' The thing keeps building and builds and builds until the people have simply had enough, where they can't take it any more. Now, it isn't a decision by me or a decision by my twenty-four people, or a decision made by Bob De-Pugh. This is a decision made by the people in general all over the country. When the people simply have had enough they have to go.

"And this is our purpose, or should be our purpose. We have to be prepared. . . . This day may never come. You have to realize this here. It could be our whole lives are dedicated to something that never happens. I hope to Christ that it don't ever happen, too. We have to be prepared that if it does happen, then we're ready to furnish the means, the leadership and the knowledge that'll go into making it successful."

At least two points raised by Lauchli, it seemed to me, deserved exploring with DePugh. One was Lauchli's accusation that DePugh lied to him so often. DePugh replied by attempting to explain the necessity at times of keeping even members of the Minutemen in the dark on certain information—for security reasons.

"If I figure that it's important that these people don't hear it," DePugh said, "then I'll lie to them. . . . Maybe we're getting ready to move these files to Springfield, Missouri, and I'll say, 'Well, let's see, how far is it from Springfield to Chicago? Is that so-and-so?' And I may plant the idea that these things are going to Springfield, Illinois. It's not just that I don't want them to know. I want to be doggone sure that these cars aren't stopped and these records seized heading south on Highway 71 (to Springfield, Missouri). And to most of the people in the Minutemen organization, this is an accepted and not dishonorable necessity."

Apparently referring to Lauchli, he added that there are always some members who cannot avoid asking too many questions.

"And the people who ask the most questions get the most deceptions," he said.

The other point concerned the "nuts" in the Minutemen organization, an issue I have raised with DePugh repeatedly in the last few years.

From the public's standpoint, DePugh offered by way of explanation, it is better to have "kooks and nuts" inside the Minutemen organization than out of it on their own. He elaborated on his theory this way:

"Out, they're liable to do most anything at any time without anybody knowing it except them. If they decide they want to go out and blow somebody up, okay, they go out and blow somebody up. But if they're part of a group, they may say something about it, like, 'Hey, I've got a good idea, I think we ought to go out and do something,' like assassinate Senator Fulbright. Well, then there's a good chance someone in the organization will know about it and they're going to take steps to bring this person under control, whereas if they weren't in the organization, there would be no restraining influence."

Unfortunately for DePugh, the image of the Minutemen as a "restraining influence" on anyone simply has not gotten across to the general public.

I could not help but ask DePugh whether he felt it was not a bit dangerous—since he admitted having such persons in his organization—to keep providing them with what they easily could interpret as a moral justification for acting out their hostilities in much the same manner as the painter's nephew wanted to do in Illinois.

"Well, to a degree you're right there," said the agreeable Minutemen leader. "And oftentimes it's been said that through the provocative nature of our literature we might provoke somebody into doing something they might not do otherwise. Well, if our literature were not fairly provocative, we wouldn't find them in the first place."

This didn't make a lot of sense to me, unless he was applying his restraint theory aggressively, seeking out the unstable and potential crackpots so as to be able to serve as a restraint on them.

"You're trying to get them in?" I asked.

"No," DePugh replied, oblivious to the fact that he was more or less contradicting himself. "Once we identify them, we give them pretty benign literature, and after a couple of years, they tend to drop off. A lot of times they change and become less violent. . . ."

"What's benign? Even 'On Target' gets pretty violent."

"Well," DePugh chuckled, "that's just because you haven't seen our violent literature."

CHAPTER 5

JOIN THE MINUTEMEN

. . . We have studied your Communist Smersh, Mao, Che, Bucharin. We have learned our lessons well and have added a few home-grown Yankee tricks of our own. Before you start your next smear campaign, before you murder again, before you railroad another patriot into a mental institution . . . better think it over.

See the old man at the corner where you buy your paper? He may have a silencer-equipped pistol under his coat. That extra fountain pen in the pocket of the insurance salesman that calls on you might be a cyanide-gas gun. What about your milkman? Arsenic works slow but sure. Your auto mechanic may stay up nights studying booby traps.

These patriots are not going to let you take their freedom away from them. They have learned the silent knife, the strangler's cord, the target rifle that hits sparrows at 200 yards. Only their leaders restrain them.

Traitors beware! Even now the cross hairs are on the back of your necks. . . .

On February 27, 1963, the existence of the House Committee on Un-American Activities was . . . challenged in the House of Representatives. . . . Twenty Congressmen voted against it. . . .

. . . Here then, are the Judases who seem willing not only to sell out their country for thirty pieces of silver but to go on record and brag about it.

IN MEMORIAM

James Roosevelt (Calif.), George Brown, Jr. (Calif.), W. D. Edwards (Calif.), Edward Roybal (Calif.), William Fitts Ryan (N.Y.), Abraham Multer (N.Y.), Leonard Farbstein (N.Y.), Benjamin Rosenthal (N.Y.), Mrs. Edith Green (Ore.), Robert Duncan (Ore.), Robert W. Kastenmeier (Wisc.), Barratt O'Hara (Ill.), Thomas L. Ashley (O.), Charles Diggs (Mich.), John Dingell (Mich.), Lucien Nedzi (Mich.), Neil Staebler (Mich.), Donald Fraser, (Minn.), Henry Gonzalez, (Tex.), Thomas Gill (Hawaii).

From the March 15, 1963, issue of "On Target."

Following the Minutemen's flashy infancy in the latter months of 1961 came two formative but relatively obscure years of adolescence. Many an organization, having tasted as inordinately spectacular a dish of fame and notoriety as the events at Shiloh had afforded the Minutemen, would have faded for lack of attention under similar circumstances. But DePugh was persistent and possessed with the patience required for the undertaking he had shouldered.

Not that every effort in the years 1962 and 1963 was an unqualified success. In fact, 1962 was very nearly a bust for DePugh. I have the distinct impression that had it not been for the Kennedy assassination and the right wing's capture of the Republication Party eight months later, the Minutemen would have died on an undernourished vine by 1964.

DePugh, perhaps oversold on his ability to attract attention to his causes, made a vain attempt to become a part of the right wing fraternity in 1962, picturing himself, I feel, as one of the potential leaders of ultraconservatism in America. Perhaps he tried to make his move too quickly. More likely, he misjudged the others of the Far Right, thinking they would accept his militant, violence-prone approach openly, and give him a sort of ideological respectability.

In January of 1962, DePugh journeyed to Tulsa, Oklahoma, to attend Billy James Hargis' annual $100-tuition, five-day "Anti-Communist Training School." Next, in the spring or early summer of that year, he traveled to Dallas for a meeting with several leaders of ultraconservatism, including Robert Welch, of the Birch society, and Frank McGehee, a Texan who had achieved a measure of success in 1961 as founder of the National Indignation Convention through his opposition to the training of Yugoslavian pilots on American soil and the sale of U.S. planes to the same Communist country.

I queried both Welch and McGehee about this meeting to confirm DePugh's version of it, but met with limited success. McGehee simply refused to discuss it, either by telephone or by letter. Welch—who DePugh said was of no help after the meeting—was only a little less reticent. First I wrote Welch at his Birch society headquarters in Belmont, Massachusetts, about this and other matters pertaining to the Minutemen and DePugh. Mrs. Mary White, his personal assistant, replied most cordially that Welch "said to tell you that he doesn't remember this at all but undoubtedly it was true that he was less than enthusiastic about any suggestions that would connect us with the Minutemen in any way."

Later, while Welch was visiting Kansas City, following a press conference, I was able to ask him about it personally.

McGehee was a friend of his, he said, and DePugh had been there. He remembered meeting with them at someone's home, in Dallas, but could not recall whose home. And nothing came of the meeting, as far as he was concerned.

As far as DePugh and McGehee were concerned, however, the meeting did produce results. From it, apparently was born the idea of the "American Freedom Rallies."

Would it not be a fine thing indeed, it was decided, if simultaneous protest rallies could be held in all the major cities of the United States each time the government made another of its damnably pro-Communist moves either on the domestic or international front?

Thousands could assemble in city after city at the same hour, it was envisioned, uttering vigorous, identical objections to each new policy. Lower a new tariff—hold protest rallies. A suspected Red visits the White House—protest rallies. A new firearms-control law is passed —protest rallies. Another liberal decision is passed by the Supreme Court—protest rallies. *That* would be a way of getting across a message to the American public. And how could the press—left wing though it is—ignore them? Not easily, to be sure.

To Kansas City in furtherance of this idea in the summer of 1962 came Miss Sue Eastman, the pretty, brunette, nineteen-year-old half sister of McGehee. Her mission: to set up the "National Coordination Center of the American Freedom Rallies." She rented a unit in a duplex in an attractive residential section of south Kansas City and fitted it out as her headquarters. Soon it became one of the busiest duplex units in town.

I did not meet Miss Eastman while she was in Kansas City, not having yet become sufficiently intrigued with the Far Right to bother, but Steve Underwood of the *Star* found her charming and affable. He reported in a long feature article about her that when she spoke of "The Fight" she felt she was waging against Communism, she glowed "with a dewy-eyed exuberance that suggests a high school girl anticipating her first prom." A few years later I located her by telephone in New Orleans. When the Freedom Rallies were mentioned, it was clear from her manner that the prom was over, the band had gone home.

Miss Eastman had arrived in Kansas City flushed with the success of her half brother's crusade. The government had quietly ceased training the Yugoslavians and selling them government aircraft. She went to work with duplicating machine, telephone, volunteer workers, a large filing case crammed with the names of conservatives over the country, a big map of the United States, pamphlets, envelopes and stamps preparing for the nationwide October rallies.

Kansas City had been picked as the coordinating center for the Freedom Rally effort, Miss Eastman later told me, because of its central geographical location, not because of the proximity of Kansas City to Norborne and the Minutemen. In fact, she said, when she arrived in Kansas City, she was not aware that DePugh was in any way involved in the Freedom Rally effort.

"I was never told that Robert DePugh was in on it," she said. "He did come to the rallies. He used to come by once in a while to the headquarters, but I didn't know what to do with him. I was never told at any time to give him any information.

"I was nineteen at the time," she said, "and I was not prepared for the situation I ran into up there."

"What kind of situation?"

"The kind of manipulations—who's going to run it. I kept calling home and said I just can't handle these people, and that's one of the reasons we left Kansas City. . . . It was a mess."

While sitting around her headquarters, DePugh would talk with the workers, she said, but not help with the work. She took particular exception to his companions.

"The people that came with him were not exactly desirable," she said. ". . . They were just kind of rough, rough-talking, low-class people who wouldn't say who they were."

As Freedom Rally preparations continued, DePugh diverted attention from them briefly by leading more than 100 Kansas City area conservatives to the Liberty Memorial monument one hot Sunday afternoon to protest the flying of foreign (especially Communist) flags there. Originally dedicated by President Calvin Coolidge as a monument to the American dead of World War I, it had been rededicated by ex-Presidents Eisenhower and Truman in 1961 to world peace. As a result the flags of the ninety-eight nations with which the United

States had diplomatic relations were flown from it—a fact that irked DePugh, among others.

The picketing caused something of a furor in Kansas City and eventually resulted in the replacement of these flags by state flags and many Old Glories, except on special occasions.

But for the conservatives to win their point, they had to picket several Sundays in a row. One Sunday I decided to go take a look at the pickets myself—hoping, frankly, to catch DePugh for an interview in the process. Until this time, I had never met a Minuteman.

About twenty-five men, women, teen-agers and children were quietly walking back and forth on the south side of the memorial with signs such as "United States—Yes. United Nations—No." One of the pickets had dressed himself in a black Halloween robe that covered his head and body and contained a skeleton's face. All of the pickets were clean-shaven and friendly to sight-seers.

I asked one of the pickets if Robert DePugh was around, as I did not know then what he looked like, and was told he was the man standing beneath one of the shade trees in his shirt sleeves with a camera hanging from around his neck.

I introduced myself, pad and pencil at the ready, but DePugh did not seem eager to be interviewed. I was surprised. Finally he began to respond guardedly to questions. No, he was not in charge of the pickets; he was there just to take photographs; and soon we had turned to the subject of the Minutemen.

"Our one purpose," he said, "is the preservation of the Constitutional Republic of the United States."

But how? Against whom? And when? These seemed the logical questions.

DePugh spoke of an "anti-Communist revolt" inside the United States, a violent civil war of sorts in which he seemed to envision the Minutemen providing the equipment and leadership necessary to make the revolt successful instead of suicidal. No, no, no, the Minutemen would not start the revolt. But they would be on hand to support it.

And who would be the enemy?

"We don't seriously think this country will be invaded by Communist troops," he said, "unless invited in by traitors within our own country. . . . The revolt might well begin with mass indignation rallies and a complete stoppage of everything against the government policy. Then anything could happen. Maybe federal troops would move into some areas to force the people to do something against their wishes."

But what could touch it off?

"When the people realize they're being sold out to their enemies," he said. ". . . If the United States, for instance, should turn over all its military power, including its nuclear weapons, to the UN."

And who was to decide when the revolt was needed?

"A lot of people think the world situation is so complex that only the eggheads can understand it and decide what we should do," he said. "I don't think so. The man on the street will know, when the time comes."

Very interesting. Thank you, Mr. DePugh.

Before the big, nationwide Freedom Rally that was set for October 13, 1962, several from the Freedom Rally group, including unidentified Minutemen, hurried to Springfield, Missouri, for a fast picketing job in behalf of General Edwin Walker, who at the moment was being held in the federal institution there for psychiatric examination.

As DePugh recalls it, "we sent down about three carloads of people" to picket the institution. The former Army general had been taken there by federal officials after he had turned up in Oxford, Mississippi, at the heights of the ruckus over whether James Meredith could register at the University of Mississippi and whether it was going to take another civil war to register him.

This action against Walker tended to confirm the fears of the Minutemen that the government was going to use destructive psychiatric skills on its critics. The former general was released after a few days and is still referred to by some of the Minutemen as having been America's first "political prisoner."

The Kansas City Freedom Rally was held as scheduled, with Miss Eastman speaking in person, DePugh and Thomas Anderson, editor of *Farm and Ranch* magazine and a Birch society council member, by tape recorder. Sixty-nine protests were presented to the audience of more than 200 persons assembled.

And that was about all there was to it. Something was lacking. Perhaps the need for a central, unifying issue rather than sixty-nine shotgun blasts all at once. Maybe just leadership.

In ultraconservative circles in Kansas City, much longer remembered than the Freedom Rally that summer will be the plot to assassinate Senator William Fulbright that was developed by a handful of men who had been attracted to the pre-rally activities and Liberty Memorial picketing.

Enough different persons have come forward to provide details about it that I feel safe in reporting it as a confirmed fact, generally speaking. The details, however, vary from source to source.

The idea was hatched among at least three men, two from the Greater Kansas City area, the third from either Texas or Oklahoma, depending on which version is to be believed. It is uncertain whether any of the three were Minutemen. They did run in Minutemen circles and were known by DePugh, however.

The Kansas Citians contributed money and a car to the would-be assassin, and for the purpose of assassination. But word leaked out quickly of what was happening, the FBI started asking questions, and so did Robert DePugh.

The three men may have called off the plot on their own. The Texan-Oklahoman may never have fully intended to go through with it. If DePugh and Jerry Brooks (about whom you will be reading a great deal later) are to be believed, DePugh may have nipped the plot in the bud.

DePugh and Brooks said that DePugh arranged a meeting with the Texan-Oklahoman at one end of the Missouri River bridge in Lexington, Missouri one night and scared him out of pursuing the plot any further.

DePugh said he told the man that "either you have somebody in your group that is deliberately provoking you into this action to get rid of you or else you're all crazy, one way or another." He said he also told him that word was out that the Minutemen were behind the plot, "and I just want to let you know on a person-to-person basis that the next time I hear of you talking about this kind of action, you're not going to have to wait for somebody else to move against you, because we'll put a stop to this real quick."

The Texan-Oklahoman hasn't been heard of since in the Kansas City area. One of the two Kansas Citians involved was later arrested in Colorado on a warrant charging unlawful flight to avoid prosecution. The all-points bulletin put out on him cautioned that he was dangerous and had threatened to assassinate Robert Kennedy and Barry Gold-water.

DePugh had another story about one of the plotters. It concerned a chance meeting at Miss Eastman's duplex. The plotter and a friend who was with him had been trying unsuccessfully to gain membership in the Minutemen but DePugh had turned them down, he said.

"I know why you don't want us in the Minutemen," DePugh said one of them told him. "You don't think I've got guts enough. You don't think I can take it. I'll show you how I can take it. I'll cut off my little finger right here and now to show you that I can really take it."

DePugh said the man thereupon took out a pocketknife and began sawing on the little finger of his left hand until DePugh stopped him.

After the 1962 Freedom Rally disappointment, Sue Eastman closed down the Kansas City office and returned to Texas, disheartened, as best I can tell from her account of the experience, while DePugh quickly set out on a new tack—publication of the semimonthly newsletter, "On Target," which soon became a monthly. Its first issue was dated January 1, 1963.

"This sample copy will introduce a new type of patriotic newsletter," the first issue of the newsletter began: "The purpose of 'On Target' is not to inform but rather to identify by name, address, and phone number the thousands of Communist traitors who are even now working to sell out their country to the enemy. . . ."

This first issue suggested that the Communists probably would consider the newsletter more than they were willing to "tolerate."

"In starting this publication," it read, "we fully realize that we are placing not only ourselves but our wives and children in a position of extreme danger. We do so in the hope that other conservatives will use the precise information contained in this newsletter effectively in their own continued fight against Communism. In any event, we are determined that a clear record shall exist in history of those traitors who have brought our great nation to its knees."

Its March 1 issue was so desperate for information that it led off with a report from a reader that to refer to the House Committee on Un-American Activities as the House Un-American Activities Committee was to be duped into using the Communists' own terminology. Putting "Un-American" in front of "Committee" carried a psychological impact which "On Target" likened to brainwashing. Then it observed:

"Our reader also pointed out a similar technique which the Communists are now beginning to attempt. This is to call the FBI the 'Federal Investigation Bureau.' The psychological difference would certainly be obvious if this agency were to be commonly referred to as the 'FIB.'"

DePugh is no longer quite so solicitous toward the FBI.

Two weeks later, "On Target" shook itself free of ultraconservative clichés and routine name-calling. It launched an audacious all-out verbal assault on twenty Congressmen—part of the text of which opened this chapter: ". . . Traitors beware! Even now the cross hairs are on the back of your necks."

Had Lee Harvey Oswald used something besides a rifle with a telescopic sight eight months later, this "On Target" issue might have gone relatively unnoticed, but Representative Henry Gonzalez (D-Tex.) raised a belated but justified storm about it after President Kennedy's assassination and asked that the attorney general investigate the Minutemen. Commenting on the "On Target" issue later, DePugh said: "I thought it was pretty good myself." While he did not write it, he said, he edited the publication and approved it. He said it was "just for propaganda purposes" and explained, "the writer chose this way to dramatically demonstrate we weren't going to let traitors sell us out."

"On Target" had now become a far more interesting publication and the April 15 issue was no letdown. It was devoted to the strange disappearance of a one-time well-to-do businessman, John Robert Harrell—known to his friends and followers as "Johnny Bob" Harrell—of Louisville, Illinois. Harrell, smiling beneath a blond crew cut, was pictured on the front page in a family portrait with his wife and four children. The headline: "Did Harrell Name His Own Assassins?" This issue offered a $5000 reward for information leading to the whereabouts of Harrell and his family or to the positive identification of those responsible for his disappearance. Included in the article was part of a letter Harrell had written DePugh on the day of his disappearance. Deleted was that section in which, "On Target" said, Harrell had written the names of those he had been warned were going to try to kill him.

Johnny Bob Harrell's hair had reached to his shoulders when he first gained national attention back in August, 1961, as the leader of an anti-Communist religious movement he called the Christian Conservative Church. An eighteen-year-old Marine stationed at Camp Lejeune, North Carolina, had heard somehow of Harrell's religious sect, had become impressed with it and went AWOL one day to seek sanctuary with Harrell from the military authorities. Upon arriving at Harrell's estate in Clay County, Illinois, he told of "debauchery, immorality and atheism" in the Marine Corps, whereupon, Harrell was to tell reporters, the Lord told him to protect the young man.

Harrell refused to let the Clay County sheriff or FBI on his premises when they sought to question the young Marine, whom he called "just another victim of Communist infiltration."

"He'll stay right here with me and they'll take him over my dead body," declared Harrell to the news media. ". . . We (the USA) can't spare one cent to fire a bullet at Khrushchev or Castro, but we'll spend billions to break the hearts of young men."

Before dawn the following day, approximately 100 law-enforcement officers raided the Harrell estate, using a half-track armored vehicle as an added dramatic. Harrell had threatened resistance and several of his followers were armed with rifles around the gates and atop four look-out towers Harrell had ordered constructed.

No shots were fired, however. As Harrell explained later, he had received no instructions from the Lord to order gunfire. The wife of the caretaker on the estate, however, did boast to a newsman later that she had managed to hit one of the state troopers on the head with a Bible.

The young Marine was arrested and charged with desertion. Harrell, his thirteen-year-old son and fifteen followers were charged with harboring a deserter and taken to jail. The womenfolk on Harrell's estate fasted until the men were freed on bond.

In about five weeks, Harrell, his oldest son and twelve of his followers were indicted by a federal grand jury in East St. Louis. When Harrell entered a plea of not guilty that October, his shoulder-length hair now trimmed, he announced that his colony had just completed construction of several fallout shelters on his estate. The Lord, he explained, had told him to complete them by October 4 and, "We just made it." A nuclear attack on the United States would occur before the end of the year, he said, adding, "In fact we will be fighting Russian troops on American soil by Christmas."

It was later this same October that DePugh gained his own measure of fame at Shiloh, about eighty miles west of Harrell's estate. Almost inevitably, the two men of similar interests became acquainted. By early 1963, Harrell was still awaiting trial in federal court but now was also having trouble with the Internal Revenue Service. Harrell said the IRS had threatened to confiscate his estate for payment of back taxes. The letter that "On Target" said Harrell had written DePugh on March 31, 1963, read, in part:

". . . Most of the family and myself are leaving within a few hours for New Mexico by the way of Springfield, Illinois, where we are to appear April 1st before Income Tax Agents as they move in another attempt to try to crush this Movement and even, I feel, confiscate our Louisville property which has been a point of irritation to them. This great irritation came after President Kennedy sent one of his Secret Service guards to talk with me two years ago this March inquiring as to why I would question the loyalty of the Leadership of the Government. This is a big joke to every Patriot in the land for as you know Christian Patriots do not have a President and haven't had for many years but rather we have Russian Ambassadors in the White House. When the Secret Service man did not receive the promises which he sought, we have known nothing but difficulties since.

"The pressures upon us as we leave are quite heavy with strong threats being made against our family and it being somewhat circulated locally that there shall never be other Basis (sic) established because we shall not live that long, however, that remains to be seen for even though they may stop some of us I am quite sure they shall not stop all who love this great land."

He concluded with an invitation to DePugh to visit him near San Fidel, New Mexico, where he said he planned to relocate his colony, and urged DePugh to "keep pegging away at this Godless system."

"Let us work, fight and pray," he wrote, "for the hour is so late and the grief I feel is great for our people cannot see far enough ahead to know what we know is behind the door," he wrote, "but shall soon close cutting off all avenues of escape and freedom with blood shed ankle deep from shore to shore and coast to coast. . . ."

A few days later, Harrell's car was found abandoned about ten miles south of Springfield, Illinois, near Route 66. The keys were in the car and papers found in it indicated it had been driven by Harrell. The state police were quoted as fearing for his safety.

DePugh quickly put out his "On Target" issue, suggesting "there is good reason to believe that John Harrell and his family have been brutally murdered by Communist agents or fellow travelers."

The Minutemen newsletter explained Harrell's dedication as having resulted from his miraculous recovery from cancer in 1959. Instead of submitting to surgery, the Minutemen said, he prayed.

"The possible reasons for his cure need not be argued here," the newsletter said. "The important thing is that John Harrell sincerely believes that his life had been saved by an act of God. He made a pledge that he would spend the rest of his life and all of his fortune working against evil. He first turned his elegant estate into a refuge for other anti-Communists and proceeded to spend hundreds of thousands of dollars on anti-Communist educational campaigns. That is when his persecution began. . . ."

After reprinting an Associated Press story about his disappearance, the newsletter speculated that most persons reading it would immediately jump to the conclusion that Harrell may have wanted to disappear.

"To those who know John Harrell well this theory does not hold water," the newsletter said, jumping onto a limb.

For the next year and a half, the disappearance of the Harrell family remained a mystery. The St. Louis *Globe-Democrat* reported learning that Harrell, who often had said he distrusted American currency, had made large purchases of gold and silver over a five-year span of time and that its value reached into six figures. Seven months after their disappearance, an attorney for Harrell in East St. Louis said that he had received a letter he believed had been written by Harrell. The lawyer said Harrell had written he was being held prisoner in Chicago or St. Louis. A few days later twenty-five of his former followers showed up unexpectedly at his by then weed-infested estate and held church services in the mansion. In November, 1963, a bench warrant for Harrell's arrest was issued because he had failed to show up for his trial in federal court. One of the twelve followers who had been indicted with Harrell entered a guilty plea. The others were tried and convicted.

Harrell was found—quite alive—on September 19, 1964. He was in Strawberry, Arkansas.

Harrell, his wife and children had been living under the name of Taylor in Strawberry, a town of 300 inhabitants, for the past year, according to the sheriff there. Their tight-lipped manner in Strawberry had aroused the suspicions of an electric-meter checker who complained he thought someone was locked inside the "Taylor" home. He also reported seeing several firearms and chain saws in the house. There had been several burglaries in the area, so police set up a roadblock and arrested Harrell at it. No one was found locked in the house and the firearms and chain saws were determined not to have been stolen. But it was too late for the meter reader to apologize. Harrell had been discovered.

He was returned to East St. Louis, sentenced to ten years in prison and fined $10,000 after pleading guilty to the charges of harboring a deserter and jumping bond on his indictment. In prison at this writing, he is now called by the Minutemen "America's second political prisoner."

Reminiscing about Harrell later, DePugh told a story of how he once kidded Harrell about Harrell's frequent personal conversations with God, with "The Lord" sending down so much advice to him.

DePugh and some others in the Minutemen were in need of $15,000 to pay the balance owed on a $25,000 purchase of TNT, DePugh said.* Knowing Harrell's financial health to be good, DePugh said he decided to telephone him from Norborne and hit him up for the $15,000.

"I told him, 'John, something's happened to me. I've been Born Again,'" DePugh said mischievously. "John was delighted. Then I told him that just last night, the Lord had talked to me. John said, 'Well, what did He say?' So I said, 'Well, the Lord said that I should ask John Harrell for the $15,000 we need and he'd probably give it to me.' Well, there was a long pause over the line, and finally John says, very softly, 'I think I'll have to hear it from the Lord myself.'"

"On Target's" cross-hairs threat did not precipitate the immediate public outcry that undoubtedly had been anticipated by the Minutemen upon its publication. The organization was, in fact, seeming to become less and less newsworthy as the months rolled by. In April, 1963, DePugh granted Wayne Nicholas, of the Richmond (Missouri) News, an interview over a tape recorder and offered one bit of melodrama that seems worth noting here:

"The thing that is really a little terrifying about it is that we could very easily be sitting on the edge of a bloodbath in this country," DePugh told Nicholas. "If something happened to spark this thing off—if for example it should be known that I was killed by a Communist, our organization would take immediate reprisal against the other side and in

---

* "What did you want with $25,000 worth of TNT?" I asked, fully expecting an unexpected reply.

"Maybe we wanted to blow up something," he replied unexpectedly.

turn, they would take reprisal against the ones of us that they know and it could spread like wildfire to the point where it would just be mass murder on both sides. That could happen—it could happen very easily. . . ."

The following Memorial Day weekend, DePugh drove to a farm near Wentzville, in northeast Missouri, for a Minutemen training session. This session was fairly routine, apparently, except for a question that later became of concern to the federal government—did DePugh drive up with only a trunkful of groceries in his car, or was there an automatic submachine gun also in the trunk? But that will be dealt with later.

In the course of ascertaining the contents of that trunk, the identities of some of those who attended the training session have become known. Troy Houghton, the West Coast coordinator, was there. So was a salesman from Hutchinson, Kansas, and an anesthetist from Omaha, Nebraska. So was a handsome, teen-age girl named Mrs. Cyndra (Cindy) Sanders Melville. Among others.

The Wentzville training session is the first Minutemen event, to my knowledge, in which Cindy figured. My knowledge of Cindy's activities is extremely limited however, for she has remained strangely reticent about them. She had joined the Minutemen through a boy friend, she is willing to reveal, but without elaboration.

"They treated her like a slave," her mother volunteered recently, in her presence, once her long Minutemen adventure had ended.

"Well," Cindy responded, "it wasn't *that* bad."

Two weeks after the Memorial Day weekend, Cindy left her mother's home in Kansas City. Mrs. Frieda Sanders, her mother, received a letter from Cindy soon afterward with a return address a post-office box in Chicago. Mrs. Sanders wrote several letters to that post-office box, but all were returned not accepted. The envelopes appeared to have been opened, however.

Mrs. Sanders went to Chicago and somehow obtained the name of the man in whose name the post-office box was registered. She contacted him and was told Cindy was "all right," and that was all.

Two months after Cindy's disappearance, the distraught mother went to the Kansas City police department's missing persons bureau and reported Cindy missing. The police record of this visit stated: "Supposed to be involved in Minutemen organization. Mother is afraid girl is being held against her will." It stated further that Cindy was married, separated and a mother. Her husband was said to have been in North Carolina.

Mrs. Sanders also went to the FBI with her fears. And she visited the office of George W. Robinson, one of Kansas City's better-known private detectives.

"Frankly," Robinson was to recall two years later, "I thought the woman was suffering from hallucinations. I didn't take the case because I didn't want to take advantage of her and take her money. She told me the Minutemen had captured her daughter, or words to that effect. . . . I advised her to see a psychiatrist. . . ."

Sometime in the fall—Sergeant Harry Hogue, of the missing persons bureau, does not remember exactly when—a man identifying himself as Robert DePugh telephoned him and asked if any charges were pending against Cindy. When told that Cindy simply had been reported missing by her mother, the caller said he would put Cindy in touch with Mrs. Sanders. Soon afterward, Mrs. Sanders told the sergeant that Cindy had visited her and had satisfied her that she was not being held against her will.

DePugh had acquired a confidential secretary who soon was to occupy a position of considerable importance, and even more considerable mystery in the Minutemen organization.

On November 22, 1963, the cross hairs of a telescopic sight settled on the back of the neck of President John F. Kennedy and he was dead.

As most of the nation mourned, the printing press at the Minutemen headquarters produced a postscript to the December 1 issue of "On Target."

"Now that John F. Kennedy is dead," it read, "we can expect to hear millions of words about his greatness. Even his most bitter political enemies will praise him.

"We will not be hypocrites—we will not soon forget that he ignored the best interests of his country from the day he took the oath of office to the day he died. Still, very little is really changed. The 'power behind the throne' remains the same as before."

The year, 1963, closed on a somber note nationally, with the impact of President Kennedy's assassination still fresh in America's consciousness. In many ways the assassination was to have particularly harmful effects on the Minutemen. Suddenly a politically oriented organization that placed cross hairs in the "O" of their official newsletter's masthead did not seem quite as quaint as it had before November 22.

To the Minutemen themselves, however, the immediate effect of the assassination seemed more of a nuisance than anything else. Looking back on it three years later, DePugh observed: "Here you had a man you could say anything about and get away with it, and he's suddenly turned into a national hero that you don't dare say anything about without people taking offense at," DePugh said. "We were really zeroing in on Kennedy at the time he was assassinated. He was our number one whipping boy, so to speak. . . .

"It took quite a while before Johnson maneuvered himself into a position where he became a legitimate target for adverse publicity. For quite a long while he rode along on John Kennedy's halo.

"So that (the assassination) was kind of a setback for us so far as our psy-war campaign was concerned. All of our recruiting literature was written up and based on the Communist infiltration of the Kennedy administration, and suddenly, the literature was of no value."

CHAPTER 6

JOIN THE MINUTEMEN
Warning to Patriots!

ALL PATRIOTIC AMERICANS THAT HAVE BEEN ACTIVE IN THE ANTI-
COMMUNIST MOVEMENT ARE NOW FACING A PERIOD OF EXTREME
DANGER. . . .

If you are EVER going to buy a gun, BUY IT NOW.
The time may come that almost any gun of any caliber will
be worth its weight in gold. Still, your life may depend on it,
so why not get the best you can possibly afford? We especially
recommend the following: Adult males: 30-06 Garands, 7.62
NATO FNs, 30-06 bolt-action Springfields or Enfields, high-
caliber sporting rifles as desired, 12-gauge double barrel, pump
or semi-automatic shotguns. Adult females: Winchester model 100
in .308-caliber, Remington model 742 in 30-06 caliber or 30-caliber
military carbines. Older children: sporting rifles in 6mm., .243,
.270, .222 calibers. Younger children: semi-automatic .22 rifles. . . .

From the April 1, 1964, issue of "On Target."

The year 1964 was only a few days old when the first fierce vollies of
criticism the Minutemen had been lacking so much the two previous
years were fired at them.

U. S. Representative Henry B. Gonzalez, a Texas Democrat from
San Antonio, and California's Attorney General Stanley Mosk set
them off almost simultaneously.

"In light of recent development," Gonzalez told the Houston *Post*,
"I have become decidedly more sensitive about some of the hate
material that is so widely distributed."

He thereupon asked Attorney General Robert Kennedy to investigate the Minutemen, citing what he called the 'thinly veiled' cross-
hairs threat against him and nineteen of his Congressional colleagues
in the by then ten-month-old "On Target."

In Norborne, DePugh quickly snapped back a reply.

"Regarding possible action by the attorney general," he told the Associated Press, "I can observe that if Robert Kennedy had in the past been as concerned over left-wing anti-Americans as he had been concerned over the right-wing pro-Americans, then his brother might be alive."

The dialogue in California was just as nasty:

"Some aspects of the Minutemen have caused them to be considered much more ridiculous than dangerous," Mosk told a group of Rotarians at the Disneyland Hotel in Anaheim on January 6. "When some San Diego leaders of the group were arrested for the failure to register as sex offenders, the current joke was that the Minutemen evidently intended to hit the Communists with their powder puffs. . . ."

And he called for new California laws tightening firearms controls and outlawing private armies and paramilitary groups such as the Minutemen.

The Minutemen were paranoid in their fear of Communism, their distrust of American institutions and their desire to own all varieties of firearms from pistols to machine guns, he said.

". . . There is a frightening parallel between the mentality of the members of these groups and that of the accused assassin of President Kennedy. Yes, I know Lee Harvey Oswald was on the Far Left, and these groups are generally on the Far Right. But we know Oswald had rejected our system. We know that he spent his nights attending all varieties of political meetings for some inner satisfaction. We know he pursued political causes with fanaticism and without regard for democratic processes. He was a political agitator who was alienated from our society and our political order.

"It is this alienation which is most disturbing in the attitudes of so-called Minutemen. . . . They feel that our system has failed. They feel that our two major political parties are shams—simply a choice between two evils. They feel our processes have been totally perverted and are of no use. They admittedly look forward to a time of armed conflict with an enemy they only vaguely identify. . . .

"We can no longer allow fanatics in our state to nurture their illusions by building private armies and menacing the safety of the people of California and America. . . ."

Houghton somehow had obtained an advance copy of Mosk's speech, enabling him to answer it in advance in a bulletin to members and in interviews with the San Diego news media. This also gave him a chance to claim other "counterintelligence" coups in the attorney general's office.

"He's been finding Minutemen stickers on the door of his office," Houghton declared, "even after the Capitol has been locked all night. He found one on his menu on an airliner recently."

Mosk labeled Houghton's espionage claims as "a pipedream."

Houghton answered Mosk's speech with such observations as: ". . . This attempt to indict patriotic Americans who are loyal to the ideals of the founding fathers of this country is typical of the smear tactics so dear to the hearts of Attorney General Mosk's Communist friends and supporters. . . ."

And back in Washington soon afterward, Representative Gonzalez asked Chief Justice Earl Warren to see whether there was any connection between the Minutemen and the presidential assassination.

It would be more than three years before James Garrison, the district attorney of New Orleans parish, would try to link any Minutemen or ex-Minutemen to the assassination conspiracy he believed had existed.

A week after Gonzalez had made his request, the New York *Post* reported that J. Lee Rankin, general counsel for the Warren Commission had said the commission would investigate the Minutemen to see if there were any relationship between it and the assassination.

In another week, Robert Kennedy wrote Congressmen Gonzalez that there was no evidence that the Minutemen had violated any federal laws but that the Justice Department would continue to study the matter.

Gonzalez was not satisfied and in releasing the Kennedy letter said he would ask again for an investigation. The FBI should infiltrate the Minutemen as it has done the Communist Party, he said.

The Minutemen could not have been happier. Again under attack, they could point with alarm once again to the "conspiracy" that sought to destroy them. Old copies of the "Reuther Memorandum" were dusted off, and the Minutemen counterattacked.

Their April "On Target" carried an especially urgent message to the effect that all "patriots" were at that moment in a period of extreme danger. It quoted "Communist" sources to the effect that Johnson would win re-election with Hubert Humphrey as his running mate and once the election was over the Communist organizations "expect to be

able to operate openly without any government interference whatsoever."

Warning of the possibility of being placed in prisons or concentration
camps after the election, "On Target" advised its readers to avoid long-
term investments that would tie them to one area ("for example you
can leave a rented house faster than one your own or are making pay-
ments on"); to find a job that did not carry too much responsibility
and take up too much of their free time; to live frugally, save every
nickel and hide a modest savings in cash away from their residence
because it "might mean the difference between life and death"; avoid
being pegged as a "fear monger" or "racist" and instead blend into
their surroundings and remain "anonymous." Also: form a secret
Minutemen team.

"Do *not* expect a 'big round-up' of Patriots," it advised. "We will be
picked up one by one for real or imaginary legal violations. You will
have little or no warning when your time comes."

Elsewhere in the April issue, it was revealed that the racist National
States Rights Party's leaders had demanded that their members disavow
the use of arms by civilians and avoid association with the Minutemen.
It quoted the NSRP as saying, "The right wing must come to power by
use of the ballot box." "On Target" replied that "for the information of
the NSRP leaders, the Minutemen have no desire to 'come to power.' "
It also implied that the NSRP was "pseudo-Nazi" and consisted of "a
bunch of tin-horn Hitlers." Most Minutemen, of course, object strenuously to the "fascist" label for themselves.*

---

* Evidence of a certain overlapping of membership between the Minutemen
and American Nazi Party cropped up in June, 1965, when United Press-International reported that some disenchanted ex-Nazis had joined the Minutemen.
Later, when asked about this, DePugh acknowledged that about a dozen had
joined in Pennsylvania after discovering they were in an organization of "hate-
mongers." He allowed them into the Minutemen, he said, only after they assured
him that they were through with the Nazis. Their leader, he added, later left
the Minutemen to join the Ku Klux Klan.
  The late George Lincoln Rockwell, national leader of the American Nazi
Party, paused in his tour of college campuses in March, 1967, just five months
before his assassination, long enough to grant me an interview about the Minutemen. He complained that DePugh had lured some of his members and three
of his best financial supporters (in Florida, Texas and Pennsylvania) away from
him into the Minutemen. "I'm all for what the Minutemen stand for," said
the penny-ante Führer. "People should be armed and prepared to defend themselves. But to use illegal firearms is suicide. . . . I won't tolerate illegal firearms.
I detest the idea of young men possessing weapons and going to jail. . . . They
say they don't, but every Minuteman I've ever met is running around with illegal
weapons, in fact were counseled to get weapons. But the Minutemen are at
least trying."

The National States Rights Party was not the only right-wing organization DePugh was having difficulty with that month. On April 7, 1964, the John Birch Society sent DePugh a check for $6 representing that part of his advance-paid dues owed him as a result of the termination of his membership in the society.

Something of an argument arose between Welch and DePugh over whether DePugh had been booted from the Birch ranks or whether he had resigned of his own free will. Whatever the case—and the weight of evidence seems to favor the Welch account—it soon became clear that if Welch and DePugh were allies, it was a dark secret shared only by the two of them.

DePugh says he does not remember when he joined the Birch society, but it was apparently sometime in 1960 or 1961. He says he joined primarily to obtain its literature and never belonged to an active Birch chapter.

I have written Robert Welch twice—in 1964 and 1967—asking him about DePugh's involvement in the Birch society and their personal relationship in the past. In response to the first query, Welch replied that the August, 1964, Birch society bulletin explained the matter, and enclosed the bulletin. In it, Welch's comments were limited to three paragraphs, the most informative part of which read:

"It is worth noting that for about two years Mr. DePugh had made the most continuous and determined effort to bring about extensive collaboration of the Minutemen with the John Birch Society that we have experienced with any other group. And that we merely brushed these efforts all aside, in as friendly a fashion as we could, until Mr. DePugh began steering the Minutemen into becoming an underground armed-guerrilla organization—which caused us to drop him from membership. . . ."

But DePugh had been "steering the Minutemen into becoming an underground armed-guerrilla organization" since 1961. When I wrote Welch a second time for a more forthright explanation, Welch's personal assistant, Mrs. Mary F. White, replied with a most friendly letter.

". . . From the time he first met Mr. DePugh through his membership in the Home Chapter of the John Birch Society he (DePugh) tried in many ways to attach himself to our organization in a more or less executive capacity such as offering to train our coordinators or later offering us the use of a building to serve as a school for training of staff people," she wrote. "However, Mr. Welch wanted no part of these suggestions at any time because he did not have any desire to work in connection with this group even though at that time we were not aware of their true aims and purposes. It was some time before we recognized the true aims of the Minutemen but just as soon as these became obvious to us Mr. DePugh was immediately dropped from membership. We never did know just when he started steering this group into the avenue of an armed-guerrilla organization but repeat here that just as soon as we discovered this a revocation of membership was entered at once."

In an on-the-run interview in Kansas City more recently, I mentioned to Welch that it was hard to imagine he had been unaware of DePugh's intentions to steer the Minutemen into becoming an underground armed-guerrilla organization until April, 1964. Welch repeated emphatically that he had learned of these intentions only then. When I observed that such intentions had been mentioned in the newspapers well before then, he replied: "Not in the ones I read."

"Another thing we didn't like," Welch volunteered, "was his wanting people to find out if their neighbors were Communists, but we didn't think this would go very far."

DePugh said that he had several conversations with Welch in addition to the one in Dallas in 1962 when they were discussing the Freedom Rallies. Some of those meetings were in Kansas City while Welch was there for speaking engagements. Once, DePugh said, he telephoned Welch in Belmont, Massachusetts, and told him he had the money to pay for a round trip there if Welch had an afternoon to devote to talking with him. Welch found the time.

At one meeting, DePugh said, they discussed the possibility of some of the Minutemen instructors making themselves available to the Birch society to instruct them in propaganda and resistance warfare techniques.

"I think the reason we didn't," DePugh said, "was not through a difference in philosophy but the fact that we weren't able to get together on the necessary security measures. In other words, he didn't want our people learning the identities of all of his members and we didn't want his people learning ours."

The break came when he decided to telephone Welch one day to find out why Welch had become so cool toward him, DePugh said, and why, when people would write the Birch society asking about Minutemen, they would receive "sarcastic" replies.

"So I called Welch finally, and I said, 'Bob, if there's something wrong here between us, let's get it out in the open and see what's the matter.' I said, 'We've got too big an enemy to fight to be fighting among ourselves.' And after considerable reluctance on his part, he sort of lost his temper and said, 'Well, all right, if you want to know, I'll tell you. You're trying to take the Birch society over and I'm not going to stand for it.'"

DePugh said he denied having such an ambition to Welch, but it made no difference.

Writing for Welch, Mrs. White said the Birch society founder had no recollection of saying this to DePugh, but she added:

"He does believe, however, that this could be a paraphrase of some statement he made that would definitely make it clear to Mr. DePugh that he just didn't want him to come in to help us in any way whatsoever. Mr. Welch was then and still is following the plans he had set down in The Blue Book of the John Birch Society as he believes these to be the very best way to turn back this atheistic Communist conspiracy and to win in this struggle for God, family and country."

DePugh's appraisal of the Birch society included praise for what it has taught younger persons through their literature, but scorn for what it has done to its older members. For them, he said, the Birch society is a "dead end."

"These people get in there and they're told to write letters and they're told to study this, read that, and it's an endless repetition of triviality to a point where in time they become frustrated. They're well educated, but they're frustrated. . . . In other words, they tell them what's wrong, but they offer no practical solution and say what to do. . . .

"They don't have the courage to stick their necks out too far and the John Birch Society gives them the oportunity to soothe their consciences. They say, 'Well, as long as I'm paying my dues each month and writing to my Congressman and reading the reports and telling other chapter members how bad things are, I'm doing my part.'"

DePugh credits the Birch society with having been a good recruiting ground for the Minutemen, however. And, indeed, this appears to have been the case.

While the Birch society and Minutemen appear to be separate entities organizationally, only a hair separates them ideologically—a cross hair.

Congressman Gonzalez's efforts to tie the Minutemen in with the Kennedy assassination having failed, he inserted into the Congressional Record in May, 1964, various comments accusing the federal government of subsidizing and encouraging the Minutemen through the Army's national board for the promotion of rifle practice, which distributes rifles at cost and ammunition free to civilians to encourage marksmanship, providing the civilians are members of the National Rifle Association.

"Who knows how many of these persons are extremists and fanatics who have dedicated themselves to the subversion and the eventual overthrow of our democracy?" Gonzalez asked.

He recalled the "cross hairs" issue of "On Target," noting that it left "no doubt about the intent of these threats or the proposed victims" and candidly adding that "the fact that my name is on the list of future victims is of special interest to me."

"Mr. Speaker," he said, "I have in the past supported our foreign-aid program including the military assistance features of that program. And I have always been a strong supporter of our defense program and of the Armed Services. But I was not aware that I was also supporting a program of military assistance to private persons in this country. I was not aware that in voting for military appropriations I was also voting for a program of military assistance to right-wing extremist groups. I was not aware that I was supporting a private army."

He also inserted a copy of a newsletter written by N. S. Riecke, Jr., founder of the Paul Revere Associated Yeomen, Inc., (PRAY) of New Orleans, which urged "all patriots and conservatives" to join the National Rifle Association . . . stock up on rifles, shotguns, pistols . . . join the Minutemen . . ."

Later, Gonzalez said the Army had told him it had sold 530.207 rifles and other firearms to NRA members since 1959 and had spent at least $12,000,000 for its program of supplying weapons and ammunition to civilians. Army spokesmen at the same time were quoted by the Associated Press as maintaining that the arms and ammunition "do not fall into unscrupulous hands."

DePugh subsequently told the St. Louis Post-Dispatch that while many Minutemen are members of the NRA, they do not join it to obtain large quantities of arms and ammunition from the government.

"When the government sells guns through its civilian marksmanship program," DePugh said, "a record is kept of who gets the guns. The weapons can be recalled by the Army in time of any emergency. The government might elect to take them back at a time when we would want them the most."

The *Post-Dispatch* also quoted DePugh to the effect that Gonzalez's "continuing tirade" against the Minutemen was "linked with a similar move by various left-wing and Communist groups throughout the country" to bring about confiscation and registration of private firearms.

"This is something the Communists have always tried to do before taking over a nation by internal revolution," DePugh said. "They always succeeded in getting firearms registered before their takeover of the country."

And at about the same time, he told the New York *Times* that it was a common tactic for Minutemen to join the NRA, or gun clubs in order to gain access to rifle ranges for target practice. Each Minuteman, he said, fires at least 500 rounds of ammunition a year to maintain proficiency as a marksman.

As has been the case with several other Minutemen, some of Troy Houghton's tales of his activities are extremely hard to believe and difficult either to confirm or disprove. Most tantalizing of Houghton's, to me, are the stories he tells of the work the California Minutemen have done in "playing cat and mouse" with the U. S. Armed Services during some of their training exercises and war games.

Knowing Houghton to be both an erratic and audacious man, I cannot automatically dismiss these tales as fabrication. According to Houghton, he and members of his organization have on several occasions "harassed" the United States Marines during their winter survival-training exercises in the California mountains. They did this for practice in a variety of ways, he said, one of their ploys having been to sneak up on the Marines as they slept and stick gummed labels on their foreheads. The labels read: "If this had been a real war, you'd be dead."

During the Army's big training operation, Desert Strike, held in California and Arizona in 1964, Houghton said he posed in full uniform as an Army colonel and drove about the area openly in a jeep, with driver, talking to and inspecting the troops. At one point during Desert Strike, he said, the Minutemen actually captured some servicemen, "just to show it could be done," releasing them unharmed as soon as he had proved his point.

"Isn't posing as a colonel in the Army illegal?" I asked him.

"Oh, yes," he replied with what seemed to me to be a rather forced nonchalance.

He said he used the name of a real colonel who was a friend of his while the real colonel was elsewhere on maneuvers in the same operation. He said he also used the colonel's jeep.

He suggested, if I checked out his story with the Army, that I ask how many guns they lost during the operation.

"They lost at least seventy," Houghton said.

"How did they lose them?" I asked.

"Just ask how many they lost," Houghton grinned.

Upon first hearing this tale, I was understandably skeptical about it. But early in 1967, I learned that a California novelist had just finished writing a satirical book about an organization similar in some ways to the Minutemen. The climax of his novel, I was told, came when this organization became inadvertently involved in some war games with the Marines in southern California. Could his fiction be based on some facts at his disposal, I wondered. I sought him out while researching the Minutemen in southern California, learning in the meantime that he was Leland Frederick Cooley, whose *Condition Pink*, the novel in question, was to be his seventh book.

I first telephoned him at his hillside home in Laguna Beach in Orange County, overlooking the Pacific Ocean, and found him in telephone conversation to be strangely cautious in his remarks. I describe the author in this manner only because at that time I was not fully aware of the extraordinary nature of southern California politics.

When I arrived in Laguna Beach the following evening, Cooley received me most cordially, for in the meantime, through telephone calls to New York and Kansas City, he had checked me out to his satisfaction. I wasn't, he now felt confident, an extremist up to some obscure mischief.

I wanted to know how had he come upon his idea for *Condition Pink*. Did he know something I should know?

The idea had evolved slowly, he replied. His inspiration to write the novel, he said, lay in his strong opposition, in his words, "to the excesses to which extremists, left and right, go on the basis of insufficient or inaccurate information."

In the spring of 1961, Cooley recalled, he happened into an idle conversation with a doctor while having his car greased at a service station. They chatted mainly about the trailer the doctor's car had been pulling until Cooley mentioned that he was a writer. This prompted the man to remark that perhaps he should try to "recruit" Cooley into the patriotic organization of which he was a member. Writers, he told Cooley, were especially needed in this organization.

Several days later the doctor telephoned Cooley at his home and offered him an "officer's commission" in this organization, the name of which he would not then divulge. Cooley turned him down with few apologies, but the two odd conversations lingered in his mind.

Later that same spring, Cooley and his wife, a former ballerina and choreographer on TV and Broadway and co-author with her husband of non-fiction books, were driving in a remote section of Hollywood Hills on Mulholland Drive, an undeveloped but scenic hilltop area that separates Hollywood from the San Fernando Valley. As they rounded a turn in the narrow dirt road that follows a ridge, they happened unexpectedly upon a uniformed party of men crossing the right of way.

"They were as surprised as we," recalled Cooley. "One of them, in camouflaged battle dress, acted as MP and held us up until the men went through. It was not until we recovered from our initial surprise that we saw the impromptu MP was carrying a heavy hunting bow and a quiver of steel-tipped hunting arrows. We thought they were some sort of 'commando' group on a training exercise."

Several months later Mr. and Mrs. Cooley journeyed to a stretch of desert north of Los Angeles to inspect a half section of land they had recently purchased. They soon became separated while roaming over the area. Suddenly Cooley heard gunfire in the distance. He ran toward the noise and eventually spied something red traveling at a fast clip below him about a half mile away in a ravine. Since his wife had worn a red hat that day, Cooley ran to intercept the moving red object. He soon found that it was indeed his wife whose choreography that day had spontaneously included as fast a sprint as possible, with her hat perched atop a long stick she was carrying. As soon as her husband had been able to halt her, Mrs. Cooley informed him that someone had just taken a shot at her.

Cautiously the winded couple retraced Mrs. Cooley's steps to the vicinity of the shooting and found on the opposite side of a hill a group of about a dozen men dressed in Army fatigues and carrying rifles. One of the men approached them and explained gruffly that they had no business being in that area of the desert. "You're apt to get shot!" he warned.

"On my own property?" Mrs. Cooley protested in bewilderment.

The rifleman returned to his companions and discussed the problem. With what seemed to the Cooleys to be considerable reluctance, the men slowly gathered their equipment, climbed into four nearby automobiles and left. In their wake the Cooleys found hundreds of expended shells of varying sizes scattered over the ground.

Cooley even today is not certain who these men were. Or who the Hollywood commandos were, with their archer. Or what patriotic group has doctors that offer writers officers' commissions.

Whatever their identities, the incidents set Cooley to thinking about para-militarism in general, in the context of southern Californian extreme right-wing alarmism. As he nosed around the area talking with fellow residents, Cooley said, he found that the rumor of Chinese Communists massing at the Mexican border in Baja California actually was still generally believed.

Then he noticed an item in one of the local newspapers about a Marine Corps exercise that had been temporarily halted when an innocent civilian found himself in the middle of a simulated battle-ground.

The prospects of a patriotic-minded para-military organization gearing for battle against an imaginary force of Red Chinese in Southern California and meeting instead a group of Marines on war games proved irresistible to Cooley's imagination and he set to work on his book. He did not have any specific group in mind at all, he told me.

But what of Houghton's tales of playing "cat and mouse" with the military? Cooley did not know, and he doubted whether the military in California would say. He did know, however, that while researching for his novel among the military brass in Southern California, he gained the unmistakable impression that they were glad he was writing on this subject, that, as one of the officers put it, "it was about time somebody did."

I later asked Bettie Houghton whether Troy had been involved in Operation Desert Strike. "I know he was up there, but I don't know what went on," she said. Had he worn a colonel's uniform? "The FBI told me about that, but I doubt it," she said, cryptically. Had they ever stuck gummed labels on servicemen? "I've never heard of that," she said, "but there's a lot of things that I'm not aware of."

A query about Houghton's story of Minutemen participation in "Desert Strike" to the Defense Department brought this reply:

". . . Neither the Army Chief of Information nor the U. S. Strike Command (which organized and conducted Operation Desert Strike) have been able to find any details about the impersonation or the alleged capture of U.S. troops by the Minutemen.

"Although the people with whom we talked were directly concerned with the public-affairs aspect of the operation, they had no knowledge or recollection of any incidents of this type. They did emphasize that in an operation of this magnitude (there were aggressor, neutral, defender, special forces—all in different uniforms), some small incident could have occurred: but they feel it was extremely unlikely. . . ."

As the Defense Department may or may not know, the Minutemen themselves are extremely unlikely.

The Republican National Convention opened at the Cow Palace in San Francisco on July 13, 1964. Among the delegates, DePugh soon was to claim, were about two dozen Minutemen. More recently he has lowered that figure to "six or seven." Which ones were they? Sorry, "security precautions" prevent disclosure of their identities, I was told. At any rate, the Republican liberals' and moderates' efforts to put the convention on record as repudiating the Birch society failed, Goldwater was nominated and "extremism in the defense of liberty" was declared by the candidate to be "no vice." Under ordinary circumstances, this last statement by Goldwater would have been little more than another politician's platitude. But by the time Goldwater had said it in his acceptance speech, the word "extremism" had become equated in the minds of most listeners at the convention (if not Goldwater himself) with the Birch society. Right-wing "extremism"—which came to be defined in bewilderingly varied ways—became a major issue of the 1964 campaign.

The Minutemen had not rated mention at the convention alongside the Birchers, Ku Klux Klan and Communist Party, but DePugh and those who were aware of the Minutemen knew that his relatively small guerrilla-warfare vigilante group fitted neatly into the "extremist" mold by most persons' definition of the word. DePugh hardly shied from the possibilities of becoming a campaign issue himself and early in August

was telling Donald Janson of the New York *Times* that the Minutemen
intended to play an active but clandestine role in support of Goldwater.
One of their projects, he told the *Times*, would be to infiltrate
campaign headquarters for President Johnson around the country and
sabotage efforts in his behalf.

Regarding the two candidates, he branded Johnson a "political
opportunist" and Goldwater a "patriot who should take a stronger
right-wing stand than he has."

That August "On Target" predicted that if Goldwater lost the election, unilateral disarmament would proceed rapidly until the Soviets
had an obvious military superiority over us, the Communist subversion
of Latin America would be virtually complete by 1968, the brainwashing
of our school children to accept a Socialist police state would be nearly
complete and, among other things, voices of dissent within the U.S.
would be stilled by economic or legal reprisals "plus an occasional
'disappearance.'"

More intriguing was its prediction of what would happen if Goldwater won. The nation would suffer a total economic collapse, it said,
engineered by others and blamed on Goldwater to the ultimate discredit of all future conservative candidates for President in the next
forty years.

By mid-August, Candidate Goldwater, perhaps aware by then of the
sort of wild "help" the Minutemen were giving him, declared after a
Republican Party "summit meeting" of leaders:

"We repudiate character assassins, vigilantes, Communists and any
group such as the Ku Klux Klan that seeks to impose its views through
terror or threats of violence."

DePugh, who had been eager to interpret the late President Kennedy's opposition to "vigilantes" in a 1961 speech as an attack on the
Minutemen, felt somehow different about this Goldwater statement.
No, he said, he didn't think Goldwater was talking about the Minutemen because he didn't think Goldwater knew much about his organization.

That August I sat down with DePugh for two interviews lasting a
total of nine hours for the purpose of a series of articles I was preparing,
finally, on the Minutemen. Some of his remarks in those interviews
already have been mentioned.

I suppose what intrigued me most at the time about DePugh was the deep strain of potential violence, up to and including assassinations, that was reflected in Minutemen literature I had read and, in a modified form at the time, in DePugh's own remarks.

"I recognize that running a military organization, and writing things that could be considered inflammatory, entail certain risks," he said, "but sitting on my tail also entails risk. I'm taking the avenue of least risk."

The "risk" of doing nothing entailed allowing a Communist take-over of the nation, he said, and he likened his predicament to that of a man about to be killed by someone with a meat cleaver. The man must decide whether to stand there and fight his assailant or run away across the street and possibly be killed in the heavy traffic.

We talked about the vague references he had made to possible assassinations by the Minutemen and the files he claimed to have on 65,000 "Communists and fellow travelers." The only persons the Minutemen had considered assassinating specifically, he said, were those in the United States the Minutemen *know* are members of the Communist "hidden government." To date, he said, this list included only twenty-five or thirty persons. Another 1500 had been singled out for continual surveillance, he said. The assassinations would not occur, he added, until after the Communists had taken over the country and installed members of their "hidden government" in city, county, state and national offices. Before such installations, he said, the present officeholders who were not Communists probably would have been murdered. There would be no problem, he said, of knowing when to kill, or whom.

"Who's in this 'hidden government'?"

"One of them is a professor at the University of Kansas," he said.

"Which one?"

"I won't name him, but if you print this, he'll know who I mean, and he'll know that we know who he is."

"How do you know?"

"By infiltration. By infiltration of the Communist Party by the Minutemen."

"How many Minutemen have infiltrated the Communist Party?"

"Several," DePugh replied.

"Have any Communists infiltrated the Minutemen?"

"Yes, and we have discovered who several of them are. We immediately put these Communists on a special mailing list, sending them some accurate and some false information."

"Could the Communists be doing the same thing to Minutemen infiltrators?"

"We don't trust them (the infiltrators) completely. We check, double-check and triple-check all the information they supply us."

I asked DePugh how he arrived at the conclusion a person was a Communist, a fellow traveler or just another liberal.

"In our files," he said, "we state just the facts. A person writes a certain article a certain way, or belongs to certain organizations, or signed a petition for a certain thing, such as abolishing the House Committee on un-American Activities. When these begin to show a consistent pattern of following the Communist line, you have to start considering them fellow travelers, and if it continues you have to start considering them Communists."

When I asked him about the remarks he had made to me two years earlier at the Liberty Memorial, when he had suggested the Minutemen might end up shooting American troops if they started shooting first, he said he had changed his thinking on this a little since then. As long as the military stayed with the government, he said, the Minutemen would not start their activities.

"The anti-Communist revolt will come when the country is so indisputably Communist that everyone over seven years old will know it," he said, and he predicted this probably would not occur for twenty or twenty-five years—which was quite a departure from other Minutemen predictions that place The Day much nearer at hand.

When the Communists take over, he also said, he was convinced they would kill eighty million Americans either by assassinations or working them to death in slave labor camps. "So our point is, we're going to kill them before they kill us."

We skipped around to many other subjects.

The FBI had begun investigating the Minutemen at the request of the Warren Commission and had plagued him with telephone taps, tampering with his mail and tailing him surreptitiously by car and on foot, he complained.

"When an FBI agent asked me for our roster," he said, "I told him that if I gave it to him, it would go on file in Washington and the Communists would have it when they took over. He said, 'All right, we'll find out anyway.' I told him I would make it as hard as possible for them and that it would cost the government tens of thousands of dollars. My conscience doesn't bother me about this, because if they didn't spend it on investigating the Minutemen, they'd probably be giving it away to Yugoslavia."

A strain of anti-Semitism seemed to exist in the Minutemen, but only occasionally would it surface for ready identification. One example of this was "On Target's" reference to Jack Ruby as Jack Rubenstein. When I asked DePugh about this, he said it was mainly to show how the news media had been pressured, probably by the Anti-Defamation League of B'nai B'rith, into calling him Ruby after he had shot Oswald.

More recently, DePugh chose to identify Karl Marx as Jewish in his *Blueprint for Victory*, while on the same page failing to mention Frederick Engel's religion. When I asked him why, DePugh replied that three or four Jewish acquaintances had jumped him about this "and to me it wasn't important one way or another, it just wasn't important."

"But the fact that they jumped me about it," he said, "I just kind of bowed my neck about it. Like the first time you jumped me about Rubenstein. . . . After you'd mentioned it, you couldn't have got me to change that to Jack Ruby for anything in the world."

"Why?"

"Just perversement," he said, "and that's one reason I haven't changed it in *Blueprint for Victory*."

While not aggressively anti-Semitic himself, as best I can tell, De-Pugh has left the door open wide for anti-Semites to join and play active roles in the Minutemen.

Hoping for some fresh insight into the Minutemen from others in the Far Right after these interviews, I dropped in on Kansas City's Freedom Center Book Store which is something of a gathering place for the city's ultraconservatives. Although it is not an official John Birch Society store as are the various American Opinion stores in many other cities, two of the five men who incorporated it openly admitted to Birch society membership at the time. It offered such selections as Welch's *Blue Book* and *The Politician*, texts on guerrilla warfare, and such fantastic literature as Frank Capell's *The Strange Death of Marilyn Monroe*, in which it is alleged that Bobby Kennedy had the Communists murder the movie queen to avoid an impending scandal. Also on display, but not in a prominent position in the store, were two issues of "On Target" and a pamphlet, "The History of the Minutemen."

I asked the pleasant saleslady who runs the store for its owners if she had any other Minutemen literature.

"Oh, no," she replied. "They're too controversial. They don't like us to sell much from them." She explained that "they" were the men for whom she worked at the store.

We talked a little longer and while I did not consciously try to make her think I was a sympathizer, she apparently concluded I was and, finally, entered the vault in the store and returned with another Minutemen booklet.

"Are you sure you want this?" she asked with what I interpreted as admiration for the raw courage I was displaying. "A lot of these hate groups don't like him, you know."

"Who?"

"Mr. DePugh."

"What hate groups?"

"The left-wing hate groups," she said. "And he seems like such a fine man."

"Do you know where I could get more information about the Minutemen?" the relentless investigator asked.

"You could drive up to Norborne or write Mr. DePugh there," she said. "But be sure not to put a return address on the outside of the envelope. He asked us to say that."

"Why?"

"The FBI."

While seeking someone else from the Minutemen ranks for an interview, I put out word through my then extremely limited sources within Kansas City's Far Right that I wanted Jerry Brooks to telephone me.

I had heard of Brooks for several months prior to that summer, the first time as a shadowy figure who had been aware of the inept Fulbright assassination plot in 1962, later as a gadfly whose activities in behalf of Minutemen causes were cloaked in intrigue, rumor and confusion. He was the only identifiable member of the organization, except for DePugh, as far as I knew at the time, in the area. I was intrigued with the possibility of sitting down and talking with anyone who was attracted by the line of reasoning followed by DePugh.

Brooks did not call me until after the series had appeared in print.

"I hear you've been trying to get hold of me," he said after brief introductions.

I tried to arrange a meeting with him later in the week. Brooks said he might be out of town part of the week—in Wichita, Miami, New York, it was impossible to say where in advance.

"Doing what?" I asked, although I realized it was none of my business.

"Keeping my eyes on the Commies," Brooks replied with a laugh that fit somewhere between a chuckle and a cackle.

A time and place for a rendezvous was set up, but he did not keep the appointment. It would be a year and a half before we met face to face.

The FBI, to the surprise of no one, declined to comment on DePugh's charges of wiretapping and mail tampering, but Russell Millin, U.S. attorney for the Western District of Missouri, in answer to a query about what the federal government was doing about the Minutemen, if anything, replied on August 19, 1964, after checking first with the Department of Justice in Washington:

"The Department of Justice has been aware of the activities of the Minutemen for several years. However, there is no action the government can take to curb those activities or to prosecute those responsible unless there is sufficient available evidence to establish that said activities are beyond the protected area of free speech, press and assembly guaranteed by the first amendment of the Constitution, and in violation of some federal law. Such evidence is not now available.

"Also, at present, there is insufficient information to justify placing this organization on the attorney general's list under executive order No. 10450 relating to the Federal Employees Security program (sometimes called the "subversive list").

"Under our neutrality laws, particularly Title 18, Section 960, United States Code, such activities as the collection of arms and the meeting together in the training of men in military tactics within the United States may be held to be in violation of the law where such activities are in preparation for setting afoot from our shores a military expedition or enterprise against a friendly foreign power. Here the purpose of the group is purportedly to train individuals to defend themselves in the event of an enemy invasion or attack.

"The possible use of other international security statutes has been considered but it has been concluded that the information currently available is insufficient to establish a violation warranting prosecutive action.

"We are continuing to follow closely the activities of this group."

Lyndon Johnson somehow survived the infiltration of his campaign headquarters by Minutemen saboteurs and defeated Barry Goldwater quite decisively at the polls that November. Of all the heartbroken far-right organizations, the Minutemen seemed to take it with the fewest tears. Unsympathetically, they told their ideological brethren: "We told you so."

"In all the conservative movement you cannot find another organization that worked harder than the Minutemen have to elect Barry Goldwater," claimed the November 4 "On Target." "Literally millions of pieces of campaign literature were distributed by our members. Our members worked as volunteers in many local Republican headquarters.

"The Minutemen organization worked for Goldwater not because we thought he would win but in spite of the fact that we knew he was sure to lose. Anyone who doubts this statement need only to read again the literature which the Minutemen have distributed for the past 3½ years."

The Goldwater defeat, this issue of their newsletter stressed, demonstrated the proof of the basic premise on which the organization was founded:

"The time is past when the American people might have saved themselves by traditional political processes."

Goldwater's defeat did not blow the far-right movement out of the water, nor did it still the voices of those who opposed the Rightists. Representative Charles S. Joelson, a New Jersey Democrat, Representative Ronald Brooks Cameron, a California Democrat, and Senator Stephen M. Young, a Democrat from Ohio, were among those in Congress who lashed out at the Minutemen in the next few months.

Senator Young, in fact, let forth with as vitriolic a denunciation of the Minutemen as they may ever have received:

". . . If the Communist leaders had hired helpers in their announced task of burying us, of creating disunity, distrust, and undermining our institutions from within, they could not have chosen a better vehicle than the Birchites or Birch saps, or Sons of Birches, as the distinguished minority whip (Senator Kuchel) terms them, and their fellow-traveling radical crackbrain followers. Among these is a particularly scurrilous group termed the 'Minutemen' . . . The wild men who lead this band of psychotics realize they will never achieve power through democratic means. Therefore they have turned to force. The Minutemen, a lunatic fringe, right-wing extremist group, have issued a call for volunteers to join a secret underground army of terrorists and saboteurs. . . . These stupid, Fascist-minded, misguided, ignorant Americans imitate language and methods of the Nazis in Germany, the Fascists in Italy, the Communists everywhere. . . ."

Senator Young's solution to the threat he felt the Minutemen posed:

"We must destroy these enemies of democracy, not with bullets, as they would use against us, but with facts, constant exposure, and relentless publicity. America is last with them. They are truly America-lasters. If the ignorance that breeds these anti-democratic groups is dispelled, they will soon go the way of the know-nothings, the Coughlinites, the America firsters, the German-American Bund and other lunatic organizations in our past history."

By November, Lynch had succeeded Mosk as California's attorney general, but the anti-Minutemen campaign by that office did not let up. In November, 1964, after the presidential election, Lynch announced he would seek legislation outlawing private military groups in California.

"This anarchism cannot be allowed," he told the Los Angeles Lawyers Guild at a luncheon. "California does not need vigilantes in 1964. . . . Armed bands equipped with automatic weapons, grenades, tear-gas devices, mortars and even cannons are a danger to the peace of our cities and a clear challenge to law enforcement."

He also reported a definite increase in the membership of "private armies" in the past year.

Among the Minutemen's retaliatory moves was the distribution of calling cards, which read, simply: "Lynch Lynch."

Through 1964, California saw sporadic arrests of persons identified in one way or another as members or associates of the Minutemen. Two men who said they were members were arrested in Burbank and charged with possession of illegal weapons in June. Later the same month another man identified with the organization was taken into custody in the Los Padres National Forest, found in possession of 33,000 rounds of assorted ammunition, M-1 rifles, carbines, shotguns, a riot gun, a .45-caliber pistol, gunpowder and dynamite caps. In October yet another man identified as a Minuteman was arrested in Los Angeles. Found in his home were seven machine guns, six rifles, four hand guns, thousands of rounds of ammunition, dynamite, dynamite caps, fuses, twenty hand grenades and seven booby traps. A month later a Van Nuys man who said he was head of anti-subversive activities of an American Legion post was arrested on suspicion of possessing tear gas after eleven cans of such gas, a red Nazi navy flag and several spent .38-caliber cartridge cases were found in the trunk of his car. While showing police his gun collection at his home, his wife, police said, telephoned one of Houghton's staunchest admirers and told him her husband was being arrested.

The Los Angeles *Times* street editions carried an eight-column banner headline on February 26, 1965: "Dynamite Seized—Explosives Cache Found in Glendale" and told of the search for Keith D. Gilbert, a twenty-seven-year-old Glendale gunshop owner in whose home had been found 1400 pounds of dynamite and other explosives which, police said, had been stolen from a powder company. Also found in his apartment were numerous weapons and piles of Minutemen tracts, including membership application forms, the police said. Gilbert later was arrested, tried before a jury, found guilty and sentenced to from one to ten years in prison.

A month after the discoveries in Gilbert's apartment, a cache of 373 machine guns, 100,000 rounds of ammunition and some silencers were confiscated by the California Bureau of Criminal Identification and Investigation and Los Angeles County Sheriff's Department at an arms company near Los Angeles. The attorney general's office soon was to report that the head of this firm was known to have had dealings with three Minutemen members, including Gilbert.

By now, the Minutemen were beginning to feel quite apprehensive about the Federal Bureau of Investigation's interest in their activities.

While the rest of the Far Right was busy quoting J. Edgar Hoover on every anti-Communist statement he had ever made, the Minutemen put out bulletins to members advising them on how to deal with inquisitive FBI agents. The October, 1964, bulletin to California Minutemen and the January, 1965, bulletin to New Jersey members fell into the hands of officials. They proved to be identical in their advice.

Members were told to appear surprised and curious at the reason for an agent's call and, when shown their FBI identification cards, to take a good look in order to learn what such cards look like. They were advised also to remember the agents' names.

"Remember their main objective is to get information," members were cautioned. "The more you talk the more they are going to get."

They were warned that one of the agents could have a hidden tape recorder on his person, recording everything said.

"Remember also that information is a two-way street," the bulletins continued. "You can get information from them by using your wits and keeping your ears open. Ask them what made them think you could conceivably be a member of the Minutemen. They probably won't tell you but look for any hint or slip of the tongue which might give you a clue on this count."

The bulletins warned the members not to be bluffed by such statements as, "We've just received the membership lists of the Minutemen and are checking out all members in this area." Ninety percent of those Minutemen known to the FBI, the bulletins noted, had been identified either because the member told the agency of the fact himself or by interception of the mail.

"As soon as the agents leave," the bulletins stated, "write out a complete and detailed account of your conversation with them. Try to remember the exact wording of every question they ask you and the exact wording of your answer. Send this report to your regular mail drop immediately. By comparing your report with several others we can obtain valuable information as to the progress of their investigation."

Members were advised to lie to the FBI by denying membership in the Minutemen. The only exception to this would be, it added, in the case of trained members capable of playing the double agent who could agree to cooperate with the bureau and then feed them misleading information.

The bulletins added a few other pieces of advice from the New Jersey and California leadership on the same subject, cautioning against being seen near other members after an FBI questioning session for fear of a "loose tail" by the FBI.

"Also, beware of the telephone," the bulletins advised. "Do not call any other members, especially from your home phone. If a phone call is necessary, use a pay station, and then be very sure you are not observed making the call."

And what did the venerable J. Edgar Hoover have to say about this organization that so many Congressmen had been viewing with such alarm? On May 19, 1965, came the answer. He devoted approximately 600 words to the Minutemen in his testimony before the House Appropriations Subcommittee, while attempting to justify his request for funds.

"We have long been aware of the Minutemen organization," said the FBI director, "and our investigation is continuing. . . .

"Our investigation aims to determine the locations of units of the organization: the identities and backgrounds of the officers of each unit as well as the principal active members of each unit: whether the activities of the organization are in violation of any Federal statutes over which the Bureau has investigative jurisdiction: and whether the organization or its members pose a threat to the life of the President or other Government officials. . . ."

He then told the appropriations subcommittee certain basic facts about the Minutemen that any newspaper reader who had followed the organization already knew.

When Hoover got around to his analysis of the Minutemen, I found in reading it that it seemed somehow familiar. So familiar, in fact, that it slowly dawned on me I had written essentially the same analysis in an article the Washington *Post* had asked me to write six months earlier—on November 18, 1964.

"Our investigation indicates this organization is a loose federation, with each unit acting independently and lacking any real central control," said Hoover. "Its numerical strength is probably greatly exaggerated. *DePugh is the only known leader of the group. He is, therefore, its sole spokesman and some of the things he says are, indeed, hard to believe.*"

I had written: "Just how seriously one should take DePugh and the Minutemen organization depends almost entirely on how thoroughly DePugh is to be believed. He is the only known leader of the group, and is one of its few known members. He is therefore its sole spokesman. And some of the things he had spoken are, indeed, hard to believe." (It was that "indeed," I think, which first tipped me.)

Hoover continued: "*DePugh, for example, avoids the responsibility of trying to prove that all he says of the Minutemen, their activities or their size is true.*"

My phraseology had been: "DePugh shrugs off the responsibility of trying to prove that all he says of the Minutemen, their activities or their size is true."

More Hoover: "While he has placed the membership of the Minutemen at 'more than 25,000,' *there is little real evidence that the Minutemen are anything more than essentially a paper organization, with just enough followers over the country so they can occasionally attract a headline, usually because of their preoccupation with violence, or weapons of war.*"

Here I had been strategically vaguer: "But DePugh has never offered any real evidence that the Minutemen are anything more than essentially a paper organization with just enough followers over the country so that they can occasionally snag a headline somewhere, usually because of their preoccupation with weapons of war."

Somehow, after comparing the Washington *Post* story and Mr. Hoover's words, I was not as overwhelmed as I perhaps should have been by his assurance at the end of his statement: "We have penetrated this organization and our sources are keeping us advised of developments."

I must admit having felt more flattered than offended at the plagiarism initially, but after a period of gloating had passed, the question then struck me: Does the government really know very much about the Minutemen? I have reason to doubt whether it did at that time. Today, I am happy to report, there are excellent reasons to believe that the FBI and ATTU do know a great deal about them.

Hoover's ghost writer continued along the same lines later, however. In Hoover's presentation to the appropriations subcommittee on February 10, 1966, he was still saying: "DePugh avoids the responsibility of trying to substantiate all the things he says of the Minutemen.

For example, while he has placed the membership of the organization at 'more than 25,000,' there is little real evidence that the Minutemen is anything more than essentially a paper organization with a membership estimated at 500." That was released on September 22, 1966.

It apparently became evident to the FBI writer that an organization with an estimated 500 members could not be at the same time "essentially a paper organization." On February 16, 1967, Hoover stated flatly, "This is an organization of about 500 members" and the phrase "essentially a paper organization" was finally abandoned.

"This is the organization that claims its primary purpose is to prepare its members to overthrow the Government of the United States in the event the Government is taken over by Communists," Hoover said. "The danger of this position, of course, is DePugh will decide when the Communist takeover has occurred."

Hoover concluded his 1967 assessment of the organization with: "The obsession with violence and expressed intent to make the determination as to the occurrence of a Communist takeover are indicative of the dangerous nature of such extremist groups as the Minutemen. They would act as vigilantes, a law unto themselves."

By February, 1968, Hoover had lowered his estimate of the Minutemen's size to "less than 500" in his plea for funds, adding that "recent information indicates there are less than fifty persons upon whom Minutemen leaders can call for overt action."

Attorney General Lynch's interest in the Minutemen continued in 1965. He released a scathing eighty-one-page report on "paramilitary organizations" in California on April 18, specifically aimed at the American Nazi Party, the National States Rights Party, the California Rangers, the Black Muslims, and the Minutemen.

Lynch observed: "The report clearly shows the threat to the peace and security of our state which is posed by the existence of these groups. They have lost faith in our system of government."

The report estimated that the total active membership in the Minutemen in California was from 100 to 600, according to the "educated guesses" of active and inactive members of the organization.

The organization's gravest potential danger, the report said, lay in the training of members as a guerrilla force. While the organization itself does not own illegal weapons, the report continued, "there appears to be every inducement and invitation to collect illegal arms."

Excerpts from a Minutemen Handbook were quoted to show how members were advised to have on hand, in case of hostilities, carbines with infrared snooperscopes, submachine guns, Browning automatic rifles, mortars, rocket launchers, bazookas and hand and rifle grenades.

Excerpts from "General Notes and Hints from September Seminar, 1963," a training exercise held September 28 and 29 near Temecula, California, and attended by about fifty members, also were offered. Among them:

"Methane gas or nerve gas is obtained when small slivers of pure teflon plastic are inserted in a cigarette. The results are always fatal, and almost immediate. The only known antidote is atropine, which must be taken immediately. . . .

"The complete formula for the manufacture of nitroglycerine is given on page two. Warning!!! NOT to be attempted by amateurs. This stuff is bad!!! Etc. . . ."

The attorney general's concluding commentary on the Minutemen included the observation that they presented "the fantastic situation of a private citizen raising a private military force to accomplish by violence whatever the objective the citizen decides in his judgment is best for the country. Such a military force is improperly labeled guerrillas; the more precise term is insurgents."

In June, 1965, shortly after J. Edgar Hoover's and then Attorney General Lynch's parries at the Minutemen, the Washington *Star* reported the discovery of a cache of dynamite "big enough to destroy a multistory building" had been uncovered in Prince William County, Virginia, a little over twenty miles from Washington. Near the dynamite, the *Star* reported, was a guerrilla warfare training school built by none other than the Minutemen.

The Washington area unit of the Minutemen had been formed in February, government sources were quoted as saying. Its membership was reported to be from twelve to fifteen. Copies of recruiting literature from DePugh and Biolab also were reported to have been obtained from inside this group.

The same newspaper carried another article quoting a judo instructor from Alexandria, Virginia, to the effect that he had been teaching guerrilla warfare tactics to this Minutemen band, including hand-to-hand combat, target practice and techniques of disarming a man holding a gun or knife. The judo expert was quoted as having joined the Minutemen in Florida while teaching judo to Cuban rebels. Representative Gonzalez was quick to read these two newspaper articles into the Congressional Record, commenting that the nation had been shocked by the revelations.

But as this was happening on the East Coast, DePugh was in the process of becoming embroiled in his first major brush with the law as Minutemen chieftain back in Missouri. This was thanks to two young ladies named Linda, sixteen years old, of Independence, and Patricia, age twenty-one, of nearby Lake Lotawana.

CHAPTER 7

JOIN THE MINUTEMEN

... It is going to be necessary for each of us to conduct both our organizational and personal affairs in a manner above reproach. If we give the Communists and their socialist dupes the least cause for criticism they are sure to take instant advantage of it. ...

From a letter to Minutemen from DePugh sent out shortly after the Shiloh training session in October, 1961.

Nearly any way you look at it, DePugh's decision to take a personal hand in recruiting Linda and Patricia into the Minutemen was a mistake—even if his explanation of how it all happened is true.

It was bad for his national image, most assuredly, once it had become known publicly. One would naturally expect the national coordinator of a supersecret, patriotic, paramilitary, anti-Communist organization that claimed 25,000 members to busy himself with more important duties than the personal recruiting and tutoring of a six-teen-year-old girl who has just run away from home. And DePugh's assertion later that he thought Linda was seventeen helped very little to soften the blow to his image.

Nor did it help the Minutemen's reputation for it to become known that teen-aged girls were being so strenuously sought for the organization. Minutemen membership carries with it the obligation to keep certain secrets. Sixteen-year-old girls, no matter how hard they may try, historically have a dismal record in the field of confidence keeping.

It was especially unwise for DePugh to have included in the girls' curriculum—or indoctrination, as he called it—any mention of a Russian espionage school that taught lady spies how to seduce the enemy in order to blackmail or obtain secrets from them. He might have anticipated how easily an impressionable young lady might have interpreted or misinterpreted even the slightest mention of sexy spying. And interpret it—or misinterpret it—they most certainly did.

Linda and Patricia will understand, it is hoped, that no criticism of them is intended by the observation that neither of them proved to be especially reliable Minutewomen. This is obvious, however, from what they told the Independence police department, the FBI, a polygraph expert, the Jackson County prosecutor, me and presumably a Jackson County grand jury.

Two basic versions of what happened to Linda and Patricia between June 4 and June 19, 1965, eventually were offered—one as related by the two young girls, the other as offered by DePugh and Cindy Melville, the young lady whose mother had complained to the police and FBI in 1963 that she was being held against her will by the Minutemen.

Parts of these two versions duplicate one another, other parts are in direct conflict with one another. The exact truth, it appears, lay somewhere in between, not simply because of some fabrications of fact, but because of the differences in perspectives of the tellers.

First the story according to Linda and Patricia. The details in separate statements given the police by the two girls are essentially the same:

> Patricia, a diminutive, brown-haired, twenty-one-year-old divorcée, moved into the Brookside Manor apartments in Independence on April 22, 1965, with some sort of understanding with the apartment manager that it was not necessary for her to worry about keeping up with her $125 monthly rent, although she had a regular job in Kansas City.
>
> Sometime in May, she met a young man of sizable girth known around Independence as "Alley Oop." He also lived in the Brookside Manor. Chatting with him one day beside the apartment complex swimming pool, she asked him what he did for a living. He promptly began lecturing her about Communism and what the Minutemen organization was doing about it. When he asked her if she would be interested in that kind of work, Patricia replied she would have to read up on it before deciding.
>
> The young man brought a large supply of "On Target" newsletters and pamphlets titled "The Combat Use of the Rifle" to her apartment about a week later and told her that if she would fold them, it would help keep the apartment

manager satisfied about her rent deficiencies. She agreed to fold them.

A few days later the young man introduced Patricia to Robert Bolivar DePugh.

"Mr. DePugh talked to me about Communism and the Minutemen organization and how he felt that young people of this country should join his organization," was Patricia's capsuled account of the half-hour conversation.

They parted with DePugh inviting Patricia to meet him in an Independence restaurant a few days later so that he could tell her more about the Minutemen. She did not keep the appointment.

On the evening of May 31, little (five feet two inches), blond-haired Linda—a girl whose appearance might, indeed, fool an older man into believing she was over sixteen—left home, not to return for three weeks. It was not the first time she had done this. She spent the first three nights out sleeping alone in a car a boy friend had loaned her. The boy friend finally took her to Patricia's apartment on the afternoon of June 3. The two girls had worked together in a café and were close friends. Linda agreed to let her spend the night.

That evening, before the girls left on a double date, DePugh visited Patricia's apartment, opening the conversation, according to Linda, with:

"I know Linda's left home, and I know that her mother is going to prosecute anyone who helps her. . . . I want you two in the Minutemen organization."

The girls did not commit themselves and soon were off on their double date, which kept them out until two-thirty the next morning. They were awakened at five that morning by a knocking on the apartment door.

Before they could answer, DePugh and Cindy, his secretary, had managed to enter the apartment and were standing in the front room. The girls assumed that he had a key, for at least one of them is certain the door had been locked. Cindy was introduced to the girls as "Bonnie." DePugh then repeated that he knew Linda was a runaway and added that the police were going to be at the apartment at seven o'clock to return Linda home and arrest Patricia for harboring her.

"At this time," Patricia said in her statement, "Mr. DePugh pulled a gun out from under his coat and started putting it in one hand and then the other hand."

"He had a gun, I don't know what kind it was, in his hand," was the way Linda described it. "He didn't point it at us, but toyed with it in his hand."

DePugh persuaded the girls to dress and accompany him and Cindy from the apartment. They drove to an Independence restaurant where they ate breakfast together. DePugh then took Patricia back to the apartment to collect her belongings while Cindy and Linda remained at the restaurant.

"Linda and I kept trying to argue with Mr. DePugh," related Patricia, "but he kept insisting that we would go with him."

A circuitous path was then followed from Independence to Richmond, Missouri, a small community of 4000 people about fifty miles northeast of Kansas City and fifteen miles east of Norborne. Cindy drove the girls, with DePugh following in another car. Once in Richmond, they were taken to a house where they spent nearly two weeks in the constant company of a young woman who went by the name of Mary Taylor—an attractive girl in her mid-20s who later acknowledged her true name to be Mary Tollerton, the daughter of a well-to-do northwest Missouri land owner. Linda, meanwhile, was given the code name of "Cassie" and Patricia was called "Michelle."

"Mr. DePugh told Linda and I we were not to stick our faces outside the door," Patricia said, "because he didn't want anyone to know we were there. He told us that someone would be there with us all the time. At this time I realized that Linda and I were being held captive." (DePugh's pistol apparently had not convinced her.)

Before leaving them that day, DePugh told the girls to study and learn about the Minutemen. He visited them nearly every day they were there, and reviewed their studies with them.

As for the curriculum . . .

Patricia: "Each day Mr. DePugh would talk to us about the organization and discuss what we had read. He told Linda and I that our purpose in the organization was to use sex as a weapon to blackmail Communists in our government. He showed us through papers he had that past Presidents such as Roosevelt,

Truman, Eisenhower, Kennedy and all other government officials were Communists."*

Linda: "During these two weeks, DePugh talked to us about what and why he wanted us in the organization. DePugh told us he wanted us to seduce men in the high government. He told us that the Communists had taken over our government and he would use us, and other girls like us, to return the government to the American people."

An occasional visitor to the house in Richmond while the two girls were residing there with Mary was a young Chicagoan who had recently joined DePugh's Norborne contingent of Minutemen—Walter Patrick (Wally) Peyson, about whom a great deal more will be discussed later. According to Patricia:

"At one time Wally showed Linda and I a machine gun and told us what would happen to informers."

At about nine-thirty on the night of June 17, Patricia and Linda decided they had had enough indoctrination and walked out the front door. They made it to the end of the driveway before DePugh drove up in a car.

"Where do you think you girls are going?" asked DePugh, and he told them to climb in his car.

A pistol lay in the front seat of the vehicle beside DePugh, the same one Linda thought she had seen in the apartment on their last morning there.

"Mr. DePugh told us that once we were in the organization, there was no getting out," related Patricia, "and if we did find a hole to crawl into, we wouldn't find any way to crawl back out. He kept telling us what happened to people who informed on him and about what he did during the war. Linda and I were scared enough by then, we went back in the house with him."

Within a few hours, DePugh was driving the girls to 613 East Alton Avenue in Independence.

Occupying the living quarters there at the time were Jack and Anne Cannon and their several small children. Cannon, it later was learned, was a gunsmith employed by the Minutemen.

* Indeed, less than a year later, DePugh was to write in *Blueprint for Victory:* "Our last five presidents have all aided and cooperated with our Communist enemies. The degree of such cooperation is almost beyond comprehension. . . ."

The girls spent only a day or two at 613, but long enough, as Linda described it, to work developing plates, typing, filing records and running the printing machine. Several weeks after giving her statement to the police, Linda elaborated on her Minutemen clerical work, saying she also opened envelopes mailed to 613 East Alton. One day's delivery, she said, contained about $200 in dues and contributions. She said she also typed up lists of Minutemen members and their secret code numbers. Although she personally only typed about nine pages, single-spaced, Linda was able somehow to reach the conclusion that the organization had between 9000 and 10,000 members.

The girls found allies in the Cannon couple, who helped them escape on the night of June 19. They slipped out the back door while the Cannons, DePugh, "Mary Taylor," and Wally Peyson were talking in the front office.

Patricia, who had left her car at a service station in Independence at DePugh's insistence (backed up against a fence so the license plate would not show), had secretly kept an extra key in her possession. The girls spent the night in the car. On the following day, a Sunday, an Independence policeman arrested them.

And that is one side of the story, take it or leave it.

James McCarty, an Independence policeman who by coincidence was to figure in a strange Minutemen escapade thirteen months later, was the officer who arrested Linda and Patricia that day.

As McCarty recalled it later, he had noticed two cars parked side by side while on patrol. Two girls were in one car, two men in the other, one of them a "minor police character." McCarty drove around the block once and, upon returning, saw the men's car pulling away. He stopped them and asked what they were doing.

"You won't believe this," he quoted one of the men as saying, "but they were trying to borrow a dollar so they could get something to eat."

This aroused McCarty's curiosity enough to prompt him to question the girls. After seeing their identification cards, he radioed to his dispatcher and was informed that Linda was wanted on a missing persons report. He told the girls he was taking them to headquarters.

"On the way in," he recalled, "they kept begging me, 'Don't take us back to DePugh.' I couldn't figure out what they were talking about at first, but the more they talked, the more interesting it got."

The girls said that DePugh had warned them it would do them no good to go to the police for help because the Minutemen had infiltrated both the Independence police department and the FBI.

When the girls reached headquarters, they immediately asked to talk with an FBI agent. Patricia was booked on a charge of vagrancy while Linda's parents were notified of her whereabouts and she was turned over to a juvenile officer.

After telling an FBI agent and policemen their story, they were disappointed to notice that no one seemed particularly impressed.

"Have you seen any James Bond movies?" Linda recalled being asked by the FBI.

"*Goldfinger*," she replied.

But as skeptical as lawmen can become, especially when listening to young girls in trouble, a tale of having been kidnaped by the Minutemen was simply too wild to be totally ignored.

By the next morning it had been decided that the girls should at least be given polygraph tests. By what appears to have been nothing more than a coincidence, the man chosen to administer the tests was George Robinson, the private detective to whom Cindy's mother had gone in 1963 seeking assistance in "freeing" Cindy from the Minutemen. After interviewing Patricia and Linda at some length without the polygraph, Robinson asked them several questions with the device in operation.

"Were you forced by threat of violence, either direct or indirect, to accompany Robert DePugh to a residency on Broadway in Richmond?"

"Yes."

"Were you held in captivity at the previous mentioned residence in Richmond, Missouri, for at least a week or more?"

"Yes."

"Were you ordered by Robert DePugh to the effect that you were not to leave the house?"

"Yes."

Robinson concluded, after studying the girls' responses to these and several routine test questions unrelated to their allegations, that they were telling the truth. In the younger Linda's case, however, he noted certain reactions during his longer interview with her and cautioned the police that any information she supplied them should be checked carefully.

After seeing the results of Robinson's polygraph test, the police

officers decided to have Linda and Patricia guide them over the entire
route they said they had been taken on June 4 with Cindy and DePugh
—to the restaurant in Independence, a service station, a junction in
Lexington, Missouri, where they had been joined by Peyson and "Mary
Taylor," to a restaurant in Lexington, to a laundromat and a super-
market in Richmond and finally to the house in Richmond where
they said they had been held. The girls appeared to know what they
were talking about.

The federal officials, while interested in the story, said they found
only one aspect of it possibly pertinent to them as a law violation:
Wally Peyson's "machine gun."

Automatic weapons fall within the jurisdiction of the National Firearms Act, and unless they are registered properly with the government and a tax paid on them, their owners can fall into serious
trouble.

What happened between June 24, when the girls led the police
on the route from the apartment to Richmond, and July 8, when the
Jackson County's prosecutor's office decided to do something about
it, is something of a mystery. Had the prosecutor acted immediately,
DePugh's troubles the rest of that year might not have become so
complex. The delay worked to his distinct disadvantage.

Sometime late in June—the exact date is difficult to establish, but
it was during this important period of delay—several (DePugh says
fifteen) Minutemen from different points over the country converged
on 613 East Alton for what DePugh later was to describe as an
intended two-week training session on surveillance and explosives. According to DePugh, the first week was spent on the subject of surveillance, with classes held in the basement at 613. The second week was
to have been spent on a southern Missouri farm where the use of
explosives could be taught.

Midway through the session, he later went on to say, he received
word from inside the Independence police department that trouble
was imminent. Forewarned, the out-of-town Minutemen fled Independence to protect their identities, leaving behind explosives they had
brought with them for fear of being arrested with them in their
cars.

Among those present for the training session were at least two
Californians, Troy Houghton, the Minutemen West Coast coordinator,
and Dennis Patrick Mower, a young Houghton side-kick. They had

driven together to Independence with a deactivated Thompson submachine gun resting in the trunk of Houghton's car. It was the property of young Mower. This weapon, as harmless as it was in its deactivated state at the time, later was to figure prominently in a tangled web of controversy in two federal courts. This was because as Houghton and Mower fled Independence for Norborne, they left the submachine gun behind at 613 East Alton.

After talking with the two girls himself, Lawrence F. Gepford, then the prosecuting attorney of Jackson County, decided to file a charge of kidnaping against DePugh—a charge that could have put the Minutemen leader behind bars for a maximum of ten years. (Kidnaping without demanding ransom, under Missouri Law, is a markedly lesser offense than kidnaping for ransom.)

The warrant for DePugh's arrest was issued early the afternoon of the eighth and three men were sent out to look for DePugh: Sergeant Harold Taylor and Detective Bob Jackson of the Independence police department, and Roy Horridge, the grand jury investigator from Gepford's office.

I accompanied Horridge on this escapade, finding him amiable, efficient, melodramatic, and annoyingly inclined to high speeds with red light and siren.

We looked around Independence all afternoon for DePugh without success. The police even had additional officers keep two of his most regular Independence haunts under surveillance, but neither reported seeing him enter or leave.

DePugh, it seems, had decided to play the hunted man for a while. He said later that as the police searched for him, he was driving from here to there, stopping periodically to make strategic calls from pay telephones. This way, he explained, he did not have to spend a night in the Independence jail, and in light of what subsequently happened to Cindy and Jack Cannon, he may have had reason for such apprehension.

But like his decision to recruit Patricia and Linda into the Minutemen, his resolve to become a fugitive backfired.

Shortly before dark, Horridge, Taylor and Jackson met near 613 East Alton and decided to pay a visit inside. I followed.

Cannon met us at the door. A handsome, square-jawed, dark-haired man, rather slight of build but muscular, grim and stoic in demeanor, he reluctantly allowed the law-enforcement officers inside and soon was joined by an aggressive young woman with an attractive face that was almost obscured by her flamboyantly coiffured hair. None too pleasantly, she asked each of the officers for their identification before allowing them to penetrate the building any further. (Not as efficient as she considered herself to be—she forgot to check mine.) After looking at the ID cards, she told the lawmen her name was Jody McPhillips, nineteen years old, and that she had come to Missouri recently from New Jersey in order to work for the Minutemen.

The only other adult found in the building was Mrs. Anne Cannon, Jack's wife, a sweet, soft-spoken woman who looked as out of place in the surroundings as Jody seemed a part of the suspicious atmosphere.

We gathered in the larger of two front offices. The building's occupants were questioned for several minutes about DePugh and the two young visitors they had entertained there the previous month. Anne Cannon recalled that two girls had been there—their names, she thought, had been "Michelle" and "Linda"—but it had been only for a short time. She seemed surprised at the officers' concern.

The office in which they were questioned was unusual in several respects. In addition to various books on Communism, Americanism, anti-Communism, weaponry, guerrilla warfare and espionage, the book shelves on the south wall also were lined with numerous thick, out-of-town telephone directories. More to the amusement than of interest to the officers was a poster noticed stuck to a glass partition that separated this from the smaller office. It was headed: "WANTED: LADY SPIES." I did not have time to read it then, but later ran across a mimeographed booklet headed "Minutemen News," dated December 15, 1964, with the same heading, "WANTED: LADY SPIES," atop one page. Beneath it was a somewhat whimsical explanation of how the best women spies in history were ugly or middle-aged, not beauties, and concluded with the observation: "But madam, just because you are beautiful, do not despair—you too can be a spy. It's just a little harder if you're glamorous."

Behind the desk, within easy reach of anyone sitting at it, was a carbine, which the police officers discovered was fully loaded and ready for firing. As one of them unloaded it, Jody told them matter-of-factly that she kept it there for protection when studying in the office late at night. Several bullets had been fired into the front of the building in the past, she said.

Hoping apparently that DePugh was hiding somewhere in the building, the officers did not devote all of their time to the interrogation, spending part of it looking now and then into other rooms. There was, as a result, considerable traffic in and out of the office. Mrs. Cannon, with several children to worry about, added to the traffic.

Suddenly the officers noticed that Jack Cannon had disappeared from the room. They looked quickly through the first floor of the building and, concluding he had sneaked out the back door, rushed outside to look for him. Additional police cars began to arrive.

I found myself at this point alone in the office with Jody. Relieved that the rifle behind her had been divested of its ammunition, I was surprised to see lying directly in front of her on the desk what looked to me like a German Luger. It had not been there when we had entered.

"What's that doing there?" I asked, trying to hide my nervousness.

The Minutewoman smiled mischievously, picked it up and tossed it to me. It was a wooden toy.

As police officers scurried about outside the building, a loud, metal-on-metal crash came from the basement. I had wandered into the largest room in the building by this time and jumped at the noise. Next I heard footsteps on the basement stairs. I was alone in the room as Cannon, pale and nervous, opened the basement door and reappeared.

"Where the hell have you been?" I asked, eloquent in crisis.

Cannon mumbled something about having put something away in the basement for fear one of his children might hurt himself with it. The gunsmith will no doubt be amused at the news that it was at this point—forgetting for the moment that he had his entire family in the building at the time—that it occurred to me that this grim young man might have planted a bomb in the basement to destroy Minutemen records in the structure. He hadn't.

The police officers were as unimpressed by Cannon's explanation for his disappearance as was I. As some of them hastened down the basement stairs, others handcuffed Cannon and ordered him and his family to remain in the kitchen.

DePugh was not in the basement. Other surprises were.

Lying about in untidy array were a weathered Japanese land mine still in its original crate, wire-tap equipment, a directional "shotgun" mike for long-distance eavesdropping, two recoilless rifles and a movie projector and screen, among other things. Behind a curtain on which the sign "Off Limits" had been hung was Cannon's workshop area. At one end was a bullet-riddled target in the shape of a man's body silhouetted over a white background.

One police officer happened to notice that two sections of the furnance pipe were not linked together properly and, upon examination, found that a Thompson submachine gun had been hidden inside the pipe with apparent haste. This, the policemen guessed, had accounted for the loud noise in the basement during Cannon's disappearance.

Only the submachine gun was confiscated that night. It later was found to have been deactivated. This was the weapon brought from California by Houghton and Mower.

The search for DePugh resumed, although by now it could reasonably be assumed that the Minutemen leader knew he was being sought and that chances of finding him were remote.

Lieutenant James R. Wingate of the Independence police department ordered several more policemen to join in the search as he, Horridge, Jackson and Taylor sped across the city to the Brookside Manor apartments. ("Roy, do you really think we have to go seventy miles an hour in this traffic?" He slowed down to sixty-five.) Somehow the rumor had reached the police that this was a hotbed of Minutemen and that one of them had a large machine gun somewhere in the apartment complex. The police urged caution in approaching the area. Police riot guns were readied. A casual passerby could well have assumed from the appearance of what was happening that a pitched battle was about to erupt between an army of police and an apartmentful of sharpshooting Minutemen stationed at every window.

Horridge, riot gun at the ready, took the lead in inspecting various apartment units, much to the irritation of some of the police officers. After a tall, gangly teen-aged boy had allowed him and other officers into the apartment manager's apartment, Horridge became suspicious at finding one door locked. Informed by the youth that he did not have a key, Horridge broke it open with a swift kick and burst into the room with his riot gun poised for action. The room, an office, was empty of people, but three shotguns were found inside.

The atmosphere was tense enough during this episode that my imagination became overcharged, I confess. While standing alone in the parking lot behind the apartments at one point, I noticed a tall, rugged-looking man in a sport shirt and slacks appear from around the corner of one building and walk cautiously toward me. He was carrying a shotgun. A Minuteman, I surmised. The battle was about to begin, and I was going to be its first casualty. We eyed each other as noncommittally as possible as he approached. Finally conversation became unavoidable.

"You'd better put that away," said I, too scared to run.

"Why?" the man asked, his eyes narrowing.

"There's a lot of policemen roaming around here with the same thing you have there," I said.

"I'm a police officer," the man said with justifiable disgust. "Who the hell are you?"

Several more apartment units were searched, but no DePugh, no machine gun, no bloodshed, in fact no real opposition to the search could be found. Various apartment residents stood about in groups whispering observations, but without any noticeable emotion.

By now I had decided to catch a taxi back to my office in Kansas City where I persuaded my editors that all of the preceding had, indeed, occurred and was worth a front-page story the following morning. Bob Phillips, another *Star* reporter, took over the search with Horridge and the police and was soon wondering—with greater justification than had I—whether he was going to be shot by Minutemen snipers.

This was when they reached Norborne. They were joined by a deputy sheriff from Carroll County and a state highway patrolman before venturing to within firing range of DePugh's two-story, white frame house. There, behind a locked screen door at the front of the house, stood three young men armed with rifles—Houghton, Peyson, and John DePugh, fifteen years old, the Minutemen leader's second-oldest son. As the police officers began to explain the reason for their visit, the three young men behind the screen injected cartridges into their rifles' chambers.

One of the officers told John DePugh to telephone his mother before they entered the house. John obliged, reaching her in California where she was visiting with the youngest DePugh children in tow.

A search of the DePugh residence revealed Dennis Mower, Houghton's young side-kick, and the attractive Mary Tollerton in an upstairs bedroom guarding Minutemen records. The lawmen resisted the temptation of confiscating them.

On the floor of the front room of the first floor were found ammunition and clips for automatic weapons.

Wally Peyson, when asked during the search of the house whether anything unusual had occurred there in recent months, was quite frank: "It depends on what you call unusual. There is chaos around this place continually."

Houghton, nearly two years later, looked back on that search of the DePugh house in an interview and gave a rather surprising account of what he said almost had happened.

He said he had been in charge of the household that night and that he had been ready to shoot it out with the police if they had entered the house illegally and tried to take away Minutemen records that were in the house. Mary Tollerton and Dennis Mower had been stationed upstairs sitting atop the valuable membership records ready to douse them with an inflammable liquid and set them afire at a moment's notice if the police had tried to take them. Mary later confirmed this, adding that this had been a decidedly foolish act to have contemplated.

"You were ready to shoot?" I asked Houghton.

"Oh, yes," he replied.

In reply to my observation that shooting police officers sometimes resulted in long prison sentences if not execution, Houghton replied that he had fully expected to be gunned down himself that night, his killing being chalked off as the justified elimination of a cop-killer.

"Those records were worth dying for?"

"Oh, yes," he replied. "We have an understanding that the records must never be compromised."

He said that during the encounter he had stationed someone at a telephone near the house in long-distance communications with someone else in the Minutemen ready to relate details of the bloodshed.

He also said that he was wearing a bulletproof vest during this episode, although a photograph Phillips took of Houghton and Peyson standing in the doorway disputes this.

The police then went to the office of DePugh's Biolab Corporation in the business district of Norborne, but the deputy sheriff and city marshal of Norborne refused to let the other officers inside without permission from someone in the DePugh family. Mrs. William DePugh, Robert DePugh's sister-in-law, finally obliged, but an inspection of the main floor and basement of the building produced no Minutemen, least of all DePugh.

On their way back to Independence in the early morning hours, the officers stopped at the house in Richmond where Linda and Patricia had said they had been held. The house was abandoned, but several samples of discarded Minutemen literature were found about the house.

Late the following morning, Prosecutor Gepford asked the FBI to join in the search for DePugh. Horridge, he said, had been told by one of DePugh's followers the night before, "You'll never find him. He's gone underground." Soon the United States Attorney's office in Kansas City announced the FBI would look for DePugh as soon as a federal warrant could be issued charging him with unlawful flight across a state line to avoid prosecution. Before J. Edgar Hoover's men had had time to rally their forces for the hunt, however, a lawyer called Gepford in behalf of DePugh and said the fugitive was ready to surrender peacefully. Relaxed and self-confident, DePugh soon appeared at the county courthouse in Kansas City, was arraigned on the kidnaping charge and posted $5000 bond.

"People have for years been trying to discredit the Minutemen," DePugh told newsmen, and answered a few questions before departing with William H. Costello, his attorney.

He did not recognize either Patricia or Linda by name, he said, and therefore could not say if he knew the girls who had accused him of kidnaping them. He denied ever carrying a gun, as the girls had alleged. Asked whether he thought the charge would hurt the Minutemen organization, DePugh replied, "We were pretty strong yesterday. I don't know how strong we are today. Any bad publicity hurts." Which, as he well knows, isn't always true.

A circuit-court judge meanwhile was signing a search warrant to enable police to revisit 613 East Alton with the right to look for and confiscate illegal explosives and weapons.

The second "raid" began at six o'clock that night, with Jody McPhillips greeting the officers at the screen door this time with even less cordiality than the night before. Her refusal to unhook the screen prompted Lieutenant Wingate to yank it open.

With Jody hanging over their shoulders, protesting bitterly, the police officers uncovered a great deal more this time than had been found the night before. Perhaps they had not noticed these items in the rush the previous night. Perhaps they had seen some of it but purposely had avoided confiscating it because they lacked a search warrant. I don't know. Whatever the case, their official list of items confiscated the second night included a bazooka in a first-floor closet of the Cannons' living quarters and the following from the basement:

Five cases of live dynamite, containing more than 200 sticks of the explosives (although DePugh later was to boast they had overlooked two other cases); seven live hand grenades; five .45-caliber homemade but inoperable grease guns; a carbine; two "explosion (rocket) launchers"; a detonating device; a box of assorted Japanese land mines; one pound of TNT explosives; six rolls of detonating wire; seven boxes of wire fuse lighters; a timing device; two boxes containing seventy-five blasting caps; a "deactivator"; a mousetrap booby-trap detonator; a .242-caliber Winchester automatic rifle; a roll of detonating cable and one box of powder for explosives.

DePugh, free on bond, arrived at the scene shortly after eight o'clock with Cindy, entered the building, apprised himself of the situation and returned outside to complain loudly to Police Chief Orson (Barney) Myers that the inventory police had just given Cannon covered only about one-third of what had been taken.

I was not there that night, but can attest to at least one such unlisted item having been confiscated: the parabolic "shotgun" mike for long-distance eavesdropping, which I admired a day or two later in the vault of the Jackson County prosecutor's office. It was later returned, however, with many other items. Not returned were Mower's submachine gun or the hand grenades, some of which were destroyed by demolition experts who were testing them to see if they were live. They were.

"I've demanded of the chief of police a complete inventory of what has been taken and he has refused," DePugh said in a loud voice outside the building as he and Myers glared at one another.

Myers asked DePugh twice if he owned the confiscated items—an admission, he said, which would have entitled him to the inventory—but DePugh replied he would have to consult his attorney before answering.

Meanwhile, the police took Cindy into custody for investigation concerning her role in the alleged kidnaping. Cindy was held in jail overnight and questioned at length. She failed to answer at length, however, and was arraigned the next day as a material witness and released on $3000 bond.

But is this really what happened between June 4 and July 9? According to DePugh and Cindy, in separate interviews, and according to the August 1 issue of "On Target," quite a bit happened quite differently.

The Minutemen account unfolded slowly in bits and pieces through the rest of July and August—first through a short interview with DePugh on the day he surrendered; then in an interview of DePugh the following day while Cindy was waiting to be arraigned (an interview that ended abruptly when DePugh fled down a flight of stairs in the courthouse, apparently fed up with questions); next in an unusual interview with Cindy that same night (which had an even more unusual ending); ten days later in a fuller interview that DePugh arranged to be held in the downtown Kansas City public library with (it was learned later) another Minuteman, Jerry Brooks, watching DePugh and me from a distance as a precaution against God-knows-what; then in "On Target"; and finally at a rally of about 125 conservatives, ultraconservatives, Minutemen and Minutemen sympathizers in a downtown Kansas City hotel on August 9, after it appeared possible that DePugh might have to go to jail the next day for contempt of court.

Knit together into one narrative, here is what happened, according to the Minutemen:

> Patricia lived at the Brookside Manor apartments and folded Minutemen literature, as she told police. She met DePugh sometime in May, as she said. DePugh asked her at this meeting whether she had been reading what she had been folding. Patricia replied that she had read it all, and that she believed it.*
>
> Exactly why Patricia's willingness to fold Minutemen literature enabled her to pay less than the required $125-a-month rent remained unexplained. The apartment manager, a friend of DePugh, refused to answer any questions when queried, and DePugh later commented, "He wouldn't give anybody a dime

---

* The May, 1965, issue of "On Target"—presumably the issue she had worked with—was headlined "Madmen Rule the World," and took a decidedly unenthusiastic view of President Johnson's victory the previous fall over Barry Goldwater. The article began:

"On November 3rd, 1964, civilization stumbled across a threshold, as forty million Americans, simply by casting their ballots, fixed upon the world the seal of approval of government by madmen. . . ."

off their rent if they folded all the Minutemen literature between here and New York. . . . He's never been a member
of the Minutemen at all."

Shortly after midnight on June 4, DePugh learned from the
apartment manager that he was going to evict Patricia because
of some "wild parties" that had been held in her apartment and
the arrest of one of her male callers in the apartment complex
parking lot for a parole violation.

He telephoned Cindy immediately and asked her to meet
him at the apartment early the next morning. In confirming
this later, Cindy noted that such telephone calls and meetings
with DePugh at odd hours were not unusual.

"I met him once at two o'clock in the morning," she said.
"That's the way he was. It's like Wally said, 'You don't think
anything's strange when everything's chaos.'"

DePugh and his confidential secretary met outside Patricia's
apartment at six o'clock (said Cindy) or sixty-thirty (said
DePugh), not five o'clock as the girls alleged, and knocked on
the door. The girls let them inside, where they talked for about
forty-five minutes about the girls' joining the Minutemen.

Both DePugh and Cindy insist DePugh had no weapon with
him at the time. DePugh, in fact, said he never carried a pistol
on his person or in his car because this would give law enforcement officers a chance to arrest him for carrying a concealed
weapon.*

Cindy related that DePugh told Patricia that morning she
was going to be evicted and the police were planning to visit
her apartment in an hour or so.

"We talked about forty-five minutes, trying to ascertain if
they had any talents that could be used in the organization,"
DePugh said, of the encounter. "I wanted to see whether they
really wanted to work or were just attracted by the intrigue.
One had had typing experience and the other had done work
in a print shop once. Cindy and I went out and talked it over.
We were both dubious, but I thought they basically had a strong,
patriotic streak to them."

* A year later, however, when DePugh was arrested in Kansas City by deputy
federal marshals on a grand jury indictment, a .38-caliber pistol was found in an
attaché case on the back seat of the car in which he was riding.

He said that "Alley Oop," the Minutemen member who originally had talked with Patricia about joining the organization, had told him she was very patriotic and could be developed into a good member of the organization.

The girls agreed to go with him and Cindy to Richmond, where, it was explained to them, they were to be indoctrinated into the Minutemen. They spent about a week there, he said, not two weeks, and then went to 613 East Alton, where they remained roughly another week, not two days as the girls had said.

At all times—in Richmond and in Independence—the girls were free to leave whenever they wished. Wally took them to a movie one night. They went out on dates every night while in Independence.

As for the allegation that DePugh had told them they were to be used to seduce Communists in government, DePugh gave this explanation:

"We were reading about the curriculum of Russian spy schools, and one subject that came up was the use of seduction by the Communists for blackmail and control of other people. The girls—half-jokingly, I thought—said, 'That sounds like the job for us,' and I told them that the time may come when we would have to resort to such measures, but that things aren't that desperate yet.

"Mary told me later that the girls talked about that the rest of the day."

More recently DePugh offered a slightly more revealing explanation of the Minutemen's use of young women in espionage work.

". . . A couple of good-looking young women are a valuable addition to the organization," he said. "You don't just pick them up like you do men and older women and so forth."

"What's the value of good-looking young women?"

"Their youth was one of the main advantages. We've found out that once a person is past twenty-five or thirty years old, it's very difficult to infiltrate them into a Communist organization. They're very suspicious of older people, and then, of course, an older person, if they don't have a history of pro-Communist activity, they're dead for sure, they're not going to get in."

"What do their good looks have to do with it?"

"The Reds are always looking for young girls, and if we can find them first and get them thoroughly indoctrinated, they're the first people that the Communists will take into their apparatus."

"For what reason?"

"Well, I suppose they figure on using them the same way that we would, as spies."

"Seductive spies?"

"I wouldn't say it's impossible. I think I said many a time that to defeat this particular enemy, there's no ends that I would consider too far."

"You mean they were right when they said you told them one of their functions would be to seduce Communists in the government?"

"No, we didn't tell them that. Maybe if they'd gotten far enough in their training program we might have told them that someday. But we weren't that far along."

Referring to one of the girls' assertions that Peyson had shown them a machine gun and "told us what would happen to informers," DePugh said that the girls had noticed a carbine in Peyson's car, had asked what it was and had been told by Wally that it was his "machine gun."

"Wally's a practical joker," DePugh explained.

DePugh took the girls back to Independence because they had grown restless in Richmond, wanted to go back to see their boy friends, and, DePugh complained, had not been concentrating on their studies.

The girls slept nights in the photography dark room at 613 after returning from their dates. DePugh became impatient with their late hours eventually and told them, "Either you're patriots or you aren't." He also warned them that their behavior could give the Minutemen a bad name.

When finally arrested by the police, why did they give out such a condemnation of DePugh? "On Target" offered this explanation under an article titled "Ingredients of a Frame-Up":

"Take two frightened young ladies, one who had run away from home and the other arrested for vagrancy. Add one chief of police with announced antagonism against the Minutemen.

Add one prosecuting attorney with political ambitions. Mix well to produce unfounded charges, nationwide smear, arrest and harassment of loyal Americans, seizure and damage of private property."

It related that Linda once had displayed bruises around her neck and shoulders and had said, "This is what I got the last time I went home."

"After finding herself in police custody it would seem like a natural thing for a girl her age to cook up a story of kidnaping to explain her absence and try to avoid further punishment," the newletter continued. "In fact, subsequent investigation has disclosed that she came up with a similar story two years ago when she charged another man with abducting her and holding her captive at a service station. Those charges were dropped when the story was presumed to be a hoax.

"Pat . . . a twenty-one-year-old divorcée, had been accused a few weeks earlier of contributing to the delinquency of a minor. Finding herself in jail for vagrancy it can be surmised that only a modest amount of persuasion was necessary for her to go along with the kidnaping story so that she would be released."

The newsletter went on to note that Police Chief Myers once had told DePugh: "We have no common ground for discussion. Your beliefs and mine are as opposite as they can get."

Myers once had called the members of the police department together and told them that if he could prove any members of his force were Minutemen, they would have five minutes to either resign their positions or be fired, the newsletter charged. (Myers confirms this, except that he recalls he said he would give them only thirty seconds.)

The newsletter called Gepford a man of "obvious political ambitions"—a conclusion that did not require an extensive undercover Minutemen investigation to reach.

"It is reported," the newsletter said, "that he wanted to run for the office of Missouri Attorney General at the last election but was turned down by the political bosses as being unknown throughout the state. What a wonderful opportunity to become widely known as the crusading prosecutor of the Minutemen.

"After their arrest the girls were questioned and their story rehearsed for several days before any charges were filed. With time they were able to answer selected questions correctly for a polygraph test. Repeated conferences were held between Chief Myers, Prosecutor Gepford and others as to if and how a charge of kidnaping could be made to stick.

"We had been warned of this conspiracy several days before a warrant was issued but considered the story so improbable that the warning was ignored."

The "On Target" issue also approvingly reprinted an article from the St. Louis *Post-Dispatch* quoting DePugh as saying: "Various governmental agencies have been trying for three years to get something on me, and there are a lot of pro-Communists in and out of public office who would love to discredit the Minutemen."

The "Reuther Memorandum," also was reprinted in part in "On Target" to imply the extent of this conspiracy.

This, then, was the Minutemen version of the alleged abduction, and it, too, can be taken or left.

In mid-August, after the countercharges of "On Target" had been printed in the *Star*, Linda's husband—she had married shortly after the Minutemen incident had become known—telephoned me and urged an interview of Linda, with him and her mother present.

From beneath a mass of unsightly middle-of-the-day hair curlers, Linda, by then seventeen, and her mother offered a refutation of the newsletter's accusations. For one thing, said her mother, Linda never had been beaten at home. She and Linda offered a different version of the incident in which Linda had accused another man of locking her in a service station.

"He was planning on abducting us or seducing us, I guess," said Linda. "I don't really know what he planned."

Linda's father had decided to press charges against the man and the charge had been contributing to the delinquency of a minor, not kidnaping, as "On Target" had said.

That part of the Minutemen account as offered by Cindy Melville was obtained under odd circumstances the Saturday night of July 10, only a few hours after she had been released from custody as a material witness under bond.

I had set out that evening to interview Cindy's mother, Mrs. Sanders, hoping for some fresh insights into Cindy's Minutemen involvements.

I reached Mrs. Sander's apartment shortly after dark, innocently parking my car on the street almost directly in front of the entrance to the apartment building. When she responded to my knock on her door, I was surprised to find that Cindy and her two young children also were there. Also to my surprise, I was admitted inside. Cindy had had few words for me at the Independence police headquarters and later at the courthouse, with DePugh hovering about all the time.

Cindy is a big-boned girl, taller than average, well proportioned. Through the hectic day of July 10, she had worn her long hair straight down, well past her shoulders, giving herself a rather spooked look that excited few newspaper readers as they obtained their first look at a photograph of the girl DePugh called his "confidential secretary." With little effort, Cindy has subsequently proven, she is able to appear in public as a fine and admirable specimen of womanhood. This night, however, she was tired and looked every bit as though she had, indeed, just spent the previous night in a jail cell.

I explained that I had gone there to talk with Mrs. Sanders, but that since Cindy was there, perhaps they both would like to tell me about the Minutemen, DePugh, Linda and Patricia, the whole shebang.

Cindy at first said she was tired from her night in jail and the rigors of the arraignment. Perhaps it was because of her mother's presence there, and a desire not to appear too secretive in front of her—I have no way of knowing her real motives—she slowly seemed to warm to the idea of discussing the case. Soon she was detailing the events of the day of the alleged abduction, admitting she had driven the two girls to Richmond, but punctuating the account several times with: "I did not kidnap anyone." The girls had gone voluntarily, she insisted.

Mrs. Sanders attempted to inject a comment several times, but usually was cut short by Cindy, not unkindly, with, "Mother, don't say anything." This did not prevent Mrs. Sanders from making it clear to me that she had "no use" for DePugh. Before Cindy could finish her story, we were interrupted by a knock on the apartment door.

"It's for you," Mrs. Sanders told Cindy, after answering the knock, and Cindy disappeared into the apartment hallway for about five minutes. When she returned, she said she could not continue the interview because "an emergency has come up."

"Concerning the Minutemen?" I asked.

"It's an emergency," she said, and indicated the interview could be resumed sometime in the future on an I'll-call-you-don't-call-me basis.

By this time, I was filled with the spirit of intrigue that surrounded the whole affair. I slipped out the back door of the apartment building so as not to be shot by a sniper who my imagination cautioned me might think I knew more than I did, walked to a bowling alley several blocks away and telephoned my office. After describing where I had been, I was amazed to learn that Bill Anderson, head of the *Star*'s Johnson County, Kansas, office, lived in the same apartment building. I returned there, by the back way (snipers, you know) slipped up to his apartment, interrupted him and his wife from a quiet evening in front of their television set, and asked if I might quietly sit by the darkened window of their kitchen, which had an excellent view of the front entranceway to the apartment building, and phone in my story.

I suppose I overdramatized the whole affair to them so thoroughly that they were either drawn to the intrigue or amused by the fledgling James Bond who was visiting them. They were most hospitable, at any rate. My hope was that DePugh or some other Minutemen would suddenly appear out of the shadows and do something worth writing about.

After waiting about an hour and a half, with nothing happening, I returned to my office, a drive of about fifteen minutes from the apartment. Upon my arrival there, I was informed that just after I had left the Andersons, Mrs. Sanders had gone upstairs from her apartment, knocked on the Andersons' door and asked them, of all persons, if they would baby-sit for her two grandchildren while she took her daughter to St. Luke's hospital. Her daughter, she said, was not feeling well. Mrs. Sanders did not know that I had just left his apartment or that Bill knew the identity of her daughter.

I waited at the office a few minutes and telephoned the emergency room at St. Luke's to inquire about Cindy. No, said the hospital, no one answering the description of Cindy or her mother had been there.

After about an hour, Bill called again. Cindy and her mother had returned, thanked him and his wife for baby-sitting, and that, apparently, was that. It was after midnight by then. On an impulse, I even suggested the police keep an eye on the apartment building that night. They did.

Several months later, Jerry Brooks, after defecting from the Minutemen, told me he was among those who had had Cindy's apartment under surveillance that night, that my car had been spotted in front of the building, and that Mary Tollerton had been sent to the door to tell Cindy to quit talking to me. Mrs. Sanders later confirmed the caller's identity as Mary. Mary, however, insists now she did not know I was there when she knocked on the door.

Brooks, whose information has to be judged very carefully as to its accuracy, also said that the Minutemen spent approximately $3000 to keep Cindy under surveillance, at one time even tapping the telephone in her mother's apartment while Cindy was staying there.*

DePugh's later description of the two raids at 613 East Alton and what "On Target" was to print about them were somewhat at variance with the police versions—and, as far as the first raid was concerned, what I saw and heard.

"During the training session (before the first raid), I was told there was going to be a raid of the place," DePugh said, "and the only thing I was interested in was the papers that were there that had names, addresses, the correspondence that we were working on at the time, because I didn't know about these other things at the time."

The "other things" were the dynamite and hand grenades.

DePugh said he suspected that the tip of the raid might have been a deliberate subterfuge to prompt him to try to hurry the

---

* Partial confirmation of this came inadvertently in the June, 1966, issue of "On Target." An article by-lined "Cindy Melville" told of an incident in which Judson Doyle, an Alcohol and Tobacco Tax Unit agent from East St. Louis, Illinois, had told her that DePugh had had her followed and her phone tapped.

"What Mr. Doyle didn't know was that Mr. DePugh had other members follow me with my knowledge. We were trying to learn the identity of other people who were also following me at the same time. Mr. Doyle hadn't realized that I had watched through a crack in the apartment door where I lived at the time and actually watched the man who did tap my phone as he was working on the phone terminals."

She did not explain why she felt she had to watch through a crack in the door. Neither did she reveal in this article who the other persons were that had been following her. According to Brooks and DePugh, it was a group of well-dressed Negroes whom they later discovered were members of the Black Muslims. That's what they said.

records out of the building so that he could be arrested on a trumped-up traffic violation and the records confiscated.

With him at the time was Wayne Morse, a Kansas City man in his sixties who in recent years has devoted most of his energies to being a peripatetic gadfly for far-right and red-neck causes. When I first called him a "peripatetic gadfly" in print, he took such pride in it that he began signing his correspondence, "Wayne Morse, P.G." While his activities have consisted primarily of picketing, he also is a pamphleteer, and for a time he offered those who would dial V-I-C-T-O-R-Y on the telephone a recorded message championing some ultraconservative or segregationist cause or attacking persons he regarded as Communists or Communist sympathizers. He describes himself as being closer to DePugh than anyone else not in the Minutemen organization.

"The first thing I did," DePugh said, "was just take a bunch of empty boxes and rushed them all out and threw them into the trunk of Wayne Morse's car and I told Wayne, 'Take off out of here like the devil was after you, like you're trying to shake anybody that's trying to follow you, and drive on home and I'll see you tomorrow. Call me when you get home and see if anybody stops you.' "

If the tip had been a means of luring someone out of the building with the records, DePugh reasoned, this would have exposed the plan. Morse, however, was not stopped.

Satisfied that the tip of an impending raid was legitimate, DePugh said, he took all the important Minutemen records from 613 East Alton and did not worry any longer about the raid. He did not know, he claims, that other persons attending the training session had stored dynamite and hand grenades in the basement. One person had brought the dynamite and grenades, he said, with the intention of selling it to one of the others there.

"What really teed me off," he said, "was that I wasn't informed of it, because we had time to get rid of it. If these people had just told me it was here."

As for the raids, "On Target" offered an emotional and generally distorted account of police brutality, illegal procedures, harassment, theft and persecution. Police Chief Myers was accused of displaying a "venomous attitude."

Myers, a soft-spoken, ex-FBI agent, reacted to this with a letter to the prosecutor seeking a grand jury inquiry into the Minutemen accusations. DePugh and other Minutemen later did testify before the grand jury, but no action was taken against the Independence police.

Before his first grand-jury appearance, DePugh had commented that he did not have to worry about revealing the identities of the Minutemen who had attended the training session at 613 because he knew them only by code number. This was a built-in protection for them, he said, done deliberately in the event of just such circumstances as then faced him.

This may have been the case with some of the visiting Minutemen, but it certainly was not the case for all. Houghton and Wayne Morse, for instance, were well known personally by DePugh. Brooks, who was also there, said he knew the names of at least ten of the participants.

A week after DePugh's appearance before the grand jury, a fresh issue was injected into the controversy and for a time it tended to overshadow the bizarre "kidnaping" furor. DePugh was served a subpoena ordering him to bring the grand jury the ledger books showing the income and expenses of the Minutemen and "On Target," the applications for membership in the Minutemen, the names and addresses of persons mailed "On Target" and lists of names and addresses of persons and organizations who contribute to the Minutemen for the years 1961 through 1965.

Soon DePugh was publicly declaring that seizure of such records would lead to the destruction of the Minutemen. If necessary, he said, he might take it before the Supreme Court of the United States, but, the former Birch society member added:

"The Supreme Court has enough people on it with a history of Communist front affiliations and sympathies that I would doubt seriously that I would get a fair hearing before them."

During this same week, letters went out to a large number of conservatives in and around Kansas City, informing them that if they wished to hear the true story of what had happened to DePugh, they should go to the Park East Hotel Sunday afternoon, August 8, when Robert Bolivar DePugh would tell them.

Approximately 125 persons showed up for the meeting. Included among them were numerous conservatives and ultraconservatives who presumably had had no direct connection with the Minutemen in the past, except to read about and perhaps sympathize with them.

James Kernodle, a Birch society section leader, praised DePugh as "intelligent" and "mild-mannered," commented sympathetically that men with such views as DePugh's often have trouble in the United States, and observed: "If you're a little pro-Communist and a little anti-American, then you can get along pretty well in this country."*

DePugh, calm and deliberate, soon took the podium and kept it for most of the remaining two hours. His remarks seemed aimed at three major goals: to convince everyone that he had been insidiously and conspiratorially framed; to whip up fresh enthusiasm for others to join the Minutemen; and to raise money for his legal defense.

Jack Cannon and Cindy spoke briefly of the indignities they felt they had suffered at the hands of the police, whereupon DePugh made a pitch for the establishment of a "mutual-defense committee" for patriots who were harassed and forced into unnecessary legal expenses in the manner in which he had been pushed.

"Jack and Cindy are Americans just like yourselves," he said. "Maybe we need this mutual-defense committee. What do you think?" (enthusiastic applause) "I may be going to jail tomorrow. I hope some in this room can carry out the plans I won't be able to. Kansas City could be a starting point of an intense effort to oppose Communism in a more effective manner."

The real purpose behind the kidnaping charges, he said, was to "smear" him and the Minutemen in the newspapers. "I went before the Jackson County grand jury and was questioned for eight and a half hours and did not take the Fifth Amendment one single time!" DePugh said. (again applause) "It became apparent this was just a fishing expedition, and the real thing they were after was the membership lists. If I turned over those lists, it would mean the destruction of the organization, the betrayal of my country, of my own conscience, of the cause of freedom. *I won't do it!*"

His audience sprang to its feet. An ovation.

"I'm a descendant of the first man hung for treason by the British in the Revolutionary war," DePugh said, calmer now. "Tomorrow

* The opening prayer was offered by another Birch society leader in Kansas City, the Reverend Robert Hatch, pastor of the First Bible Presbyterian church, a Carl McIntire disciple and Birch chapter leader. Both Kernodle and the Reverend Hatch were later scolded by the Birch society's area coordinator for having openly participated in this event on grounds that it could have hurt Birch recruiting efforts had it become widely known.

I guess I'll stick *my* neck out." (Asked about this later, DePugh said he could not remember this ancestor's name.) He told them that by refusing to turn over the Minutemen records, he would face a possible contempt-of-court charge, which he described as a continuing offense. This meant it could result in his spending a long time behind bars without bond, he said. He even praised the Reverend Dr. Martin Luther King because, "I admire a man who'll go to jail for what he believes in."

Soon a little man in a white suit and sunglasses was standing at the podium, having been introduced by DePugh only as "a friend from out of town." After discussing the plight of other "political prisoners" in the United States, such as General Edwin Walker in 1962 and Johnny Bob Harrell, the man in the white suit told the audience: "Conservatives should ask, 'Who's next?' Whatever prison Bob's in should be picketed every day!"

Distributed at the meeting were two separate sheets of paper, one headed "The Robert B. DePugh Defense Committee," the other "Legal Defense Committee." The "Legal Defense Committee" was described as "a voluntary association of individuals for the purpose of providing continuous legal, financial, and public support for any patriotic American citizen that now, or in the future, may be subjected to legal persecution or illegal harassment." Applicants for membership were to enclose $1 membership fee and note which of numerous suggested duties they would be willing to perform on the committee: provide automobile transportation for other workers, hold small meetings in home or office, speak at meetings, solicit contributions, distribute literature, picket, serve on a "telephone alert committee" or address envelopes and mail literature. Two days later, DePugh said that $1700 had been raised for his defense as a result of the meeting and subsequent solicitations.

On the day following the meeting, DePugh appeared outside the grand jury chambers, as he had been ordered to do, but without the records he had been ordered to bring. Jackson County's sheriff was expecting a new visitor to his jail before the afternoon was over. DePugh appeared ready for imprisonment, but after only a half hour in session, the grand jurors unexpectedly and stoically trooped out of their meeting room and went home without having called in DePugh.

"I'm ready to spend the rest of my life in jail," DePugh told newsmen. "To bring them (the records) in would be a gross infringement of my personal and constitutional rights. I had prepared for the worst. I am disappointed that things have been put off for a week."

Then with a note of compassion in his voice for the public officials he had earlier implied were involved in some Communist conspiracy: "I have no doubt there is a lot of pressure on local officials from pretty high up in Washington about this. These fellows (the local officials) have been caught in the middle. Their case is as full of holes as Swiss cheese and they don't know what to do."

Meanwhile, the Kansas City chapter of the American Civil Liberties Union had begun to look into the matter quietly, and DePugh's attorney was boning up on the 1958 United States Supreme Court case of the NAACP vs. the State of Alabama.

In that case, the Supreme Court had held that when an Alabama court had found the NAACP guilty of contempt of court for not having produced records of its membership in Alabama, they had tended to restrain the NAACP members from exercising their right of freedom of association.

DePugh appeared outside the grand jury room six days later, again without any records, and again apparently expecting to be charged with contempt of court and jailed. He waited for two hours to be called in this time, but again the grand jurors adjourned without demanding the records.

The jurors this time proceeded to a circuit court room where they handed Judge Paul Vardeman several indictments, two of which were aimed at DePugh. One charged him with the possession of bombs, a felony, and the other with contributing to the delinquency of a minor. The latter indictment included the assertion that he had "enticed" Linda and "placed her in an environment and associations that were injurious and detrimental to her welfare."

Gepford immediately dismissed the kidnaping charge, offering the rather bland explanation: "The grand jury felt, after investigating the matter thoroughly, that contributing to the delinquency of a minor was the charge that should be made against DePugh."

As for the subpoena for the Minutemen records, the prosecutor said it still was in effect but that he did not know when or if DePugh would be called again before the grand jury.

Absent from the grand jury room on the day it voted its indictments against DePugh, but present for earlier testimony, was the late Charles W. Fisher, a city councilman in Kansas City from 1959 to 1963 and a Democrat, serving on his third grand jury.

To Fisher, DePugh was "very intelligent" and "essentially a super-patriot," a term, he added, which he did not use derogatorily. He made this appraisal about two weeks after the indictments, adding: "They let Communists run wild, yet here's a man who has manifested patriotism beyond the call of duty and above the average man on the street."

Speaking out about the case after the investigation had been completed, Fisher also said he felt efforts to subpoena Minutemen records had been "just harassment by authorities." He said that had he been present, he did not think he would have voted for the indictments. (Only nine votes are needed.) The other eleven grand jurors maintained a decorous silence, letting the indictments speak for themselves.

By the end of September, a new county grand jury had been impaneled and nothing more was heard about the subpoena for the Minutemen's membership and financial records. Nor has anything been heard of it since.

Despite the blow to his image from the revelation of his recruiting efforts with a juvenile, the whole affair was not a complete disaster for DePugh.

It netted him publicity, to be sure, for the wire services carried lengthy accounts of his initial arrest and the charges against him. Once the grand jury had indicated in its choice of indictments that it did not entirely buy everything Linda and Patricia had originally alleged—choosing contributing to delinquency over kidnaping as the charge—it began to occur to some that perhaps DePugh had been victimized somewhat by authorities. His staunch insistence that he would not turn over Minutemen membership records, even at the risk of rotting away in jail, no doubt imbued many a Minuteman with new respect for their leader.

The possession of bombs charge hung over DePugh for more than a year and a half until on March 9, 1967, Judge Charles Shangler of the Jackson County Circuit Court upheld a motion by the defense to dismiss it on grounds that as drawn up, it was a "fatally defective" indictment. It had failed to allege intent to use the explosives against anyone or anything. Therefore, the judge ruled, the Missouri statute cited in the indictment had not been violated. Mere possession of bombs did not constitute a crime.

Geptord had been defeated in his bid for re-election as prosecutor by then and the new prosecutor, Joseph Teasdale, did not bother to refile the charge or take it back to a new grand jury.

Less than a month later, the new prosecutor asked that the contributing charge be dropped too. The Jackson County criminal docket was clogged at that time with many long-pending cases and, the prosecutor observed, a review of the evidence in the case showed that the state's position was weak.

This wiped the slate clean for DePugh as far as state charges against him were concerned, but by then—as will be shown—DePugh was in far more complex trouble with federal authorities.

CHAPTER 8

JOIN THE MINUTEMEN
[sic]

RAT	RED
RED	RAT
RATS	RED
RED	RATS
RAT	RED
RED	RAT
RATS	RED
RED	RATS
RATS	RED

ONE IN THE SAME

RED	RATS
RATS	RED
RED	RATS

ANARCKY

RED	RED
RATUS	RATUS

YEAH AMERICA

Doodles on the inside back cover of a "Steno" notebook apparently used by someone attending a training session of the Minutemen in Independence.

The first Kansas City *Star* reporter to discover DePugh and recognize him as a fit subject for concern was William Bulger, then of the newspaper's office in Independence. A few days before DePugh began making nationwide headlines at Shiloh, Illinois, Bill interviewed De-Pugh and filed a long report on him for our editors:

". . . He impressed me as a man educated enough to be dangerous, who had a psychology of fear and a determination to fight an enemy he has imagined to be far more powerful than it really is. . . ."

During the second night's raid on 613 East Alton in July, 1965, Bill parked his car about 200 feet south of the building on a side street before joining police to cover the story. It was an ordinary vehicle with no markings to indicate a newspaper reporter drove it, although a two-way radio could have been seen through the window beneath the dashboard had there been adequate lighting.

It was not until several weeks later that Bill noticed something yellow protruding from beneath the seat in the back of his car. Pulling it out, he found that it was a stenographer's notebook, covered with a thin layer of dust. Written in large letters on the inside of the front cover was the name "John DePugh." Thumbing through the notebook, Bill saw numerous references to the Minutemen. It appeared to him to be notes taken at a lecture of some sort.

He decided to look more closely under his car seat following this discovery and to his surprise found yet another stenographer's notebook, a red one this time, but with no name conveniently identifying its owner. The handwriting in the red notebook was different from John's and considerably more legible.

Enough dust had covered both notebooks that Bill concluded he had been driving around with them for some time. As for who had put them there, and why, he could only guess.

The most logical possibility was that someone from the Minutemen had slipped them inside his car on the night of the raid, not aware of whose car it was and planning later in the evening to retrieve them. The police were nosing around inside 613 at the time and confiscating a good deal more than the Minutemen had expected. Possibly this person had concluded Bill's car was that of a neighbor and would be there all night.

Another possibility is that they were intentionally planted there by the Minutemen in a devious attempt to attract more publicity to the organization. Or, conceivably, some policeman—knowing he could not legally confiscate the notebooks—slipped them from the building and into Bill's car as a way to help expose the Minutemen. Neither of these seem as likely as the first.

The contents of the two notebooks, as far as I can tell, revealed nothing especially new except that mention was made of someone having mailed a scorpion to a "left wing radio announcer" once. Still, what was written in the more detailed red notebook provides an intriguing insight into the Minutemen because of the unusual perspective it offers, a perspective that would appear to be that of a Minuteman jotting down what he regarded as important or interesting at a lecture or series of lectures by a leader or leaders in the organization.

Apparently these are notes from the week-long training session at 613 in June, 1965—at which DePugh, Cindy Melville, Troy Houghton and Wally Peyson were supposed to have lectured. Possibly they were from other lectures. Whatever the case, this is how the notes from the red notebook began [all *sic*]:

"The primary operation of Guerrilla Warfare is Psychological effect.

"We must win through Psychological Warfare. . . .

"We must break the moral of the enemy.

"Build the moral of the Minutemen.

"It is a tragic waste of time, of which time is scarce to argue among ourselves The Minutemen.

"We cannot see our enemy So we take our hatred out on other Minutemen, this is *very* bad.

"If we had a physical enemy then we could work on our enemy.

"Various types of Harassment.

"A boxed scorpion was sent to a left-wing radio announcer. He wasn't bit.

"Telephone harassment is good.

"Enemy has a mental conflict when taking out silent no. (number). Then when you dial silent ⚡ it has a psychological affect.

"Physical harassment—shine light in window of Communist.

"Learn picking of locks, this isn't too difficult.

"You can saw through a typical padlock. examine it carefully. Take a tempered block spring, use for lock pick. all but Yale locks are easy to pick.

"Go in Peace groups-take-note-of-all-office-furnishings-write-letters-letting-them-know-you-know-what.

"Mail-harassment-is-very-good.

"If - mail - harassment - comes - at - time - when - moral - is - kind - of - low, - then - stop - & - give - it - some - long - thought.

"One - of - the - set - rules - of - Guerrilla - Warfare - is - don't - operate - with - a - set - pattern - or - plan.

"EXPLOSIVES

"Tincture of Iodine or Iodine Crystals. pour out in place, evaporate in front of fan, pour on Kleenex—take Ammonia pow on paper keep wet at all times, this forms *Ammonia Tri Iodide is* highly explosve. It is too dangerous. It is self detonated. Put this under the door.

"Make Black Powder. use match heads for sulfur. sodium nitrate. potasium nitrate. charcol

"If we are lucky we can form nucleus for an underground.

"The best Defense is a Offense.

"Any time a member of Minutemen is killed, he must do in 1,000 of the enemy to make up for his life being taken.

"A tiger has an excellent chain of command.

"A jelly fish, or a sponge, has a very neblius coordination—you can cut it up & it will grow a new sponge.

"Once an organization is set for Revolution; it must be used. . . ."

And on and on it went, often with familiar phrases and ideas that can be found in Minutemen literature. Under the heading of "Espionage," the Minutemen trainee had jotted down the following on the left side of the page:

"(All illegal means of gaining information.

"(Telephone tap—)

"(tamper mail—)

"(burglar home—)

"(search files—)—CRACK SAFE

"(infiltrate country—) of Enemy

"(agent tricks & steal information—)

"(blackmail—)

"(bribery—)"

On the right side of the page was a fascinating example of doodling that suggests the trainee at this point may have been bored, or possibly bothered a bit by talk of mail tampering, blackmail, etc. The doodle read:

"Hail To The Lord
Old Lord
Pray For Us
Now And
In Time & Need"

"In Time & Need" was written in tiny letters so as to fit in his doodle space without overlapping the words "CRACK SAFE."

The trainees seem to have been urged to do much reading, not all of it conventional.

"By subscribing to police journals etc. you get many hints and tips," the trainee wrote. "Electronic information obtained from Electronics magazines. Journal of Toxicology on toxins—poisons—methods of assassination etc."

Cryptography also seems to have been discussed in some detail, although I will confess to ignorance on what to make of the notes concerning it. A sample:

"Intercept, Decode messages of the Enemy. Computers are not needed for a secure code. It is organized confusion.

"The cipher rather than the code.

"Cipher is similar to hiroglythics.

"Code is another actual word."

A	T	T	A
C	K	A	T
D	A	W	N

T	O	R	E
4	2	3	1
A	T	T	A
C	K	A	T
D	A	W	N

Or try this for clarification:

AT — AQORE		
ATTACK — ARERA	ONE	
DAWN — CUVAB	PART	
AT — BULAX		
ATTACH — ONIZA	TWO	
DAWN — FOVEP	PART	

A good deal of time apparently was devoted to "Internal Security" in the training session, judging by the notes. For instance:

"Pre-membership screening & Internal Security.

"Internal security—Limits damage that enemy can & may do to any Patriotic group.

"If a band leader in N. Jersey wants contact with a member in Calif., he has to contact Nat. Leadership. . . .

"The Need to Know Rule.

"I don't read other members mail open letters.

"We must volunteer no info.

"Observe need to know rule.

"Does a member seek to know other members that he doesn't need to know. These and other factors that determine whether a man is an infiltrator.

"The man you have to look for will know how to get along so to infiltration. Maybe this fellow is an infiltrator.

"We have tried various truth serums. They aren't any good. You can get people to talk. But after they contradict themselves 20-30 times in 1 ho. of questioning.

"The best laid plans of mice and men can go astray.

"Human factors usually can be the blame for plans are destroyed.

"Security leaks are from high in organization, the same goes for embezzlement & systematic thefts come from people in trust.

"Security comes naturally & comes by indoctrination. Yet a person not born with security so they become Security risks. Some persons are naturally friendly are talkers, so they are Security Risk. An egotist is Security Risk. A bad inferiority complex is a Security Risk.

"Maintain a certain psychological distance, if you don't you must refrain from too close assn', with any & all members. In this way you become a security risk.

"The person you trust today you may not trust next day.

"People come from all walks of life. People are all different.

"It is almost impossible to teach Security. . . .

"Without Security, how do we get around brainwashing.

"We are being brainwashed every day.

"Can we be right when other people are wrong: everything looks so normal."

The subject of explosives is dealt with at considerable length next, and the trainee filled four pages with details. Somehow, reading these notes by an unknown Minuteman in a hurried script inside a stenographer's red notebook acquired in such a strange fashion was more alarming to me, personally, than seeing or hearing it in any other form. It seemed to have a chilling ring or authenticity to it. The notes on explosives began:

"First of all there are types of explosives

"1. Black powder—explodes fuse or match spark—flame.

"2. Dynamite 40-50-60-70% strength & lesser strength.

"3. T.N.T.

"4. Nitro starch.

"5. Composition B & C & C_3 & C_4

"6. prima cord

"7. Mercury Fulmanit

"8. Fuse & electrical type detonating caps.

"280 Grains DuPont Powder for filling grenade.

"buy for Flintlock guns

"Bullseye is a good powder.

"Black Powder is best. put in 2″ pipe—drill hole insert fuse light fuse & throw & run."

Also recorded in the little notebook are vague hints on how to conduct successful surveillance by means of a visual, photographic or physical "stake out." The trainee was instructed to "check visitors" to the subject's home and to use a rented or borrowed car when following him.

"The LAW has a great advantage," it is noted at the bottom of the stake-out section.

The notes conclude with more cryptography.

The final notation is as follows:

IIPO	TAII	SNPE	
LESE	HCDR	HITN	
KRBT	NNET	CTAC	ESRI
APIN	ENNI	NERS	
EWIE	AIEE	TPEK	
SRSH	HSHR	HLIN	PETT
LTOD	PLOD	LRYE	NWLY

And if this revelation breaks the Minutemen code, so be it.

BOOK TWO

The Federal Crackdown

CHAPTER 9

JOIN THE MINUTEMEN

SILENCERS

The advantages of a gun that makes no noise when fired are obvious. In underground warfare the availability of such weapons would be invaluable to individuals or small combat teams forced to operate against a superior enemy force. . . . The time may come when citizens may profit from a knowledge of how to construct such devices. . . . Telescopic sights are often helpful. Some companies make mounting rings that hold the telescopic sight well above the barrel of the rifle. This may be sufficient for a silencer that is about two and one-half inches in diameter. Special scope mounts may be purchased or constructed for silencers having a larger diameter. . . . Since we do not wish to go to jail as accessory to the crime we hereby state that nothing in this article should be taken as a suggestion that the reader actually build any of the devices described herein.

> From Minutemen pamphlet on how to build your own gun silencer, with numerous illustrations.

The federal investigative agencies had not totally ignored the Minutemen in their formative years, but they had not expended any great effort to keep track of them either. Then came Oswald in Dallas, the resonant desperation of the Far Right in the election year of 1964, the Warren Commission report with its criticisms of the protection afforded President Kennedy and fresh cries of alarm about the Minutemen by certain members of Congress.

Soon DePugh's organization began to receive the kind of official scrutiny Minutemen egotists relished, yet had good reason to fear. The effects of this new attentiveness by federal investigative agencies became especially noticeable to the Minutemen in early 1966 when numerous members of the organization and persons with whom it had had encounters of one sort or another began to receive subpoenas to appear before a federal grand jury in Kansas City. What amounted to a federal crackdown on the Minutemen had begun.

Before the end of that year, Robert DePugh, Troy Houghton and Wally Peyson found themselves sitting uncomfortably in a U. S. District Courtroom in Kansas City for six days while twelve of their peers in the jury box sat in judgment of them.

Of immense value to the government in its work were persons who had infiltrated the Minutemen ranks for investigative purposes and others who had joined in good faith but who later had defected, disenchanted and talkative.

Also of importance in this crackdown was the fact that in the 1930s Congress had become so sensitive to the likes of John Dillinger and "Machine Gun" Kelly that it passed a set of laws placing certain restrictions on automatic weapons—the kind that fire more than one round with the single depression of the trigger—by requiring manufacturers and owners of such weapons to pay taxes on them and register them with the Treasury Department. Congress did not make it unlawful to possess such weapons, but it did express a specific desire to be kept informed of who possessed them. Also covered by these laws were silencers. The ATTU was assigned to enforce these new laws.

As DePugh, Houghton and Peyson sat through their trial in November, 1966, they were faced with one count in their indictment that alleged thirty-five overt acts in a conspiracy to violate the firearms laws. Three of those acts concerned events in southern California back in August, 1965, shortly after Houghton had returned from his exploits in Independence and Norborne.

Intimately involved in those events was forty-three-year-old James W. Clark, of Temple City, California, a calm, reserved man of less than average height and weight. Beneath his crew cut was a face of deliberate impassiveness that suggests he would be a formidable opponent at poker or bridge. He does not look the sort who would join the Minutemen, but then neither do a great many of its bonafide, dyed-in-the-wool members. Clark joined the organization through Houghton in April, 1964, in order to investigate it. He is a special agent for the Bureau of Criminal Identification and Investigation of the State of California Justice Department.

Clark began by writing a letter to post office box 5294 in San Diego indicating his interest in the organization. He used his true name and home address, fearing that evidence obtained through his infiltration might be judged "tainted" if he used an assumed name.

He fudged only in listing his occupation. As he recalled, he identified himself as a self-employed "records researcher." In his letter, Clark said, he wrote that he liked the way the Minutemen were doing something about the nation's drift toward Communism. Soon he was sent an application blank, which he filled out, started sending in $2 a month dues and paid $5 for a year's subscription to "On Target." He was assigned Minuteman number 28722.

Clark first met Houghton in August of 1964 in Van Nuys, California, after Houghton had addressed a crowd of about 150 persons at a meeting sponsored by young Dennis Mower's own new organization, the Southern California Freedom Councils. As Clark recalls it, he shook hands with Houghton and told him he had delivered a "wonderful speech." He remembers that Houghton was gracious in the face of such praise and was "very much the perfect gentleman." He also recalls that the speech had bordered on the ridiculous.

Clark was by now receiving monthly bulletins from "930"—Houghton—regularly, was filing monthly reports as required of members and had enrolled in phase number one of the Minutemen correspondence course.

Another of his duties was to attend meetings of the "San Gabriel Valley Bird Watchers Association" in a savings-and-loan building in a Los Angeles suburb. The Minutemen most often preferred gun clubs as their front organizations, but the bird watchers of San Gabriel Valley, although concerned exclusively with guerrilla warfare and propaganda, were a more complicated organization.

As Clark described it, they consisted of some dissident, anti-Houghton Minutemen who had organized it, more than one Houghton faithful who were there to spy on the anti-Houghtons, and of course Clark himself, whom the CII had planted in it to spy on everybody else.

The following month, Clark was among the Minutemen who received notice of a special meeting in San Diego where certain Minutemen were to visit with Houghton. It was held the same day that a statewide group of California Republicans were gathering for a convention at the El Cortez Hotel in downtown San Diego. Clark remembers it now as "cloak-and-dagger day," with a grin.

Acting on instructions, Clark drove to San Diego and telephoned Houghton's home, asking, he said, to speak with No. 17883, who turned out to be Bettie Houghton. He telephoned her at ten-thirty that morning and was told mysteriously to call back at two o'clock that afternoon. She gave him a name to ask for and the number of a motel room. Clark checked at the motel and found nothing had been scheduled there for that afternoon. He called Bettie back ahead of time and was told the meeting place had been changed. He was then given the name of a woman at the El Cortez Hotel whom he should contact and who, he said, identified herself as the wife of one of the convention's assistant sergeants-at-arms.

That afternoon, Clark—who was working under a Democratic attorney general, it might be noted here—found himself with a badge that gained him entry to various meetings of the Republicans at the convention.

It was arranged for Clark to meet Houghton and his wife in the hotel lobby at eight o'clock that evening, he said. Once together, they drank coffee in the hotel's coffee shop and talked. Houghton, he recalled, sported a button on his coat reading "S.O.B."—for "Sweep Out Brown."

Aware that Houghton probably knew he had attended the San Gabriel Valley Bird Watchers Association meetings, and hoping to establish rapport with the California Minutemen leader, Clark cautioned Houghton about the possibility of dissidence within his organization as reflected by the bird watchers.

As Clark described it, the meeting was rather pointless. The whole trip, for that matter, appeared from Clark's description to be without much real purpose, but he explained this was not uncommon in Minutemen circles. Frequently, he said, he heard other members complain that they would be told of important up-and-coming meetings to which they would drive long distances only to find the meetings canceled.

As far as Clark was able to tell, the Minutemen—despite the elaborate security precautions they claim to take—still did not know at this point that he was an agent for the CII. Houghton later claimed to have known Clark's true identity as far back as three days after he had submitted his application, but Bettie Houghton, in a separate interview, said they were still only "suspicious" of Clark as of August, 1965, a full fifteen months after he had joined the Minutemen. In August, 1965, California Minutemen received notices of a nine-day Minutemen training session to be held in the California wilderness. Members were told to indicate whether they could attend the entire session or be present on one or both of the weekends that opened and closed the unusual event. Clark was among those responding that he wished to attend the weekend sessions.

Clark received instructions to bring camouflage clothing, a sleeping bag or ground cloth, two blankets, a change of clothing, notebook, pen or pencil, coffee cup and silverware. Cost of the training was $7.50 a day, he was told, and he sent in a $5 deposit as required. Enclosed with the communication was a numbered card—his was No. 18—which was to be used as his means of identification when meeting at a specified pick-up point. He subsequently was given a button with the same number to wear. Two maps were sent him, showing his pick-up point was at College and University avenues in San Diego. He was to be there at nine o'clock Friday night, August 27, or twelve-thirty the following morning. Once there Clark was to look for a car or truck with a red, white and blue striped rag tied to the door handle on the vehicle's passenger side. A sign and counter-sign were supplied him.

Clark did as instructed. After he had waited fifteen or twenty minutes, a car drove up with a red, white and blue rag tied to it appropriately. Clark left his car, approached the driver and asked:

"How do I get to the Sportsmen's Lodge?"

"Follow me," the driver replied, "I'm going there myself."

This had been the prearranged sign and countersign. Inside the car were a young, unidentified man and Bettie Houghton. Bettie gave Clark a hand-drawn sign that read, "Car Out of Order. Will Pick Up Tomorrow," and told him to leave it on his car. They then drove him to the Houghton home where several other trainees were gathered, waiting for transportation.

It was decided that several of the men would drive to the training site in a pick-up truck owned by Kenneth L. Templeton, a middle-aged heavy-equipment operator from San Diego, who had joined the Minutemen seven months prior to the training session after a long association with the John Birch Society.

It was later confirmed that when Templeton had applied for membership in the Minutemen, he had written on his application blank:

"I am a right-wing conservative who believes our wonderful country is becoming socialistic. The next step down in Communism. I am a member of the John Birch Society and we're doing a good job but not good enough. I believe the last Jew administrations have been selling us down the tube and the present one intends to finish the job. I think our foreign policy stinks. . . ."

With Templeton driving, Troy Houghton and another young man riding in the front cab, and Clark and several others sitting with their equipment in the back of the truck, the vehicle headed east out of San Diego on Highway 80 to a camping ground about sixty miles east of San Diego, a mile north of the Mexican border near Jacumba, California. A dirt road took the Minutemen trainees into an arid area dotted with scrub oak, some small oak trees and manzanita bushes. A small clearing had been made for their camp site.

The men climbed from the truck, spread out their sleeping bags and promptly fell asleep. A few hours later, at six-thirty that morning, Clark arose and took a better look at the camp. Camouflage netting had been placed over parts of the camp. Attached to one of these nets was a sign reading "The Rolando Park Sporting Outdoor Survival Club." Two lister bags had been placed nearby for the trainees' water supply. The kitchen area boasted a three-burner, butane-fed stove.

The CII agent noticed from forty to forty-five men and from twelve to fourteen women at the camp, all of them Caucasian and ranging in age from the late teens to about sixty-five. All were dressed in old clothes, military fatigues or camouflage clothing. Nearly all had a rifle or hand gun with them, but Clark said he saw no illegal weapons at the camp.

It appeared to Clark that the formal training sessions were supposed to start that morning, but nothing more than informal discussions were held at first. Some of the Minutemen appeared to become restless by mid-morning, until one of the men finally decided to conduct a class. His lecture was on the prevention and treatment of snake bites, then desert survival.

Houghton, who had been absent from the camp most of the morning, arrived shortly before noon, Clark recalled. He informed the crowd that he and two others had leased the property on which they were training and that sufficient liability insurance had been purchased to protect everyone there. He passed around for inspection samples of food in tin cans with a self-contained heating unit attached to the bottoms of each, samples of Army C rations and several types of survival packs.

Clark said Houghton also told of his own personal "escape and evasion kit" including chloral hydrate crystals, a handcuff key, three dimes and a $20 bill. All this could be contained in either a little .35 mm. film container or a waterproof match holder.

Houghton talked more about survival after lunch, then moved on to other topics that included hints on how to hide out, how to use mail drops, telephone tapping, other bugging techniques and methods of making security checks on members. After dinner, movies on survival were shown, followed by an anti-Communist movie narrated on the sound track by General Edwin Walker. The training ended at eleven o'clock that night.

In between sessions, Clark reported, some informal target practice was held by the Minutemen. At the end of one lecture, he said, the speaker told Clark he had to hurry off so as to keep an eye on an FBI agent who had infiltrated the meeting posing as a Minuteman. The "agent" was never identified to Clark, if he existed.

Clark said he took his turn standing guard at the camp entrance armed with a loaded rifle. The idea for sentries had not been Houghton's but Templeton's and a twenty-eight-year-old roofer and painter named Lloyd Pullen, of Long Beach, California.

Pullen had joined the Minutemen about three months previous to that time after noticing a Minutemen sticker on a lamppost. He had written Norborne, received a reply from DePugh and was then contacted by a Minutemen coordinator from Orange County. Houghton had asked him to attend the training session to lecture to the group on what his contingent of Minutemen had done earlier that summer during the Watts riots.

According to Pullen, an ex-Marine with "USMC" tatooed on his right wrist, the Minutemen under his command mobilized to protect outlying areas after the riots had started. They donned paratrooper boots, unmarked Army fatigues and green berets, armed themselves with rifles and set out to protect the population. But first, Pullen said, he checked with the Long Beach police to let them know what they were doing.

Twice, Pullen told the gathering at the desert training session, his Minutemen performed useful services, in one instance rescuing two girls in a car from a band of roaming Negroes, and later saving a shopping center near Compton, California, from a possible bombing by a carload of roving Negroes armed with two rifles and two Molotov cocktails.

After his talk, Pullen paid little attention to Houghton's other activities, and instead spent his time chatting with others who, he found, were growing as disgusted with the training session as he had.

"It was a real terrible session down there," Pullen later told me. "I mean, Houghton wasn't even there at first, and then when he came, he had white levis on and a fire-engine-red shirt, and he's a little plump, and the levis and shirt were a little small for him and his gut was hanging out from his waist and he carried a little .25 automatic and it kept falling out of his hip pocket and I thought, 'This is a guerrilla war leader? This is a top fighting man? I don't want any part of it.'"

Among the matters discussed by Houghton which especially irked Pullen, the ex-Marine said, was Houghton's tips on how to infiltrate left-wing organizations and harass left-wingers. Along these lines, Clark said Houghton provided his audience with the name and address of a fireworks company in Missouri that made some prankster type smoke or whistle bombs that could be planted in left-wingers' cars.

"Houghton described and demonstrated the use of metallic sodium, which explodes in water," Clark said. "He described a prior instance where gasoline was poured into a left-winger's swimming pool and then metallic sodium was placed in the pool. This caused the water and gasoline to explode and burn."

Middle-of-the-night long-distance phone calls, reversing the charges, also were suggested, as were distribution of large-headed roofing tacks in parking lots outside Communist meeting places, and the obnoxious impersonation of peace marchers.

Houghton's Sunday morning lecture then began to move into more violent areas. Clark said Houghton announced plans that the Minutemen organization expected to send out instructions on how to make a Sten (submachine) gun from material available from any hardware store. Only the weapon's magazine could not be obtained at the hardware store, he said. Houghton next told of using one and a half sticks of 40 percent dynamite placed as far as possible up the exhaust pipe of an automobile, with a blasting cap attached, Clark said. The heat from the exhaust would detonate the cap in six minutes, the agent quoted Houghton as saying.

Hypodermic needles containing poison and attached to the tips of arrows were described, he said. It was explained that Communist sympathizers also could be done in by putting four ounces of denatured alcohol or antifreeze in an otherwise palatable drink, Clark said, since an autopsy of someone killed in this fashion would indicate the cause of death as diabetes.

What was to prove most damaging to Houghton fifteen months later at his trial was that part of Clark's report to the attorney general's office regarding a silencer-equipped pistol.

"After the bow-and-arrow lecture," Clark reported, "Houghton spoke concerning the use of silencers in connection with firearms. He provided a twelve-page bulletin on silencers which was distributed among Minutemen members present. . . . Houghton borrowed a .22 caliber pistol from one of the members present. He then fired the pistol and immediately afterward fired a .22 caliber pistol equipped with a silencer to demonstrate the difference. . . ."

But as far as federal authorities could tell, Houghton had not registered a silencer with the Treasury Department.

In the Sunday afternoon session, Clark went on to relate, Houghton took some of the members a good distance from their encampment and detonated an antipersonnel mine to show how it worked.

From conversations he overheard during the training session, Clark said, it appeared some of the participants had journeyed long distances to attend. Some, he said, were from Oregon, Nevada and Arizona, as well as different distant parts of California.

Clark rode back to San Diego that Sunday evening with several others in Templeton's pick-up. This time he rode in the cab.

Pullen left the same day and soon started his own organization in competition with the Minutemen ("Staff—Home Defense Organization"), a group by no means as secretive as the Minutemen. Its stated purpose: "To prepare to maintain law and order, back up the local police and provide protection for lives, property and neighbors in the event of riots, racial disorders, fires, prowlers, guerrilla warfare, insurrection and other emergencies when the local law enforcement agencies are not available or unable to provide protection or assistance."

Bad blood developed between Pullen and the Minutemen and a good deal of harassment, short of violence, came into play before an uneasy truce was established.

Since the training session, Houghton has insisted that he did not fire a pistol with a silencer that weekend. Bettie Houghton backs her husband on this point. Of Clark's infiltration, Mrs. Houghton said:

"He stuck out like a sore thumb at the training session. We suspected him, but weren't sure before the training session. We were quite sure after the first day. He looked over everyone's shoulder and he contributed nothing."

Troy Houghton said that at the training session he even announced to the group that he knew there was an agent from the attorney general's office among them. Clark acknowledges that Houghton told the group there was "an informant" among them, but said he doubts whether Houghton knew this for certain. It adds excitement to any gathering such as that, he observed, to say such a thing.

There is no question that Clark's identity was known soon after the training session. Attorney General Lynch revealed the successful infiltration of the training session by an agent and soon afterward a Minutemen bulletin was distributed commenting on it.

"I would like to state at this time for those who attended the above-mentioned training session," the bulletin read, "and for the membership in general, that we have known of this informer since before March of this year, and have known of another since July, and two more with applications pending. The reason for not exposing this informer prior to this time is that we prefer to neutralize the activities of such persons by keeping them under surveillance which also reduces the risk of them infiltrating someone new into the organization.

"Some of the members who attended the August 28–29 weekend training session may recall that I mentioned that there was an informant present. Also you will recall that I delegated the task of watching him to six individuals there. This informant was given 'special' attention from the time he arrived at his pick-up point. His car was left at the pick-up point rather than being re-parked at the home of a friend of the organization, and similar precautions were taken when he was returned to his vehicle at the end of the session. . . ."

Beneath this was a drawing of a tombstone and a grave. On the tombstone were the words *Jim Clark, 10627 E. Olive, Temple City, California*. Bettie Houghton later acknowledged having drawn the tombstone for the bulletin. It was not meant as a threat, she said, but just a way of showing that "he's dead in the Minutemen."

"Why did you let Clark attend the training session in the first place if you knew all along he was an informant?" seemed the logical question to Houghton later.

"It was just before the paramilitary bill went through," was Houghton's reply. "This was my way of (and he thumbed his nose) at the attorney general."

Fifteen months later, as Houghton was ready to go to trial in Kansas City, three men were subpoenaed there from California by the government to testify against him—Clark, Templeton and Pullen.

CHAPTER 10

JOIN THE MINUTEMEN

Machine guns and submachine guns are very useful in certain phases of guerrilla warfare. Generally speaking, they waste ammunition to such an extent that they are not recommended as weapons for individual members of a resistance movement. In any event, a submachine gun is about the easiest of all firearms to manufacture with simple tools and readily available raw materials.

From the December, 1966, issue of "On Target," devoted to "Family Survival Techniques."

The two-story frame house at 408 South Pine in Norborne, Missouri, carried the loose title of national headquarters of the Minutemen in the fall of 1965, although the same designation might well have applied to the Biolab office a few blocks away, the DePugh home less than a block away, or DePugh's building at 613 East Alton in Independence.

Indeed, a great deal of Minutemen work was performed inside 408 South Pine that fall, and at nights it served as the temporary home of five persons:

•Jerry Milton Brooks, who will be discussed in detail in the next chapter.

•Walter Patrick Peyson, who, it may be recalled, showed Linda and Pat his "machine gun" while they were in Richmond.

•Mary Tollerton, the "Mary Taylor" who was Linda's and Pat's hostess in Richmond, and later guarded Minutemen records in Norborne during a police raid.

•Jerry's invalid mother.

•And Raithby Roosevelt Husted, a former Marine Corps buddy of Peyson's from California, who went by the name of "Ray Shannon" while in Norborne.

Mary, the college-educated daughter of a well-to-do northwest Missouri landowner, has sparkling feline eyes, small heart-shaped lips, a few nicely placed freckles and a slender, well-developed figure that easily could have earned her the title of Minuteman I'd Most Like to Bury Weapons With.

According to "Shannon," she was "the liberal one of the group" at 408—"when talk of assassinations, violence, bombings and such came up, she would more than likely take the why-do-you-have-to-do-that attitude."

It was more than a year later before I met Mary, although her name had cropped up repeatedly in accounts of various Minutemen adventures as, less frequently, had the names of two of her brothers, James and Robert Tollerton.

I first met her when she was staying briefly at 613 East Alton in Independence in the winter of 1966–67. Dressed fashionably in tight slacks, her hair cropped just below the ears, she impressed me as an authentic and refreshing individualist, despite her political leanings. At that time, she said, she was the only member of her family still devoted to the Minutemen cause. The others—especially her mother—had grown angrily disgusted with DePugh and the organization.

"Why did I join the Minutemen?" she said. "For kicks, I suppose, and because I believe very strongly in individualism as opposed to collectivism."

She spoke of having read a good deal of Ayn Rand and agreeing with much of the Randian philosophy. She said she differed with the writer mainly over what she regarded as the Randian advocacy of selfishness.

"I'm more of a humanitarian," she said. "And I don't go for violence."

A few months after this brief encounter, Mary turned up in West Palm Beach, Florida, charged by police there with carrying a concealed weapon.

She had graduated into a more important role with the Minutemen by then and had gone to Florida on some sort of mission for the organization, the exact nature of which I was unable to learn. It involved meeting numerous Florida members of the organization, Mary said later.

While she was living in Miami, the Miami police intelligence division sent officers to her apartment to question her.

"They wanted to know if I was stirring up the Cubans," she laughed. "I wasn't. They're already stirred up."

She said she spent the greater part of the interview trying to convert the Miami police officers to her cause.

While driving in West Palm Beach a week or so later, Mary was stopped for a traffic violation. When a .38-caliber pistol was found in the glove compartment of her car, she was taken to police headquarters for further interrogation. This was because the arresting officer was under the impression that she had taken the weapon from her purse and placed it in the glove compartment as he was approaching the car. Mary insisted the pistol had been in the glove compartment from the start. She had put a road map in the glove compartment as the officer approached, she said.

"Why?" was the inevitable question.

Because the road map had markings on it she did not wish the police to see. By slipping it in the glove compartment with numerous other unmarked road maps, she said, she had hoped it would go unnoticed. Markings? Yes—Minutemen "dead drops" over the state of Florida. (A "dead drop" is a place messages can be hidden for the eventual pick-up by their intended recipient or his courier. It may be just about anything—a hollow tree trunk, a bus depot locker . . .)

When Mary entered the office of Detective John Jamison that night, Jamison later was to relate, she quickly stuffed pieces of paper in her mouth, chewed them up and swallowed them. She eventually told me the pieces of paper had been three halves of dollar bills, the serial numbers of which would have identified her to contacts in Florida.

Mary said that Jamison had a dossier on her when she reached his office. She assumed this had been obtained from the federal government. Jamison's opening remark to her, she said, was, "Well, Mary, what have you been up to?" and "How's Mr. DePugh?"

Jamison disputes this.

Mary spent the night in jail at West Palm Beach, but was supplied a lawyer and $500 bond money after calling Wally Peyson in Norborne. She neglected to show up for her trial on the charge in June and forfeited the $500.

Mary, incidentally, explained quite plausibly that she usually carried a .38 in her car for protection when driving alone.

Her Florida tribulations—and more complex adventures even later in Colorado—were still ahead of her in the fall and winter of 1965. In Norborne, she stayed part of the time in the DePugh home and other times at 408 South Pine (before the DePugh family moved into 408 itself). Mary's job at this time was secretarial, mostly involving typing up communications from national headquarters.

The source of her bond in Florida, Walter Patrick Peyson, twenty-three, of Chicago originally, had joined the Minutemen while in the Marine Corps. In the Corps, as he tells it, he did his best to convert as many fellow Marines as possible to the cause of vigorous anti-Communism.

His buddies at the 29 Palms Marine Corps base in California were apathetic, generally, to the menace that Wally saw, and his efforts to lecture them in the barracks while standing atop a footlocker were not greeted with widespread enthusiasm from the troops.

As Wally later was to tell the story, he began subscribing to various conservative magazines, such as *Human Events*. After reading the material, he anonymously mailed selected pages to various Marine Corps officers stationed at the base. This was not an official Minutemen function, he said, but his own idea, a way of spreading the word.

He next expanded his horizons by purchasing at wholesale bulk rates various paperbound books of a conservative or anti-Communist persuasion and mailed these to various officers, from the generals on down the line.

A private first class, Wally was transferred to Camp Pendleton in the midst of these efforts, but continued his mailings and enlisted a few others from the barracks to help him.

But even before Wally had left 29 Palms, an investigation by Marine Corps intelligence had been launched to discover the source of books various officers had been receiving so mysteriously in the mail, Wally said.

While at Camp Pendleton, Wally learned of the Church of Jesus Christ, Christian, headed by Dr. Wesley Swift of Lancaster, California. He began attending the Reverend Swift's church services on Sundays, although it was a lengthy drive there from the camp. Dr. Swift had an unusual message for his followers. Adamantly anti-Communist, it also involved the theory that Christian Caucasians were superior to those of other races, spiritually and biologically.

It is Wally's theory that the Marine intelligence agents followed him to Lancaster on more than one occasion during their investigation and saw him talking with Dr. Swift and a retired Army colonel, who at the time was very big in the minuscule California Rangers organization, another paramilitary outfit similar to but much smaller than the Minutemen. They must have concluded that he had been mailing the right-wing material at the behest of one or both of these men, Wally thinks.

Finally, only a few days before he was due to be discharged, military intelligence took him in for questioning. At first, Wally said, he refused to admit anything, but changed his mind when one of the investigators told him he thought it might be best if he be taken to a Marine psychiatrist for a talk. Adhering to the theory of some on the Far Right that the government may start using mental institutions as a means of suppressing political dissent, Wally admitted having mailed the literature.

No disciplinary action was taken against Wally over the matter, he said. At any rate, he was honorably discharged in August, 1963. He returned to Chicago briefly, trying his hand in the real estate business, then returned to California with the intention of resuming studies he had began with Dr. Swift in Lancaster. This did not last long and soon Wally was in Norborne, sitting at the right hand of Robert DePugh, ready and willing to become that right hand.

Wally is a wiry, articulate, dark-complexioned young man with sharp but handsome features. He invariably is well-groomed, his coal-black hair neatly combed, his clothing tight-fitting and in fashion. In the setting of rural Missouri, he no doubt was regarded as a somewhat mysterious but pleasant sharpie. He later married a young Norborne girl.

In our first conversation, Wally talked at length about "Onward Christian Soldiers," a small organization he claimed to have formed at DePugh's suggestion to accommodate Minutemen who wanted religion mixed with their anti-Communism. He spoke of it as a "movement," rather than an organization and did not pretend it was anything particularly big, tightly knit or well organized.

Later, over chili and a malted milk at a Norborne café, he talked more openly about himself and some of his beliefs. Concerning Dr. Swift's teachings, he said he did not go along all the way with his former tutor but did agree with him on the superiority of Caucasians over Orientals and Negroes.

Wally stressed that this belief carried with it no hint of arrogance. Rather, he said, it imbued him with a sense of responsibility to help those so unfortunate as to have been born members of inferior races.

This did not exactly place him in enthusiastic support of the civil rights movement, but still, in his own way, I don't overlook the possibility that he regards himself as sincerely humble in his role as a representative of this "superior" race.

One of Wally's duties in the service had been to play the snare drum in the Marine Corps band, and in California, he became close friends with the band's piccolo and flute player, Raithby Roosevelt Husted, who said he was a distant cousin on his mother's side to Teddy and Franklin Delano Roosevelt. His and Wally's agreement on various facets of conservatism drew them to one another and at times Wally would take Raithby to Dr. Swift's lectures in Lancaster.

Wally was discharged from the Marines ahead of Ray, but they corresponded regularly. After Ray left the service he obtained a job with the National Forestry Service in California, but when Wally's invitations to travel to Norborne and join the Minutemen persisted, Ray finally decided to accept.

By mid-October, the furor over the "kidnaping" had subsided somewhat and the Norborne Minutemen were able to settle down again to the more routine work of keeping the organization moving. It was at this time that Raithby Roosevelt Husted arrived by train in Kansas City.

On the way to Norborne, he and Wally discussed what alias he should use, for most visiting Minutemen workers of Norborne went by ficticious names for security purposes. Ray preferred C. Leroy Shannon, but Wally insisted that Ray Shannon would be safer. He had called Raithby "Ray" in the Marines and was afraid he might slip and call him that in front of other Minutemen.

Ray had been led to believe that his job in the Minutemen would be that of an investigator, and this had appealed greatly to him. While still in the Marines, he had taken several correspondence courses in the arts of detective and investigative work.

When I asked him recently why he liked investigative work and how he first had become interested in it, Ray replied, "I just, oh, you might say I liked watching *Secret Agent*, *The Man From U.N.C.L.E.*, that sort of thing. I've always been interested in police work but never could qualify as a policeman."

Indeed, Ray might one day yet make somebody a good spy. Although handsome enough a young man, he has the sort of face that blends easily into a crowd and can be quickly forgotten. His demeanor qualifies him even more, for he usually chooses his words carefully before speaking and gives the impression of being somewhat reserved, if not shy. His glasses provide him a fairly studious look, and he does not resemble the sort of person the Minutemen would entrust with a sniper's rifle and earmark as a potential assassin. Yet this is what he says they did.

Once in Norborne, "Ray Shannon," was introduced around and given a bedroom on the second floor of 408 South Pine.

Ray did most of the cooking for Wally and Mary, while Jerry usually prepared his own and his mother's meals. Most days, Ray and one or more of the others would work on the first floor at 408 preparing "On Targets" and Minutemen bulletins for mailing and wrapping books that had been ordered by members—*The Devil's Advocate* by Taylor Caldwell, *The Craft of Intelligence* by Allen Dulles, *None Dare Call It Treason* by John Stormer and a few others.

Jerry's mother remained in her bedroom upstairs most of the time, unable to descend the stairs unaided. She was a lonely woman, Ray recalls, although Jerry was kind and attentive to her. She was undoubtedly aware of what was going on in the house, Ray said, but he had no way of determining what she thought about it. Jerry, apprehensive for her safety, had instructed her to "ask nothing, say nothing except hello and goodbye if they speak, and if they don't, why, that's all right."

While Mary was busy typing correspondence for the Minutemen, Wally concentrated more heavily than Ray liked on "field trips," especially, Ray complained, when there was heavy work to do around 408.

Jerry also told of a great deal of talk about assassinations of public figures at 408 while Ray was there, and that Ray, in fact, had been picked as the man who would do the killing. I asked Ray about this and received this set of replies:

"There was talk about it being done when the time was right."

"Did they say when?"

"No."

"How immediate was this talk?"

"At some times they would say there wasn't much time left. And at other times they would make you believe it was a little while away yet."

"Who did they talk about wanting to assassinate?"

"Oh, I really couldn't say who they wanted to. They had several people they said they'd like to."

"Who?"

"Fulbright. Senator Wayne Morse. They didn't like President Johnson at all."

"Did they talk of assassinating him?"

"No. Just one of the people that had to be eliminated."

"But not assassinated?"

"No. Not as such," Ray said.

"Then how would they eliminate him?"

"Well, that'd be by how you'd do it, or how you would have to do it. But so far as his name and assassination, no."

"What about Humphrey, Kennedy?" I asked, since their names seemed to crop up more than most others when Minutemen got together to talk about menaces to the country.

"Oh, yeah," said Ray, "they didn't like Humphrey, Katzenbach or Goldberg."

"Did they talk about assassinating any of them?"

"Yeah, as far as someone ought to. Their favorite expression was 'putting the hammer to them.'"

"What does that mean?"

"I associated that with someone ought to kill them . . . using a hammer as though you'd hit a mouse or something."

"The story I got was that they were actually training you to be an assassin," I said.

"Right. I had a rifle for it," he answered.

"For assassinations?"

"That's right."

"Did they say that in so many words?"

"I had a sniper rifle."

"Telescopic lens?"

"Yeah."

"What kind of rifle?"

"A Winchester model seventy."

"Did they tell you what it was for?"

"Yeah, to be a sniper. . . . And people were to be the targets. They never said who."

"Did they give you some training, or were you a good marksman?"

"I didn't need any training in marksmanship."

"You are an expert marksman?"

"Well, I generally hit what I'm shooting at."

"Did they intend to send you to Washington?"

"Well, the way I got it, when all the shooting started, that was when I was supposed to go to work."

"What do you mean by 'all the shooting'?"

"Their revolution."

"They talked of revolution?"

"Yeah. . . . They thought the Communists, the Red Chinese to be more specific, were arming the colored element and inciting to riot and causing all this racial trouble and they said just give it some time and when it breaks out, it'll be a full-fledged revolt and then they would step in."

"Would they provoke it?"

"Not that I know of."

I mentioned that DePugh talks in terms of a "counterrevolution" rather than a "revolution" with respect to Minutemen activity.

"Right," Ray replied. "It would have already been started by this other element. . . . They'd (the Minutemen) would come in like kind of a savior and all that."

"Who gave you the rifle? DePugh?"

"Yeah."

"What did he say to you?"

" 'Here's your sniper rifle' . . . and he made the comment on what a fine caliber it was, and it was a pretty good weapon."

Later I asked him if the talk of assassinations had bothered him.

"No," he replied.

"You didn't feel that was out of line?"

"Well, it may have been out of line, but as far as shock or revulsion at it, no."

"Why not?"

"Oh, I can't really say. Maybe it's that I've never been placed in that situation, but I really couldn't tell you how come it didn't."

"How did you feel about being given a rifle and picked as an assassin?"

"Oh, I thought they were putting confidence in my marksmanship. Maybe I didn't think it would ever get that far. Maybe I was living in a fairy-tale dream or something, but even now, thinking about it again, I can't really say I have any qualms about it. I follow the philosophy, all's fair in love and war."

"You were thinking in terms of an actual war?"

"Yeah, or guerrilla action."

Aside from this assignment, vague as it was, Ray found little else in Norborne that was especially exciting. He was not being groomed for investigative work, he disliked the assignment of helping paint the exterior of the house at 408, he discovered that the Minutemen were not as well organized as he had expected and he grew irritated at the amount of "racist talk" he heard, especially from Peyson. He blames Dr. Swift for having "warped" Wally's mind about racial matters.

"Why did you go to Norborne in the first place?" I asked him.

"Oh, you might say I was in for a little excitement. From what I'd read of their material, I thought they were right. Of course, when I got there I found out different. . . . I had thought they were just a downright anti-Communist organization, a little more militant than the rest, collecting arms, ammunition, taking survival training, collecting survival books, this sort of thing, instead of just talking about it."

It was the hole he and Wally spent a week digging, however, that finally prompted him to become an informant for the FBI. ("I have this thing about digging holes in the middle of the night," he said.)

Wally had gone to a farmer named Clellie Calvert who lived near Triplett, Missouri, representing himself as "Walter Petri," and told him he wished to rent a farmhouse.

"This fella said he wanted a place where it was quiet," Mr. Calvert said later. ". . . He said he was a writer or a poet. I believe that's what he said—a poet—and I told him I thought I had a place for him."

He moved into a house known in the area near Brunswick in northwest Missouri as "the old Bill Robinson place," which Calvert had owned for eleven years.

Wally later was to tell me he had given serious thought to living off and on in the house so he could have solitude for writing and reading. Life in Norborne, he said, was too hectic at that time.

On about the first day of November, Wally asked Ray if he wanted to take a trip, not specifying the destination. They drove to Linneus, Missouri, a little town near the Missouri-Iowa line, where they met Jim Tollerton, one of Mary's brothers, and ate dinner. They then proceeded to three separate hiding places in northwest Missouri—near Loredo, Linneus and a nearby house in which the Tollerton family once had lived. From a kitchen cupboard, a cellar and an attic, respectively, they recovered numerous packages that were placed in either Wally's or Tollerton's car. Some of the packages, Tollerton later was to acknowledge he was told, contained either ammunition or machine guns. They hid some of the packages in the attic of the "old Bill Robinson place."

Wally and Ray began digging a hole the next day beneath a closet floor of the farmhouse, a hole to measure roughly 10×6×6 feet. This task took the two young men a week to perform. The earth was packed solid from years beneath the old house. Ray and Wally used small hand tools and carried the dirt in buckets from the closet to a stream near the house to avoid discovery. It proved especially irritating to Ray who still would have preferred sniffing out Communists as a Minutemen investigator.

A dispute still exists over the acutal purpose of this hole. The strongest evidence indicates its immediate purpose had been to serve as the secret repository of a .50-caliber machine gun.

Jerry Brooks, however, gave me a more colorful version of what use the hole was eventually to be put in an interview in December, 1966.

"What did DePugh say the hole was to be for?"

"He told me what it was to be for."

"What?"

"He said we might want it for interrogation purposes."

"The hole?"

"Uh huh. You could always expand it."

"You mean they'd put somebody down in the hole and interrogate him?"

". . . Bob said for interrogation or to store stuff, but he didn't say he was gonna put guns there."

"Did he mention hiding people in it?"

"Oh," said Jerry, "you can use it for interrogation. You can use it for anything."

"Who? And when would he interrogate anyone in a hole under a farmhouse?" I asked.

Jerry then offered the name of a Russian he said was living in Washington. He provided the suite number and address for him—although in checking this out later, I found no such person known to be living in Washington.

"Kidnap him and put him in the hole?" I asked.

"Snatch him up. Take him right to the hole."

"They talked about this?"

"Correct. . . . He's director of intelligence for the Russian government. He's the head of it from North and South America to Peking, China."

DePugh, on the other hand, said the hole was to have served as a "hide."

"We've been establishing a series of 'hides,' as we call them, around over the country," DePugh said. "They're designed to be stop-over places for couriers or hide-outs for people being hunted under any type of enemy occupation, so this was supposed to be a camouflaged hide-out six feet wide and six feet deep and ten feet long. I had given directions it was to be big enough to hold two men and enough food and provisions to last 30 days."

"How'd the .50-caliber machine gun get in there?"

"Well, I didn't put it in there, and I don't know who did," DePugh said.

Ray, meanwhile, confirms part of DePugh's story, although he said he and Peyson had put the machine gun in the hole.

"The hole was also for a food cache," he said, "and was to be enlarged eventually to hide people in it."

He said he never heard it discussed as a place in which Russian spies or anyone else could be interrogated, however.

Midway through their hole-digging, Ray said, DePugh, Cindy Melville and Cindy's two young children visited them with food and provisions to get them through the rest of the week. He said DePugh carefully inspected the hole.

Once he and Wally had greased and wrapped the machine gun parts, buried them, covered the hole with lumber and a black plastic tarpaulin and put the closet floor back in place, Ray said, they took a three-day break from arms caching, only to return to it in a cemetery near little Coloma, Missouri.

DePugh drove them to the cemetery, Ray said, let them out near it and left. They went to a clump of bushes where four submachine guns had been left, then dug holes beside the cemetery and buried the weapons. DePugh returned to pick up the young men, informing them that he had been followed by two government cars while separated from them. DePugh has subsequently acknowledged that he drove Ray and Wally to the cemetery, but said that he had been under the impression certain secret Minutemen records were to have been buried there, not machine guns.

A day or so after this burial—on November 11—Ray wrote a letter to the FBI, sneaked over to nearby Carrollton, Missouri, and stuck it in a mailbox. He was working with the Minutemen, he wrote. Would they be interested in knowing anything about this organization?

George Arnett, the FBI agent in Kansas City who has worked most tirelessly and effectively on the Minutemen case, met Ray at the post office in Carrollton and chatted with him for about an hour in his car.

"He said to let him know what they had planned, any illegal acts," Ray said. "And he asked if I could get hold of the membership lists."

Ray said he did obtain the names of some Minutemen coordinators for Arnett—persons to whom he mailed packages of Minutemen monthly bulletins. The bulletins, for members only, were mailed in bulk to different Minutemen coordinators to prevent the government from obtaining membership lists by snooping on their mail. Coordinators received the packages in Louisiana, Mississippi, Florida, Connecticut and New York, Ray said, adding that he was unable to remember their names or other locations any longer. He mailed out only ten such packages, he said, indicating that he had not handled the entire Minutemen membership mailing.

His mailing responsibilities extended to only about 500 Minutemen, he said, plus about 2500 others who subscribed to "On Target" without holding memberships. The Minutemen, he guessed, are larger than the 500 he could account for. There may be that many members of the Minutemen in the Los Angeles area alone, he said, although this was only hearsay. Southern California, he said, seemed to be the primary stronghold of the Minutemen from what he had heard while in Norborne.

"Why did DePugh trust you?" I asked.

"I often wondered about that myself," Ray said. "I asked Peyson why he would let me handle such material after being there such a short time. He said DePugh just took his (Peyson's) word."

Early in December, the house at 408 South Pine lost two of its residents—Jerry Brooks and his mother. Among the reasons Jerry departed, Jerry later told me, was that he had grown suspicious of Ray Shannon.

"I thought he didn't fit in with these other men," Jerry said. "He acted dedicated, but when he was kinda off by himself—I mean, they continually talked, about to drive you buggy, you know—and he'd always go to his room and start reading, which is all right, but he didn't really seem interested and dedicated like the other guys. . . . Husted is a good, loyal American. I wouldn't say he's going to go out and crack somebody's head because he thinks Medicare is a Commy plot. . . . But he always said he'd like to be a detective. One time he showed me a badge there, but I don't know what kind it was. That really got me thinking. I thought, well this guy might be some kind of policeman. . . ."

Ten days after Jerry Brooks left Norborne, 408 South Pine lost yet another tenant. This was on December 14, 1965.

In prose reminiscent of the "On Target" issue devoted to the "disappearance" of Johnny Bob Harrell in 1963, a Minutemen tract distributed in the fall of 1966 described what was supposed to have happened to Ray:

". . . Ray worked for about three months in a quiet and efficient manner. In every way he demonstrated his continued belief in the principles of individual freedom and national sovereignty as advocated by the Minutemen organization.

"The day began like most others in the small town of Norborne, Missouri, where the Minutemen headquarters are located. Walter Peyson spent the morning operating the printing press. Bob DePugh was going over his notes for a talk that he gave that afternoon before the student body at the University of Kansas. Ray was scheduled to instruct at a survival class to be held that evening in Independence, Missouri, and he spent the morning in preparing his study outline.

"In the afternoon they traveled to Independence where they picked up another member. Ray was dropped off at 613 East Alton at about four o'clock. Sometime between five and six P.M. he drove Wally's car to the Kansas City, Kansas, post office where he mailed a number of packages. That car was returned to 613 East Alton sometime between six forty-five and seven P.M. . . ."

The account next told of a strange burglary of the Minutemen headquarters between seven and ten o'clock that night. Items taken, the report showed, included $206, a pair of old hobnailed boots belonging to Ray, and a can of spray deodorant.

Left behind, inexplicably, were $40 in silver that had belonged to Ray, his good suit and his $100 camera.

"His friends wondered about the peculiar items that were taken as compared with those left behind," the Minutemen report continued. "They are speculating that perhaps he was trying to signal them in this way that his actions were not voluntary."

It was noted that Wally's car remained at 613 East Alton between seven and ten that night and that its speedometer indicated it had been driven only to Kansas City, Kansas, and back to Independence.

"Obviously, if it was Ray who broke into the headquarters," the report said, "someone else had to drive him from Independence to Norborne."

Not long after Ray's "disappearance," Wally was arrested by federal agents and charged with illegal possession of a machine gun—the .50-caliber weapon in the hole beneath "the old Billy Robinson place."

It was later revealed that Ray had defected to the FBI in Kansas City and soon afterward decided to enlist in the Air Force, hoping, he told me, that this could land him a tour of duty in Europe as well as serving to get him away from the Missouri Minutemen.

On the evening of the day of his defection—December 14—he asked the FBI agents to follow him as he returned Wally Peyson's car to 613 East Alton. Then he asked the agents to drive him to 408 South Pine in Norborne, he said, so he could collect his belongings. The house was locked when he arrived, he said, so he broke in through a basement window while the FBI waited for him on a side street. He said he took $200 of Minutemen money, but left behind his $100 camera and other belongings in return for it.

The next day, the FBI took him to the ATTU, the federal agency assigned to enforce the Firearms Law. He gave a key to the "Billy Robinson place" to one of the agents, telling him about the .50-caliber machine gun under the closet there, and he led agents to the submachine guns buried near the Coloma cemetery.

On the following day he finished enlisting in the Air Force and was shipped out to the Westover Air Force Base in Massachusetts where he became a senior cook.

CHAPTER 11

JOIN THE MINUTEMEN

Brooks has testified that he was a "top lieutenant" in the Minutemen organization. Actually he was never a member or even a provisional member. His vocation as a stool pigeon and peddler of information—to anyone that would buy it—has been fully realized by the Minutemen organization. For two or three years we used Jerry to deliberately leak misinformation to other groups but we never let him get to any real information about our own organization. . . .

Footnote in the June, 1966, issue of "On Target."

For most of the time I have known him, the teeth that were left in the front of Jerry Milton Brooks's mouth appeared to have been fashioned by a hurried carver of jack-o-lanterns. His nose curves in a decided hook that is not necessarily unflattering to him, but over which he is inordinately self-conscious. He is gaunt to the point of appearing perpetually hungry. His eyes at times glisten when he is relating a particularly intriguing set of facts or anticipating some new mischief that he has conceived; at other times they dart about with the quickness of a hunted fox. Erratic, likable, instinctively devious, his motives are so complex that it is hard to imagine that he understands them all himself.

It is not safe for anyone to vouch too strenuously for his veracity, nor can anyone interested in the Minutemen afford to dismiss all he has said as fabrication. Some of his information checked out as accurate. Some of it is simply impossible to verify or believe.

Jerry joined forces with the Minutemen in the fall of 1961 and defected four years later. Contrary to the preceding "On Target" description of him, Jerry did get close to real information about the Minutemen, as even DePugh admitted several months after that issue of "On Target" had been printed.

DePugh describes Jerry aptly as "an enigma." "Jerry was completely unpredictable," he said. "In some respects he was as smart as a whip. He had an almost photographic memory. He's got an animal cunning that just won't quit. I don't think a policeman or a plain clothesman or an FBI agent could get within two miles of him without his knowing it. He is just instinct, you know. . . .

"Lots of times I've seen him go down to the federal building where all the cars are parked in the official lots—the marshals and FBI slots and so forth. He'd just walk up the street at a good fast clip from one end to the other, then he'd sit down there at the restaurant and take a piece of paper and he'd write down, 'a green and white 1962 Oldsmobile in the FBI slot, license number so and so and so,' right on down the line, every car that was there. He used to go around the Black Muslim temple and hang around and get all the license numbers and he'd come up with lots of other information. . . ."

Jerry existed on the periphery of the East St. Louis underworld for several years, amassing a police record that included convictions for attempted burglary in 1948, burglary and larceny in 1950 and extortion (threatening to kill a man if he didn't cough up $3000) in 1957. He has spent little time behind bars, however, because of the· leniency of judges or, he says, an occasional "fix" that had been put in by friends.

Aside from DePugh, Jerry was the most widely known Minuteman in the Greater Kansas City area in late 1962, 1963 and 1964. This does not mean his name was a household word used to frighten small children, but simply that the other Minutemen were quite secretive about their affiliation while Jerry boasted about it. At one time he even went about the city distributing a red, white and blue Minutemen calling card identifying himself as a part of the organization's "counter-intelligence" unit. DePugh finally put a stop to that.

My various efforts to meet Jerry in 1964 and 1965 had been fruitless. We had talked briefly on the telephone in the summer of 1965 as Jerry —at DePugh's behest—was trying to provide me information about the Black Muslims in Kansas City.

Then early in February, 1966, Jerry walked unannounced into the news room of the *Star* and approached my desk.

"Jones? Brooks!" he announced. "I've quit the Minutemen and I'm ready to talk. Interested?"

The answer was yes, naturally. For the next six hours, Charles Powers, another *Star* reporter, and I listened to largely unverifiable tales of conspiracies, counterconspiracies, intrigue, planned violence, assassination plots, weapons caches, accusations and fears. This also provided me with my first inkling that the federal government might be taking a hard look at the Minutemen.

Dressed in a khaki work shirt that was puffed by the sweat shirt beneath it, thin, frayed trousers inadequate for the cold temperatures outside, and a pair of Western boots, Jerry, eyes glittering with excitement, left me with the impression that he was sincerely apprehensive over his safety, no matter whether the danger was real or imagined. He did not try to sell me the information, although I had half expected him to.

Jerry's narrative was hopelessly circuitous and without regard to chronology. He repeatedly would skip back and forth from year to year within the framework of one interminable sentence, rattling off a rapid fire recitation that was punctuated with the name, age, physical description, address, telephone number, color and model of car and even the number of the car's license plate for many of the nearly 100 persons he named as Minutemen or Minutemen supporters. These persons lived, for the most part, in Missouri, but some he named were from such distant points as Trenton, Arlington, Chicago, New Orleans, Tucson, and Spokane.

With some of these he would parenthetically add little enticing personal details for further identification: ". . . He carries a rod in his attaché case (a man from Topeka, Kansas). . . . He makes crooked dice in the basement (Kansas City). . . . A gun dealer, buys 7000 to 8000 guns a year, legit (rural Missouri). . . . He hands out *Thunderbolt* (a Southern racist newspaper) and hates Jews (Kansas City). . . . Head of the KKK in his district too (Trenton, New Jersey). . . . Works for the American Civil Liberties Union (Ohio). . . . Talks about the Mafia like, man, they're the greatest thing since Seven-Up (Kansas City). . . . A plastics manufacturer (Michigan). . . . Likes to shoot muskets (Lee's Summit, Missouri). . . . an ex-FBI man (St. Louis). . . ."

"Would you be willing to tell a grand jury what you've told us?" he was asked in the sixth hour.

Certainly, he said. He already had told FBI and Alcohol and Tobacco Tax Unit agents essentially the same stories, he added. An appointment with Jackson County Prosecuting Attorney Gepford was made for two days hence, primarily as a test to see if he would tell such stories to an official without stumbling over some of his details. Jerry arrived early for the appointment and did not veer even remotely from his earlier accounts.

Reporting here even part of what Jerry Brooks said about the Minutemen is done with some hesitation. Even that part which is mentioned here may slip from fact into fantasy at times. Some of the more specific accusations that Jerry made against individuals have been omitted entirely. In other cases, the names of the Minutemen he said were involved have been deleted, the accusation retained.

Much of what Jerry said is in character with what else I have learned of the Minutemen. The government dared to use him as one of its witnesses against DePugh, Houghton and Peyson in federal court.* And Jerry signed transcripts of the two long interviews he gave the county prosecutor in February, 1965, initialing each page after a careful reading. The reader, nevertheless, is cautioned to view his story skeptically.

"I joined the Minutemen right after the raid at Shiloh, Illinois," he began. "I joined through Rich Lauchli. . . . He lived at 2010 North Keebler, Collinsville, Illinois. I read in the paper in regards to the raid at Shiloh. I called Rich Lauchli at Dickens 4-3195, which was his phone at the time, and I said I'd like a meeting. He came to the house at 1736 College and I joined the Minutemen that night. And I worked up until 1962, October 4, 1962, with Rich Lauchli . . ."

It was this way for two hours. Names, addresses, telephone numbers, many specific dates. An amazing memory.

He told of meeting DePugh for the first time in 1962 while DePugh was involved in the Freedom Rally effort and picketing at Kansas City's Liberty Memorial.

Then he told of being sent on a $99 bus tour of the United States with orders to assassinate Communists with strychnine. He made it through the Deep South to Miami where he stayed with a relative, then proceeded to Washington, D.C., poisoning no one en route. News that his mother had suffered a stroke in East St. Louis, Illinois,

---

* Russell Millin, U. S. Attorney for the Western District of Missouri, immediately brought out Brooks's police record when he began questioning him lest the defense attorneys expose it themselves in cross-examination. In his closing argument to the jury, Millin commented that while Jerry might not be "the most admirable, upright person" and in fact might be classified as a "kook," it was remarkable that he had stayed out of trouble with the law the previous nine years in light of the environment in which he had been living. For half of those nine years, that environment had been largely one created by the Minutemen.

brought him to her side and temporarily interrupted his Minutemen career, he said.

A certain disappointment was expressed within the Minutemen ranks, he said, because he had not carried out the original plans.

"Right after that," he said, "my brother, Charlie Brooks, was knocked on the head real bad, nearly bled to death, Caseyville, Illinois, 519 North Long Street, was rushed to St. Mary's Hospital, East St. Louis, Illinois, for attention to the cracked noggin. Bled, bled, like bad.

"And now, my brother looks enough like me, you wouldn't have to see us two feet apart to say, 'Hey, there's your brother,' if you seen him in Kansas City. And they sent some guys out from Colorado . . . a judo-karate man, an ex-paratrooper, weighed about 300 pounds . . . came to Caseyville, Illinois, looking for me. Soon afterwards my brother was laying prone, mucho blood, and they never found out who did it. And I asked DePugh and he never did comment. But I know they do take care of their own by a few workings-over and things, because . . . they've got the boys to do it."

Rich Lauchli later was to recall that while Brooks was in Florida on that $99 bus tour, he wrote a letter to Fidel Castro.

"He said, 'Look, I've been with the right wing for a couple of years,'" Lauchli said, "'I know all about them. Here's some examples,' and he gives my name and Bob's. He says, 'I know all these guys and if I can go over and be with you and show you how much I believe in your cause,' he says, 'I'll give you all the information.' He could have given him quite a bit, you know. Well, Uncle Sam isn't that dumb. He's got connections over there too. So they pick up the letter in Havana and kick it back to Washington and the first thing we know the FBI's going around asking, 'What do you know about this and so forth?' Well, that's how we come to find out about Jerry."

"To tell you the truth now," Lauchli added, "I was told Jerry was going to be planted, put away, you know."

"What do you mean?"

"Killed."

"By whom?"

"Well, done, that's all," Lauchli said. "I didn't want to know nothing about it. I mean all you do is get in trouble on a deal like that, see. So as far as I know, that's the end of Jerry. I don't see him no more. I don't get no more phone calls from him, and I'm happy. If I never see Jerry again in my life I'm still happy."

When I asked Jerry about the letter to Castro, he admitted writing one, but made it clear he had done so in an effort to infiltrate.

"What did you write him?"

"Oh, just something kooky."

In a follow-up interview with Jerry in the prosecutor's office a week later—the transcript of which he also signed—Jerry was asked to give locations where ammunition and bombs were hidden.

"Well," he replied, "they had much ammunition . . . lots of ammunition at San Fidel, New Mexico, all New Mexico; and out at Grant, New Mexico; Phoenix, Arizona; Tucson, Arizona; Englewood, Colorado; Evergreen, Colorado; Rolla, Missouri; Success, Missouri; Louisville, Illinois; Collinsville, Illinois; Madison, Illinois; and Arlington, Virginia."

Earlier he also had mentioned Seattle, Washington; Hickory, Missouri; Cross Timbers, Missouri; Norborne, Missouri; Chillicothe, Missouri; and Baldwin, Missouri.

Jerry talked at length about the training session at 613 shortly before it was raided by the Independence police in mid-1965.

"The training session was one of many held by the Minutemen, was it not?" Gepford asked.

"Right," said Jerry.

"And was it the purpose of this training session to . . . instruct the participants, the members who attended, how to use dynamite, grenades . . . ?"

"Oh yes. Demolitions, the lecture by Troy Houghton was in the use of Primacord, real bad, bad explosive, also nitroglycerine, which they had on the scene, also machine guns, which they had on the scene, approximately six of them."

"Live ones?"

"Live ones. And one Sten gun, one grease gun, live, plus ammunition, plus live grenades, plus dynamite, plus C-4 and C-2 plastic explosive, detonating caps, and the use of said explosives and how to blow up railroads, how to blow up communications, and this wasn't for a guy who reads 'On Target' . . . this was for some of the leaders. It was team captains and stuff like that and coordinators, and I was there to see, to observe the meeting and see if I could cause a little dissension and distress, and look things over and hear what goes on and see what I think is good or bad. That was my job in security: surveillance and intelligence work. Kept me kind of busy, about eighteen hours a day."

"Were there any other lectures given?" Jerry was asked.

"Yes, sir. Robert Bolivar DePugh . . . lectured on security, research and analysis of information, of course, on the enemy, and surveillance, how to use the shotgun mike, which Jack Cannon made, how to tap phones, how to work a tape recorder, how to make mike surveillance, how to use induction taps, and Wally Peyson gave lectures on how to organize teams and how to organize coordinators, how to work with your band, how to do surveillance on bands, and also, Cyndra Melville Sanders gave lectures on cryptography, in which she's pretty well versed, and they had one guy named Andy, he talked a little bit about violence there, but he didn't give a lecture. . . .

"Andy talked about using cyanide on the United Nations, putting it in the air-conditioning system, or in the water. Tapping a water line and putting it in, and carrying it out. When liquid hits the powder, poof, you're gone. A pint takes care of 5000 feet and works pretty nice."

"In what context did he talk about putting cyanide in the United Nations?"

"He spoke of this like it's a good idea, and we should do it, and it wouldn't be a good idea to wait too long, because time is of the essence, so to speak."

Nine months after giving this statement, Jerry took the witness stand for the federal government in the firearms trial of DePugh, Houghton and Peyson and was asked under cross-examination by William Gilwee, a defense attorney:

"Your trouble with Mr. DePugh started when you came up with the idea of putting cyanide in the air-conditioning unit of the UN building?"

"No, sir," Jerry replied.

"Well, didn't you advance the idea?" Gilwee asked.

"I'll say it was discussed at the training sessions," he answered. "A lot of things were discussed . . . I'll say I brought it up."

"And you also brought up the idea of assassinating Senator Fulbright, didn't you?" the lawyer asked.

"No, sir," Jerry answered emphatically.

Millin, the U. S. Attorney subsequently asked him what DePugh had said after the Fulbright and UN matters had been brought up.

"He said, 'The Rabbi will now give a lecture on assassinations,'" Jerry replied. "The Rabbi" was his nickname in the Minutemen.

"What happened after that?" Millin asked.

"I was moved to Norborne to work for the Minutemen," Jerry said.

Back in his February, 1965, interview, Gepford asked Jerry whether the training session in Independence was to teach Minutemen how to use demolitions, telephone taps and other such equipment.

"Right," said Jerry.

"In the event of what?"

"Well, in the event that they decided that the revolution is going to take place. Now. . . ."

"That's the revolution against the United States government or any local government?" Gepford asked.

"That's right. Any part thereof, states, county, city, community and so on."

"Was that purpose pretty well understood by all the members who were there?"

"Yes, I'm as sure as it is my understanding you're Mr. Gepford, the state attorney."

Asked whether the dynamite found at 613 had been intended for use in field exercises in southern Missouri, as DePugh had claimed, Jerry disputed DePugh.

"That I know of, there wasn't, because the dynamite was there. I seen it on numerous occasions. . . . I was in and out of the office there, and many times, maybe fifteen or twenty, I didn't write it down, I saw dynamite, because at this time I was still for them. And the dynamite was still there. Five or six boxes. . . ."

Gepford also questioned Jerry about Linda and Patricia's stay at 613 East Alton.

"These two girls said they were held against their will," the prosecutor said, "and yet they had freedom to come and go. That's a matter of record."

"Right," said Jerry.

"What is your feeling or belief with regard to their being afraid or having fear for their safety? Can you give any credence to this fear?"

"Yes, I can. . . . We all—when we join the Minutemen, not when you subscribe to any of their publications, but when you join and you become an active member—after you take Training Phase 5, you're notified that you cannot quit, by mail, or in person, either way. I mean, a fellow member will contact you and say, 'There's no turning back.' Anyone that discloses anything about Minutemen on the inside, not publications, but where they hold meetings, will die, period. This is understood when you go into the Minutemen. You will be—after you take the five training phases, you're then a member, and don't quit. It's just like the Mafia, only in the Mafia, you don't take training phases. You join that, and you're an Italian, [somebody] talks, waaap, you're dead. Okay. It's the same way with them. . . ."

Gepford asked Brooks about a shotgun blast that was fired through a window of Roy Horridge's home a few months after the grand jury investigator's search for DePugh and the raid on 613.

One of the Minutemen "wants Horridge," Jerry said.

"Now, I never heard DePugh make a threat against (him) . . . I never heard him say, 'I'm going to kill Gepford, I'm going to kill his family.' I never heard him say, 'I'm going to kill Horridge, Jackson or Wingate.' But I did hear (another Minuteman) and was in his presence . . . you know, he's a judo-karate man, and he said, 'Man, let me at that crummy Horridge, I'll kill him.' Now, that's all, it could be just talk, but he was bad with karate.

"One time I went to the door, pushed the buzzer, he had a gun on me. They pull that stuff to shake you up, to see if it will scare you into talking, and I went in. He said, 'Come on in, I want to talk to you. You've been talking.' And he said, 'Stand over there against the wall,' so I did. And so he used the—oh, I guess five different approaches to me with karate, and one, he come up about that far from my head (indicating less than an inch), you know, you take the stance, he said, 'I'll look ten feet beyond your head,' and, man, that's when you start worrying with karate. I know a little karate myself. I thought he'd do me in. He gave me one down here, barely hit me, just enough, and I had pains for a long time. He said, 'I'll crack the [rib] cage there and one here and one across the back, and just practice.' He said, 'That's how to be had.' Well, he was. He about killed some of the guys that came out and took judo instructions from him. And he was always talking, 'Wingate, kill him. Horridge.' He hates Jews, see. They may not be Jews. He thought I was a Jew because I had a hooked nose. And he didn't trust me at first. You know, anybody that—he said, 'Anybody that's opposed to the Minutemen must be a Jew.' You know, he's carried away. And he'd say, 'Horridge, kill him,' he didn't say all the time he was going to, but he'd say, 'Wingate, kill him, Jackson, kill him. . . .' "

Jerry said that after moving with his mother to 408 South Pine, members of the Minutemen told him: "Your mom, she could run into a piece of piano wire."

Gepford, irked at numerous harassing telephone calls he had received at his home since first charging DePugh with kidnaping, asked Jerry about phone harassment procedures in the Minutemen. Jerry named four Kansas Citians whose job it was, he said, to make harassing phone calls—he called it the "phone committee." Jerry also admitted that he had made harassing phone calls himself, but only to known "Communists."

Jerry was apparently broke at the time. For the next two months, he would telephone or drop by the newspaper office with new nuggets of information about someone he said was either a Communist or a Minuteman. He was also making regular visits to the FBI and ATTU offices in downtown Kansas City.

He kept the address of the apartment in which he and his mother were living a closely guarded secret, known only to a few.

Early in April, he was placed under federal subpoena to appear before the federal grand jury at an unspecified date in the future—a move that Jerry said he felt offered him a measure of protection from his enemies who he hoped would not dare harm a federal witness. This also bolstered the *Star*'s confidence in him enough to publish a copyrighted article by reporter Charles Powers relating a portion of the information he had provided. The Associated Press picked it up, making the Fulbright assassination plot its lead, and Jerry Brooks gained a small measure of national fame.

This fame attracted the special attention in nearby Lawrence, Kansas, of Laird M. Wilcox, the then twenty-three-year-old editor of the sporadic Kansas Free Press, a former University of Kansas student, and a self-proclaimed Socialist and "radical" at the time.

Wilcox and Conrad Creitz, also a former young K.U. student, rushed to Jerry's side the day after the article had appeared and the three men began conjuring up foolishness with which to harass the Minutemen.

Their first thrust was to telephone the DePugh home in Norborne and mysteriously say that at a certain hour that evening, Jerry and his mother would board a bus for St. Louis at the downtown Kansas City bus depot. They passed similar misinformation on to a few other

Minutemen in the city, then, armed with a portable tape recorder and camera, jumped into Wilcox's pick-up truck and headed for the bus depot.

From all reports, what followed was sheer slapstick. Inside the main lobby of the bus terminal as the three men arrived were Wayne Morse, the notorious right-wing picket; Theodore J. Lyman, a Minutemen sympathizer who is over seventy years old; and Gilbert Theetge, a forty-year-old Minuteman.

After frightening Theetge and Lyman away by their unexpected presence, Wilcox and Creitz converged on Morse as soon as he had begun to speak to Jerry, Creitz with flashbulbs popping, Wilcox with his recorder's microphone shoved pugnaciously before Morse's gaping mouth.

Finally they fled the scene in the pick-up, leaving Morse and his companions shaking their fists into their exhaust fumes

Morse and Lyman attempted to retaliate that weekend by driving to Lawrence and scribbling down the license-plate numbers of cars parked in front of and near Wilcox's apartment. When Wilcox and Creitz discovered this, the Free Press editor grabbed a pistol, his sidekick seized a sawed-off shotgun and the two men hopped into Wilcox's pick-up. They followed Morse and Lyman almost bumper to bumper, "just to shake them," as Wilcox described it.

The two older men tolerated this only long enough to pull abruptly into a service station and jump from their car. As Morse stormed toward the pick-up truck, he suddenly realized that Creitz had a shotgun. Morse wheeled around, ran at an uncommonly fast speed into a telephone booth and called the Lawrence police department.

The police officers found the two young men's weapons empty of shells and the shotgun of legal length. Morse and Lyman were instructed to leave Lawrence. They left.*

Wilcox, a bearded and muscular red-headed intellectual, is a voracious student of the Far Right and Far Left. DePugh, in 1964, was quoted in the St. Louis *Post-Dispatch*, while discussing Communism on campuses,

---

* "There's a lot of things going on around town lately you don't know about," Morse told me the following Monday afternoon when I happened across him as he was picketing the Kansas City board of education, and he proceeded to relate his narrow "brush with death" over the weekend.

Brooks, Wilcox and Creitz later told essentially the same story—between guffaws—except that Wilcox and Creitz denied the riot gun actually had been pointed at Morse. Lyman, without guffaws, also confirmed the essentials of the story.

as singling out Wilcox as a "professional leftist agitator," which delighted Wilcox. (He more recently has abandoned "Socialist" as a part of his self-identification.)

Once Wilcox had discovered Jerry, he and Creitz spent nearly every day for more than a week with him, harassing Minutemen by telephone with conversations that would begin usually with, "This comes straight from 551 . . ." (DePugh's code number), and the Minuteman would be advised of an urgent meeting at 613 East Alton or in Norborne. Wilcox boasts he watched one Lawrence, Kansas, Minuteman hurry to his car after such a call and head for Norborne, about a two-hour drive.

Other times they sat around in the pick-up truck or at Jerry's apartment talking.

"Jerry was really impoverished," Wilcox said later. "I remember sitting in the kitchen with him and his mother when he opened the door of the refrigerator. All that was in there was a jar of jam. Just one jar. Their dinner consisted of putting the jam on some bread and eating it. We gave him several dollars from time to time."

He put thirteen hours of Jerry's tales on tape, so impressed was he with his colorful Minutemenorabilia, and later used a segment of it to expose a young woman student at the university who played an active role in a left-wing campus organization but was in reality an infiltrator for the Minutemen.

The troubles Jerry was to create for both the Minutemen and the United States government had only begun. The same could be said for Ray Husted.

CHAPTER 12

JOIN THE MINUTEMEN

. . . What Has Happened to Ray Husted?

It is now obvious that the present indictments against Minutemen leaders are based largely on the testimony given by Ray while under the influence of drugs or later from him by threats or coercion.

More important right now is the personal safety of Ray Husted. Has he been shipped to some other military post where he is terrorized into silence? Is he being held in some insane asylum while his mind is being destroyed by shock treatments and more drugs?

> From a Minutemen pamphlet distributed widely in the fall of 1966, titled, "Federal Witness Says FBI Agents Used Padded Cell and Drug Injections to Get His Signed Statement."

Ray Husted had spent the first half of 1966 at the Westover Air Force Base in Massachusetts as a cook, his whereabouts presumably a mystery to all his old Minutemen chums in Missouri.

It was not until August 16 that the Minutemen learned what had happened to the quiet Californian who had disappeared from their midst so suddenly the previous December. Or at least they thought they had learned what had happened to him.

Ray returned to Kansas City in mid-August in answer to a federal grand jury subpoena. The grand jury was in its final days of investigating the Minutemen organization, and what Ray, the defector who had led federal agents to buried submachine guns, had to say was of great importance to the government in shaping up their case against the Minutemen.

Mary Tollerton was under subpoena to appear before the same grand jury in connection with the investigation, and so it was that they happened to meet in the hallway of the federal courthouse building on August 16. They nodded to one another in a friendly fashion but were hastily separated by federal agents who whisked Ray on his way.

Later, when the agents were not looking, Ray quickly printed the words, "Pickwick Hotel" on a scrap of paper and pinned it onto his suitcoat so that it would be hidden by his lapel. The next time he passed Mary in the hall, he flipped his lapel out far enough for her to read the message.

According to Ray, the telephone rang in his Pickwick Motor Inn room around ten-thirty or eleven o'clock that night.

"Do you know who this is?" came a woman's voice.

"No," said Ray.

"This is Mary. Do you want to talk?"

"Yes, I'll be down in a minute."

Ray met her in the lobby and took her to the coffee shop at the nearby Greyhound bus depot where they renewed their acquaintance from Norborne.

What had happened to him, Mary asked. Why had he left so suddenly? Where had he been? What was he doing back in Kansas City now, in the company of federal agents, obviously preparing to testify before the grand jury?

Since he recited the story he told her at least five times in the next few hours, there undoubtedly were some variations from one to the other. The statement he wrote and signed for the Minutemen, and which was subsequently reproduced and circulated widely by the organization, read as follows:

17 August 1966

On the 13th or 14th of December, 1965, I was to hold a weapons class at East Alton. Before the class started I had some time to kill so I went into Kansas City, Mo. On my way back from K.C. one car got in front of me and one behind me and they stopped me. One man got out of the front car and came to me and asked my name and showed FBI ID papers. The fellow told me to follow him. He took me back to East Alton and then had me get in the lead car— At the time the second car left— Then he took me to the MM HQ in Norborne. On the way up he said I was getting out. I was to raid the place. I broke in and took some MM money and some of my stuff. I was to leave the back door open and did so. I went back to the car and we went back toward K.C.

Somewhere in the K.C. area I was taken to what appeared

to be a Medical Clinic or hospital. I was placed in a padded room. A short time later a doctor came into the room and gave me a physical exam and some shots. After the shots I don't remember much. About all I remember is signing a statement, taking some FBI, & ATTU men to a cemetery and enlisting in the USAF. Outside of being told to "follow me" and "you're getting out" I cannot remember being told to do anything. Everything was suggested. It was implied if I didn't go along with them I would be put in a mental hospital. Total time was about three days. All I can remember about the clinic was it wasn't very big. On the way to Norborne it was suggested I take any money, records or guns I found in the house.

Raithby R. Husted.

After hearing this story, Mary asked Ray if he wanted to see his old pal Wally Peyson again. Ray said he did. They walked to another bus station a block away where Wally was waiting. After Ray told the story over again, Wally asked him if he wanted to tell it once more to Robert DePugh. Ray agreed.

They drove in Wally's Volkswagen to 613 East Alton. It was approaching midnight now and heavy rain had begun to fall. Wally left Ray and Mary in the car while he went inside the building and brought out DePugh. The Minutemen leader climbed into the back seat of the little car beside Ray and they drove to the Coffee Stop Restaurant, an all-night café on Highway 24 in Independence. There Ray told his story over again as they sat in one of the booths.

"DePugh said that it was incredible," Ray recalled, "and he indicated, but didn't say so, that he thought there was some agency—the FBI, the Treasury agency or some investigative department—at the café, and said he didn't want to leave there until he had some help, and he left the table, supposedly to make a phone call."

Unknown to Ray, Wally, Mary or DePugh at that time, two Independence police department detectives, James McCarty and Ray Whitaker, with a little time to kill before going off duty at two o'clock in the morning, had dropped by the Coffee Stop shortly after DePugh and company had arrived.* The two police officers, wearing

---

* McCarty, by coincidence, had been the policeman who had arrested Linda and Pat after their "escape" from 613 East Alton fourteen months earlier.

civilian clothes, sat down at a booth some distance from the Minute-men and ordered breakfast, oblivious to the identities of the others in the restaurant. As McCarty recalled later, they were surprised a short time later to see Bill Herdlinger, acting chief of the Independence police department, enter the restaurant, his yellow raincoat dripping from the summer downpour.

The detectives asked Herdlinger to join them and offered to buy his breakfast. The police chief settled for a cup of coffee and sat down with them, his back to DePugh and friends. After the necessary amount of small talk, Herdlinger, motioning behind him, asked the detectives:

"You know who that is?"

"No."

"DePugh."

In the next fifteen to thirty minutes, McCarty said, Herdlinger table-hopped several times. After one visit to the Minutemen table, he said, the police chief whispered to the detectives: "You know, he (DePugh) thinks you're a couple of feds out to assassinate him."

They laughed heartily over this.

"I'm the only guy on the police department he trusts," Herdlinger continued, as McCarty remembers the conversation.

McCarty recalled that Herdlinger asked him and Whitaker whether they would like to work overtime, explaining, "This crazy nut thinks someone's out to assassinate him tonight. We've got to protect the kooks as well as the other citizens."*

Acting Chief of Police Herdlinger had gone to bed early that wet night and had been somewhat perturbed when the telephone rang at his home shortly after midnight. It had been DePugh.

The Minutemen leader had asked him to hurry to the restaurant to help him.

---

* Herdlinger discussed his trip to the Coffee Stop with me reluctantly, but con-firmed the events and remarks as related by McCarty.

Orson (Barney) Myers, who was chief of police in Independence from late 1963 until shortly before the night Ray Husted returned to Independence, has proven himself an outstanding law-enforcement officer, but he admits to having made one big mistake—assigning Herdlinger, then a lieutenant, to "infiltrate" the Minutemen so as to feed him and the FBI information. The trouble with the arrangement was that Herdlinger already had joined the Minutemen, on his own.

Herdlinger lost his job with the police department as a result of the events in the early morning hours of August 17, a discouraged but hopefully wiser man.

"I'm not mad at anybody," he told me later. "I'm just fed up."

"Why did you call Herdlinger?" I asked DePugh many months later.

"Well," DePugh said, "as Ray began to tell the story [of his 'brainwashing,' etc.] I thought, well now, here this fellow is called as a federal witness, you know, subpoenaed before this federal grand jury. So I wondered if we were being set up for tampering with a witness. So when we got to the café, I called Herdlinger. He was acting chief of police at the time, and I asked him if he'd come out there, which he did, of course.

"I didn't tell him anything except that I've got a fellow here with us that's a witness before a grand jury and I just wanted to have somebody here to verify the fact that he's here on his own free will and that nobody's using any arm-twisting tactics to get this story out of him. . . ."

Herdlinger disputes this on one important point. He insists that he did not know that Husted was a federal witness.

"In fairness to DePugh," he added, "DePugh started to tell me, but I stopped him. I said, 'I don't want to get involved.' I just thought it was some more of this cloak-and-dagger stuff."

DePugh, Ray, Wally and Mary soon left the restaurant and drove a quarter of a mile west on U.S. 24 to the Moonlight Motel, where they joined Mary's two brothers, Jim and Bob Tollerton, inside.

Herdlinger and the two detectives also drove to the motel. On the police chief's instructions, the two detectives stationed themselves outside in their car to guard the Minutemen leader, they thought. Inside, the Minutemen were obtaining a signed statement from Ray on how the FBI had "brainwashed" him.

DePugh told Herdlinger, "There's certain people who, if they knew what I had, they'd blow my head off," Herdlinger recalled, but he did not let the Minutemen leader continue with the details. He said he also declined DePugh's invitation to join the others in the motel room.

After Ray had signed the statement, DePugh and Wally left the motel to drive to Norborne for a tape recorder. They wanted Ray to repeat his story once more. As Ray and the three young Tollertons waited in the motel room, Ray recalled, Mary told him, "Well, you're in good hands. The chief of police of Independence is standing guard and there is a detective outside."

The chief, however, had left by then, and the detectives, McCarty said, were growing increasingly suspicious of their unusual assignment. Unaware that the Tollerton brothers had been inside the motel room before they arrived on the scene, the detectives were under the impression that after DePugh and Wally had left, Ray and Mary were alone in the room, unchaperoned. After contemplating this arrangement and the fact that the man they had been assigned to guard against assassination was no longer in the motel, the detectives decided enough was enough, McCarty said, and they went home.

"I suppose the moment that stands out the most in my mind of that evening was a rather emotional moment, both for myself and Ray," Mary Tollerton later said. "Bob and Wally had left to get a tape recorder, and Ray had lain down on one of the beds there in the room and was trying to sleep when I noticed that his eyes were still open.

"I said something to him, I said, 'Ray, are you having trouble getting to sleep?' All of a sudden he got off the bed, came over to the chair where I was sitting and sat down on the floor. He put his arms around me, put his head in my lap and started to cry. This young man was afraid! He said, 'Mary, I am so frightened. I don't know what is going to happen to me. I am afraid for my life.'

"He was crying and he was not the kind of man to break down and cry easily. It was at this moment I think the real impact of the whole thing hit me and I really felt that he was telling the truth."

(Mary's moving testimony was later printed in "Richard Cotten's Conservative Viewpoint," from a taped interview with Cotten, an ultraconservative radio propagandist with a following primarily in parts of the South and California.)

Meanwhile, early that rainy morning a telephone call was placed to Hannibal, Missouri, about 300 miles east of Independence, where the two attorneys Peyson had employed months earlier to fight his machine-gun indictment lived. They hurried across the state and arrived at the motel in time to question Ray themselves. Cindy Melville arrived at the motel at about the same time with her two youngsters.

It was nine o'clock in the morning by then, just a half hour before Ray was scheduled to testify against the Minutemen before the grand jury. The Alcohol and Tobacco Tax Unit, however, had already found out what had happened and two agents were at the Independence police headquarters bright and early questioning Herdlinger. McCarty recalls being awakened at seven-thirty by an urgent call from his police chief, telling him to hurry to headquarters. Once there, he said, Herdlinger told him, "Don't try to protect me." He didn't. McCarty subsequently testified before the grand jury three times.

The Hannibal lawyers, DePugh, Cindy and children, Wally, Mary and her two brothers accompanied Ray to the office of an Independence lawyer in a three-car caravan later that morning. The Hannibal lawyers introduced Ray to the Independence attorney, Ray said, with the information that "I was telling the truth or was a very clever liar."

The Independence lawyer simply instructed Ray to tell the truth to the grand jury. Over iced tea in a restaurant later that morning, Ray said, he told DePugh and Cindy that he would plead the Fifth Amendment before the grand jury.

He didn't live up to the promise. Before the day was over, he had testified, without taking the Fifth Amendment apparently, and subsequent events indicate that his testimony was most damaging to the Minutemen. He also provided a long statement to the FBI concerning his activities the previous night.

"Apparently they re-established, through fear or some other means, a complete control over Ray," DePugh later told Cotten, "because apparently he did not tell the grand jury the same story that he told us, though he had been willing just a few hours before to have us call out newspaper reporters or TV cameramen or anyone, as he was very anxious for his story to become public. I think one of the big mistakes that we made was the fact that we did not publicize it to the very utmost at the time."

It was several months later before Husted's strange behavior at the Moonlight Motel was explained, either to me or the Minutemen.

"Why did you do it?" I asked.

"I thought I could get back into the Minutemen," he replied. "Maybe not as far as I had been, but get back into it and still supply information, which I'm still convinced I could have done, but our fine federal government (and there was an unmistakable note of resentment in his voice here) had other ideas."

"Why did you want to do this?"

"Oh, I like that type of work. I'm interested in that sort of thing."

CHAPTER 13

JOIN THE MINUTEMEN

> . . . The shadow of the police state lies across our land. If we
> are railroaded into the penitentiary, then your turn will surely
> come sooner or later. . . .
>
> From fall, 1966, Minutemen pamphlet headed "Federal Witness
> Says FBI Agents Used Padded Cell and Drug Injections to Get
> His Signed Statement."

A few days after Ray Husted's performance in the Moonlight Motel,
the federal grand jury that had worked so many fascinating hours
hearing witnesses testify about the Minutemen organization voted
some weighty indictments.

Robert DePugh, Wally Peyson, Troy Houghton, James Tollerton
and John Blumer, of Manchester, Missouri, were indicted on a charge
of conspiring to violate the National Firearms Act. DePugh, Peyson
and Tollerton were charged additionally with direct violations of the
act. Cindy Melville and Ray Husted were named as co-conspirators
in the conspiracy indictment, but were not charged.

The federal crackdown on the Minutemen organization had moved
into a new, more threatening phase. Jerry Brooks had talked. Ray
Husted had talked. And so had quite a few others whom the Minutemen once had trusted. Black days were ahead.

Immediately it became the job of the federal marshal's office in
Kansas City to round up the defendants. DePugh was first on their
list.

ATTU agents, presumably in anticipation of the grand-jury action,
had been trying to keep abreast of DePugh's activities that Saturday.
Checking the home of DePugh's parents in Independence, they noticed that Cindy and DePugh were just climbing into a car, with
Cindy at the wheel. (DePugh's driver's license had long since been
revoked.) The federal marshals were alerted and the pursuit was on.

By the time Cindy had headed the car west on I-70, a relatively new, high-speed superhighway that connects St. Louis and Kansas City, the marshals and ATTU agents were ready to act.

Soon after they had buzzed across the Independence city limits and into Kansas City, Missouri, DePugh and his secretary noticed they were being followed and a man in the car behind them was waving Cindy to stop.

Cindy was dressed in a tight, sleeveless blouse that hot August afternoon, an equally tight pair of blue jeans, and white moccasins. Her hair hung straight down almost to her waist.

She obligingly pulled the car onto a siding at the behest of the federal officers, but when the marshals and ATTU agents walked over to the car, they found DePugh's arrest was not going to be as routine as they might have anticipated. Neither DePugh nor his confidential secretary would roll down a window or unlock the doors of the car.

Orders were shouted at the pair and credentials were waved at them. Eventually DePugh rolled down his window an inch so that they could converse. He insisted that each agent hold up his credentials, one by one, and as they did so he scribbled notes concerning their identities. But DePugh still refused to open his window any further or unlock his door. One agent obtained a large club from his car. Marshal F. M. Wilson told DePugh that if he did not come out, the agent would break the windows. This persuaded the Minutemen leader to open the door and submit to a search. Cindy was told she could remain in the car.

A double-barreled shotgun was found on the floor of the car and two shotgun shells were found in one of DePugh's pockets.

"It's legal, boys," said DePugh as the officers inspected the shotgun, and he was right. It was one-half an inch longer than the legal minimum.

In the back seat of the car, the officers noticed an attaché case which, when they opened it, was found to contain a .38-caliber pistol. Presumably because of his conduct and perhaps the weapons, DePugh was then handcuffed, preparatory to delivery to the federal courthouse building.

As this point, as federal officials later described it, Cindy exploded from her side of the car and pounced onto Frank I. Belecky, the agent in charge of the ATTU in western Missouri.

"She lit right on him," Wilson said, "both fists going like a man. Then she started kicking too."

According to the officials' version, Belecky tried to ward off the blows as another agent (who later said he had thought she was going for the shotgun) leaped to his rescue. Marshal Wilson moved in behind her, grabbed her around the waist and slipped a handcuff around one of her wrists.

"Then we had more trouble than ever getting the other handcuffed," Wilson recalled. "Oh, it didn't take long, but it sure seemed like a long time."

Cindy quickly calmed down, the federal officials said, and Wilson removed the handcuffs.

A somewhat different version of this incident was offered much later by Cindy Melville.

As she recalled it, she had attacked no one. The Husted statement was fresh in her mind and she was terrified, she said. "I had visions of hypodermic needles and drug injections," she said. "I was just trying to run away." She remembered exchanging angry words with Belecky and jerking away when Belecky finally took hold of one of her arms. At that point, she said, "they all pounced on me."

Whichever the case, DePugh and Cindy were taken before the U.S. commissioner in Kansas City. DePugh stood with his hands behind him at a parade rest as he scanned the three-count indictment against him, his attorney, William Costello, by his side. Cindy was brought next before the commissioner on a charge of assaulting a federal officer—Agent Belecky. DePugh's bond was set at $7500 and Cindy's at $5000. Both posted bond and were released.

Russell Millin, U. S. District Attorney for western Missouri, by then had called the grand jury back into session, reviewed the assault charge against Cindy and an indictment was returned against her, superseding the earlier charge.

The indictments had been returned almost two years from the day that Millin, the D.A., had said, in a statement:

"The Department of Justice has been aware of the activities of the Minutemen for several years. However, there is no action the government can take to curb those activities or to prosecute those responsible unless there is sufficient available evidence to establish that said activities are beyond the protected area of free speech, press and assembly guaranteed by the First Amendment of the Constitution, and in violation of some federal law. Such evidence is not now available . . ."

Now there appeared to be evidence.

As the other four men who had been indicted with DePugh were surrendering themselves peacefully over the next few days, DePugh was busy making preparations for a press conference and speech to some of his admirers at Kansas City's U-Smile Motel.

As wild as Husted's story was, DePugh may well have thought it was true at this time, just eight days after Husted had given it to him. As Ray said later, he had chosen the drug-and-padded-cell story because, "I thought it was something they'd believe," and indeed, the Minutemen are never lacking in suspicions of conspiratorial activity.

"The purpose of this meeting," DePugh told his audience, "is to ask you to join with me in asking for a congressional investigation of the gestapo tactics being used by the Federal Bureau of Investigation and similar law enforcement agencies."

He played the tape of Husted's statement and then asked, "Where is Ray Husted now?"

Wally Peyson had been unable to make bond immediately, and DePugh urged the audience to contribute money to free him. He complained that even known American Communists were bailed out on less than had been set on him and the other Minutemen.

He charged that the search of the car, upon his arrest, had been illegal and that Cindy had asked for a search warrant from the officers because the car was registered in her name. He called this "perhaps the most flagrant violation of a citizen's rights that I know of." He then asked Cindy to show the audience bruises he said she had suffered at the hands of the federal officers. DePugh conceded that Cindy was a "pretty husky girl," but observed that she was no match for three federal officers.

Sometime the following week, a letter may have gone out to members of the Minutemen over the signature of Mrs. Ramona Van DePugh, Robert DePugh's wife, asking for funds. I say "may have" because when I mentioned one paragraph of it to DePugh, he said he did not believe such a letter was sent. Sometimes, he said, fake letters on Minutemen stationery are mailed to some members by adversaries who try to cause trouble or confusion. This could have been such a letter. (I obtained a copy from someone I regard as trustworthy, but cannot vouch for its authenticity, since my source cannot either.)

The letter stated that the charges against DePugh and several of "our workers" were based on "manufactured evidence and the perjured testimony of paid government witnesses."

"We believe the time may come that loyal American citizens will be required to fight in the streets of our land to preserve this Constitutional Republic," the letter said. "If we have distributed information as to how weapons may be manufactured in such time of need, that is our right so long as freedom of speech and freedom of the press exist."

The letter then proceeded to contradict itself rather seriously. It stated first that DePugh "was out on bond the last part of this past week" and had held his press conference. Three paragraphs later, it declared:

"However, our work is going to be greatly handicapped *until Mr. DePugh* [my italics] and other workers—which include our printer—can be released on bond. The only reason they are in jail now is that we do not have the money to pay the fees. We must get them out as quickly as possible so we can work effectively in this critical time. Please send the largest possible contribution that you can for our Legal Defense Fund."

In other words, send in your money, folks, and free Bob DePugh from a jail he does not occupy. But then, as DePugh suggests, maybe this was a phony letter. It was suggested that all contributions be sent to the *Biolab Corp.*, P. O. Box 68, Norborne, Missouri, however.

District Attorney Millin filed a motion in U. S. District Court on September 2 seeking a psychiatric examination of DePugh to determine whether he was mentally able to stand trial.

This motion contained the report on DePugh's Army discharge in 1944, including how an Army psychiatrist had diagnosed DePugh's mental condition at the time.

DePugh's behavior since 1944, in the government's opinion, had not been such that it was assured—assuming he had been mentally ill in the Army—that his condition had improved much in the last twenty-two years.

"As titular head of an organization known as the Minutemen," the government had observed in this motion, "defendant DePugh has published or caused to be published and distributed material advocating bizarre and violent action against numerous and sundry persons.

"The court has been informed that defendant DePugh's mental condition has been seriously questioned by close friends and associates, and a police officer with the Independence police department has characterized him as 'a kook, a wild man and off his rocker.'"

The identity of the Independence police officer was not revealed, nor were his credentials as a psychiatrist.

Judge Elmo B. Hunter sustained the motion and ordered DePugh to be examined by a psychiatrist appointed by the court.

A legitimate question can be raised here, I think, as to the propriety of this motion's being made, of its being made a matter of public record, of it having been carried on page one of the Star, and of my inclusion of the psychiatric report in this book.

I handled rewrite of the story in the Star at the time and considered it front page news, as did my editors. And obviously I regard it as proper to mention here. But I have some reservations about this too. What kind of obligation were we under to print it? Did the public have a right to know? Or was this an invasion of privacy—by us, by the government?

Millin and Calvin Hamilton, his chief assistant (who succeeded Millin as D.A. in 1967), explained that the motion was made in the interests of giving DePugh a fair trial. If he was not mentally capable of understanding the charges against him or not able to assist in his own defense, they said, then this should be determined before the trial. Inclusion of the Army medical report was important if the judge was to have all the available evidence to help him in determining whether he should order a psychiatric examination. Had they omitted this from the motion, they said, they would have been derelict in their duties, for they would have not adequately informed the judge of all the facts.

This does not justify the use of an anonymous Independence policeman's diagnosis of DePugh as being "off his rocker," but to my mind does in most ways justify use of the 1944 report by the D.A.

As for our taking the report and telling others about it—DePugh's rights of privacy are severely limited because he has presumed to advise and guide those Americans who will follow him along a course of action which could prove of great danger to innocent persons in this country. It is not simply that he is a public figure. He has placed his personal integrity and his personal judgment up for review by the American people. If he was judged mentally ill twenty-two years ago, I feel as obligated to report this as Millin felt it necessary to tell Judge Hunter.

Army psychiatrists (whether in a hurry, as DePugh claimed, or not) can be wrong. And even if right, mental illness can be cured. But the examination was conducted, the diagnosis was made and it now has been made a part of public record in court. These are facts. And these are facts about a man who preaches revolution, in effect, in the United States, no matter what name he wishes to give it. Had he stuck to making Fidomin or Enzodine tablets for dogs— and had he not been indicted on charges that he had illegally involved himself with automatic weapons—there would have been no justification for anyone's going into his service jacket and revealing it, or for our reporting it. The court-appointed psychiatrist in 1966 found "there was nothing wrong with him in any respect mentally," as Judge Hunter eventually revealed in open court.

DePugh won his first court victory as a Minuteman in September in the Jackson County magistrate court of Harry E. Whitney. When DePugh was arrested on the federal indictments and the .38-caliber revolver was found in an attaché case in the car in which he was riding, a state charge of carrying a concealed weapon was filed against him. Magistrate Whitney ruled that evidence obtained at the time of the arrest had constituted illegal search and seizure and that the .38 had not been readily accessible as required for violation of the state's concealed-weapon statute. He dismissed the charge.

That was on September 13. A little more than two weeks later, the federal grand jury returned another indictment against DePugh, this time charging him with causing the same .38 to be transported from Des Moines to Kansas City while under indictment in state court on the charge of having committed a felony (the possession of bombs charge).

DePugh's legal problems by now were not only mounting but were becoming entangled with one another. Had DePugh not been indicted by the federal grand jury on the National Firearms Act charges, the federal officers would have had no occasion to arrest him and the .38 probably would never have been found. Had he not been under a county grand jury indictment for possessing bombs, there would have been nothing deemed unlawful about his having transported the .38 across the Iowa-Missouri state line.

DePugh meanwhile was having Ray Husted's signed statement reproduced and distributed over the country via the Patriotic Party, a Minutemen front organization he had set up in the meantime that year. With the reproduction of the statement was an article elaborating on it at length.

Near the end of the pamphlet was an emotional appeal for funds to help DePugh and other Minutemen meet their legal expenses. Readers also were urged to mail copies of the pamphlet to their Congressmen and Senators.

"Demand a congressional investigation of these gestapo tactics by United States Federal Agents," it urged. ". . . Time may be running out for your fellow patriots."

At the bottom was a special message from DePugh in which he stated that their legal expenses to date had amounted to $4800 and that bail-bond fees had totaled even more. The coming legal battle, he predicted, would cost between $20,000 and $50,000.

"Unless we receive a great deal of financial help from other American citizens, then we are sure to lose this case for lack of money to maintain a good legal defense," he wrote.

". . . You cannot secure your freedom by ignoring such a threat to the freedom of others. If you help us finance our legal battles today, it may save you a similar experience in the future. Do not deceive yourself into thinking that you can avoid this threat by 'staying out of trouble' or by remaining silent. We desperately need your financial assistance now. Send as large a contribution as you possibly can."

Richard Cotten, the radio commentator, rushed to DePugh's defense. His broadcast of September 7, 1966, told of a press conference at which DePugh had related the Moonlight Motel version of the Ray Husted story.

"This one of 200 people who were present listened in wide-eyed amazement and dead silence as did the reporters while Bob DePugh told the story of his harassment," Cotten said, "the allegations about the padded cell, the drug injections, etc., and at the end of that time they sat down and wrote letters to their Senators and Congressmen demanding a Congressional investigation which I believe is long overdue. . . ."

How much money was raised with such appeals has not been disclosed. That they prompted conservatives to write their Congressmen, however, is clear. J. Edgar Hoover was bombarded with inquiries about it.

As November 17, 1966, the date for the start of the federal firearms trial in Kansas City, approached, I was fascinated by the prospects of DePugh's defense attorneys introducing Husted's pro-Minutemen statement, and what its repercussions might be.

CHAPTER 14

JOIN THE MINUTEMEN

... Do *not* expect a "big round-up" of patriots. We will be picked up one by one for real or imaginary violations. You will have little or no warning when your time comes. . . .

From April 1, 1964, "On Target."

The federal firearms trial of Robert DePugh, Troy Houghton and Wally Peyson began as scheduled on Monday, November 7, 1966, despite pleas by their attorneys for a continuance.

The three Minutemen formed a pensive triangle at one end of the long defense table for the six days of the trial—five weekdays of one week and the Monday of the next. They dressed neatly each day, DePugh with a red, white and blue-tipped handkerchief peeping out of the breast pocket of his suit coat on some of those trying days. Wally was his usual natty self. Houghton, with a more limited wardrobe at his disposal because he was living out of a suitcase, was a trifle more rumpled in appearance, but nevertheless respectable. They conducted themselves with decorum in the jury's presence, attracting as little unnecessary attention to themselves as possible either by movements or facial expression. Frequently stoic, always attentive to what was being said from the witness stand, they occasionally smiled at one another or whispered confidences, but without cockiness or overconfidence and in as nonconspiratorial a manner as possible. None of the testimony visibly shook them, and considering some of the testimony, this took considerable restraint.

While the Minutemen organization technically was not on trial —as was pointed out in the trial more than once the nature of the government's case against its two best-known leaders and one of its top lieutenants was such that it became quickly clear this was not simply the trial of three gun buffs who had not paid enough attention to the complicated federal regulations on automatic weapons and pistol silencers.

Attempts by Judge Hunter to impanel a jury that had not been prejudiced by news media began immediately with the questioning of the seventy-nine men and women who had been brought together as the jury panel. The whittling down process took only about two hours. Three men were excused because they knew one of the defendants or a member of his family. Twenty-four were excused because they had heard, read or seen something about one or more of the defendants. Five more were excused because they had heard, read or seen something about a defendant in connection with his membership in "any organization." Eighteen more were temporarily excused when they answered they had heard or read about "an unincorporated association called the Minutemen," but they were then questioned individually and most remained on the panel.

Under questioning by Judge Hunter, out of the other prospective jurors' presence, various members of the panel displayed a wide range of impressions of the Minutemen. One panel member said he recalled that he had heard the Minutemen were "influenced by the Communist Party." Another, blushing slightly, told the judge he had heard a joke about the Minutemen, but was not required to tell it after explaining it was "of a sexual nature." Another panel member said flatly he did not think the Minutemen organization was "good for the United States government." While some had a generally accurate grasp of what the organization was all about, the over-all impression I received from the answers given was that I and the rest of the news media were not doing an adequate job in reporting on the Minutemen.

Of most immediate concern in the questioning was whether the jury panel had been influenced by news the previous week about a major development concerning the Minutemen in New York state. Those who had read of it and considered themselves influenced by what they had read, of course, were disqualified from serving on the jury.*

* The New York case is discussed more fully in Chapter 17. Eight days before this trial began, nineteen New Yorkers were arrested in raids and accused of having planned to bomb and burn three camps that had been used by left-wingers or Communists in the East. The nineteen were identified by the Queens district attorney as Minutemen. A huge arsenal of weapons and ammunition was confiscated. The story made the front pages of most daily newspapers. I hurried to New York and wrote several articles about the case from there for the *Star*. The big question for Kansas City readers, I reasoned, was whether these men were indeed members of DePugh's Missouri-based organization. I found concrete evidence that they were and reported it.

The "fair-trial–free-press" issue is involved here. We knew that DePugh was

Before narrowing the panel to sixteen, Judge Hunter asked them a variety of other questions. Had they ever received any Minutemen literature? Were any of them members of the Patriotic Party? Had they ever contributed money or worked in behalf of the Minutemen organization? Were any connected with the National Rifle Association? (Some said they were.) Were any of them connected with the W. E. B. Du Bois Clubs, the New England Committee for Non-Violent Action, The American-Russian Institute, the Communist Party, the National Council of American-Soviet Friendship, the Young Communist League? Did any of them subscribe to *The Worker, World News and Views, The Party Organizer, The National Guardian, People's World?*

By late Monday morning, the sixteen jurors and alternates had been sealed.

"I have got a problem, your Honor," volunteered one of the jurors. "I'm supposed to go quail hunting Thursday morning."

"If you had told me that earlier, that is the one excuse I think I would have honored," Judge Hunter said. "But unfortunately it comes a little too late, so there are going to be more quail at the end of this season than there ordinarily would be."

Before testimony began, the three counts of the indictments were explained to the jury and the thirty-five "overt acts" detailed in the conspiracy count were read.

All three defendants were charged in Count No. 1, which accused

<hr>

scheduled for trial the following week in Kansas City, and we knew that news stories that tied DePugh to the New York case would tend to be prejudicial against DePugh if the jury sitting in judgment of him had read them. But we also knew we had an obligation to report what had happened in New York, and to ascertain whether these New York Minutemen were connected in any way with the Missourian who called himself the Minutemen's national coordinator.

To me, there was no question what to do: Report the news. Judge Hunter, I reasoned incorrectly, probably would continue the trial until a later date, waiting for the New York case to blow over and DePugh's name to disappear from the front page of the *Star*. The judge, however, relied on the fact that there are plenty of potential jurors who do not read newspapers carefully (or, if they do, bypass articles about such subjects as the Minutemen) and do not listen to radio or TV news (or if they do, let a lot of information pass through one ear and out the other).

Four days before the trial was to begin, the judge did ask all the Kansas City news media to impose a voluntary blackout on Minutemen news until a jury was selected and locked up. We all agreed. The New York story had cooled by then anyway and nothing new of grave importance developed the next four days forcing a reconsideration of the agreement.

them of conspiracy to violate the National Firearms Act between May 31, 1963, and August 20, 1966, by transferring, making, receiving and possessing firearms that had not been registered as required by law. At issue were silencers and automatic weapons.

Count No. 2 was against DePugh and Peyson, charging that they had possessed an MP/40 Schmeisser machine pistol that had been made in violation of the law and on which the $200 "making tax" had not been paid.

Count No. 3 was also against DePugh and Peyson, charging they had possessed two machine guns and another machine pistol not registered with the government.

James Tollerton also had been charged on all three counts and John Blumer had been charged on the conspiracy count, but they were not being tried at this time. Tollerton appeared in the courtroom later that week as a government witness.

Most of the thirty-five "overt acts" in the conspiracy charge involved the defendants singly or in various combinations near Wentzville, Missouri (in northeastern Missouri), in Independence and Norborne, or at the Minutemen training session in August, 1965, a mile from the Mexican border in southern California. By the time the jury had heard all of the acts recited, they were well aware that this would be a long and complex case to hear.

In charge of presenting the government's case in such a way that the jurors could make sense of all of its complexities were Russell Millin, the U. S. Attorney for the Western District of Missouri, and Calvin K. Hamilton, his first assistant.

Millin had become district attorney in 1961 at the age of thirty-seven primarily with the backing of Senator Stuart Symington (D-Mo.). Tall (six feet, four inches) and quietly handsome, Millin is not given to dramatic histrionics but has a calm deliberateness in his courtroom manner that is decidedly persuasive. Throughout the trial, both he and Hamilton presented the picture of lawyers sure of themselves and their evidence.

Judge Elmo Hunter had been appointed a U. S. District Court judge in August, 1965, at the age of forty-nine, moving up from the Kansas City Court of Appeals. He enjoyed a reputation for fairness and careful attention to detail in the courtroom and the defendants had no reason to expect anything but a fair trial from him. However, they did have reason to fear that if convicted, their sentences could be considerably tougher than would be expected from some of the other federal judges in Missouri's Western District. His handling of organized crime cases had shown this beyond question. No one ever thought of him as a coddler of criminals.

It was ludicrous that before the trial I received worried inquiries about Judge Hunter from some liberal out-of-towners who were unfamiliar with the high respect he enjoyed in Kansas City. Their fear was that Hunter might be prejudiced in favor of the right wing. Why? They had learned to their horror that Judge Hunter's daughter had married a son of H. L. Hunt, the Texas billionaire who dabbles so frequently in ultraconservative causes. I assured these suspicion-prone doubters they had nothing to fear.

At the defense table with the three Minutemen throughout the trial were two veterans at criminal trial law in Kansas City—William H. Costello and William J. Gilwee, whom DePugh had picked himself. Some friction developed between the defense attorneys and their clients during the trial, especially the irascible Houghton, but the basic cause for this seemed to be that the defendants fancied themselves better versed in courtroom strategy and criminal law than they were, and the defense attorneys were saddled with a more difficult case to defend than the defendants wished to admit to themselves or their followers.

Among the defense's knottiest problems was how to successfully discredit government witnesses who once had been members of the Minutemen, without putting the organization and its leaders, who had accepted them once, in a bad light. Six of the government's most important witnesses once had belonged to or worked for the Minutemen.

The conspiracy count in the indictment was by far the most complicated to prove. Judge Hunter, in his closing instructions to the jury, explained that in a conspiracy according to the law, the accused must knowingly and willfully have become a member of the conspiracy and thereafter must have knowingly committed at least one of the overt acts charged in the indictment. The overt act must have been committed "in furtherance of some object or purpose of the conspiracy as charged," he also said.

". . . Conspiracy is a combination of two or more persons by a concerted action to accomplish some unlawful purpose or to accomplish a lawful purpose by unlawful means," the Judge said. "Thus a conspiracy is a kind of partnership in criminal purpose in which each member becomes the agent of every other member. The gist of the offense is a combination or agreement to violate or disregard the law."

The first five overt acts in the conspiracy count stated that DePugh, Houghton and Blumer had traveled to a point hear Wentzville, Missouri, on the Memorial Day weekend of 1963, and that DePugh and Blumer had possessed a machine gun there.

Two former Minutemen—an anesthetist at a hospital in Omaha, Nebraska, and the credit manager of a department store in St. Joseph, Missouri—were the government's two witnesses who had been at the training session near Wentzville. A thirty-five-year-old tool setter at the Lake City arsenal near Kansas City and his twenty-four-year-old wife were put on the stand by the defense to refute this Wentzville testimony.

At issue was simply one point: Was an automatic M3 submachine gun (called a "grease gun") in the trunk of DePugh's car at the training session near Wentzville? K. B. Kendall, the anesthetist, said it was. Al Sommerford, the St. Joseph credit manager, was not asked and did not say. David and Janette Agin, two defense witnesses, said it was not.

After Sommerford had testified to seeing Kendall, DePugh, Blumer, Houghton and Cindy Melville at the Wentzville training session, Kendall took the stand and testified at greater length about what he remembered having happened there.

He said he had met DePugh in the autumn of 1960 (he may have meant 1961) when DePugh was speaking at the Civic Auditorium in Omaha and had then joined the Minutemen. He had learned of the Wentzville session by mail.

"We were to drive to Wentzville," he said, "and were advised to pull into a parking lot at this certain restaurant there and at a given time there would be a car come in with a white cloth attached to the radio antenna of the car and we were to follow this car."

He did as instructed, he said, and arrived at the training site in predawn darkness. Later in the morning, DePugh arrived. When Kendall was asked whether he had seen DePugh with an automatic weapon while there, he replied:

"After Mr. DePugh got there, well, there was this other man and myself walked down by his car and there were some people. They were taking some pamphlets or literature, you know, printed matter, out of the trunk of the car."

In the trunk, Kendall said, was a fully assembled grease gun. Later, he added, he saw Blumer hold up a grease gun before the group that had assembled in a garage on the farm.

Agin (who said he was not a Minuteman, incidentally) and his wife testified that they had helped unload the trunk of DePugh's car at this training session and had found it filled completely with groceries. Neither had seen an automatic weapon in the car trunk or anywhere else at the training session, they said. Agin was able to remember in meticulous detail what type of foodstuffs had been contained in the trunk.

Another phase of the trial concerned DePugh in the summer of 1964 at Norborne. Sommerford, the department store credit manager, was the key witness on this matter.

After the trial, the November Minutemen bulletin to members commented on Sommerford's scathing testimony against DePugh as follows:

"Many members of the organization will remember Al Summerford [sic]. He attended the 1963 meeting at Wentzville and gave a very fine talk on underground warfare. He impressed everyone with his sincerity, ability and his professional knowledge. So much so, in fact, that he was later given a job in the National Headquarters. Other members will remember Al Summerford as one of the men who conducted the 1964 training sessions at Independence, Missouri. He is about forty years old, somewhat round-faced, has ears that stick nearly straight out from his head and usually wears his hair in a crew cut. Al speaks with a slow, soft voice and in a convincing manner. He is the person who gives the talk on the last half of side one and the first half of side two of Training Tape A-1.

"It would appear that Al worked a long time to infiltrate the organization. His efforts were terminated last week when he appeared as a government witness against the three defendants. Not only did Al Summerford testify to everything he could that would be damaging to the organization but he did so in a hateful and vindictive manner in which he referred to members of the organization as 'kooks and nuts.'"

Indeed he had, but the Minutemen bulletin could have been more specific. Defense attorney Costello, while cross-examining Sommerford, asked him under what circumstances he and DePugh had parted company.

"We had a dispute over a number of things that had been building up for several months," Sommerford said. "I can give you a long list for why I left the Minutemen."

"And?"

"One of the last straws that broke the camel's back was I refused to train a bunch of nuts and kooks into being assassins."

Costello immediately objected to the answer, claiming it was not responsive.

"He asked for it," Hamilton countered.

"Overruled," said Judge Hunter. ". . . I think it was within the question you asked him."

Neither Millin nor I (and perhaps the jury) had heard all of Sommerford's answer, for he had said it in a low voice. After the court session that day, I asked the court reporter what his full sentence had been. All I had heard was "nuts" and, I thought, "kooks." When she read back "into being assassins," Millin, who happened to be nearby, overheard it and became elated.

Before this remark by Sommerford, the ex-Minuteman had given damaging testimony concerning automatic weapons and silencers he said had been in DePugh's possession in mid-1964. Sommerford had left a job in Hutchinson, Kansas, to go to work at $115 a week for the Minutemen. He spent most of his time at Minutemen work but also performed chores for Biolab. He was paid with checks written on the Biolab account, he said.

Sommerford also testified about a document titled "How to Organize a Combat Team." DePugh had shown this to him, Sommerford said, and asked him for his opinion because of his experience in combat during the Korean war. Sommerford said he objected to the table of organization that had the team leader carrying a "machine pistol and 250 rounds in clips." A team leader has no time to fire an automatic weapon under fire in combat, he said, because he has his hands full directing his men. With this, Sommerford said, DePugh explained that this pamphlet had been prepared by the St. Louis coordinator, and he quoted DePugh as adding, "Well, you know how they are machine-gun crazy over there."

"Machine-gun crazy over there?" asked the government attorney.

"Yes," Sommerford said, "and he passed it off at that."

Another overt act in the conspiracy indictment stated that in April of 1965, DePugh had employed a gunsmith to design and manufacture machine guns at Independence. This was with reference to Jack Cannon, the grim young man who had been at 613 East Alton the evening Horridge, two Independence policemen and I had gone there in search of "kidnaper" DePugh. Cannon was never produced as a witness in the trial, however, because, the government said, it could not find him to serve him with a subpoena.

It is known that after the troubles in the summer of 1965 in Independence, Cannon, his wife and children had moved to Colorado where he had worked for a time in some capacity for Kenneth Goff, an ex-Communist turned right-wing minister and leader of the "Soldiers of the Cross" organization.

Ben A. Spann, manager of the Colorado School of Trade in Denver, was called as a government witness to testify that Cannon had learned gunsmithing in a sixteen-month course offered there in 1953 and 1954.

Jerry Brooks testified that DePugh had told him Cannon had been brought to Independence to manufacture fifty machine guns and that he was paid about $1000, plus room and board at 613 for him and his family.

Jerry Brooks also proved to be an important witness regarding five other overt acts alleged in the conspiracy part of the indictment. These concerned the training session at 613 in June, 1965, just before the kidnaping charges had been filed against DePugh and 613 had been raided. Jerry testified that Houghton had discussed automatic weapons at this training session, that he had seen five or six .45-caliber Thompson submachine guns, a Sten gun and a grease gun at 613 during this time, and that Houghton had fired a pistol equipped with a silencer into a barrel to demonstrate the effectiveness of silencers.

"What kind of a sound did it make?" Millin asked.

"Phhhsssst," Jerry replied wetly.

He was next asked whether the submachine guns he had seen had been operative.

"I'm not a gun expert," he replied.

"Did you look at the weapons?"

"Yes, sir."

"Did they have any plug in the barrel, a metal plug?"

"That I noticed, no."

Jerry also testified that he had heard DePugh tell Houghton and

Cindy Melville "that he had to get the machine guns out of there" at 613 because "there was going to be a raid."

In cross-examination, after ascertaining that Jerry had left DePugh and the Minutemen on December 4, 1965, Gilwee asked:

"You were trying to extort $300 from him, weren't you?"

"No, sir," replied Jerry.

"Did you tell him and his wife that if he didn't give you $300 he would be in bad trouble?"

"No, sir."

The purpose of Gilwee's question became clearer when Mrs. DePugh, wife of the national coordinator, took the stand.

She testified that she and Robert DePugh had brought Jerry and his mother to Norborne in October, 1964, to live in a house she owned. His mother, she said, was crippled and did not have the use of one arm or hand. Jerry, she said, was trained as a printer to work for the Biolab Corporation.

Shortly before Jerry left Norborne, she said, they had eaten lunch together in a dinette in the town. Jerry told her and her husband that he needed $300 in a hurry, for income tax he had not paid and for bad checks he had written. She quoted Jerry as telling her and DePugh:

"If you don't want bad trouble, I'll need $300 tomorrow, $300 the next day and more later—or else!"

They did not give him the money, she said, and in three days Jerry and his mother were gone.

Three overt acts in the indictment involved Houghton alone. They related back to the August, 1965, training session that James Clark had infiltrated for the California attorney general's office. Clark and Kenneth Dale Templeton, the thirty-nine-year-old Fairmount, California, heavy equipment operator who had defected from the Minutemen after the training session, testified against Houghton in this phase of the trial.

Clark and Templeton both told of seeing Houghton fire a silencer-equipped .22-caliber pistol in a demonstration before the group and Templeton said that he had fired it himself as well. Both men also told of that part of Houghton's lecture in which he discussed forthcoming instructions on how to make your own submachine gun.

Gilwee scored one point when he asked Templeton in cross-examination to read one line from the letter he had received inviting him to the training session—"All guns must be legal and not fully automatic. No exceptions"—but then, the government was not alleging automatic weapons had been present. Just a silencer.

The defense tried to make an issue over the question of why no state charges had been filed against Houghton for possession of a silencer. Clark replied that he had mentioned the silencer in his report to the attorney general's office, it being that office's responsibility, not his, to file charges. (I read a copy of Clark's report while in the California attorney general's office in Los Angeles and confirmed that he had, indeed, mentioned the silencer.)

Gilwee and Costello put four witnesses on the stand to rebut Clark and Templeton—Bettie Houghton, Troy's wife: Frederick W. Hawes, a fifty-six-year-old retired Navy captain and graduate of the Naval Academy at Annapolis: Kenneth Stanley Waite, a thirty-eight-year-old Arcadia, California, city employee, and Mrs. Francis Taber, the middle-aged wife of an El Monte, California, steamfitter.

All four said they had attended the training session, but had not seen a silencer-equipped pistol there. Bettie Houghton, dressed strikingly in a black suit and black gloves, confirmed that her husband had had a pistol at the session, but that no silencer had been attached to it.

The retired naval captain was obviously Houghton's prestige witness and he was impressive from the stand. He had known Houghton for five years, he said.

"I met him at a patriotic meeting," he told the jury, "got some of his literature; I read it; I approved of it. I have known him quite well."

He quoted Houghton on automatic weapons at the training session, saying that Houghton had told the group "there were so many restrictions and red tape to it that it was practically impossible for the normal citizen to have one."

Fifteen of the overt acts dealt with the November, 1966, activities of Ray Husted, Wally Peyson and, to a lesser extent, DePugh and James Tollerton, as they related to the four submachine guns and one .50-caliber machine gun that had been found buried in northwest Missouri.

It was this complex story that took the longest to tell. Husted's testimony—much of which already has been described here earlier—tied nearly everything else offered on this subject together. Jim Tollerton also helped in this respect.

The government attorneys wove testimony about those five automatic weapons together neatly. The sheriff of Carroll County, Missouri, told how Husted had led him and FBI and ATTU agents to the submachine guns by the Coloma cemetery. ATTU agent John F. Smith told of this trip and identified the submachine guns in the courtroom as those that had been dug up. An employee of Klein's Sporting Goods store in Chicago told of how one of the four weapons from the cemetery cache had been a "DEWAT" (deactivated war trophy) once in the possession of his store, and how it had been stolen while on display in April, 1963. (The weapon in the courtroom had a new barrel and could fire, but the serial numbers matched.) A Chicago policeman was brought in to verify that the DEWAT had been reported stolen from Klein's.

It was not established who had stolen the weapon, but the picture was becoming clear. There are many DEWATS over the country. The Minutemen urge members to acquire them. The Minutemen employ gunsmiths. A gunsmith easily can reactivate a DEWAT. Eventually the reactivated weapons are buried. As simple as that.

Clellie Calvert, the farmer who had rented "the old Billy Robinson place" to Wally, made a refreshing witness as he told about his relationship with Wally as "Walter Petri," who had identified himself as a would-be poet in search of peace and quiet.

After Husted had led agents to the caches and had informed Mr. Calvert of what they had found in the hole beneath the closet of the house, the farmer happened across Peyson and offered him some fatherly advice.

"Well, I first said to him, 'Boy,'—I always called him, 'Boy,' he seemed to like it, to me—I said, 'Boy, I believe that whatever you are doing or whatever you are into, I believe I would pull away. You are a nice kid,' and I thought a lot of him, I still do. I said, 'I would pull away from that deal. It's no good for you.' And he didn't answer me. I'm going to be honest. He didn't answer me."

When Gilwee cross-examined Mr. Calvert, he asked him: "You think he is a pretty nice fella, don't you?"

"I think he's a nice boy," answered Mr. Calvert. "He appeared to be one of the nicest boys I believe I ever met in my life, and I've seen a lot of boys."

"You still think that?" asked Gilwee.

"I still think he's a nice boy. Can be, yes sir."

Two employees of the lumber company that sold Wally two-bytwelves, which he had used to make a roof for the hole under the closet at the Billy Robinson place, were questioned about the sale. A handwriting expert for the ATTU, Howard Doulder of Chicago, was used to compare the signatures of Walter Patrick Peyson and "Walter Petri."

Gerald D. Johnson, a Chicago citizen, testified that he once had owned an MP/40 Schmeisser submachine gun, serial number 6575, but that it had been inoperable when he sold it to a souvenir shop in 1962. An operable MP/40 Schmeisser submachine gun with that serial number happened to be government exhibit No. 13 in the trial, another of the weapons dug up near Coloma.

Sidney Anderson, another ATTU agent, testified with the most effective prop at the trial—the big .50-caliber machine gun he said he had found in the hole at the Billy Robinson place.

As deputy federal marshals carried the weapon and the 953 rounds of ammunition that had been found with it into the courtroom, the jury was visibly impressed with its size and fearsome appearance.

Many of the weapon's shells were in belts, which the deputy marshals had slung over their shoulders in order to free their arms for carrying other loose rounds. The clips clicked noisily against one another on the belts, adding to the awesome nature of this, the government's key "silent witness," as Millin called it, exhibit No. 74.

Much ado was made by defense counsel over the "prejudicial" nature of this weapon's mere appearance in court and the jury was instructed not to consider it as it related to the case against Peyson. (There had been some question raised in pre-trial motions over the legality of the search that had uncovered this weapon.) After Anderson was through telling how he had found it, the weapon was removed from the courtroom and in just as noisy a fashion as it had been introduced.

Anderson testified that everything needed to make an operable .50-caliber machine gun had been found in three packages in the hole. All that was missing, he said, was a traversing mechanism that served as the linkage between the weapon and its tripod. Gilwee made a point of this in his closing argument, pointing out that without that linkage, the machine gun would not fire accurately, for it was big enough to make its firer "shake like a go-go girl."

But Husted's testimony was most critically important, a fact that the defense feared from the start.

For those in the courtroom who were aware of the Moonlight Motel episode in August, 1966, additional drama began to build as time approached for the defense counsel's cross-examination. Would they dare bring out Husted's statement of padded cells and drug injections?

Gilwee objected to Husted's testifying at all before the young Air Force cook began. ". . . It is apparent from the holding of the court," he said, "that this man was working with a government agent and had entrapped the defendants."

This did not sound like an argument that would lead the jury inside the Moonlight Motel. Not at all. For Husted could not have "entrapped" the Minutemen in November, 1965, if it was not until December that the FBI "brainwashed" him.

Another phrase Gilwee used frequently as Husted's testimony began to hang more heavily over the defense table was that Husted had worked "at the instance" of the government when he went to the farmhouse with Wally to dig their massive hole.

The defense objections were overruled and Ray Husted was allowed to testify. He nailed down the government's case solidly. The Moonlight Motel was never mentioned, nor was anything that had happened there that rainy August night.

(Gilwee explained to me after the trial why he had stayed away from it. Once it was brought out in testimony that Husted had written the FBI more than a month before he had defected from Norborne, offering his services, Gilwee did not feel safe in bringing up the brainwash statement. Besides, he said, he was trying to prove, through Husted, that DePugh had been the victim of entrapment by the government in November. To allege at the same time that the FBI had forced Ray to give them information in mid-December would have destroyed the entrapment argument. I cannot help but imagine that the defense counsel felt also that they would have had an exceedingly hard time persuading the jury that the FBI would use such tactics.)

Under direct examination, Husted—cool, precise, a bit condescending toward the defense attorneys—told of how he had happened to go to work with the Minutemen in Norborne, of his chores at 408 South Pine, of his nighttime trips with Wally and James Tollerton as they rounded up the various submachine guns and ammunition and finally took them to the old Billy Robinson place. He quoted Wally as saying, "We are going to build a weapons cache." Once he and Wally had entered the farmhouse, he began securing the house with extra locks on the doors and nailing the windows, he said, all at Wally's suggestion.

He tied DePugh with the weapons in three ways: He saw one automatic weapon and parts of others at the Biolab office while in the
presence of Wally, Jerry and young John DePugh (Jerry testified to
the same thing); DePugh had visited the farmhouse midway through
their hole-digging and had inspected the hole; and DePugh had driven
them to the cemetery near Coloma before they buried the submachine
guns and had picked them up near there afterward.

He told of writing a letter to the FBI on November 11, more than a
month before he departed the scene, of leading agents to the cemetery,
giving Sidney Anderson a key to the farmhouse, breaking into 408
South Pine while two FBI agents waited for him on a side street in
Norborne, and enlisting in the Air Force (he called this "a sudden
decision").

Gilwee pounced on Husted for his break-in, referring to it repeatedly
as a burglary and trying to tie the FBI into it as something of a silent
accessory. Husted held up fairly well, however, and Millin brought out
in redirect examination that Husted had simply asked the FBI agents
for a ride to Norborne to collect his belongings without letting them
know he had had to break into the house to obtain them. Husted had
left other valuables of his own behind in "exchange" for the ready cash,
it was also brought out, as was the fact that Husted had been paid no
salary by the Minutemen for his work in Norborne.

Later, Millin asked Husted whether Peyson had made any statements
to him about any other weapons caches. Husted replied he had.
"He described the procedure for getting the Billy Robinson place and
told me it was a way he had gotten to find other places for other
caches," Husted said.

James Tollerton, under indictment himself, but not on trial at the
moment, seemed more reluctant to talk about the acquisition and
disposal of the weapons. After meeting Wally and Ray for dinner at
Linneus, they had driven together to start picking up "packages" at
various points. Husted, he said, did most of the talking on the way. He
quoted Husted as saying, "We're going to pick up machine guns and
ammunition."

"What did Mr. Peyson say, if anything?"

"I can't remember what he said. . . . It was all just a general discussion."

"Did Mr. Peyson participate in the discussion?"

"Well, yes. We all discussed this."

"You all discussed that you were going to pick up machine guns?"

"Yes."

No rebuttal witnesses were offered to counter testimony on these fifteen overt acts.

The November 14 Minutemen bulletin, discussing revelations and problems of the trial after it was over, gave this version of the testimony of James Moore, ATTU agent from Omaha, who covered one other overt act mentioned in the indictment:

"Members who attended the July third and fourth meeting of the Patriotic Party may remember a likable young man about thirty who walked with a cane. He was thin, about six feet tall, neatly dressed and wore glasses. He went under the name of Jim Wilson. After that, Jim Wilson stopped in at our headquarters three or four times to tell Mr. DePugh that he knew where some machine guns could be obtained and urged us to buy them. Mr. DePugh told Mr. Wilson that he wasn't interested.

"As the trial proceeded, Jim Wilson minus his cane and glasses and going under his right name of Jim Moore properly identified himself as an undercover agent of the Treasury Department's Alcohol and Tobacco Tax Division."

Moore took the defendants by surprise when he walked into the courtroom, for until that moment, the Minutemen had thought Wilson to be a faithful party worker. As mentioned earlier though, DePugh remained cool as Wilson-Moore stepped into view.

Moore told of a conversation with Houghton in Independence during a Minutemen training session that apparently had been held in conjunction with the Patriotic Party's first national convention:

"One of the members of the group—I don't recall who—brought up the subject [of automatic weapons] and Mr. Houghton stated that he had one particular machine gun which was as he termed it rather 'junky' or constructed from parts of other firearms, but which nevertheless fired fully automatic.

"He stated on one particular occasion that he kept no automatic firearms in his home. If an agent searched his home he would find nothing, and that he kept a cache of what he termed 'critical materials' in the High Sierras."

"High Sierras?"

"Yes, sir. He also distributed a group of training texts, one of which related to machine guns."

"Did you obtain one of these which related to machine guns?"

"Yes, sir, I did," and Moore identified it as the same one James Clark had obtained from Houghton at the training session he had infiltrated in California.

Moore continued by stating he had asked Houghton what was the best way to obtain guns without having a record made of the purchaser so as to avoid its being traced back to him.

". . . He pulled from his wallet what I recognized as a federal firearms dealer's license," Moore said. ". . . He showed this to me briefly and I could see that it was not his name on it, although I don't remember what the name was. . . . As he displayed this, he said, 'This is what I use.' I tried to get a better look at it but Mr. Houghton smiled and held on to it and said, 'Well, I have got it under a different name.'"

Moore also had a parting parry for Peyson. During a break between lectures the previous summer, as the participants stood around in small groups talking, Moore said, he overheard someone ask Wally a question that related to machine guns. He said he heard Wally reply:

"It's getting so hard to get them that we have taken to making our own."

Gilwee, intent on making a case of illegal entrapment against the government to save his clients, was more interested, while cross-examining Moore, in the relationship between Moore and DePugh *after* DePugh had been indicted in August.

". . . Did you attempt to sell him [DePugh] or offer to sell him or offer to procure machine guns for him?" Gilwee asked.

"I said that I was planning to procure some machine guns," answered Moore coolly.

"You were planning to procure some machine guns?"

"Yes, sir, and I did ask Mr. DePugh if he was interested in them."

"And you were then with the Alcoholic Tax Unit?" Gilwee asked, presumably not intending to be funny.

"Yes, sir."

"And you went down there with the intention of entrapping him into buying machine guns, didn't you?"

"No, sir, I did not."

Following a long series of questions and answers on this subject, Moore summed it up with:

"I told Mr. DePugh I thought I might have an opportunity to acquire some machine guns and I asked him what would be a proper amount to pay for them and Mr. DePugh answered that for Thompson submachine guns the usual price was $150, for a Schmeisser or a grease gun, I believe he said $75 to $100. He then told me that sometimes you can find a machine gun in the possession of a dealer or a collector who was afraid to have it and wanted to get rid of it, in which case you could get it for lower prices, which he quoted. He then said, 'I [DePugh] had done this.'"

"Those are the collector's items?" asked Gilwee.

"We were talking about live machine guns, sir," replied Moore.

"Well, you don't buy live machine guns from gun collectors, do you?" asked Gilwee.

"If they have live machine guns," said the agent.

The overt acts of the conspiracy count and the particulars of the other two counts had been covered, but the nature of the Minutemen organization, in which this conspiracy had been nurtured and had blossomed, had been revealed in a variety of ways to the jury at the same time.

In cross-examination, Jerry Brooks had provided the jury with some of the most unusual testimony it could expect to have received. After admitting he had brought up the idea of putting cyanide in the air-conditioning vents of the UN building in New York, he was asked by Gilwee whether he also had not brought up the idea to assassinate Senator Fulbright. Jerry would have none of that. Under redirect examination by Millin, Jerry tried to elaborate on his denial.

"And was there anything else said that you can recall by Mr. DePugh about assassinating people?" asked Millin.

"Yes, sir," Jerry replied. "There were discussions regarding—" and he turned to Judge Hunter. "Your Honor, I don't know if I would be out of order, but the defense attorney asked me if I was the one that promoted the idea of killing Senator William Fulbright of Arkansas. I would like to say that the . . ."

Gilwee objected, but Judge Hunter allowed Jerry to explain.

"The FBI of Kansas City, Missouri, questioned me," Jerry said. "Mr. George Arnett and Maurice Daniels, agents of the FBI, came to my house in Kansas City, Missouri, at 3021 McGee Street and asked me if I knew anything of a plot to kill William Fulbright, that they had heard rumors. I could name the people involved if you want me to do that also."

"I don't think that is necessary," said Millin.

"They were aware of the plot," Jerry continued, "and they were well aware of the people who were going to fulfill the plot, and it was not made [carried out]."

"Did you furnish them information?" asked Millin.

"Yes, sir."

"No further questions."

As he had done with Brooks, Gilwee tried to discredit Kenneth Templeton, the Californian, by bringing out some of his background. He read an excerpt from Templeton's application to join the Minutemen (". . . I believe that the last Jew administrations have been selling us down the tube and the present one intends to finish the job. . . ."), but Hamilton was able to throw this back at Houghton and DePugh.

"Were you accepted into this organization on the basis of this application setting forth your views?" Hamilton asked him.

"Yes, I was," replied Templeton.

"Did Mr. DePugh or Mr. Houghton express any objections to the views that you expressed?"

"Apparently not."

"Were you asked to change your views?"

"No."

". . . Was anything said by them whether or not these were their views?"

"Well, I was under the impression that everyone in the organization held about the same views."

The government rested its case on Thursday afternoon after three and a half days of testimony. The defense took over on Friday morning. The Agin couple testified first about Wentzville. Then up to the witness stand stepped young Dennis Patrick Mower, pink-cheeked, chubby and, as Millin soon showed, quite vulnerable to cross-examination.

Dennis was the young side-kick of Houghton who had driven with Houghton to Independence in the summer of 1965 to attend the training session at 613 East Alton. It had been Mower's deactivated submachine gun that had been found hidden in a furnace pipe in the building's basement while police were looking for "kidnaper" DePugh. And Mower—according to Houghton—had been upstairs at 408 South Pine in Norborne ready to destroy Minutemen records when police raided that house later, still looking for DePugh. Now he had made a second trip to Missouri with Houghton.

Under questioning by defense counsel, Dennis made a fairly good impression. He was a theology student, he said, from Lancaster, California. He had known Troy Houghton for five years.

But why would a theology student take a deactivated Thompson submachine gun to Independence? Why, to let Houghton use it on a lecture on gun safety at the training session, said young Dennis, naturally. And maybe to sell it.

This weapon had been referred to in Brooks' testimony earlier. But what little the defense had hoped to gain by putting Mower on the stand was quickly lost when Millin began his cross-examination.

Millin started slowly, asking about Dennis's role in the Minutemen. Dennis said he was a former member. Millin asked him if he now had his own organization in California. Yes, Dennis replied, the Southern California Freedom Councils. Had he ever had any business dealings with Houghton? Well, yes, in their "patriotic work" together.

Soon Dennis was led artfully into the subject of his theological studies. They were under Dr. Wesley Swift of the Church of Jesus Christ, Christian, Dennis said. And how many students studied under Dr. Swift? Well, two at the moment, but other ministers of the church elsewhere have other students, Dennis said. And what kind of study was involved? Theological research, said Dennis. There were lots of books to read.

"Dr. Swift's thesis is that the white race is the lost children of Israel," Millin said suddenly, "and all other races are inferior. Correct?"

"Yes, sir," said Dennis after a pause.

"You were a defense witness in a case of a Mr. Gilbert who was charged with illegal possession of explosives, weren't you?" Millin asked.

"Yes."

"Objection!" but the dam had burst on Dennis Mower.

Millin asked him about instructions his Southern California Freedom Councils had once put out urging members not to talk with FBI agents. Dennis allowed that such instructions had more or less been put out, yes.

But Millin had more. Had Dennis known Walter Patrick Peyson when Wally was a student under Dr. Swift?

Yes.

And yet more.

"Have you seen Troy Houghton taking pictures of witnesses as they came out of the courthouse this week?" he asked.

"No," said Dennis.

Others had.

In his closing argument, Millin conceded to the jury that he may have gone a bit far in cross-examining the young theology student, "but I wanted you to see what was behind that bland, affidavit face," he explained, and indeed, the jury had been shown just that.

Millin was more generous with the other defense witnesses, especially Mrs. DePugh and Mrs. Houghton. He barely questioned Bettie Houghton at all, and limited cross-examination of Mrs. De-Pugh to only a few exploratory questions, apparently nibbling around to see just how sympathetic a picture she presented to the jury, this mother of six, with one boy in Vietnam.

Suddenly, by late afternoon, Friday, the defense was out of witnesses. Just seven had appeared. The defendants were not going to take the stand. But the defense was not ready to rest. There then occurred a sequence of events that in any other trial would have seemed remarkable. With the Minutemen, however, only the unpredictable is predictable.

Houghton had been growing annoyed all week at his attorneys. He had not shown it in front of the jury, but in the hallway, during recesses, he did not try to hide his irritation with the way the trial was going. By Friday afternoon he was stomping back and forth in the corridor, snapping at the lawyers, then pleading with them, then walking away from them in seething anger.

After the last defense witness had left the courtroom, the defense asked that the jury be sent out of the room so that a new problem could be discussed with the judge. Houghton, it seemed, wanted a continuance of the trial until Monday.

This was a lock-up jury. Great pains had been taken to keep them from newspapers, television, radio and their friends and families. To continue this over Saturday and Sunday, from the defense standpoint, was a dangerous move. Jurors do have feelings, after all, and can become as annoyed as anyone else. But Houghton persisted. He had four more witnesses in California whom he wished to bring to Kansas City. They could not arrive until Sunday or Monday.

After hearing what Houghton had to say about the importance of his four absent California witnesses, the judge asked DePugh how he felt about a two-day continuance.

"I was just asking my attorney if we would be limited to these people Monday," DePugh replied.

"Yes, sir, you certainly will," Judge Hunter said. "All other witnesses that you have, you have the opportunity of putting on right now."

"Well, frankly, your Honor, we have had so little time in this matter that I have had very little opportunity to confer with my counsels," DePugh complained.

"You have been here all week with them," the judge said.

"We have been awful busy, your Honor," said DePugh.

Judge Hunter was not visibly moved, but did tell DePugh and Peyson that he did not want to grant a two-day continuance if they opposed it. He also told them that if they had any other witnesses to produce, put them on the stand that afternoon or not at all. DePugh asked for a ten-minute recess so he could talk with his lawyers. The judge agreed to this, but before they left the courtroom, DePugh asked to address the court.

He complained that he had been led to believe the trial would last two or three weeks, giving him one and possibly two weekends in which to talk with his attorneys about bringing forth an entire block of additional defense witnesses.

". . . I simply have the personal feeling that I, for one, would not have a fair trial unless I have an opportunity to counsel at considerable length with my attorneys as to the advisability of bringing in these other witnesses," DePugh said. ". . . I remember your Honor's statement to me one time that it was your intention to afford us a fair trial and I have voiced my honest opinion in this matter."

"Mr. DePugh, do you have any feeling that your trial hasn't been fair so far as I am concerned to date?" Judge Hunter asked.

"Not so far as your Honor is concerned, no," said DePugh, "but I feel that the circumstances have been such that I was possibly inadvertently misinformed as to the length of this trial and due to the unanticipated speed with which the other witnesses have been dealt with, I simply have not been afforded the opportunity of counsel that I feel could be very important to the outcome of this case."

"All right, sir, now let me make a reply to your very frank statement," the judge said. "This indictment . . . as I recall, was returned on or about the twenty-fourth of August. If my memory is correct, you gentlemen were all here and arraigned on or about September second of this year. At the time of the arraignment, I set this case for trial for November seventh. I explained to you gentlemen in some detail that that was a firm trial setting and that I intended to stand by it and that one of the reasons that I wanted to stand by it was that I was having difficulty with you causing publicity and I did not want to have any publicity occur whether occasioned by you or anyone else that might deprive you of a fair trial. And for that reason it would be a firm date to hold down on the publicity that might be engendered and to get this case moving along.

"That was over two months that you had to prepare your case, because you then had counsel of your own employment and had them available. So you have had counsel available to you for over two months.

"Now I am like many other people—I have noted in the newspaper where you have been traveling about the country various places carrying on your business as usual, I presume, and you could have used some of that time to have been consulting with your attorneys and to be preparing your case. Two months is an adequate time in my judgment, and I felt that any further delay would not be to your interests, but would be contrary to your interests. So I set that date and I certainly made it clear it was firm. Since that time we have had I guess somewhere between twenty and thirty motions filed against the case of one nature or another, and at every hearing we have had in relation to those motions, I have again announced that this case would be tried on November seventh."

Judge Hunter then observed that no one can predict with certainty how long a trial will last.

"For example, Mr. DePugh, if you and your co-defendants had elected to take the stand this case might well have gone on for another three, four, five, six or even seven days," he said. "If your attorneys had gone into more lengthy cross-examination this case could have lasted a good deal longer. If the government had used other witnesses or had prolonged its cross-examination, it would have prolonged the trial of this case. These are all matters of trial tactics. They are decisions that are made during the course of the trial. Nobody can say with any certainty how long a case will take to try. . . ."

After the ten-minute recess DePugh and Peyson registered no objection to Houghton's request and the judge called the jury back into the courtroom.

"Members of the jury," Judge Hunter began, "when you left the courtroom, it was for the purpose of the court hearing a motion presented by defendant Houghton asking that the case be continued over until Monday morning in order to give him additional opportunity . . ."

It was fascinating to watch the faces of the jurors at this point.

". . . to present four witnesses which he advises that he believes he can have present Monday morning. . . ."

Was "disappointment" the best word to describe those expressions?

". . . I well realize that the burden of granting such a continuance falls on you, gentlemen. The case is completed except for these four witnesses and I had planned that we would finish this case tonight or if there were any additional witnesses that we would finish it in the morning . . ."

Houghton had goofed.

". . . and submit it to you early tomorrow afternoon. But in view of the request of defendant Houghton he be granted this continuance and to assure him of a fair trial in every respect, I have granted the request. I regret that I can't release you from sequestration order. . . ."

So did they.

". . . I must continue to have you under it for the duration of the trial. I will do what I can to see if we can't provide you gentlemen with some reading material that has nothing to do with any aspect of this case. I will see perhaps if we can work it out so that you can watch the football games on television. I might even be able to work it out so you can see a picture show if you want, all in the custody of one of our assistant marshals. I can simply say to you I will see you Monday morning at nine-thirty when we will continue with the remaining witnesses in this case. . . ."

Houghton's four California witnesses, it was agreed among by-standers as the courtroom emptied Friday night, had better be strong.

They weren't. Two of them didn't even show up.

Kenneth Stanley Waite, thirty-eight years old, of Arcadia, California, an engineering draftsman employed by the city of Arcadia, said he had met Houghton at the August, 1965, training session near the Mexican border. Yes, he once had been a member of the Minutemen. No, he hadn't seen Houghton with a silencer at the training session. Yes, Houghton had discussed automatic weapons, but only on what was legal and what wasn't—in fact, he said, everyone had been cautioned not to buy illegal ones.

An attempt to establish Waite's credibility was made by referring to "undercover" work he was doing at the moment for the district attorney for Los Angeles County. This boiled down to the fact that he was being used as contact man, properly wired for sound, with a man who was trying to pedal machine guns. Only part of his "undercover" story was deemed allowable for the jury's ears.

Houghton's other Monday witness, Mrs. Fran Taber, the steam-fitter's wife, was brief and in line with what the other defense witnesses had said about the training session in California with Houghton. The defense rested.

Following closing arguments and Judge Hunter's long instructions to the jury, the jurors were sent to deliberate. It was 3:27 o'clock Monday afternoon.

That period of time after 3:27 o'clock naturally was tense on the sixth floor of the federal courthouse building. Observing the judge's dictum on not talking with the defendants until the end of the trial, I found the most likely Minuteman to chat with was the Reverend Robert LeRoy, who carried the unlikely title of "chaplain" of the Minutemen. I had seen the Reverend LeRoy at a meeting two months earlier, but had not met him. He was a rather humorless but nonetheless pleasant fundamentalist in his early forties.

Whatever the outcome, he said, Romans 8:28 seemed to him to apply to the case: "And we know that all things work together for good to them that love God, to them who are the called according to His purpose."

He was determined to be optimistic, although it seemed to most of us who had watched the trial that the only defendant with the slightest chance for acquittal was Houghton, since he was charged only in the conspiracy count.

"Even if they must spend time in prison," the Reverend LeRoy said, "it could give them an opportunity to be nearer to God."

This led inevitably into an analysis of the defendants' religious make-up.

He didn't know Houghton well enough to say, but Wally Peyson he knew, and Wally was a "devout Christian," the Reverend LeRoy said. As for DePugh: "He takes his religion seriously, I'll put it that way."

The jury returned seventy-one minutes after leaving the courtroom. The defendants and their attorneys walked back to the defense table and Millin and Hamilton took their familiar positions. The spectators crowded in behind them.

The verdict: All three defendants were guilty, on all counts charged.

There would be a pre-sentence investigation—a study of the defendants' backgrounds—before passing sentence, Judge Hunter said, and defense counsel were given thirty days in which to file motions for a new trial. The defendants would remain free on bond. The judge thanked the jury and the courtroom slowly cleared.

"No comment," DePugh told newsmen politely.

"No comment," said Peyson, also politely.

"No comment," said Houghton with a weak smile.

"If they're sent to prison," predicted the Reverend LeRoy, "the prison will be picketed."

The maximum penalty for DePugh and Peyson was fifteen years in prison, for Houghton, five years.

Speculation on what they would receive seemed to run from a suspended sentence and long period of probation to one or two years in prison for each. But no one really knew what to expect. In chambers, Judge Hunter said he would probably pass sentence in about three weeks.

And everyone went home.

CHAPTER 15

JOIN THE MINUTEMEN

There is no travesty of justice too rank to be carried out in the sanctimonious dignity of a courtroom.

Blueprint for Victory

This was a black day for the Minutemen organization. After a week-long trial, Robert DePugh, Walter Peyson and Troy Houghton were found guilty on the charge of conspiracy to violate the National Firearms Act. . . .

The loss of one battle does not mean that we have lost the war. Other people will continue the work of both the Minutemen and the Patriotic Party to the best of their ability. We will never surrender and who knows—we may even win. . . .

Meanwhile, we don't feel that anyone can give us quite the same degree of optimism and inspiration that we have received from Bob DePugh. It will be tragic indeed if the conservative movement is deprived of his leadership for lack of sufficient money to finance this necessary appeal to a higher court. Whatever sacrifice we may be called on to make to keep him out of jail will be well worth it.

Every member should redouble his efforts to recruit and organize locally. Each member must make a special effort to support the National organization to the full extent of their financial ability. Each member should train himself for the long struggle ahead. We may retreat but we will never surrender.

From the November 14, 1966, Minutemen Bulletin to members.

The defense decision not to bring out Ray Husted's Moonlight Motel statement came in for considerable discussion after the initial shock of the jury's decision had begun to wear off the partisan Minutemen rooters and a search for scapegoats had begun.

The jury foreman's remark after the trial that he thought Husted had been the key witness ["everyone was influenced by the testimony by Mr. Husted"] added urgency to the need for the Minutemen to belabor this point, criticizing Gilwee and Costello unfairly in the process.

I immediately tried to seek Husted out for an interview but found that he had quickly flown off for Massachusetts and more Air Force duty.

In the course of finding Husted by telephone, I learned to my surprise that J. Edgar Hoover was decidedly annoyed about Husted and in fact had made unofficial replies to numerous queries about Husted's allegations against his agents in Kansas City. Normally Hoover would not dignify such charges with a reply, I had been led to believe.

"I can emphatically state that they are complete fabrications with absolutely no foundation in fact," Hoover had replied. "I have never tolerated any misconduct in the FBI and I can certainly assure you that if a special agent of this bureau behaved in such a manner, he would be summarily dismissed from the service."

The two agents whom the Minutemen had accused of such skulduggery were, indeed, still at work in the Kansas City FBI office at this writing.

This hardly placated the Minutemen. Richard Cotten, the radio commentator, decided to intensify his campaign in behalf of what he felt was justice for DePugh, Houghton and Peyson, all of whom he said he knew as friends. In one of his December radio broadcasts, he proclaimed:

"The question that comes to my mind is this: Had the jury known that their 'star witness'—this man whom they trusted because they saw him place his hand on a Bible and swear a holy oath—on another occasion had placed his hand on a Bible and sworn an *equally* holy oath that the FBI had kidnaped, drugged and threatened him *unless* he gave his testimony, would they have given his testimony the same credence? Of course they wouldn't! And the question we must ask is *why* was the jury not informed as to the nature of this 'star witness'?"*

Before making this broadcast, Cotten had telephoned me from Shreveport, Louisiana, and asked for a first-hand account of what had happened at the trial. I made it clear to him that the defense attorneys could have introduced Husted's Moonlight Motel statement into the trial if they had wished to do so, but they had elected not to for reasons of their own. I am still uncertain whether this was a wise decision by the lawyers, but am inclined to think they were prudent in leaving it alone.

* A Bible, incidentally, was not used in swearing in witnesses at the trial. (Cotten had not been present for the trial.)

Introduction of the motel statement into evidence by the defense would have opened up entirely new areas of exploration to the government attorneys. The performance of the D.A. and his first assistant in the trial showed clearly they were well prepared. Considering how effectively they presented their case and cross-examined some of the defense witnesses, it seems logical to assume that they could have turned the motel statement to their own advantage before they were through. It is debatable, of course.

On January 4, 1967, DePugh, Houghton and Peyson returned to Judge Hunter's courtroom for a hearing on motions for a new trial. Vainly, DePugh and Houghton and both their defense attorneys attempted to establish that their telephones had been tapped at various times before and after the indictment.

But none could prove his allegation. The lawyers and the two Minutemen leaders spoke at length of the strange behavior of their telephones at various times and each Minuteman said that FBI agents had indicated to him through their questioning that they had information obtainable only through a telephone tap.

Frank Belecky, the ATTU supervisor in Kansas City, was put on the stand briefly and asked by Millin:

"I want to ask you whether or not, to your knowledge, any kind of electronic device was used in obtaining evidence that led to this indictment? And when I say any type of electronic device, I include any bug or any tap on a telephone or any such equipment?"

Belecky's reply was an unqualified, "No, sir. None whatsoever."

"Have you discussed the matter with your agents since this motion was filed and have you reached the positive conclusion that no such evidence was obtained in this case?"

"Yes, sir, I have," replied Belecky.

Judge Hunter ended the hearing with the information that on January 17, he would announce his ruling on the motions for a new trial and, if he overruled those motions, would at that time pass sentence.

All three defendants returned on that date as scheduled, none of them optimistic over what they expected to befall them. They did not expect the judge to grant them a new trial. And they had cause for apprehension over their sentences.

DePugh, Houghton and Peyson took their familiar positions at the defense table. Wally, as usual, was dressed the most immaculately, thin lapels, well-pressed suit, blue sweater beneath his suit coat (it was twelve degrees above zero outside), a neat, three-point, white handkerchief emerging from his breast pocket. He was too sharp a dresser to sport one that was red, white and blue. Houghton was well-combed but his suit was a bit wrinkled, reflecting his trip from California. DePugh looked rumpled, too, and his face showed more lines than usual, suggesting both worry and a lack of sleep.

Judge Hunter began by announcing he was overruling their motions for a new trial and a motion for an arrest of judgment. He then instructed the three men to approach the bench. Costello and Gilwee, Millin and Hamilton flanked them.

The judge began their ordeal by observing that neither DePugh nor Peyson had prior records of convictions and that he would take this into account. He added that Houghton did have a record, and that this would be taken into account too. Then he asked Millin if he had any remarks to make before sentence was passed.

"The government would only point out in respect to all the defendants that are being sentenced here this morning," Millin began, "that they are guilty of a criminal activity which strikes at the nerve center of law and order—the possession of unregistered firearms. . . .

"Now, these guns were designed for one purpose—to murder humanity. You don't shoot duck or quail or deer or even elephants with such an arsenal. You kill people with these types of guns. . . .

"The guns that were found were introduced into evidence. The number and location of other such weapons may never be known. To this day, none of the defendants has evidenced the slightest desire to furnish information to their government or to cooperate in any degree. To the contrary, their attitude has been and continues to be hostile to the forces of law and order.

"The National Firearms Act laws were enacted to prevent such murderous arsenals from secretly finding their way into the hands of criminals, lunatics, incompetents, and other potential enemies of the public and I think that recent events illustrate the wholesale death that can result from the control of guns by such persons, and the need for perhaps even more stringent legislation. . . .

"To contend that the defendants' violation of law was excusable because carried out under the guise of patriotism is to disregard facts of the case, to ignore the machinery that is designed to redress wrongs and grievances in this country, and to forget lessons of history as taught by such zealots as Adolph Hitler and Benito Mussolini.

"The true patriot obeys the law of the land wherein he dwells and respects the rights and properties of his fellow citizens. Our system of government considers no man to be above the law. All are subject to its mandates, the weak and the powerful, the rich and the poor, the learned and the unlearned. None can pick and choose the laws he will obey and the laws he will not obey. To do so invites the penalties prescribed by law—the penalties which these defendants now face."

Hitler and Mussolini? A bit strong, but Millin was certainly not the first man to have implied a similarity between the Fascists of Germany or Italy and the Minutemen approach to American life. Gilwee did not let it pass unnoticed. When his turn came, the defense attorney delivered an oration which, at its peak, prompted one of the Minutewomen who was seated in the front row of the spectator's section, to dab at her eyes.

"The only thing, if your Honor please, is that I think Mr. Millin went rather far afield in comparing the defendants to Hitler and Mussolini in his suggestion to the court," Gilwee said. "These men have never been convicted—Mr. Peyson and Mr. DePugh—of any offense against anybody or any governmental authority."

And now passion began to enter his deep voice, the passion of old-school courtroom oratory.

"We are living in an age where it seems to be the not popular—but the condition that exists—where Communist organizations are disrupting our universities," he said. "They are training people in this country to sabotage the country. They have created a feeling throughout this country of insecurity. They have attacked every institution of this country verbally if not actually. They have subverted information and security of foreign governments, and it was once said that this country will never be destroyed from without but from within.

"Most of us until the last few years have always been taught love of country and it is trying to be taught now. Many have given their lives to protect the institutions which we all revere.

"I don't think it was any intention on the part of these defendants to try to cause an insurrection against the institutions of our country, but more or less to protect themselves and their homes against an uprising of an underground force which is being advocated at least—I don't want to go too far—advocating at least the overthrow of our present form of government from the nation all the way through.

"We have been fighting around the world trying to protect other people from this same force. And I think whatever DePugh and Peyson did, they did not with the idea of causing any overthrow of the government, but to protect the institutions of our country in case of necessity.

"That is all I have to say."

Between these two speeches, Judge Hunter had reviewed Houghton's police record at length. He made it clear at the outset that he was not taking into consideration arrests that had not resulted in convictions, although there were a couple, he said, that he wanted to discuss with Houghton. After reviewing a conviction for tampering with a vehicle in 1952, when Houghton was still a teen-ager, the judge turned to the indecent exposure charge in 1957 which had come back to haunt him so many times. He read the lengthy police report on the incident, then asked Houghton about it.

"Your honor," Houghton replied, ". . . they were going to bring charges against my wife also, and I pled guilty at the time and no charges were pressed against my wife. But also, my wife had our oldest son at the time, which was a baby, with us, too."

"But the record is correct to this extent," asked the judge, "that you did plead guilty as related here?"

"This is true, sir."

The judge then turned to one charge that did not result in a conviction, but which he felt deserved an explanation from Houghton. He had been taken into custody on suspicion of rape in San Diego but not formally charged.

The judge then read from a police report telling of how Houghton had said he had been propositioned by a woman who later brought charges against him when he refused to avail himself of her services. The woman had stated, however, that she had advertised in the newspaper for the return of a lost cosmetic case valued at $80. A man had telephoned her telling her he had found the case.

"When she offered a $20 reward for its return," the police report continued, "the man indicated he would rather have something else. He then asked if she were married and if she was skinny. He then indicated he would like to spend the night with her and advised he would bring the case to her home."

That night, the judge continued, reading from the report, Houghton showed up at her front door carrying a briefcase. The police, who had been alerted, arrested him. Inside the briefcase were a package of women's night clothes, assorted bottles of liquor and club soda, two glasses, olives and even toothpicks.

While several observers in the courtroom muffled their snickers, Houghton told the judge that the woman had placed an ad in the newspaper, all right, but not for a cosmetics case.

"And is the rest of the report accurate?" Judge Hunter asked.

"I think it is, your Honor," the chagrined Minuteman replied.

The judge then asked him about an incident in May, 1960, when he was arrested for improper display of license plates while parked in front of the Swallow's Nudist Camp. Police then discovered several traffic warrants outstanding against him and he forfeited bond.

Houghton at this point concluded that the judge was interested in why he had been parked in front of a nudist camp.

"I had—we had belonged to the club for a couple of years, sir," Houghton said.

"You belonged to the club?" Judge Hunter asked.

Houghton nodded.

"Did you forfeit bond?" asked the judge. "That was the part I was interested in."

"Oh . . . I don't honestly know, your Honor."

Then the judge went into Houghton's failure to register as a sex offender in November, 1961. Houghton told the judge that this had been prompted by the Minutemen publicity in California, that a San Diego police official had admitted as much and that even the judge in the case had said, "You are being arrested and prosecuted here for something entirely separate than what this is." Houghton added that at the time of the "sunbathing" incident in 1957, the crime of which he was charged was not one of those requiring subsequent registration as a sex offender. The registration law was broadened later, he said, but he had not been aware of it when charged with not having registered.

"All right," Judge Hunter said. "I will accept your explanation."

Peyson, with his spotless record of the past, limited his observations to:

"Judge Hunter, I just have this to say in regard to one statement that Mr. Millin made. I don't believe that I personally have ever exhibited any hostility for any law-enforcement agencies or agents thereof and I do resent that personally. I have respect for governmental agencies, local and federal, and the people that work as public servants, and that is the only thing I wanted to clarify."

Houghton thereupon made a similar statement, assuring the judge that he, too, liked and respected law-enforcement officers.

DePugh remained silent, his hands folded behind his back, his fingers moving nervously over one another.

Judge Hunter then proceeded to pass sentence.

"Gentlemen," he said, "I have now given you, I hope, all the opportunity that you want to make any statement. If there is nothing further, I would like to, by way of review . . ."

And he reviewed the charges, and verdict.

"In sentencing you," he said, "I want to make it clear that you are being sentenced solely for your personal actions that were in violation of the Federal Firearms Act as found by the jury.

"In this case, no one has claimed that the Minutemen organization was on trial. Nor was it on trial. In this case, no one has claimed that it was unlawful to be a member of that organization or, for that matter, of any organization. No one was on trial here because of any political philosophy or personal or economic beliefs that he may have. No one in this trial has contended that it is unlawful or wrong to be either a conservative or a liberal. No one has contended that it is not proper to be ever alert to the threat of Communism or to be constantly vigilant and to guard our and our nation's freedom and liberties.

"In passing this sentence as a court, I am not nor am I permitted by law to be concerned with whether any of you three defendants is a liberal or a conservative or holds any type of economic or political belief. The sole question that was involved in this trial was, 'Did you men by your personal conduct violate specific, valid federal criminal statutes as charged?'

"If you did, it is no answer to say you did so in order to further some political or economic view which you or the Minutemen organization in which you have admittedly said that you hold membership hold.

"No one, no matter how sincere his beliefs in some cause or movement, has the right to commit unlawful and felonious acts in his effort to support that cause or movement.

"It is no defense to a charge of violating federal criminal laws to say that the end that one has in mind justifies the employment of illegal means to accomplish that end.

"The evidence in this case has made it abundantly clear that you men have intentionally employed illegal means as charged in the indictment in your endeavor to further your personal views. The evidence has indicated that you well knew that you were violating the federal laws. You were intentionally secretive about it and, of course, you did not expect to get caught. But you were caught. You were tried and convicted by the jury and it is now my duty under the law to sentence you for the unlawful acts that you have been found guilty of committing. It is not an easy matter for me to do, but it is one that I must do."

Judge Hunter's eyes then turned toward DePugh.

"Starting with Mr. DePugh, on count one," he said, "you are sentenced to the custody of the Attorney General of the United States for a period of four years. . . ."

And to Houghton . . .

". . . Three years!"

And to Peyson . . .

". . . Two years!"

In prison.

But there was more. Probation, following their time in prison. To DePugh, Judge Hunter explained the probation would be for five years, to Peyson, three years.

"Now the probation conditions for that sentence are the usual ones that will be handed to you by the probation department," the judge said, "and in addition I am placing special conditions of probations on you which you must fully comply with or be subject to having your probation revoked.

"These special conditions which you must obey are, first, you are not to be a member of, or a participant in any organization or group that teaches or encourages the acquisition or transfer or manufacture of guns or firearms in violation of the federal firearms act, or in violation of any federal or state law. Secondly, you must in writing keep your probation officer fully and currently advised of all organizations or groups that are of a military nature or that collect or use or train in the use of firearms or explosives to which you belong or in which you participate and, if known to you, the list of the officers or leaders of such organization or group, and the location of its meeting places. Third, you must obey all federal and state criminal laws."

Emotions did not show on the faces of any of the three men. Mrs. DePugh, who was seated in the audience, also remained impassive. Their plans for an appeal to a higher court were discussed. Appeal bonds were kept low—$5000 on each—and each said he would post bond. Houghton said he now had a new attorney, from California. The judge left the courtroom. A hushed conversation between defendants and defense attorneys. A calm departure by all from the courtroom.

"Any comment?" I asked DePugh.

"No, only that we'll appeal," DePugh replied and smiled weakly.

"We're set up downstairs," said Claude Dorsey, a television newscaster for station KMBC, and DePugh nodded.

"Any comment?" to Peyson.

"Would you like to hear me give a rendition of 'Every Cloud Has a Silver Lining'?" Peyson replied amiably.

Houghton telephoned his wife in San Diego with the news.

"I thought you'd have something to say now," I told DePugh.

"I think," DePugh said, with no further coaxing, "that Judge Hunter made a real effort to stay within the letter of the law, but sometimes there can be a disparity between the letter of the law and real justice. I think that this trial was the result of a massive effort by government agents that was politically inspired and was designed to put us in prison by any means necessary."

Houghton and Peyson entered the elevator together and at the ground floor were greeted by photographers, television cameras and microphones. Houghton did not avoid the news photographer but pleasantly declined the opportunity to talk on camera. Wally was not so shy.

Wally tried to perpetuate the idea that this was nothing more than a tax-evasion case—they had failed to pay a tax on the machine guns and therefore had broken the law.

"From the standpoint of tax evasion," he said, "I think it was a bit harsh. From my standpoint, it was a bit harsh."

Then it was DePugh's turn. He had entered the lobby from a later elevator. He repeated what he had told me upstairs almost word for word, and then began to elaborate.

"I think that some of the means used were unconstitutional and set a precedent that is dangerous to the freedom of all citizens of this country," he said.

"What will happen to the Minutemen organization in the interim?" one of the television newsmen asked.

"Should I go to prison," DePugh responded, "no doubt the Minutemen will select someone else as their leader. Certainly I'm not the indispensable man."

"Do you consider the terms of probation imposed by the court a mandate that you leave the Minutemen organization?"

"Well, technically, perhaps they're not, but in actual practice I'm sure they would be interpreted as such."

"Do you intend to leave the Minutemen?"—mike closer to mouth.

"Well, that's a matter that's now under advisement and perhaps I'll know in a few days."

The next question alluded to the terms of probation and firearms.

"Well, of course, it's a fallacy to think that firearms are necessary to the purposes of the Minutemen organization," DePugh said, and suddenly, without even taking a breath, "I think that the Liberal-Communist-Socialist conspiracy *that now effectively controls our federal government* will pass any laws, or interpret any laws that they have to, to effectively silence opposition to the present bureaucracy, regardless of what form that opposition might take."

Until that moment, DePugh had always couched his language in terms of a future take-over by the Communists. Until then, he had talked of *"when"* the conspiracy took control, *"then"* would be the time for Minutemen to take action. Until then the conspiracy had been in the process of "taking control." But now, it was *in* control.

Claude Dorsey seemed to catch the implication immediately.

"You say this conspiracy does now effectively control our federal government?"

"I think that the Communist-Socialist conspiracy now controls our government to such a point," DePugh replied, "that it controls all major policy, both domestic and foreign."

"Do you think that this also controlled your trial?" Dorsey persisted.

"Yes, I do, most definitely," DePugh said, but then hastened to spare himself the possibility of Judge Hunter's wrath. "Perhaps not the trial procedure itself, but certainly the unfair and unconstitutional investigative procedure that was used to bring the trial to court."

That afternoon, interviewed in the WDAF television studio, DePugh held to this new line:

". . . From the very beginning, it was clear to me that the efforts of the Communist-Socialist conspiracy control our federal government right today and these people are determined to put me in prison and destroy the Minutemen organization any way they can. . . ."

BOOK THREE

The New Militancy

CHAPTER 16

JOIN THE MINUTEMEN

. . . By 1972 the enemies of freedom must be challenged by a strong experienced political party. That party, if it is to succeed, cannot stand alone. It must be the political arm of a United Front Against Communism.

Along with the political party, that united front must have developed into a complete resistance movement, including a well-trained underground organization. The underground will provide the tangible guarantee of honest elections. Without this guarantee the Patriotic candidates are certain to be "counted out" in the polling places and in the electronic computers that tabulate final national figures. . . .

In times like these, milk-toast methods cannot succeed. The true patriotism of our forefathers cannot fail.

Concluding observations in *Blueprint for Victory*

DePugh's declaration that the United States was now under Communist-Socialist control failed to set off rioting in the streets and no hapless liberal was shot, strangled with a piano wire or incapacitated by nerve gas on the night of his sentencing. The Day—thank goodness—still was not at hand.

But from that day forth, a new militancy began to grip the Minutemen organization and it has continued to grow since then. Their leader faced a four-year prison sentence and did not speak optimistically to them of his chances on appeal. These were grim times. Urgent times. Something must be done And sooner than they once had thought.

Quickly an internal reorganization of the Minutemen began, more secretive than before, more ominous. The Minutemen rhetoric became yet more violent and now was coated with a sense of immediacy and fear that had been less pronounced until then.

"Resistance networks" were formed to replace the old "band" and "team" structure. Members became more suspicious of outsiders, of each other. Recruiting of new members was done on a more clandestine basis. The "enemy" was more fearsome, now, closing in relentlessly.

To understand how this all came about, it is necessary to backtrack to the early months of 1966, well before the DePugh-Houghton-Peyson trial. The kidnaping episode in DePugh's life was still fresh in his mind and the state charges that had resulted from it still hung over him. First Jerry Brooks, then Ray Husted had disappeared or defected from Norborne with valuable information. The federal investigative agencies were breathing down the Minutemen's necks.

As DePugh tells it—and there seems little reason for him to have embroidered on the story especially—he journeyed to the New Mexico-Arizona area in January or February of 1966 and moved into a motel room near an old mine belonging to an elderly woman of his acquaintance, a woman he affectionately refers to as "sort of a lady hermit."

When not visiting with the elderly friend, DePugh said, he shot a few javelinas—wild hogs native to the region—just to keep his target eye sharp. And while not shooting javelinas or chatting, he said, he spent his time sitting either in his motel room or atop a rubble heap at the mine entrance writing.

In a few weeks, he said, he had drafted in longhand *Blueprint for Victory*, the $1-a-copy, 106-page paperbound book with which he soon was to launch the Patriotic Party on July 3 and 4, 1966, in Independence, Missouri. The self-published book went on sale that spring, just as the federal grand jury was beginning to hear numerous witnesses concerning DePugh and his Minutemen organization.

Blueprint for Victory was an up-dated amalgamation of segments from Minutemen bulletins, pamphlets, speeches and "On Target," but with a new, self-contradictory revisionism of sorts. The book asserted that salvation of the nation through politics is futile. Yet it called for the formation of a new political party to save the nation.

DePugh tried to reconcile these conflicting points by stating the new Patriotic Party would have to function as an arm of the Minutemen's total underground "resistance movement," but a careful reading of the book indicates he could have spent a little less time shooting javelinas while working out this rationale and a little more time wrestling with the logic behind his appeal.

"Our nation has been occupied by the enemy," he wrote. "Today the chains of slavery lay lightly on our people but with every passing day the chains become stronger and the American people are more tightly bound. We must either break these chains soon while they are yet weak or else we must face an uncertain future, frightful to behold."

How?

". . . We must study the methods which our enemeis are using against us and we must use their own strategies against them."

And he defined the enemies' strategies and methods as most terrible and horrifying.

But who are the enemies?

At various points, DePugh used a variety of names to identify them: Communists, collectivists, Socialists, liberals and bureaucrats, whom he called "parasites."

The real battle, he added, is best described as "an endless conflict between individualism and collectivism," because "the forces of collectivism are determined to destroy the American way of life by destroying its very foundation—the American system of free enterprise."

Despite such passages, DePugh at other times tried to draw a vague distinction between, for instance, outright Communists and liberals. In his advice to readers on the art of effective propaganda, for instance, he urged them not to alienate newspaper publishers, journalists or radio announcers because "most may be liberal but few are actual Communists."*

DePugh took an exceedingly unpleasant view of government bureaucrats, seeing them in league with the Communists for the sake of self-preservation. The bureaucracy, he wrote, is controlled by a small elite who are "insanely lusting for power."

DePugh offered as the climax of his book the idea that a Patriotic Party should be established with the intention of running a presidential candidate by 1972. His best prediction as to when the collectivists' control of the country will be virtually complete was 1973. Thus, the 1972 try for the White House was described as a last-ditch, do-or-die effort.

Realizing that the bulk of *Blueprint* had made it seem rather futile to think of political action, DePugh wrote:

"Many pessimistic statements have appeared throughout this book such as this: 'Our nation has been occupied by the enemy'; and

---

* Hopefully, his readers will draw from that the additional conclusion that they should not shoot journalists. As for radio announcers—readers can use their own judgment.

this: 'The American people can no longer defend their freedom by the traditional means of politics and public opinion'; and this: 'Words won't win—action will.'

"Now it may seem that we advocate what we have previously argued against; namely, the organization of still another political party. Worse yet, it might seem that we suggest forming such a party with one breath, then with the next breath we say it cannot win."

In trying to work his way out of this hole by defining the proposed party as the political arm of the resistance movement, he explained, with a touch of menace, "Words sound less hollow when the speaker has an armed alternative to words."

The fifty-one planks of the party's platform were fairly well summarized as follows:

"If our nation is to be saved, then the entire bureaucratic tree must be pruned from top to bottom. Subversives must be jailed. Unnecessary jobs must be eliminated. Incompetent workers must be fired. Padded payrolls, graft, waste, kickbacks and special favors must be made things of the past. A thousand obsolete bureaus, committees, departments and agencies must be done away with.

"Economic sanity must prevail. Oppressive taxation must be eliminated. Free enterprise must be encouraged. Government snooping in the private lives of the people cannot be permitted.

"Trade with the enemy must stop. The dismantling of our armed forces must stop. The drift toward world government and loss of national sovereignty must stop. Treason in government must stop. The basic rights of the citizens must not only be guaranteed—they must be upheld."

The party's plans? They did not lack for an ambition. The party should be listed on the 1968 ballots in every state of the union and should win two or three Senate races, ten to twenty House contests and many state, county and city offices that year. In 1970, add victory at the polls for four to eight more senators, fifty to eighty more members of the House, several top state officials and hundreds of lesser state, county and city officials. And then:

"In 1972 we will make a one-time try at the presidency. This must be a 'do-or-die' effort. No party can possibly put a real patriot in the White House before that date and our free Republic cannot last much after."

Using the Patriotic Party's original platform as printed in *Blueprint for Victory* for a guide (with exact wording from the platform italicized), imagine for the next few pages that it is now summertime, 1973.

The Patriotic Party, which nearly everyone had laughed at when 400 people showed up in Independence, Missouri, to found it back in 1966, won a smashing victory at the polls last November, putting *genuinely loyal, patriotic, pro-American candidates* into the White House, majorities in the Senate and House and thirty gubernatorial posts. Working smoothly together, the President and Congress—utilizing the valuable advice of Secretary of Defense Robert B. DePugh—already have put into practice many of the fifty-one original platform planks.

It was a hectic, historic election day, to be sure, the first in the nation's history in which there was no election fraud. The Minutemen had seen to that.

True, many Democratic and Republican precinct workers, election judges and policemen were shot outside the polls that day, but as Secretary DePugh explained on TV afterward, the killers had been "nuts and kooks" he had cashiered out of the Minutemen years before or had never allowed to join in the first place. They had misinterpreted what he had meant by "insuring" honest elections, apparently.

The changes that have taken place in this country since the inauguration have been sweeping and phenomenal. Even party critics have to admit that for once in the history of this country, an administration is keeping its campaign promises.

The President, less than an hour after the inauguration, *put our armed forces on immediate alert to guard against surprise attack by any foreign aggressor*, and within two months, nearly all our boys in *Europe and Asia were returned to the Western hemisphere*. What parades we had! What glorious home-comings! It's just too bad we couldn't bring back every single one of them, but, of course, a few had to stay behind in those *small, balanced units equipped with atomic weapons*.

Now that the *military* is our *fourth major branch of government*, the *general staff* is displaying *greater latitude in forming their own plans and deciding on the best weapons systems without the interference of inexperienced civilian advisors*. Of course, the military is *still under the control of civilian authority*—the President and Secretary DePugh.

All those *military installations* which that Commie-lover McNamara had *closed* in the '6os have been *reopened* by now and are being *modernized*. At the same time *our Armed Forces now stationed in the United States have been dispersed into small, self-sufficient combat groups so that a maximum percentage of our military strength* can *survive any surprise atomic attack.*

It has been interesting to hear all the generals, admirals and other *top military officers* exercising their regained *freedom of speech* on TV the last six months. It is certainly clear, when you hear them, that Secretary DePugh meant what he said when he promised that *patriotism, experience and ability* would *be the criteria* by which they would be *selected*—and in that order.

Soon, Secretary DePugh promised over TV the other night, *our defense and military forces* will have *reached a stage of development comparable to our nation's industrial might in other fields.* Then, he said, we will *make no further effort to maintain a static defense of Europe, Asia or Africa,* but *instead we* will *notify the Communist powers that any further invasion, direct or indirect, into those areas will result in their prompt destruction.* That ought to put the fear of Uncle Sam into 'em.

It's also been exciting watching the new *Department of Internal Security* at work these last six months. Its *investigations* into *all other government agencies and departments* for *evidence of disloyalty or subversion* have made interesting reading. It's good to know the new department is *under the joint direction of appropriate committees of the Senate and Congress*—the HCUA and the Senate Internal Security subcommittee—because something like that could get out of line if not in responsible hands.

And how about all those *grand-jury investigations* going on around the country? Some of those grand juries, I hear, are working fourteen- and sixteen-hour days hearing testimony about *all* those *known and suspected Communists* that were *discharged from their jobs in government and essential industry* earlier this year. Some people were surprised that so many government employees were *known or suspected Communists,* but that's probably because they didn't understand who it was that was going to do the suspecting.

The treason trials have been fascinating too, and . . .

(But here the fantasy must be interrupted briefly. Plank No. 16 of the Patriotic Party platform has to be seen in its entirety to be believed:

16. *Where evidence of treason is found, those suspected of such acts should be tried before civilian courts but if it is found that the courts themselves have been infiltrated to such an extent as to make the conviction of traitors impossible, then the Constitution should be amended to allow such persons to be tried before military courts or before new Federal Judges especially appointed for this purpose.*)

. . . have certainly accounted for a lot of interesting new appointments to the federal bench.

Frankly, I think the pay for serving on grand juries should be raised. After the grand jurors get through with investigating all those former government employees, they're going to have to start *extensive investigations into the loyalty of all other officials in government, the defense industry, tax-free foundations, labor unions, the communications industry, news media and similar fields vital to the nation's internal security.* It's a good thing Secretary DePugh didn't throw in businessmen with that list to be investigated or the grand juries' job never would be done.

As one of the admirals said on TV the other night—or was it one of the generals—anyway, the party platform certainly was drawn up comprehensively. Think, for instance, what might have happened to all those investigations and trials and convictions of suspected Communists and traitors if Secretary DePugh had neglected to include the *removal from office* of all the old *Supreme Court* Justices. Judging by the list of men and women who have filed in the *election* for the new court, no matter who's elected in November, the new court can't possibly be as bad as that last bunch of Commies. I still keep expecting Bob Welch to file, but he insists he's too busy to serve. Frankly, I think he's afraid Secretary DePugh won't endorse him. They never did get along too well.

Some people call our new foreign policy isolationism, and in a way maybe it is, but at the same time we're very much interested in waging *all-out psychological, political and economic warfare against the Communist conspiracy* so as to realize our *goal of freedom and dignity for mankind everywhere.*

The flow of *strategic and non-strategic material to Communist bloc nations or their satellites out of this country* certainly stopped in a big, fat hurry after it was declared that such shipments would *be considered an act of treason and punished as such.* Some of the other nations have stopped their shipments to the Commies too, since they don't want their *American military and economic aid stopped.*

Quite a few of our mutual-defense agreements around the world have been voided too, as promised, since so many of our so-called allies weren't willing to *reciprocate our efforts fully* and didn't *maintain a strong anti-Communist position in both their foreign and domestic affairs.*

Things are certainly buzzing down in Florida now, with the Cuban exiles reportedly on the verge of invading Cuba. It will be interesting to see just what the Cuban *Free Government in Exile* will receive from us in terms of *whatever help may be necessary to regain their political freedom,* as Secretary DePugh promised in his speech about *enforcing the Monroe Doctrine.*

The administration is still working hard selling or *transferring all the so-called "public lands" now controlled by the government to the states.* Hopefully the *states* will decide to buy the land at *a modest rate.* The money will *provide an emergency reserve fund that the federal government could draw on temporarily when its expenses unavoidably exceed its income. (Thus the government* will *have no excuse for going into debt.) And when this happens, it* will *be mandatory that either the tax structure or the federal budget be adjusted so that the amount drawn from the fund* will *be repaid in not more than two years. Where limited tracts are needed for defense purposes, they can be leased by the federal government from the states.* It will be interesting to see how much the states charge.

The federal government has gone out of the business of *making or guaranteeing loans to private companies, individuals, cooperatives, states, counties or cities.* It has been rather hard to *collect* all *such debts in* both *a firm* and *orderly* manner, but people are simply going to have to realize that these *funds* will be *used to pay off the national debt legally owed to private citizens and companies that hold government bonds.* It's just a simple case of redistributing a little wealth here and there.

The federal government also has stopped *making loans, gifts or grants to state and local governments and to public and private institutions.* We no longer have to worry about *unwanted federal control in such fields as education and in the administration of local political affairs. All government subsidies* are on their way out too. Already they have been *reduced by a third* for 1973 and in two more years they will be *outlawed entirely. This will allow the proven principles of the free-enterprise system to operate more effectively, free from government control and regimentation.*

That is only one of many cutbacks in the works. All of *the departments of government which deal with internal affairs* have had to cut their number of employees by 20 *percent* this year and in five years will have cut back so far in personnel that they will have only *small staffs of administrative and technical personnel available on an advisory basis* if requested by a *comparable state agency.* Among the departments affected by this are the *Department of Commerce, Agriculture and Health, Education and Welfare.*

Just about the biggest change we'll feel, though, will be *the end of all hidden taxes, such as corporation taxes, business taxes, real estate taxes, personal income taxes, etc.* as soon as the administration can see to it that they are *made unconstitutional. A tax on income encourages waste and extravagance while tax on purchases encourages thrift and savings,* as nearly everyone knows. Therefore, *all governments, at every level, will be required to raise their necessary revenues by sales taxes which, regardless of how high they will be—* and they may get pretty high, as a matter of fact—*will be plainly labeled as such and added to each product purchased by the citizen. In this way the people will be constantly reminded of the "cost of government" and more likely to insist on government honesty, efficiency and moderation.*

As Secretary DePugh has pointed out repeatedly, governmental control over our lives is just naturally a bad thing, but that doesn't mean that government shouldn't have a say in how corporations, labor unions or the news media conduct themselves.

As soon as the new *Supreme Court is elected,* we'll undoubtedly see how the administration's rhubarb with the news media turns out. It's just a matter of which of the innumerable appeals they'll consider first. The administration has made it very clear that *in no way should government be allowed to restrict freedom of the press.* Yet—and this is what the fuss has been all about—the administration also has demonstrated it intends to *take every precaution that these news media are not controlled by any foreign ideology or special-interest group.*

Defining "foreign ideology" and "special interest group" seems to be the problem.

Certain changes are in store for the wording of the Constitution and the Bill of Rights. The phrase, *"and provide for the general welfare"* is to be *striken from the Constitution entirely, all agencies that have been formed under this clause* will *be abolished, and all laws and federal regulations that have resulted from it* will be *declared null and void. That clause has been used as an excuse by ambitious government officials to create a multitude of illegal agencies and laws that extend the government's power over citizens.*

As for the *second amendment in the Bill of Rights,* it needs some rewording too, the administration feels. While it provides *the citizens with the right to own and bear arms, its wording is such that in many areas this right has been regulated almost out of existence.* The new wording prohibits *the restraint* of any person with *the right to vote as a citizen of the United States* from *owning, bearing,* or *transporting arms* and *ammunition, provided, of course, that he takes reasonable and prudent care for the safety of other citizens and their property.* The real, true, patriotic citizens, especially.

The administration is probably wise in not having any stated policy on civil rights—the racial issue is terribly touchy—but I think that most of the complaints of whites who objected to what had happened through the 1960s have been handled adroitly. No longer, for instance, can the government interfere with anyone's *right to buy or sell property or merchandise* and the Constitution soon will be amended so that we may regain our *freedom in the selection of employees.* It's all in the way you word things like that.

We are also looking forward to *guarantees* of our *freedom from oppressive taxation* (unless the new sales taxes become oppressive), *freedom from invasion of personal privacy* (except where necessary to determine our loyalty), *freedom of choice* (within limits, of course, such as the choice of a political belief the administration feels is disloyal) and *freedom from bureaucratic restraint* (except when the restraints are necessary to make us more free).

Most significant of all, I suppose, is the way the administration is *strengthening our Christian heritage* while simultaneously *preserving the separation of church and state.* The Jews aren't too wild about this, but they are chronic bellyachers anyway.

About the only problem that seems to still perplex the new administration, according to informed sources in Norborne, are all the riots we're having this year—not just the Negro riots, either, for they're small by comparison with the integrated and all-white ones. Secretary DePugh, these informed sources say, is thinking of rewriting one plank in the party platform although he hates to do it because it would mean one campaign promise would have to be broken. I'm referring, of course, to the plank promising that the Armed Forces would "never again be used against our own citizens." After a few more riots like we had last week in New York, Atlanta, Akron, San Francisco, Chicago, Nashville, Los Angeles, Cleveland, Philadelphia, Hattiesberg, St. Louis, Kenosha, Butte, Salt Lake City, Tucson, El Paso and St. Paul, to mention a few, my guess is the people will be happy to have that promise broken. Just let our GIs in there for a day or two and they'll take care of those damned dissenters.

Was it the prospects of such a summer in 1973 that attracted approximately 400 men and women from many parts of the nation to arrive in Kansas City on the Fourth of July, 1966, weekend for the first annual national convention of the Patriotic Party? To a certain degree, it had to be. One thing that could be said about this political party, anyway—you knew where it stood.

Many attending the convention were Minutemen, most assuredly, but some were from other small, undistinguished anti-Communist organizations of the Far Right. Most attended by invitation only, because of DePugh's justified fears of infiltration.

Meetings were held at Kansas City's U-Smile Motel for two days. I missed this convention, but reports by other reporters from the *Star* and several other newspapers indicated it was a spirited, at times spellbinding event. The shining light, as was to be expected, was Robert DePugh.

The Reverend Robert LeRoy, whom I was to meet later at the DePugh trial, had opened the meeting with a prayer and pledge of allegiance to the flag. Other speakers included the Reverend Kenneth Goff, of Englewood, Colorado, who heads the "Soldiers of the Cross"; an anonymous representative of something called the "Spirit of '76 Committee"; and Walter Patrick Peyson.

A Communist for three years in the 1930s, the Reverend Goff sprinkled his speech with such observations as: "The anti-Christ totalitarianism of the Fabian Socialist one-worlders will banish God from

the skies and capitalism from the face of the earth. . . . Instead of
'Give me liberty or give me death,' they say, 'Gimme, gimme,
gimme. . . .' The only Good Communist is a dead Communist. . . .
I am not a pink-panty preacher. . . . We need a party in America
stamped, 'Made in America,' not 'in the Kremlin.'"

About two-thirds of the persons present that day signed up as
members of the new party, submitting at least $5 in dues.

A month after the convention—the size of which surprised just
about about everyone—simultaneous area meetings of the party were
held in Seattle; Chicago; Scottsdale, Arizona; Dallas; Montgomery,
Alabama; and Washington, D.C., where DePugh attempted to speak
to everyone simultaneously by means of a telephone-coaxial cable
hookup.

Soon the party had been divided into three districts and to each
was appointed a district organizer. Jerry and Carol Dunn, husband
and wife, of Prairie Village, Kansas, were assigned to the Western
states. The Reverend LeRoy was given the Midwest. Tom Hart, of
Milford, Connecticut, was promoted from state chairman to district
organizer for the Eastern states.

DePugh, in the meantime, had been indicted by the federal grand
jury in Kansas City. In a mimeographed bulletin sent to Patriotic
Party members, a faithful party official who had been a housewife
wrote with what I am told was the utmost sincerity:

"My husband and I have given up everything and invested all
our time in the Patriotic Party, and have borrowed on everything
we own, because we know the Patriotic Party is our only chance.
Of course, hospital bills and medicine have been high. A few of
you know I have lymphosarcoma—cancer of the lymph nodes and
the bone marrow. To be perfectly honest, we don't even know how
we are going to refill my prescriptions when they run out. I was
supposed to go back to the hospital before the area conventions but
I didn't have time or money. Our Founding Fathers and many others
have sacrificed more than we. I am not asking for myself. I am
dispensable—but I don't feel that Bob DePugh and the Patriotic
Party are."

A plea for contributions was included, specifically $5800 was said
to be needed for bond fees and legal expenses in order to get "our
people" back to work after the disruption of party progress by the

indictments. The indictments, she wrote, had given the party bad publicity, "but at this stage bad publicity is better than no publicity." Another "third party," it seemed, had been born.

The fate of the Minutemen's leader in court and some apparent financial problems hurt the party in its first year of growth. As the Fourth of July weekend approached in 1967, a party newsletter proclaimed that the Patriotic Party was the largest third party in the United States. DePugh claimed a party membership now of 3000, and the caterer at the Town House Motor Inn in Kansas City, Kansas, where the 1967 convention was to be held, was alerted to prepare the big ballroom for 600 conventioneers.

When Sunday afternoon, July 2, rolled around, the length of the ballroom had been shortened considerably by a sliding partition, only 350 chairs were set up and only 150 of them filled as the convention opened. With numerous Kansas City area conventioneers compelled to work Monday, the crowd shrunk to between 120 and 130 that morning and did not increase in size before Tuesday noon, the Fourth, when the convention adjourned.

I attended this convention from start to finish, and found upon emerging from the ballroom for the last time early Tuesday afternoon that it was actually hard to readjust to the outside world of reality.

It is one thing to worry about international Communism, inflation, racial integration, growing bureaucracy, Vietnam and all the other existing controversial subjects confronting us, but it was something else again to approach them in the manner this convention did—in impassioned bewilderment, frustrated determination and grotesque superpatriotism.

On the rostrum in front of the speaker's table were from ten to twelve tape recorders, some of them expensive models, spinning, spinning each time someone stood before the microphone. The owners of these machines sat on the front row, springing forward together to start them whirring at the start of each session, moving intermittently forward and back again during speeches as one or the other's tape would be exhausted and a new one needed to be inserted. Each man would return home later and play them in his living room for the party faithful who had not been able to scrape together enough money, enthusiasm, or nerve (the "heat" was by now on the Minutemen) for the trip to Kansas City, Kansas.

Behind the speaker's table hung a large banner with the American Eagle on one side of a quote from Patrick Henry: "The Battle Has Begun. Our Brethren Are in the Field. Why Stand We Here Idle?" An American flag was on the speaker's right, a yellow flag bearing the words, "Don't Tread on Me" to their left.

Merle Thayer, executive director of the Congress of Freedom, of Davenport, Iowa, splinter party candidate for Congress in 1966, offered the invocation. He led them in a pledge of allegiance to the flag and made a few superfluous remarks before turning the mike over to Tom Hart, of Connecticut, who announced the convention's schedule.

Next came DePugh, in humble determination. The conventioneers rose to applaud him as he approached the speaker's table. He told them he had been pleased to notice that a few of the members, when polled by mail on their preference for President of the United States in 1968, "facetiously" had written down the name of Robert DePugh.

"I say, 'facetiously,'" he said, "because I'm not qualified to serve. I'm a convicted felon."

Several in the audience laughed at this as DePugh smiled encouragement to them to laugh harder, for this was ludicrous, was it not, the national chairman of the Patriotic Party a *convicted felon?*

"I can't even vote," he added, milking chuckles. But then the laughter faded, and DePugh began what was to reach its climax nearly two days later. "But I expect to play a part in who's going to be President of the United States after 1968."

Soon he had traveled back to 1776, and Captain Parker of the original Minutemen was on stage telling his men to hold the line, but if there was to be a fight, let it be here. One of DePugh's ancestors had fought with the Minutemen and had been hung by the British as a traitor, DePugh said, and not a war had been fought by the United States that someone from his family was not in it. His father had been gassed in World War I, he said. He himself, had enlisted, not waiting to be drafted in World War II.

"There are no draft-card burners in my family!" he declared and the audience registered loud approval.

DePugh closed with a poem, "In Flanders Fields," and some patriotic platitudes about torches flickering, etc., which I failed to jot down on my note pad, having become slightly ill over the recitation of his "patriotism" in World War II.

"He certainly does have a way with words," said Hart admiringly after DePugh had stepped down to another standing ovation.

Standing ovations were to become the rule rather than the exception throughout the convention, and anyone who did not receive one had reason to retire from oratorical endeavors forever. Few were disappointed.

It soon became apparent just how badly organized the convention was. State Chairman Glen Jackson, of Orange, California, the second speaker, apologized that he had not known he was to be called upon to make a speech until that afternoon, and then proved this beyond any doubt in the process of delivering one.

In the lobby and in one corner of the ballroom a great quantity of books and pamphlets were on display, for sale, but bigger things were in store for the conventioneers' pocketbooks. Hart provided them with the first inkling.

Because of his many legal problems, Mr. DePugh was going to resign as national chairman of the party during the convention, he said. (Odd that DePugh wouldn't have mentioned this himself, or that he would let Hart do it for him, something as important as that). And so, folks, as a "parting gift" for Mr. DePugh, whose legal expenses are absolutely terrific . . .

And Mary Tollerton and another pretty little slip of a girl were suddenly standing side by side in the middle of the aisle with large containers, ready to pass them among the audience. By DePugh's figures, which for once I trust, $316 was raised that time around.

The speakers ranged from the nationally unknown to the nationally little-known, but most came with long, if not impressive, credentials. First there was "Bishop" C. Fain Kyle, of Richmond, California, the only Negro at the convention. His calling cards, which he offered freely, showed him to be the founder of the Conservative Christian Churches of America, Inc., chairman of the California Recall Committee, and executive director of the Dedicated Independent Society Committee Against Racial Demonstrations, Inc. (the initials of which, it should be noted, are D.I.S.C.A.R.D.). Outspoken against the civil-rights movement, he was received more warmly than anyone else, with the exception of DePugh. In fact, they called upon him to deliver a second major address on Monday, they had liked his Sunday afternoon offering so well.

"I'm anti-King, anti-Carmichael, anti all the so-called civil-rights organizations and anti everything else that is un-American," he said, prompting applause.

He told the white patriots that when critics called him an Uncle Tom, he did not mind, "because Uncle Tom was an honorable man."

In his second speech, he drew more applause, many cheers and some rebel yells with the declaration; "You can see why some people hate me. They say I'm a traitor. But I think I'm a good American!"

After assuring his admirers that he would never wish to live in a white neighborhood (applause) and scoffing at the NAACP for never having had a Negro president (more applause), he ended his final speech with: "What this country needs is a bill to nullify all the civil-rights bills."

Before the roar of his standing ovation had subsided, Merle Thayer was leaning into the microphone asking, "Do you know why a chicken crosses halfway across the road? TO LAY IT ON THE LINE!" and before the laughter was over, "That man just laid it on the line. Didn't he folks?" (More cheers.)

Myron C. Fagan, the seventy-nine-year-old national director of the Cinema Education Guild, Hollywood, California, delivered a long speech on fighting the Reds in the movie industry and the evil plot of the dread "Illuminati," which he said now masquerades as the Council on Foreign Relations.

Wally Peyson spoke on "The Spirit of the Revolution" to open Tuesday's meeting. He said the spirit of revolution was alive in the land today and predicted that conservatives eventually would follow the man who says, "This is enough. No more retreat. Let's attack!"

Richard Cotten, the glib "Conservative Viewpoint" radio commentator who had taken such an interest in the Husted case, offered strong encouragement for the Patriotic Party to back George Wallace for President in 1968 as a part of a huge protest vote he predicted against "Socialist Parties A and B," which, of course, were the Democratic and Republican parties. Cotten was quite rough on the Zionists (a Zionist brought the dread Beatles to the United States but did not take them to Israel, he noted). He was also foursquare against "mongrelization" of the races.

The Reverend Goff was back for the second year now with the

news that the CIA had had Oswald and Ruby kill President Kennedy and that "20,000 Russian spies" were in Montreal, Canada, brainwashing and training American tourists visiting Expo '67.

The Reverend Goff opened his speech with news of his wife's successful operation the previous weekend. In the recovery room, he said, a doctor asked her who the President of the United States was, to see if her mind was all right. Her reply, he said, confirmed it was just fine: "Unless he has been removed by assassination since I went into the operation, unfortunately it is Lyndon B. Johnson."

Monday evening, DePugh conducted a disorganized business meeting in which party strategy and organization were discussed at great length. While trying to decide how new party officers would be elected elsewhere than at the convention, a delegate from Ohio rose to insist voting could not be done by mail.

"I wouldn't send five cents to anyone I didn't want Comrade Johnson or Comrade Humphrey to know about," he declared.

Another man in the back of the room objected to DePugh's resignation as chairman: "This party is made up of loyalty to you. You founded it." This brought the audience to its feet to applaud.

The man from Ohio suggested that if Jimmy Hoffa could run the teamsters from prison, DePugh could run the Patriotic Party from prison too.

A gray-haired man from Florida asked how party members from his city could learn the identities of others in the organization. DePugh responded by telling him a financial pinch had prohibited the party from mailing out all the information it would have liked the previous twelve months. And while talking about money . . .

"Are those containers we passed around last night handy?" he asked.

Sure 'nuff, they were. The collection this time netted $708, he later announced.

DePugh agreed, incidentally, not to resign as chairman after all. He would wait until a successor was picked in September, he said, but neglected to return the $316 "parting gift" that had been raised for his legal defense fund the previous night. Not that anyone was going to even suggest that he return it.

Through Sunday's and Monday's sessions, there had been talk of a "surprise" Tuesday—either in the form of an unexpected speaker or in something DePugh would announce. DePugh delivered on that promise as scheduled. It came as the convention considered who to back for President and Vice-President of the United States in 1968.

DePugh introduced the subject (after another standing ovation naturally) by immodestly telling the audience that he had been "noticeable by my absence" from the convention most of Monday. He had been meeting somewhere else in the city, he said, with leaders of other ultraconservative organizations, the names of which he could not reveal, and it was agreed that these organizations would have to band together in 1968 to stand a chance of winning the White House.

He had had to compromise, he said, and the man agreed upon for Vice-President was the man he would have preferred for President. Still, one had to be practical, and so the former governor of Alabama, George Wallace, was the choice for President.

Roughly half, maybe more, but not everyone, leaped to their feet with joy. Rebel yells echoed through the ballroom. Applause was spirited. But wait—and DePugh had not smiled to the Wallace cheers—this was a "package deal." Wallace would have to accept their vice-presidential choice to keep this endorsement. And the vice-presidential choice was "someone many of you may not have ever heard of before, William Penn Patrick!!!"

"Yes, yes," said a few—a very few—voices in the crowd.

DePugh then offered a brief biography of William Penn Patrick, who only that week had been the subject of a column-length story in the business section of *Newsweek* magazine because of his being an "overnight millionaire" at thirty-seven, chairman of the board of Holiday Magic Cosmetics, Inc., and a confirmed ultraconservative who had received less than three percent of the vote in the Republican gubernatorial primary in 1966 when Ronald Reagan won, and was now helping finance recall efforts against Senator Frank Church of Idaho. A businessman was needed to run the government, DePugh said, and Patrick was that kind of businessman.

"I don't want to presume to tell you who to back," DePugh said, "but if we don't back these two, we'll be out of step with the hard core of conservatives of the nation."

He then called for a vote, without debate, and the Wallace-Patrick ticket passed with almost unanimous approval.

DePugh then looked in the direction of the few dissenters and graciously asked if any of them wished to speak. One middle-aged man who would not identify himself to me later timidly rose and asked the convention how many present knew William Penn Patrick. Ten hands were raised.

"He might be a disappointment. I think the party needs to investigate him a little bit more," he said, and it was apparent from his manner that he was summoning up courage he didn't know he had.

DePugh thanked him, reminded him that the vote already had been taken and then informed the convention that Patrick agreed with every plank in the Patriotic Party platform.

"When I talk to Bill Patrick," said DePugh, "I feel like I'm talking to a mirror."

I was writing news accounts of the convention for the morning and evening editions of the *Star*, but found myself unwilling to report that anyone agreed with the Patriotic Party platform without checking with the person first. Efforts to reach Patrick by telephone that day were unsuccessful. The following day I located him in San Rafael, California. "Do you embrace all fifty-one planks of the platform?"

"As you know, I'm a conservative," the overnight millionaire replied. "I've read all fifty-one and, yes, I do."

I was amazed, to be frank. When I asked him if he did so without qualifications, he replied that perhaps he did have some qualifications, but he volunteered none.

"Do you support the Minutemen?"

"That's not at issue, so I have no comment."

He said he had heard of DePugh several years before but had been in contact with him only a few months.

When I asked DePugh afterward about his relationship with William Penn Patrick, he told me he had first heard of him at the 1966 Patriotic Party convention, had investigated him and found him an attractive possibility for President. When I asked him whether Patrick had ever contributed any money to him or his organization, DePugh replied, "No, not one cent."

"Do you have any other millionaires in your camp?" I asked.

"I've found that a lot of people believe in the free enterprise system when they've succeeded in it," he replied. "How's that for giving an indirect answer to a direct question?"

It was not the Patrick endorsement or any of the speeches that stuck longest in my mind after that convention. It was the audience.

Most had driven goodly distances to attend. States represented there included New York, Florida, Texas, California, Washington, Montana and many others that were nearer. They had come, and they had believed, and they had believed intently. A few "amens" had greeted specific verities from speakers, and the clapping and cheers had been enthusiastic. But it was in moments of audience silence that these folks' true dedication showed through best. None dozed. Nearly everyone stayed in his seat in grim attentiveness. I found myself drawn especially to the Ohioan who had wanted DePugh to run the party from prison, for his attention to DePugh's speeches was so rapt that his head instinctively nodded agreement with nearly every point, every new revelation. They had faith, and were willing to back it up with their time, their money and their energy. They had faith in their fears, in the many plots and conspiracies the speakers described to them, and they seemed even to have faith that somehow, in some way, they could overcome all the obstacles they envisioned as standing in their way. They believed.

Two months later, DePugh tape-recorded a message to the regional meetings held on September 3 in Dearborn, Michigan; Hot Springs, Arkansas; and King of Prussia, Pennsylvania. Part of that message will be discussed later, but one part is pertinent here.

". . . About two months ago, I probably made one of the worst mistakes in my entire life. And I made that mistake quite frankly because I failed to live up to my own principles. I had worked for a year to make the Patriotic Party a success and I saw that it was going to fail, that it was going to fall apart because we simply did not have the money to keep it going. . . .

"I allowed myself to be talked into publicly recommending two specific candidates to receive the support of the Patriotic Party. And I'll tell you frankly why I did so. I was willing to publicly recommend George Wallace as our presidential candidate because I felt that he more than any other candidate available would be able to draw the most votes. And I was willing to recommend William Penn Patrick . . . because he had promised to provide the money necessary to keep the Patriotic Party alive, to open Patriotic Party headquarters throughout most of the major cities in the United States and to finance the printing, the transportation, the telephones and all of the other expenses that were necessary. . . ."

He then complained that Wallace wasn't doing a good enough job pushing conservatism and that Patrick had not provided any money to the party. Wallace was not dropped, but Patrick was abandoned. Poor Patrick.

I later wrote Patrick, asking him what had transpired between him and DePugh before and after the convention, and whether he still was in general agreement with the Patriotic Party's fifty-one-plank platform. His reply was puzzlingly terse. In its entirety, it read:

"In answer to your letter of October 5th, regarding my alleged involvement with the Patriotic Party, I can only say that I have not solicited nor accepted their endorsement."

Whatever that meant.

CHAPTER 17

JOIN THE MINUTEMEN

> After careful consideration, we the nineteen who have been accused of "Conspiracy to commit arson on Communist training camps," have decided that all funds should be forwarded to national headquarters for your defense.
>
> We feel that national headquarters is more essential than we are. If you fail, it will take a great deal of time to reorganize. This way, if funds can help bring your case to a victory, headquarters will still be in operation.
>
> I know that we have caused you considerable inconvenience but we are all agreed on the pre-mentioned plans.
>
> God speed to you on your defense. Best of luck from all of us.
>
> Letter to DePugh from a New York Minuteman as reprinted, without signature, in "On Target."

One of DePugh's sillier claims of strength, it had seemed to me, was that New York was one of his best states in total membership. It was practically insulting to my intelligence, I reasoned, for him to insist upon this. New Yorkers, after all, were too sophisticated for that sort of thing. California? Sure. Anything could crop up there. And Missouri? Why not? Whoever accused Missourians of being sophisticated? But New York?

In October, 1967, New York's Attorney General Louis J. Lefkowitz issued a special, somewhat confidential report on a ten-month investigation his office had made of the Minutemen in his state. He made public a few of his conclusions about the organization and mailed off neatly printed copies of the report to Governor Nelson Rockefeller, U. S. Attorney General Ramsey Clark, Secretary of Defense Robert McNamara, several other governors and Lord knows who else.

DePugh had not been fooling.

Around 150 witnesses had been questioned, Lefkowitz revealed, and hearings had been held all over the state—Syracuse, Albany, Buffalo, Rochester, Utica and New York City.

The Minutemen, Lefkowitz concluded, were a potential threat to the peace and security of New York and other states. They existed in thirty-three New York counties and at least fourteen other states, he warned. Nationwide in scope, they are constantly recruiting new members, he cautioned. Members in his state included policemen, National Guardsmen, members of the armed forces, doctors, teachers, employees in sensitive industries and public employees, he advised.

"Training, reading, thinking and living guns, bombs and violence, they are actively preparing for a private war," the state attorney general added. ". . . Minutemen are prepared to fight 'the conspiracy' they alleged is fostered by our President, our Vice-President, the United States Supreme Court, the Governor of New York and its senators as well as the mayor of New York City."

Members of the Minutemen had told his investigators that they would not hesitate to assassinate Vice-President Hubert Humphrey, Chief Justice Earl Warren, Governor Rockefeller or others they termed "Communist sympathizers," he warned.

Paramilitary activity in such organizations should be made a felony, he recommended, punishable by up to fifteen years in jail.

Brief reference already has been made to why Lefkowitz had reason to be concerned about the Minutemen of New York. Almost a year to the day before his report was issued, New York's Minutemen were the talk of America's biggest city.

I arrived in New York a day and a half after the action had begun, a copy of the morning edition of the *Star* under my arm. Under a three-column headline on page one, "SEIZE MINUTEMEN ARMS," was an Associated Press story that began:

> New York (AP)—Police seized 20 men and tons of bombs, guns, rockets and bullets yesterday in pre-dawn raids that smashed a Minutemen terrorist plot, Nat H. Hentel, district attorney of Queens, announced.
>
> Hentel said the plot involved sending squads of heavily armed men disguised as hunters to blow up three privately operated camps in New York, Connecticut and New Jersey. The plan was to be carried out yesterday, a few days after the opening of the hunting season, Hentel said.
>
> He would not reveal the identity of the target camps. But

he said the Minutemen organization is dedicated to destroying "Communist, left-wing and liberal" installations. . . .

Most of the New York newspapers on sale at Kennedy International Airport still carried news of the Minutemen on their front pages the Monday night I arrived. All four Manhattan dailies had blanketed the subject by then and were busy scurrying around for second-day leads. All but the New York *Times* had given the Minutemen banner headline treatment and the *Times* had page-oned them with its customary thoroughness.

Once settled in a Manhattan hotel, I placed a call to the New York police in Queens, only to learn that all information about the Minutemen case was being released exclusively by Mr. Hentel, the Queens D.A., and I was given the nighttime "hot line" number to that office. Soon I was in touch with Hentel's first assistant, Howard Cerny, who was willing to go so far as to say that the evidence in the Sunday raids did show a firm link between the men who had been arrested and the Minutemen headquarters in Norborne. The evidence indicated that all twenty were members of the national Minutemen organization, he said.

Having noticed the banner headline in the now defunct *World Journal Tribune*, "Report UN on Bomb List," I asked Cerny whether Minutemen had actually intended to blow up the UN, but Cerny would neither confirm nor deny this.

I did not know it then, but was soon to learn that I and the New York reporters covering the case were to fall victim to a careful spoon-feeding of news and near-news about the Minutemen the rest of that week at the hands of a district attorney who was fighting a strenuous battle to win election to his first full term in that office the following week.

Hentel had been appointed to the job by Governor Rockefeller in mid-term and thus was the first Republican to hold the office in heavily Democratic Queens for forty-two years. Hentel had the support of the Republican and Liberal parties but his opponent, Thomas J. Mackell, a state senator, was a political pro well known in the borough. Hentel needed as good a press as possible that last week, and it was obvious that one way he felt he could get it was through his exposures of the Minutemen. This is not to say that Hentel or Cerny made un-principled use of the Minutemen case for political purposes—as the

Minutemen and Mackell soon were to charge—but the forthcoming
election did hang heavily over the Queens County Criminal Courts
building at Kew Gardens, location of the D.A.'s office, and just about
anything he did was considered politically significant, whether it should
have been or not.

I telephoned a rather shallow story for our morning edition that night
after talking with Cerny and then settled down to a more careful
reading of the New York *Times, Daily News, Post* and *World Journal
Tribune.* Their sources of information ranged from Hentel press conferences to interviews with various law-enforcement offiers who had
been involved in the raids or in what Hentel described as a ten-
month investigation of the Minutemen. A good deal of their information had come from sources "close to the investigation" or otherwise non-attributable, as the New York reporters had endeavored to
find out more than Hentel was telling, and to beat each other to
new, exclusive stories. By reading these news accounts, attending
the rest of the press conferences that week and interviewing those I
could, I left New York Friday with some knowledge—limited though
it was—as to what had happened.

First of all, only nineteen men, not twenty, had been arrested
and charged the first day. A twentieth was found and arrested the
following day in Syracuse, New York. According to J. Edgar Hoover's
1967 report to the House Appropriations Committee, twenty-four
alleged members of the Minutemen had been arrested that day while
en route to "assault left-wing camps in a three-state area." The
additional four were material witnesses, Hoover disclosed.

The raids on the Minutemen had begun before dawn on Sunday
morning October 30, with more than 100 law-enforcement officers
participating.

Five of the nineteen were arrested at about six o'clock Sunday morning after they had entered Goldy's Diner in South Ozone Park,
Queens, all dressed in hunting garb. Detectives dressed as cabbies and
truck drivers had fanned out over the area and surrounded the diner
in case of trouble, the *Post* reported, but the "hunters" offered no
resistance.

One of these five, a thirty-four-year-old landscape artist from Bellmore,
Long Island, was identified by Hentel as a Minutemen band leader. The
other four were Bethpage, Long Island, truck drivers, brothers twenty-
nine and thirty years old respectively; a twenty-nine-year-old heavy-equip-

ment operator from Franklin Square, and a twenty-four-year-old Brooklyn cab driver.

Found in the trunk of the leader's car, which was parked outside Goldy's, were four homemade bombs.

The other fourteen men apparently were rounded up individually, several, if not all of them, at their homes. They included a twenty-nine-year-old milkman whom the D.A.'s office said was found to have stored explosives in his refrigerator to keep them at a safely cool temperature while he was away from home delivering milk. He was identified by Hentel as another Minutemen band leader.

"The ice box incident," Hentel was later to observe at one of his press conferences, "underscores the threat to themselves and innocent neighbors. When people cannot sleep in a peaceful community, like Queens is, then we are going back to the frontier days."

The milkman, while being booked, said that his nickname was "Nathan Hale." On the stock of one of the semi-automatic rifles confiscated in the raids were stamped the words: "Liberty or Death."

The milkman's younger brother was another of the nineteen men arrested. The *World Journal Tribune* sought out their mother and interviewed her about her boys as she waited on customers at her small Queens grocery.

"I got the understanding when I talked to them," she was quoted as saying, "that they belonged to the John Birch Society, but I never knew them to be Minutemen. . . . They may be Birchers, but they're not extremists."

In Katonah, New York, north of the big city, police arrested a balding, forty-year-old former Kansas Citian who had become an advertising copywriter in New York City but later had decided to return to college in Connecticut for more education. Openly on display on the front porch of his home were two howitzers. An American flag with thirteen stars hung over his front door.

The *Times* reported that the New York state police seized from the man's home ten machine guns, fifteen rifles, a sawed-off shotgun, three mortars, a bazooka, twelve walkie-talkie communications sets, a tank radio transmitter, an anti-tank projectile, 10,000 rounds of assorted high-velocity ammunition and a quantity of illegal fireworks.

Newsday took a special interest in this man, interviewing his father at length. Sample quotes:

"He's a good kid who's always been interested in civics and good

government. Much more than I. I was always too busy making a
living. . . . He's a tremendous reader, a helluva student. He's always
taken an undue interest, even as a kid, in political activities, without
actually getting into politics. . . . I don't know what triggered him.
He writes letters to the editor and had quite a few published. He's
not a real rabid guy, but he does have some convictions. And he was
very interested in Civil Defense. When Rocky said, 'Build a bomb
shelter,' he built one. He's been a nut about guns. He had the stuff
on display. But it wasn't an arsenal like the newspapers said. Everything
he had was on gun racks, out on display. He had three over the fire-
place. He belongs to the National Rifle Association and shoots on the
range. . . . [He] firmly believes he doesn't want to live under Communism, as we all do, I hope. Or at least most of us. . . .

"He's a very gentle person. He doesn't blow his top. A couple of
years ago he had some of that Minutemen material sent to him, but
in the last year, he's been so busy he just hasn't had time. He went
back to college last January because he wants to be a teacher. His
wife's a teacher and [he] wants to teach science. He'd make a good
teacher, I think. Good with children. They have triplets. Five kids
altogether. They had five under three years old. . . ."

The *World Journal Tribune* quoted an unnamed neighbor of this
man to the effect that he once had seen him firing cans of peas
from a mortar at a field of cows while another man with a walkie-
talkie acted as a forward artillery observer. The anonymous neighbor
said he did not think any cows had been hit.

A thirty-four-year-old draftsman from Smithtown, Long Island,
was another of those taken prisoner that day. Detective Captain James
Brooks, commander of the Suffolk County Intelligence squad, identified
him to the Long Island *Press* as the chief "chemist" for the Minutemen group in Suffolk. A dozen rifles, five pounds of gunpowder, a
loaded Beretta automatic (found under his pillow) and various
documents were reported discovered in the draftsman's home.

One of the documents was a thick, looseleaf book containing diagrams
of road obstacles, schematics for making exploding doorknobs, various
kinds of bombs and grenades, according to Captain Brooks.

The others arrested and charged that day included a moldmaker, an
airport steward, a gardener, a horse groom, a driver for the Transit
Authority, a New York City fireman, a plasterer, two mechanics and

a clerk, all but one of whom ranged in age from eighteen to thirty-one years.

As the nineteen Minutemen were being taken into the criminal courthouse building at Queens for arraignment that Sunday, an impressive quantity of weapons and ammunition also was being hauled in with them. A preliminary inventory released by Hentel soon after the raids showed: 125 rifles, single or automatic; ten pipe bombs; five mortars; twelve .30-caliber machine guns; twenty-five hand guns; twenty sets of brass knuckles with knives attached; 220 knives of varying sorts; one bazooka; three grenade launchers; six hand grenades; fifty 80-millimeter mortar shells; one million rounds of ammunition of all kinds; chemicals for preparing bomb detonators, including picric acid; thirty walkie-talkies and various other communications devices including short-wave equipment capable of intercepting police bands; fifty camouflage suits with boots and steel helmets; and a crossbow.

All of this—plus innumerable records and other printed material— had been confiscated from between twenty and twenty-five locations, Cerny said. Some of it had been buried in the ground. All of the weapons were operative or easily could have been reactivated, he said. *Life* magazine later characterized the haul as "enough artillery and ammunition to wipe out entire city blocks and their residents . . . a haul of unprecedented variety and magnitude."

A good deal of right-wing literature also was seized in the raid. Among the books noticed in one of the rooms in which the material had been stored were the inevitable *None Dare Call It Treason*, Hoover's reputable *Masters of Deceit*, the Birch "Blue Book" and one of the Birch society's "White Books," a compilation of monthly Birch Society bulletins to members from Robert Welch. Forlornly in one corner of the room was one of the familiar bumper stickers put out by the Birch society: "Support Your Local Police."*

Some of the many documents taken in the New York raids included coded messages which police cryptographers set to work on in an attempt to decipher, officials said.

The nineteen men were united only briefly at the Queens County Criminal Courts building for arraignment before Judge Bernard Dubin, who had signed search warrants for the raids the day before. The

---

* Three months later, I noticed a loose bumper sticker resting on the top of DePugh's dashboard. His admiration for the police had apparently lost some of its passion by then. The sticker read: "Support Your Local Fuzz."

arraignments took an hour and a half. All nineteen men were charged with conspiracy to commit arson. Other charges included possession of illegal weapons. The scene in the crowded courtroom was not without drama.

F. Courts Bouse, a Woodbury, Long Island, lawyer representing three of the defendants, and a former candidate for Congress on the Conservative Party ticket, declared that the whole affair was an "election day gimmick."

"Between now and election day there will be an indictment, and then, after election, this thing will blow up," Bouse charged.

"I resent that remark," snapped Cerny, "and counsel knows better than that."

Judge Dubin cut off the argument with the remark: "A lot of bombs have been gathered, a lot of guns. What has that to do with the election?"

The judge added that if the allegations against the men were true, "these individuals showed an utter disregard for their neighbors and their property and their community and for their own lives. . . . A misfortune could have occurred where innocent bystanders could have been involved."

The New York *Post* listened to unnamed investigators and policemen who had been in on the raid.

"It was pretty dangerous stuff," one told the *Post*. "We knew we were working with armed, determined people and we never could tell what might set them off."

"It was mad, totally mad," said another. "But they were serious. These guys really intended to attack what they considered dangerous left-wingers."

Back in the courtroom, Howard Cerny asked the judge to set bond at $20,000 each on the two alleged band leaders, and $10,000 on each of the others. Judge Dubin made the total only $81,000—$7500 each for the band leaders; $5000 on six others; $3500 on ten others; and $1000 on an eighteen-year-old Queens clerk (whose mother said he wanted to become a doctor).

After the arraignments, two *Newsday* photographers complained to the district attorney that two of the defendants had roughed them up on their way out and that the police had made no move to arrest the offenders.

Each of the defendants was taken to a different precinct in Queens

for the stated reason that the D.A.'s office did not want them conferring
with one another. Most were freed on bond by Monday, but not all.

Elsewhere in the big courthouse building, Hentel, Cerny and Robert
Schwartz, an assistant D.A. close to the case, were grimly posing with
some of the awesome weapons as flashbulbs popped and Thomas
Mackell, Hentel's Democratic opponent, doubtless gritted his teeth
somewhere else in Queens.

"This is the biggest haul of weapons and death-dealing material
seized in this area in the memory of veteran law-enforcement officers,"
Hentel declared. ". . . We have effectively broken up the secret organization in this area and have removed literally tons of death-inflicting
weapons, ending the possibility of great loss of life and property."

The obvious question was put to Hentel promptly—why the raid
now, with the election so near at hand?

The police had learned that the attacks on the three camps were to
take place that day, replied the district attorney—and "once we learned
they were making their move, we had to make ours."

A police officer "close to the investigation" later in the week un-
derscored this point. The plot, he told me, had been planned originally
for execution October 23—the previous Sunday—and the police had
been ready to move in on them at that time. At the last minute the
Minutemen raids were canceled for a week, he said, so the police
raids were canceled for a week as well.

Other obvious questions were not answered quite so readily. How
did you know the Minutemen were planning their attacks that day?
Informants from the Minutemen ranks? Infiltrators? Wire-taps? No official answer was given, but the New York press corps, using their
other contacts and non-attributable sources, came up with several hints
as to what had happened.

The *Post* reported that a nineteen-year-old college student had
gotten cold feet while in the Minutemen and had become an undercover informant for the police, helping break up the plot. He had been
providing the Minutemen with explosives for homemade incendiary
grenades, stealing them from his college science lab, the *Post* said,
but he had thought they would be used just for training. Finally
he discovered they were to be used for actual attacks, the *Post*
reported, so the lad talked things over with his mother and decided
to become an informant.

The *Daily News* meanwhile was reporting that an unidentified girl friend of a Minutemen member had given police one of their best tips when she informed them that a Minutemen band in Suffolk County was constructing bombs. This young woman furnished names of friends of members of the Minutemen to police and Captain Brooks of Suffolk County was quoted as saying this eventually led to the arrest of eight of the nineteen men in custody.

The *Times* reported that a major role in the Minutemen investigation was played by the secretive Bureau of Special Services of the New York police department—a unit nicknamed "Bossy." An undercover policeman had successfully infiltrated the Minutemen several months before the raid, the *Times* said, and steadily supplied the police department and Queens D.A. with news of their weapons build-up.

Spoon-fed information about the Minutemen continued to pour forth from "well-placed sources" here and there and at Hentel press conferences. Belatedly, the identities of the three camps the defendants were alleged to have planned to bomb and burn were leaked by someone and subsequently confirmed by Hentel. The D.A. added there also had been a fourth intended target of the Minutemen that day— the Brooklyn campaign headquarters of Herbert Aptheker, an avowed Communist who was running for Congress as a representative of the "Peace and Freedom Party."

One of the alleged target camps was located near New York City in New Jersey. J. Edgar Hoover had named it as a Communist front for the indoctrination of the young. Its director was quoted by the *Post* as having denied this charge, observing that political discussions were held on weekends, but in the spirit of free inquiry. If Communists wished to attend, they were welcome, he was quoted as saying.

"The real reason for the attacks (by Hoover and right-wing groups) is that we are an interracial camp," he said.

Another alleged target for Minutemen attack that day was a 200-cabin camp, in New York State. It had been rented the last four summers to a New York high school music teacher and his wife for use "to challenge the creative abilities of 200 children, Negro and white." Two days after this camp was closed for the summer, the Communist Party had rented its facilities for an "educational and recreational conference" attended by 200 teen-agers and college students for two weeks. Several were members of the W. E. B. Du Bois Club.

The third camp was run by the Committee for Non-Violent Action in Connecticut. It had served as a center for conferences on nonviolence and pacifism and was sometimes used as temporary lodging for transient anti-war demonstrators who had no place else to stay. The camp had been plagued with cross-burnings, window-breaking and invading toughs who had journeyed there in the past to start fights. A staff member of the committee was quoted as saying, "We have been threatened before and the Connecticut state police have told us that our attackers have not always been misguided youths from the neighborhood."

Hentel, aware that not everyone in New York was going to be especially sympathetic toward the intended targets of the alleged plot, commented after the arraignment:

"I don't like Communism, just as I assume any free man doesn't like it. But it would be chaos if vigilantes went about on their own. The material seized was so lethal as to be a threat to everyone in the [Queens Criminal Court] building."

Numerous examples of past Minutemen activity in New York came to light in the wake of the raids, some of it from Hentel, some of it from unquotable but presumably reliable sources. The one that tantalized me the most, for some reason, was strictly non-violent and unimportant. It concerned a baseball game police were supposed to have photographed during their surveillance of the Minutemen. The *Daily News* reported that the game had been between members of the Minutemen and the John Birch Society, and that the Minutemen had won, 1 to 0.

Other activities were not so frivolous.

The "Report UN on Bomb List" headline across the top of the October 31 New York *World Journal Tribune*, for instance, prompted cries of alarm from within the United Nations Security Council, where Ambassador Jamil M. Baroody of Saudi Arabia asked that UN guards be alerted in case any Minutemen took any "drastic action," the *Times* later reported.

The *World Journal Tribune's* article had quoted "authorities" that the UN building had been high on the bombing list of "right-wing extremists."

"Sources close to the ten-month-old investigation that led to the dramatic round-up revealed detectives had trailed members of the militant ultraright group into the UN at First Avenue and Forty-second Street recently," reported the newspaper. ". . . They said apparently the plot to bomb the camps was just a dress rehearsal for bigger terrorist actions. . . ."

The same newspaper reported soon afterward that Ambassador Baroody had needled UN Ambassador Arthur Goldberg in the Security Council by demanding more protection, commenting: "The United Nations is an accessible open forum and far from being an impregnable fortress. . . . I do not know what a Minuteman with lightning speed might do."

Goldberg, who was president of the Security Council that month, was reported to have replied: "Let me observe to the representative of Saudi Arabia that I am sure the personnel assigned by the secretary-general, as always in the past, will perform their duties."

New York Police Commissioner Howard R. Leary and Chief Inspector Sanford D. Garelik went to Secretary U Thant personally and spent from ten to fifteen minutes with him. The *Times* reported that a UN spokesman later said the two police officials had assured the Secretary General that "there was no basis for published reports that the activities of the Minutemen had included the United Nations as a possible target."

Hentel also denied any knowledge of a Minutemen plot against the UN, the *Times* reported.

Ambassador Baroody waited about a week after having received assurances of safety from the New York police and then let fly with a new, stronger cry of alarm about the Minutemen. This apparently was triggered by the fact that Jerry Brooks had testified, in the meantime, in federal court in Kansas City that he had once suggested putting cyanide in the air-conditioning vents of the UN. This had been carried by the New York newspapers.

Ambassador Baroody now wanted the UN to "find a new home before another extremist group succeeds in inflicting great harm where the Minutemen failed."

"There is always the danger of a time bomb being planted in the building by some radical individuals," the *World Journal Tribune* quoted the Saudi Arabian as saying. "Security here is good but not foolproof. There are too many pressure groups and fanatics in a city this size to again take such a risk. It would be better to establish headquarters in a neutral country."

Unnamed members of the Minutemen also were accused by Hentel that first week of having tried to foment racial strife in Roosevelt,

Long Island, and Laurelton, in Queens, by distributing hate literature that ostensibly had been prepared by Negro extremists. A sample: ". . . KILL THE WHITE DEVILS. . . . We will kill the white man. We will have the white women for our pleasure. We will smash out the brains of the white babies against the nearest tree. The time to begin is soon—watch for the sign. . . ."

The Minutemen who had done this were unaware of it at the time, but they were under police surveillance while they scattered the leaflets. Hentel elaborated:

"They sped through Laurelton early one morning in a car and threw thousands of these onto sidewalks and into the street. It's the vilest kind of hate literature I have ever seen."

The *World Journal Tribune* reported that the leaflets had so upset the peaceful, eighty-five-percent-white Laurelton community that citizens had considered forming vigilante brigades to protect themselves.

The police had looked for a twentieth man in their forays over parts of the state Sunday. They had been able to find and raid his homes in Syracuse and Brewerton, New York, but they did not find the man himself immediately. Records seized in one of these two raids provided the investigators with a great deal of interesting information. This man, Hentel said, was the East Coast coordinator of the Minutemen. (DePugh later was to identify him as only one of four or five Minutemen coordinators in the state of New York.)

The coordinator was a thirty-eight-year-old pharmaceutical-house technician. When he was finally located and arrested, the charge filed against him was illegal possession of hypodermic needles and non-narcotic syringes, all of which had been found during the Sunday raids. He pleaded not guilty and was released on $1000 bond pending a hearing in December.

A few days after his arrest, Queens authorities were reported by the *Times* as saying that a state policeman had stolen heavy weapons for the Minutemen for two years and had tipped off the Minutemen on state and federal investigations.

Hentel was quoted as saying this man had been one of three state troopers who had formed a Minutemen drill team in upstate New York. The D.A. said that according to the trooper's own admission in the letters that had been found, he had stolen anti-tank cannons, grenades, a mortar, a recoilless rifle and other weapons; had passed on at least one state investigation report on Communists to the Minutemen, had supplied the Minutemen with a trooper's uniform and the license plate numbers of FBI agents, and had served as organizer for them, recruiting two National Guardsmen as possible future Minutemen organizers.

Information about this trooper's activities was found in one of the Syracuse coordinator's homes, Hentel said, and consisted of a voluminous file of correspondence between the trooper and the coordinator in 1964 and 1965.

Among excerpts from the trooper's letters were:

". . . I would be very careful of what you say as he [a high New York state police official] may be investigating you. He also maintains a file of Minutemen in Oneida [New York].

". . . Feds are questioning our people in the Buffalo area.

". . . Re. stuff you mentioned in letter, have four hand grenades of same. Kind of old, though, but you are welcome to these."

Governor Rockefeller already had disclosed that three state troopers were found to have been involved in Minutemen activities, one of them as a member, and that all three had left active service with the state police as a result. It was not disclosed whether the trooper Hentel had mentioned was one of these three.

It was next revealed that on the Wednesday following the Sunday raids on the Minutemen, state troopers had discovered several explosive devices that had been planted in various buildings at the camp in New York state that had been identified as a Minutemen target for October 30.

The devices included several jugs half filled with gasoline and attached to crude timing devices consisting of cheap watches with their hour hands bent to make electrical contact with flashlight batteries that were supposed to energize detonating caps. Other jugs had candles sticking from their necks with cotton strips leading from them to some plastic-foam material that floated atop the gasoline. Inside the plastic foam was a bullet, which presumably would have ignited the gasoline when it exploded.

My own information gathering efforts inside the criminal courts building consisted primarily of confirming first-hand much of what already had been written, with a special eye on connections between the New York Minutemen and national headquarters in Missouri. Eventually I did obtain conclusive evidence from non-attributable sources there that the New York Minutemen were tied in with De-Pugh's national organization, a fact that Hentel eventually confirmed on the day before the election, when he announced that he was going to invite DePugh to New York to testify before his grand jury. (DePugh never accepted the "invitation," if it was ever extended to him personally.)

Since the federal agencies had demonstrated so much interest in the Minutemen in Missouri, it seemed especially curious that federal involvement was not being mentioned in connection with the Queens case. But each time I would ask about federal participation or whether the FBI or ATTU had even known about the Hentel investigation, I found the answers vague.

Finally at one of Hentel's later press conferences that week, the question was put to him directly. Were the FBI or ATTU aware of what was happening?

"Federal authorities are now obtaining information on the case and ATTU agents are examining the weapons," Hentel replied.

"Were the federal agents ever in on this?"

"No," Hentel said. "It started in January on confidential information from the New York City police department."

"The FBI never came in?"

"No," said Hentel. "Our information indicated it was a local operation."

But Walter Winchell's March 6, 1967, column later was to include the following:

"The FBI was furious with the D.A. of Queens County last October for staging that ill-advised raid which jailed several gun-toting Minutemen. They scared off nearby plotters under G-men surveillance for months. Now they must start all over again. The Minutemen had no plot to attack the alleged Red camps. . . ."

Meanwhile J. Edgar Hoover (who the Minutemen implied had leaked that item to Winchell) told the House Appropriations Committee in February:

"On October 30, 1966, New York police officers arrested twenty-four persons who were allegedly Minutemen en route to 'assault left-wing camps in a three state area.' Our New York office had furnished local authorities information that Minutemen groups in that area were planning military-type maneuvers on that date. . . ."

As I flew out of New York Friday night, November 4, I left a city that a week earlier could not have cared less about the Minutemen but by now had been banner-headlined into a firm cognizance of their existence.

Hentel's revelations had created a pronounced public awareness of the organization and spurred many a public figure into comments on the supersecret group.

"These people are misguided in their patriotism," said Governor Nelson Rockefeller, a political ally of Hentel and a man who was also faced with what was viewed as a tough election-day battle the following week.

Others who sprang forward to comment included Senator Thomas J. Dodd (D-Conn.), Representative Ogden R. Reid (R-N.Y.) and Attorney General Lefkowitz, who ordered his own investigation of the Minutemen.

Most officials who spoke out followed the same denunciatory line, but Representative Edwin E. Willis (D-La.) chairman of the HCUA, was reported to have told the Columbia Broadcasting Company that the Minutemen organization "is too insignificant to warrant a full-scale investigation, which perhaps could be used as a forum to enlist and encourage membership."

He perhaps was thinking back to how a congressional investigation of the Ku Klux Klan nearly fifty years earlier had accomplished just such a side-effect for the KKKers. He had a good point.

State Senator Mackell, Hentel's opponent in the D.A. election, held a news conference in the Commodore Hotel to counteract Hentel's publicity boon. He announced the release of a report by the Joint Legislative Committee on Interstate Co-operation, which Mackell headed, calling for tighter weapons laws in New York state, and the realization of a regional compact for interstate control of arms and ammunition.

This report called New York's firearms laws the most stringent in the country, but Mackell commented that these laws still failed to cover howitzers and cannons. He also observed that some states bordering New York had virtually no weapons regulations, making it easy for New Yorkers to obtain weapons it would be illegal for them to purchase in their home state.

The report said that 750,000 American civilians had been killed by firearms since 1900, a toll "actually greater than the 530,000 American servicemen killed in line of duty for all of the wars in our history. . . ."

Mackell also took time at his news conference to lambaste Hentel for delaying his Minutemen raids for "political gain," charging that Hentel had known about the arms caches since January. This had jeopardized the safety of people in the community, he said, in that a power failure, for instance, could have led to an explosion of the combustibles kept in one of the Minutemen's ice boxes.

This prompted Hentel to retort that "public health and safety were safeguarded at all times" and that Mackell's charges were "political" and "must also tar the New York City police department." His raids were held when the suspects were allegedly starting out to attack the camps, he reiterated.

The national spotlight that had shone on the New York Minutemen that week shifted to Kansas City the following Monday for the six-day DePugh-Houghton-Peyson trial. As testimony was being given in the case Tuesday, voters in Queens were defeating Hentel at the polls. More was soon to be heard about the New York case, nevertheless.

While the Kansas City trial was still under way, the downcast Queens district attorney's office released the contents of some of the mail Hentel had been receiving regarding the Minutemen.

It was running two-to-one against Hentel, the *Post* reported, with such sentiments as:

"You have the flag of the U.S. on your living room floor for a rug. . . ."

"You should be given an Iron Cross, one heavy enough to drown you. . . ."

"Long live the Zionist, Bolshevik and glorious Russia."

"How come you never raid Commie groups in Queens?"

"Fine so far. Now when are you going to do something about those Communist guerrilla camps? Please come up with an alibi that is either good or funny."

"Now, really, what's so wrong with killing the dirty, treacherous Communists? You should give a medal to the Minutemen for wiping out these Commie camps."

In late November, the *World Journal Tribune* reported that the Defense Department had confirmed in Washington that three of the defendants in the Minutemen case—including the two band leaders—

had brought their rifles and 6000 rounds of ammunition from the Army through their memberships in the National Rifle Association. A spokesman for the NRA was quoted as acknowledging that nine or ten of the defendants had been NRA members.

In the second week of December, DePugh surprised me in a long interview in Independence by confirming that part of Hentel's allegation which had described all twenty defendants in New York as members of the Minutemen.

The December 4 bulletin to members also acknowledged this: "It can now be disclosed that the persons arrested were members of this organization and the quantity of arms seized was essentially that which the papers reported."

Even more surprising was the assertion in this bulletin:

"According to our New York informant, plans had been drawn up for raids on these three camps but they were not actually scheduled or even anticipated under present circumstances. On the morning of the arrests, these teams were preparing to go out on practice maneuvers such as they did almost every Sunday."

DePugh elaborated on this for me. "Now, the story that I got on the thing," he said, "was that they had drawn up plans to raid these places, but they weren't planning to do it at any specific time. They did it more as a training exercise, just giving themselves some live targets to make the thing more interesting, and in the normal course, I doubt very seriously whether they ever would have carried them out. Maybe they would have. I don't know what their plans and intentions were."

"Do you know how much of your records the police got?"

"No. My understanding is that they got the records of approximately three hundred people."

"What does that do to you?"

"Well, it's bad for that three hundred, that's for sure. . . . That's about a fifth of the organization there."

The bulk of the Minutemen's December 4 bulletin attempted— without saying so in so many words—to justify attacks on such camps as the New York group had been accused of planning to burn.

"We don't know for certain whether or not the New York Minutemen really intended to raid these camps," the bulletin had concluded. "We do know that both state and federal authorities have been aware of these conditions [in the camps] for many years and have never made the slightest effort to correct them. Just how long do they expect decent citizens to restrain themselves?"

It was an interesting defense of their New York brethren. Commented F. Courts Bouse, attorney for several of the New Yorkers, concerning DePugh's public comments about the New York case: "What's the matter with that guy, anyway?"

On the day I was interviewing DePugh about the New York affair, coincidentally, sixteen of the twenty New York Minutemen were being indicted in Queens. The charges ranged from conspiracy to commit arson to unlawful possession of firearms. Only the gardener, the plasterer, the port steward and one of the mechanics escaped indictment and the earlier charges against them were dismissed. The man from Syracuse was not arrested immediately but the other fifteen were arraigned together and continued on bond.

As the arraignments were held, relatives of the defendants picketed outside the building with such signs as: "Would Our Boys in Vietnam Want a Minuteman Arrested?" "Investigate the Commie Camp," and "God Bless the Minutemen."

Having been assured that I would be given considerably more information about the New York case at the D.A.'s office, I returned to New York a few days before Christmas. I wanted to be there before Hentel's staff left office, since they were familiar with the case. Nor did I know yet how strenuously the Mackell staff would pursue the case.

Howard Cerny squeezed in an interview as a policeman hurried him by car from Queens to Manhattan for an appointment one afternoon. Excerpts from my notes on that hectic interview include:

"The grand jury heard ten days of testimony that covered 2000 pages in transcript form. . . . DePugh's figure of 300 members' records having been found is pretty good. . . . The machine guns either were not muzzled or weren't muzzled properly. . . . Evidence that all nineteen men were quite sincere in their beliefs. . . . No hard evidence of plans for any assassinations. . . ."

I was able to talk with Hentel only briefly. He said he was urging Mackell to continue the investigation and to continue to make the Queens D.A.'s office the clearinghouse for the statewide investigation.

Robert Schwartz, who had handled the grand jury investigations on the alleged Minutemen raids, said they had been scheduled to occur simultaneously and were to have a "symbolic" significance. He said he received the impression that the Minutemen would have tried in some way to take credit publicly, as an organization, for having burned the camps.

The assistant D.A. estimated the hard-core national membership of the Minutemen at "several thousand" and said he would guess there were "more than 10,000" just plain members in the country.

"I think they're extremely dangerous, in part to themselves, and in a greater part to our system of democracy," he said. "Not only in destruction of property, but in what they arouse in the average person. They're secretive, fanatical. You can't argue with them."

They will accept anyone into the organization, he said, but are careful about whom they allow to engage in their covert activity, fearing infiltration by Communists and sincere members with loose tongues.

"They're very security conscious," he said, "although they break security all the time. Many of them don't know the identities of others in the Minutemen. They'd write the coordinator in Syracuse and ask, 'What's the name of number such-and-such? I'd like to get to know him,' and he would say, 'I'll get in touch with him and see if he wants to meet you'."

Schwartz said it was his impression that the Minutemen were better organized than either the Ku Klux Klan or the American Nazi Party, adding, "A lot of thought has gone into setting up the Minutemen. I can see how it would appeal to a lot of people—exciting, fun, you get to fire guns, drill, it's secretive, read material, follow people around, make cards on people. They seem to have a great *esprit de corps*.

"Our first reaction to them was that they were funny, silly people," Schwartz added, "that they couldn't have bombs. But then we found they did have bombs, and the capability of using them."

A few days before Christmas, Attorney General Lefkowitz told the New York *Daily News* that his office was continuing its investigation of the Minutemen "for as long as it takes."

"Perhaps we will find we can't arrest them for being members but something will be done," he said. "Just to expose them might be enough."

"Sources close to the probe" were quoted as saying that the names of more than 200 New York Minutemen had been uncovered, that bankers, lawyers and policemen had been found to be members and that they would be exposed eventually at public hearings. A close source was quoted as saying: "The more we dig into the Minutemen operations, the larger the operation looms. We don't know where it will all end up."

Subsequently, "On Target," keeping its readers up-to-date on the New York problems, reported "flagrant" violations of the defendants' constitutional rights. It went on to note that a special defense fund for the New York members had been started the previous month, but that one of the New York team captains under indictment had written back that the national headquarters should keep the money.

"On Target" then declared: "Without money for attorney fees and additional bonds, they are certain of being in prison for many years. In spite of this, they have requested that all the money taken in for legal defense should be used to protect those associated with the national headquarters. What more can any group do in days like these to show their sincerity? We must not let them down."

And "On Target" promised the New Yorkers would get "their share" of all contributions.

"We urge each of you once again," it pleaded, "to contribute all you are able to the Patriots Defense Fund, 613 East Alton, Independence, Missouri."

CHAPTER 18

JOIN THE MINUTEMEN

. . . I believe in States Rights, freedom, liberty, separation of the races, free press, free speech, true nationalism, etc., but outside of picketing our enemies, *we do NOT believe in physical battle just yet.* Perhaps if the pro-Red element ever takes over in this country, we will have to fight for our lives, but we hope Christ returns before that day arrives. I think *we should go to war with Russia NOW* and get it over with—even at the great loss of a third of our population and larger cities—for if we wait another five or ten years, it may be forever too late. Japan has made a quick recovery, after a great loss of cities and millions of people. *America can and must survive one more war. . . .*

> From the summer, 1963, issue of "Alarming Cry," Bobby LeRoy, editor, author of the above, and former chaplain of the Minutemen.

With the New York Minutemen revelations and the DePugh-Houghton-Peyson trial and convictions still fresh in the minds of newspaper readers nationally, the Minutemen "image" was at low ebb.

To the rescue rushed the Reverend Robert LeRoy, chaplain of the secret organization.

Shortly before Thanksgiving, 1966, the minister telephoned me with the suggestion that it seemed proper and fitting to him that the American public should be reminded to count the existence of the Minutemen as one of its blessings on Thanksgiving Day as families gathered around the dinner table for their annual feasts. "Thank God for the Minutemen," the nation should whisper, heads bowed? Yes, he was serious.

I already had seen the Reverend LeRoy in action, once before an audience, offering prayers at a Patriotic Party meeting, and later at the federal trial earlier in November. He was a handsome, sincere man with a round, open and somewhat boyish face. He wore his prematurely salt-and-pepper gray hair in a crew cut which, if dyed, would have enabled him to pass for a seminary student in his twenties. As it was, he was forty-three, an age he made a point of noting was identical to that of his leader, Robert Bolivar DePugh. The Reverend LeRoy described himself as an independent Baptist minister, but at the moment without a church in which to serve as pastor. Instead, his flock was the Minutemen. He appeared neither sanctimonious nor irritatingly self-righteous, as one might have expected. Instead he radiated a bouncy affability and a persistence in his evangelistic approach to others that defied discouragement.

I had called him after the trial with an interview in mind, fully expecting his cooperation. He was not shy. Already we had received a press release from him headlined, "Right Wing Chaplain Calls for Winning the War in Vietnam Immediately," with the Reverend LeRoy quoted as offering the reassuring thought that God wants the United States to win all the wars in which it becomes involved.

Before sitting down with the Minutemen chaplain, I was able to obtain a back issue of the "Alarming Cry," a periodical published through his Biblical Evangelism, Inc. It was helpful in that it pictured the Reverend LeRoy in several different, revealing lights:

•Bobby LeRoy, editor of the "Alarming Cry," founded in 1954 "to promote Soul Winning, Christian Education, and the Twentieth Century Reformation (Dr. Carl McIntire's organization)."

•Bob LeRoy, author of a column titled, "Out of the West," accompanied by a photograph of the Reverend in a broad-brimmed western hat and polka-dot neckerchief. The headline atop his column in this particular issue read, "What the Hell Is Going On in My Country?"

•The Reverend LeRoy, ordained minister, as shown in a photograph of him receiving his ordination certificate in August, 1950, in Tacoma, Washington. The picture was reproduced in his periodical, according to the caption, to "answer critics who claim LeRoy was never offically ordained."

•The Reverend LeRoy, "the Parachute Preacher" of Oshkosh, pictured in helmet, goggles and parachute rig in connection with an advertisement urging readers to "Pray for Parachute Preacher Program" over certain Midwest radio stations.

•Editor LeRoy, who felt compelled, beneath a news item about Representative Adam Clayton Powell's feud with the NAACP, to add: "Editor's note: Some of the NAACP founders were pro-Red Jews."

He suggested elsewhere that we should maintain a life separated from ". . . the spirit of satanic teachings like Communism, Romanism, Liberalism and other anti-Christ spirits in our world today."

When the Reverend LeRoy arrived for the interview, he came armed with numerous pieces of Minutemen and Patriotic Party literature, plus a poster showing a family in church giving thanks for the Minutemen on Thanksgiving.

After three hours of conversation, I reached the conclusion that the Reverend LeRoy was, in his own narrow, sincere terms, an honest man—so honest, in fact, that he had no business in an orgniza-tion that believes deception (lying) is a necessarily patriotic function.

After traveling through the Midwest the past three months, he told me, he had met about 1000 members of the Minutemen. He had concluded, he said, that about ten percent of them were "trigger happy—the type who think that the only good Communist is a dead Communist."

The Reverend LeRoy described his mission then as: "to tone up the Bible and tone down the guns in the Minutemen." The majority of members he had met, he said, do not go along with ideas of assassinations and most are good Christians. Since the founding of the Minutemen, he said, he believed DePugh too had modified his earlier thesis that bullets, not ballots, count most in the struggle against Communism in America, and the Patriotic Party's formation was the best proof of this. Mr. LeRoy's personal choice for the party's presidential candidate in 1972? Senator Strom Thurmond, or possibly Governor Ronald Reagan.

Mr. LeRoy discussed his World War II record, telling of his days as a paratrooper in the South Pacific. He handed me a pamphlet he had prepared about those days. A sample paragraph:

". . . Pfc. LeRoy was shot through the left shoulder by a concealed rifleman. Sergeant Lowe . . . was the first to his side. He quickly stopped the flow of blood squirting from the deep wounds. The enemy's bullet had passed by this young man's heart, by less than one inch. Some believe that God Almighty stood guard within that small space—guiding the 'piece of death' away from LeRoy's heart, so that his physical life might be spared. He is still alive, and now serving God as a Teacher and Evangelist. . . ."

He told me he had made fourteen leaps from airplanes as a

parachutist, his last in 1960 in Littleton, Colorado, to dramatize a sermon he gave to about 100 young persons after landing.

A fundamentalist and "independent Baptist," he had joined Dr. McIntire's Twentieth Century Reformation Hour, Inc., and had been a member of the American Council of Churches since Dr. McIntire founded it in 1941 to fight the liberal influences in the Protestant churches.*

It was through Dr. McIntire, Mr. LeRoy said, that he first heard of the Minutemen. In the spring of 1962, he recalled, he heard Dr. McIntire mention over the radio the "Reuther Memorandum's" attack on the Minutemen. He wrote a letter of inquiry to DePugh and eventually, in 1963, began taking the five-phase correspondence course offered Minutemen. Soon he was placed in charge of Minutemen affairs in western Nebraska. He first met DePugh personally at the Patriotic Party convention in Independence in 1966.

He told of various meetings in rural areas at which he had been the featured speaker in recent months, drumming up an interest in the Patriotic Party. He offered press clippings about his appearances in southern Missouri and North Dakota. One news story told of his speaking to a near-capacity crowd at the Eudora, Missouri, Community Center, and having been introduced by the principal of a nearby Bible school.

Another clipping, this one from North Dakota, told of his foray into Bismarck with the help of a local Minuteman identified as a member of the Farmers Liberty League. Mr. LeRoy was quoted as saying the Minutemen hoped to build a national force of five million members by 1968.

Our conversation that day touched many fields, including evolution and racial issues.

He has written a book on evolution, titled *The Scientific and Psychological Approach to the Creation Story*, (Pageant Press, Inc.) in which, according to one of his brochures, he shows that the biblical version of the creation cannot be reconciled with the theory of evolution. Therefore, he deduces, Darwin must be wrong. Originally, the

* Dr. McIntire is, among other things, a dynamic radio preacher with a wide audience across the nation. He obviously has a large following and to those who agree with him, he undoubtedly is a great inspiration. I enjoy listening to him whenever possible because of his style of delivery. Most fascinating is Dr. McIntire's use of a straight man he frequently refers to as "Amen Charlie," whose chief function is to punctuate the preacher's strongest points with a soulful, "Ahhhhhh-men," several times during each half-hour broadcast.

book was written as a thesis to earn a Master's degree from Chadron State College in Chadron, Nebraska, but it was turned down and he did not receive his degree. His brochure on the book quotes the chairman of the philosophy department at the school as saying that its publication would set progressive education back 100 years. No fan of John Dewey, Mr. LeRoy takes a certain pride in that denunciation.

"Teaching children they are descended from animals," he said, "makes them act like animals."

His views on race were a bit more complex. At first he said he believed in a Sunday school verse he learned as a child:

Red and yellow,
Black and white,
All are precious,
In God's sight.

However . . .

He also said he believed that Negroes have been cursed by God. He quoted from Genesis 9:18–28 to substantiate this. Ham, one of Noah's three sons, looked upon the nakedness of his father after Noah had become intoxicated, the Reverend LeRoy said. As punishment, God cursed Ham and all his descendants by making their skin black and turning them into a "servant race."

"Most conservative theologians believe that the black race is descended from Ham," the Reverend LeRoy enlightened me. "So this would follow that the black race is basically to be the servant of the white."

He qualified this by saying that today some Negroes can excel anyway and should be given the chance to excel.

"The biblical curse has left a scar on the black people," he added. "It still exists in the minds of many people today."

Pressed on this question, the Reverend LeRoy said that while he personally believes the "skin curse" still exists, he does not think the "servant curse" does any more. He offered an explanation as to why and when he believed God had removed one of these "curses" and not the other, but it was too far over my head to try to report here.

The article resulting from this interview seemed to please the Reverend LeRoy, but—as best I could tell—angered DePugh, especially the part about the curse on Negroes. By the end of November I had begun a three-month leave of absence to finish researching the Minutemen and write much of this book. In the process, I sat down with DePugh for two long, tape-recorded interviews in his office at 613 East Alton. In the first of these—in mid-December—I asked DePugh whether Mr. LeRoy represented a new approach by the Minutemen.

"It was an experiment I don't think we'll repeat," DePugh replied. "I told him his job was to sell the Patriotic Party, not to save souls. But with a man like that, it's pretty hard to get him to stick to the subject.

"We had figured that perhaps through the Patriotic Party we could appeal to the audience of people like Carl McIntire and others of that category who generally are considered pretty conservative."

Shortly before Christmas I ran across Mr. LeRoy in the big Katz drugstore in Overland Park, a Kansas City suburb. I found the Minutemen's chaplain selling electric knives and electric razors from a card table set up in one of the busy aisles. Just earning a little extra cash over the holidays, he said pleasantly, and then he tried to sell me a razor.

"What about Reverend LeRoy?" I asked DePugh in mid-January.

He was "out" as Minutemen chaplain, DePugh replied. Definitely, irrevocably "out."

"Does he know this?" I asked, for the Reverend LeRoy had told me in the drugstore he was still very much "in."

"I've told him about twenty times," DePugh said. "Now, whether it's sunk through, I'm not real sure. But he should have got the message."

"Is he out of the Minutemen as a member too?"

"Yes."

"Why?"

"Well, mostly because he just insisted on acting as—on interjecting his own personal beliefs as reflecting the programs and policies of the organization," said DePugh. ". . . It's an unfortunate thing, because LeRoy made a heck of a good appearance, and could be valuable to anyone who needs a good public relations man."

A few days later, DePugh, Houghton and Peyson were sentenced to prison by Judge Hunter. As DePugh stood before the television cameras after the sentencing and declared that the Communist-Socialist

conspiracy was now in control of the United States, the Reverend
LeRoy stood nearby, trying (DePugh later told me—I didn't notice)
to squeeze himself within camera range.

The following day I received a telephone call at home from Mr.
LeRoy. He was looking for some advance publicity in the *Star* to
attract a crowd to a "Faith and Freedom Rally" he planned to hold
at 7:30 that Friday night, January 20, in the library room of the
World War II Memorial Building in Kansas City, he said.

"Are you still chaplain of the Minutemen?" I asked him.

"Why, yes," he replied, and there was a painful pause. "Why do
you ask?"

"I had been led to believe that perhaps you didn't hold that position
any longer," I said, trying to be nice about it.

"Who told you that?"

"DePugh."

"Well, he's never said anything to me about it," the Reverend
LeRoy replied.

I suggested he talk with DePugh about it since there seemed to
be some slight discrepancy. Mr. LeRoy said that he most certainly
would do so.

As for the Friday night "rally," LeRoy promised in a postcard
mailed to conservatives around town that he would discuss "what
is really behind the arrest of Mr. DePugh and what does the future
hold for conservatives?" He identified himself on the card as "Evangelist
and Patriot, midwestern representative of the Patriotic Party."

The main purpose of the meeting, however, turned out to be an
effort to raise enough money for Mr. LeRoy to expand his "national"
weekly radio broadcasts from three stations to four. Specifically, he
was looking for donations totaling $25 a week to obtain a half-hour
each Sunday morning over station KCLO in Leavenworth, Kansas.

The Reverend LeRoy, who had grown accustomed to the more
bland type of opposition offered by civil libertarians over the years,
was somewhat shocked at 5:30 Friday afternoon—two hours before the
meeting was scheduled to begin—when Willis R. Rohr, manager of
the World War II Memorial Building, telephoned him and told him
he could not hold his meeting there.

The building is owned and run by the American Legion.

The Reverend LeRoy asked Rohr why.

"You're connected with the Minutemen, aren't you?" Rohr asked him.

"I'm their chaplain, interested in their spiritual side," Mr. LeRoy replied. But this was not good enough.

Mr. LeRoy hastily rescheduled the meeting for the Hotel Bellerive and persons arriving at the war memorial building were informed of the change by the parking lot attendant. By 8:05 that evening, twenty-three persons had found their way to the hotel's little meeting room in which Mr. LeRoy was prepared finally to speak.

He barely touched on either of his announced topics in the next two hours and forty-five minutes, possibly because he found it necessary to spend nearly an hour, all told, discussing how the American Legion in Kansas City had denied him his right of free speech.

"I was converted thirty years ago at the age of thirteen and I've been an evangelist for fifteen years," he said, "but this is the first time I have been kicked out of a building, and with just *two hours* notice! . . . I have fought for this country. I have shed blood for this country in World War II. . . . This is not Russia! This is not Poland!! This is not behind the Iron Curtain!!! This is the LAND OF THE FREE!!!!"

Wayne Morse, the veteran Kansas City picket, was in the audience and promptly announced he would drag a Communist flag behind him on the ground in front of the war memorial building the next day.

A cooler, gray-headed man in the back of the room suggested that each of them instead start a campaign to "convert, not convict" the American Legion posts in the city and give the Legion another chance to let them hold a meeting inside the building.

Mr. LeRoy used the incident as just another example of how Socialism was coming into the United States "drop by drop," moving the nation's people away from God and "moving them to the left wing that Moscow and Peking want fellowship with."

"It's not just Bob DePugh that's being harassed. There are others!" he declared.

The audience seemed entirely in agreement with Mr. LeRoy and several nodded their heads affirmatively in response to various points he raised. Applause came only once, however, when he called for removal of the United Nations headquarters from the United States and the United States' withdrawal from the United Nations. He suggested giving our seat to Red China.

Mr. LeRoy's method of delivery seemed aimed at a higher level of intelligence than is usual for men with such messages. He did not rant and seldom raised his voice, the exception being when he talked about the World War II Memorial Building. His delivery was reasonably relaxed, but seldom accompanied by a smile. The story of a conversation between two skeletons hanging in a closet ("if we had any guts we'd get out of this predicament") was the closest he came to humor.

He ranged over a wide field of topics, all of them concerning the Communist threat. The Minutemen were barely mentioned, although he did identify himself as their chaplain. Nor did the Patriotic Party, as such, receive much attention. Instead, Mr. LeRoy recited a multitude of observations and opinions that most of the audience undoubtedly had heard or read before.

He talked about the high rate of divorce, delinquency, liquor consumption and gambling in this country. He offered copies of "None Dare Call It Treason" for fifty cents. He read excerpts from *The Communist Manifesto*. He accused the Communists of being behind race riots. He observed that urban renewal is a plot to integrate white neighborhoods and that the man in charge of it in Washington is a Negro. He predicted this would be the possible cause of a revolution in the South. He quoted two ex-FBI employees who now were in the Far Right to the effect that Dr. Martin Luther King had belonged to more Communist-front organizations than anyone in the United States. As evidence that Robert Welch was right in his assessment of former President Eisenhower, he pointed out that after Ike's retirement from the Army, he became president of Columbia University, which, he said, was one of the most left-wing universities in the country. John Dewey taught at Columbia, he said, and the Reverend LeRoy talked a long while about John Dewey. And he quoted another minister to the effect that there are more than 7000 Protestant clergymen preaching Communism in churches in the United States.

Mr. LeRoy moved into the subject of firearms-control laws during the question-and-answer period, warning that Senator Thomas Dodd was readying a new bill on this. A woman in the audience raised her hand.

"Well, why don't we write our senators and tell them we're opposed to it?" she suggested.

"Good," the Reverend LeRoy replied. "Terrific idea."

A little, elderly lady observed, while discussing Ambassador Arthur Goldberg's shortcomings, that everyone whom President Johnson had appointed to an office was "a Red."

"They're dirty rats!" shouted a middle-aged man in the last row.

"Well, I don't deal in personalities in quite that sharp a focus," Mr. LeRoy responded.

It eventually became painfully clear that the Reverend LeRoy—while he was saying all the "right" things—was not saying them in a manner that would tend to inspire. This was proven when late in the meeting he began his effort to raise pledges of twenty-five dollars a week for the radio program in Leavenworth.

"I'm going to start with one dollar," he said, "who'll give one dollar a week? I'm not going to do like Billy James Hargis. He'd start with one hundred dollars. I'm just going to start with one. Who's ready to give one dollar a week to hear this sort of message over the radio here?"

Two hands went up—a little, white-haired woman in her seventies who had earlier urged from the floor that American mothers refuse to let their boys fight in Vietnam, and a man in his fifties who had remained silent throughout the meeting.

"Fine. That's two dollars a week already. Who'll make it three?"

No hands were raised. The Reverend LeRoy continued talking. His voice was needed in the Kansas City area, he said. Kansas City was the place where the American Legion had refused to let a patriotic, evangelistic World War II veteran speak. Finally a third hand was raised. It was that of the man who had wanted to "convert, not convict" the Legion. Mr. LeRoy expressed great pleasure over this and as he addressed his next remarks to this man, he seemed to see the man raise his hand again, although he had simply scratched his head.

"Did I see you raise your hand again?" he asked. "Good, pal. That's fine. That makes four dollars. I'll put in a dollar myself. That makes five dollars a week to get on this radio station. Who'll make it six? You're buying a minute a week of patriotism in Kansas City."

The Reverend McIntire—who had around 600 radio stations carrying his daily message and was pushing for 1000—could die any

day, Mr. LeRoy said. Younger men were going to be needed to take
his place. He then told in detail of the recent death of a middle-aged
man who belonged to the same church he attended. This man had
been in excellent health up until the moment he keeled over dead of
a heart attack. Death can come to anyone at any time, the Reverend
McIntire included. Who would make it $6 (actually $4)? But the
possibility of Dr. McIntire's death and his subsequent replacement
by the Reverend LeRoy prompted no new hands to be raised.

Mr. LeRoy was becoming plainly desperate, but it was in no way
funny to watch. Normally I would be inclined to delight in a
pitch man's failure. But Mr. LeRoy—while playing the pitch man
—reflected pathos. Yet he persisted. He told of his own financial condition. This radio program was not for his own personal profit, he said—
he makes his living off the offerings he receives at meetings such as
this, nothing more.

Three hands went up.

"EIGHT! NOW we've broken the ice," he said in delight. I found
myself suddenly happy for him, hoping he'd make it to $25.

On and on he talked, but the audience simply had not been
moved. McIntire or Hargis would have had them clamoring to give
money by then.

Finally a middle-aged man from Topeka said he would give $2
for the first month, pointing out that he already was supporting Mr.
LeRoy's weekly broadcast on a Topeka station. Mr. LeRoy stopped
counting the money in terms of a dollar a week, and zeroed in now
on simply the dollar figure—for how many weeks, it did not matter.
This way, at least, he could salvage some dignity.

"Ten dollars! Wonderful. Who'll make it eleven? I think if we
can just get half, they'll let us go on the air and we can raise the
rest with Faith. Who'll make it eleven?"

Someone else offered a dollar for two months.

"Twelve!"

The little woman who had been the first to raise her hand said
she had a friend who was not present but whom she was sure she
could persuade into donating a dollar a week.

"Thirteen. Wonderful," and he began to speak with renewed vigor.
Another woman apologized that she already was donating a large
amount to support another patriotic Christian minister (a Birch society chapter leader) on his weekday fifteen-minute programs on

KCLO and simply could not afford it. Someone else reminded him that the people who listened to such programs usually were on Social Security and could not afford such donations. Mr. LeRoy assured her that radio preachers derive the bulk of their support from just such persons, and that these persons find it quite easy to take one dollar from each of their Social Security checks in order to support such broadcasts.

"Fourteen? Who'll make it fourteen?"

But there was no response.

"Maybe you can get another one to give," he told the little woman who had told of her fund-raising abilities. "We'll call it fourteen. I think we'll stop at $15 tonight. Does anybody . . ."

But although he continued to try, no one offered the fifteenth dollar and Mr. LeRoy reluctantly abandoned the project, slipping quietly into his next appeal—to help Bob DePugh with his postage expenses. He held up a large batch of sealed, addressed envelopes and informed his audience that all they needed now were stamps and mailing. These were snapped up quickly by several persons before Mr. LeRoy had even told them what was inside them.

The meeting ended shortly after 10:30 with affirmation of the intention by several present to start putting the pressure on the American Legion. Wayne Morse promised to delay his picketing until after the Legion had been given a second chance.*

But, alas, the Reverend LeRoy's brand of religious evangelism and the Minutemen way of life were incompatible. In less than a week, Mr. LeRoy officially resigned as Minutemen chaplain.

In a letter to DePugh, with copies to the news media, the preacher made the astonishing observation that "I do not feel that the basic activities of the Minutemen organization are conducive to spiritual growth." He went on to explain his reasoning:

"The emphasis has been on 'fire power' more than spiritual power. God is still running this universe, so our fellowship with

---

* Given that second chance the following summer, Willis Rohr and the high-ranking Legionnaires who control the building, refused to allow the national Patriotic Party convention in their hall. Rohr did extend an invitation to them, however, to attend the next American Legion meeting in the hall.

"But they better bring their own police protection with them," he said, "because I can't guarantee their safety. Some of these boys out here who've had an arm or leg blown off fighting for this country aren't going to stand for that kind of stuff. They'll tear 'em apart."

Him, through His son Jesus Christ, is more important than anything else. . . ."

Elsewhere in the letter were several kind remarks about DePugh and the organization, but Mr. LeRoy had made the break, and I'm sure that more than a few of the angels who look after men like the Reverend LeRoy smiled.

The Minutemen had been something of an anchor for the Reverend, however, and I could not help but wonder what would happen to him now that he had freed himself. Worry was unnecessary. Mr. LeRoy is a remarkably resilient man. About a month after his resignation, he began broadcasts over KCLO in Leavenworth, and not just on Sunday mornings, but three times weekly, a half-hour after the Reverend McIntire signed off for the day. Somehow he had found the money he had been so ineffective in raising that night in the hotel.

On the few broadcasts I heard, he offered free copies of *Blueprint for Victory* on a while-they-last basis and more than once he praised DePugh. A postcard advertising his "Faith and Freedom Hour" program included identification of Mr. LeRoy as "former chaplain of the Minutemen." This seemed odd, in a way, but having moved to Kansas City, Kansas, thus losing his Nebraska following, the Reverend needed some way of attracting a new audience.

He lost his radio time on KCLO abruptly in a few months. Rather than sticking to his normal line of religion and patriotism, he had decided to launch a full-scale attack on organized crime in Kansas City, Kansas. In doing so, he decided to name names and identified a prominent lawyer as the "top, reputed underworld leader" of the city. It was a brash move for several reasons, not the least of which was that he not only lacked evidence but was unconvincing even in theory. The lawyer naturally complained and KCLO canceled the Reverend LeRoy.

I asked him why in the world he had done this when we ran across each other at the second annual Patriotic Party convention, and he replied that some Kansas City, Kansas, Minutemen had provided him with evidence and that it was indeed a shame that freedom of speech is so restricted in the United States that he had been canceled. (The lawyer, incidentally, did not sue the Reverend. He said he felt a suit would serve only to give the preacher publicity.)

Still undaunted, the Reverend LeRoy soon opened a conservative bookstore in Kansas City, Kansas, the "Faith and Freedom Center," located in an old store beneath an apartment in which he moved his family.

During a visit there in October, 1967, I found him optimistic and friendly as usual. He was holding Bible meetings at night in the back room of the store. He was teaching guitar on the side. He had obtained a representative collection of books, magazines and pamphlets of fundamentalist or right-wing persuasion. The anti-Semitic tracts that were on display were not for sale but just there "for the interest of browsers." *Blueprint for Victory* was for sale, however, as was the bumper sticker I purchased for twenty-five cents, copyrighted by Poor Richard's Book Store of Hamilton, Montana:

"SUPPORT RED AGENTS—ATTEND BOLSHOI BALLET."

The Reverend LeRoy was still in there trying. And undoubtedly always will be.

CHAPTER 19

JOIN THE MINUTEMEN

Effective this date I am resigning my position as national co-ordinator of the Minutemen organization. . . .

Letter from Robert B. DePugh to all members in January, 1967.

BOB DEPUGH'S RESIGNATION—We should all bear in mind the old and worn strategy of "what we do and what we say may be two different things."

Letter to California Minutemen from "930," otherwise known as Troy Houghton, in May, 1967.

Shortly before the November, 1966, federal Minutemen trial in Kansas City, I received an unexpected telephone call from Columbia, Missouri. The caller identified himself as Kenneth B. Patrick, a twenty-two-year-old senior in his final semester at the University of Missouri in Columbia. He said he had chosen the Minutemen as the subject of two term papers he had to write before graduating in January. Would I be available for an interview about the Minutemen, he asked. Sure, I said, although not quite certain yet whether this was wise.

For all I knew then, Ken Patrick was another Minuteman, perhaps one of the college lads DePugh had claimed the Minutemen had trained one summer on how to rout out Commies on the campuses.

Was this student on some sort of a Minutemen counterintelligence mission? Had DePugh sent him to me to discover what kind of book I was writing about his organization? It seemed unlikely, but possible. (DePugh knew my attitude without sending in spies.) Still, I could not help but wonder.

We met for the first time at the trial and talked briefly during recesses. Later he visited my home several times, at first to interview me formally about the Minutemen, then for more informal chitchat.

Ken had established rapport with DePugh and a few others at 613 East Alton in interviewing them for his term papers and had been told some things which no one had ever bothered telling me. He was becoming if not my "spy," at least a good source of double-check information. Or was he a double-agent, reporting to DePugh everything I said just as it seemed he was telling me what DePugh was saying? I found that Ken's visits became increasingly interesting when such doubts were applied to everything we said to one another.

On our first long visit, Ken made a point of informing me that he was an ultraconservative. "You might even call me a radical," he said, and confessed membership in the Young Americans for Freedom at the university. But his interest in the Minutemen was academic, he insisted. He disapproved of both the Minutemen and the Birchers, he said, because he felt they brought discredit upon conservatism.

By the time he had left Kansas City for the Marine Corps in March, I had concluded that this tall, easy-going, good-looking young conservative was exactly what he had presented himself as being, and I felt a bit ashamed at having doubted him at first. When I told him this, he seemed to understand. His father's attitude and what one of his university professors told me about him helped strengthen my trust in him near the end. Before he left Kansas City, however, Ken had created some doubts in the minds of quite a few others besides myself as to exactly what the nature of his interest in the Minutemen was.

During one of our sessions in which we exchanged information in late December, Ken told me DePugh had mentioned something about the possibility that if he were sentenced to prison, there were Minutemen around who might take rash, retaliatory action of some sort. I thought it interesting that DePugh would have told the college student this since, as far as I could tell, he had no assurance Ken would not repeat it—possibly even to federal authorities. Was DePugh actually trying to frighten the government out of sending him to prison? It was hard to imagine he would be that naïve, but I could not help wonder.

Four days after the new year, 1967, Troy Houghton flew into Kansas City to be with his co-defendants for the hearing on motions for a new trial. I attempted at that time to persuade the California Minutemen leader to sit down for an interview before he left town again, but he was unreceptive to the idea.

The following day was a cold Thursday in Kansas City. The date was January 5, and now a date and hour of day and night become

important—to Houghton, to Patrick, to me, and to the police in Cheyenne, Wyoming.

Somewhere between seven-thirty and nine o'clock (I can establish
the time within this hour and a half, but no more definitely),
Ken Patrick telephoned my home. Jo, my wife, told him I would
be back shortly after nine, but he said he had to drive back to
Columbia that night. Would she deliver the message? Certainly. Ken
said he had just driven Houghton to the bus depot in Kansas City
and in the process had managed to interview the California Minuteman.

One of the items of interest Ken had picked up in their conversation
was that Houghton—like DePugh—thought (or said he thought) that
if DePugh received a heavy sentence or went to prison, there were
Minutemen around who might possibly "start shooting."

Jo passed this on to me when I returned home and I filed it away
in my mind without much thought. Ken had known I was getting
nowhere trying to interview Houghton myself (Houghton thought I
was working with or for the FBI, Ken said) and so the college student
had been quite pleased with himself for having managed to interview
the Californian.

Four days later—Monday, January 9—I picked up the evening *Star*
and read that Houghton had been arrested in Cheyenne, Wyoming,
the previous Saturday night on a charge of indecent exposure before
two teen-age girls.

James W. Byrd, Cheyenne chief of police, was quoted as saying
the alleged incident had occurred the previous Thursday night at a
Wyoming shopping center while the girls were seated in a motor car
in the parking lot.

I soon discovered there was good reason to suspect that Houghton
was innocent of the crime.

It had been committed within a few minutes of ten o'clock (Kansas
City time) the night of January 5. Yet Ken Patrick had telephoned
my home well before ten o'clock with the news that he had dropped
Houghton off at the bus depot at eight o'clock that night. Houghton
had not had time to reach Cheyenne in time to commit the crime—
unless Patrick had lied when he called me.

But why would he have lied? Whoever heard of anyone setting
up a false alibi ahead of time to enable someone to indecently expose
himself in front of two teen-age girls in a shopping-center parking

lot? For a murder, a robbery, a kidnaping—certainly. But indecent exposure? It made no sense. Patrick had to be telling the truth.

I conducted my own, self-styled investigation, the details of which, I fear, would be boring to everyone not directly involved. At any rate, I concluded that Houghton had been the inadvertent victim of mistaken identity.

Houghton, however, seemed convinced that "the conspiracy" was back at work, and he conjured up a dark and devious plot involving federal agents who he thought had followed him all the way from Kansas City to Cheyenne by bus (where he picked up a car) and then from Cheyenne to San Diego, just to frame him.

"Ken Patrick tells me you think the Minutemen might start shooting if they put you in prison," I asked DePugh later.

"Well, that's what some of them have told me," DePugh responded. "I didn't expect him [Patrick] to tell you or anyone."

"Who do your members say they are going to shoot?"

"Oh, nobody in particular."

"Everybody in general?"

"I don't know. . . . I'll admit I told Patrick this, but I did it in a facetious manner and I didn't really think the guy would take it seriously, and I didn't take the people seriously who made the statement, although they may have tried to make it sound serious. There's going to be a hell of a lot of people in the organization who are going to be as mad as can be, but I'm certainly going to take steps before I ever go to jail to see that the chain of command is passed on in a smooth, orderly manner . . . to another one of the members of the [and he smiled] non-existent council."

The next leader of the Minutemen, he added, would be anonymous and would probably try diligently to remain that way. If he were imprisoned, DePugh said, Minutemen members would be left with considerably more freedom of action than existed at that time.

"But I think that within the organization," he said, "the goals and objectives and the approximate timetable, the broad outline, will be propagated from what I've written."

That had been shortly before Judge Hunter had sentenced him to four years in prison, pending appeal.

About a week after receiving this sobering news, DePugh called me from Norborne to tell me that he had decided to step down from his post as national coordinator of the Minutemen.

"Why?" I asked.

"I'm mailing out a letter now to all members explaining why," he said, and he read me the letter, the main points of which were:

•He was resigning as national coordinator immediately and avoiding any contact or communication with the future leaders of the Minutemen.

•The new leaders, from whom future directives would be issued, would be the still anonymous members of the "executive council." It was doubtful, he added, that any one leader would be identified as such in the future.

•Minutemen were to accept this anonymous leadership. ("I have absolute confidence in both the loyalty and the ability of those who now accept the responsibilities of leadership. I ask all of our members to show them the same loyalty which they have shown me and for which I have been both grateful and honored.")

•He was still strongly in favor of Minutemen principles and was resigning only to strengthen the organization. Initially the Minutemen had needed a known leader, but it no longer did so and in fact would be able to function better with a secret leadership.

•The Minutemen henceforth would become entirely clandestine in their operations.

•While still free on bond, DePugh would continue to work in behalf of the Patriotic Party (and thus, he did not need to add, retain a platform from which to state his views publicly, and a base from which he could recruit more persons into the Minutemen.)

The letter, which also contained a good deal of routine prose on patriotism, the Commie threat and so forth, left several questions unanswered. How, for instance, was the average Minuteman-in-the-street going to know what to do? How would he receive his orders? How would he know, if receiving orders, that the orders came from a legitimate source? How could he trust an anonymous leadership, it being hard enough as it was knowing whether to trust persons whose names you knew?

DePugh answered that the Minutemen were going through a thorough reorganization that would solve most of these problems. All members had new identification numbers, he said. Those numbers would become known only to the executive council and a courier. Messages would be delivered to members from the executive council through couriers using knowledge of the new identification number as proof of their reliability. Team captains and other leaders would have an additional secret means of identification.

Ken Patrick soon was graduated from the University of Missouri (with an "A" on his term paper titled "The Minutemen as a Social Movement" for Sociology course 315—collective behavior).* With time to kill between graduation and his entry into the Marine Corps (he wanted to go fight the Viet Cong), Ken expressed a desire to join me on a trip to Joplin, Missouri, on January 31. This was the date set for DePugh's trial on transporting a .38-caliber Smith & Wesson snub-nosed revolver from Des Moines to Kansas City while under a state indictment for a felony. He had entered a plea of not guilty and with a trial expected, Judge Hunter had transferred the case south to Joplin to get some miles between prospective jurors and the Kansas City news media.

One of the most compelling reasons for our going to Joplin was to see whether Cindy Melville would testify in the case, and if she did, for whom.

Cindy had been with DePugh when federal officers found the .38 in his attaché case. She thereupon had thrown something of a fit with Agent Belecky as the subject for her wrath, and as a result she had been indicted by the federal grand jury for this indiscretion. Since then, little had been seen or heard of the usually ubiquitous longtime secretary to DePugh.

Earlier that month I had asked DePugh what had happened to Cindy, but DePugh insisted I switch off my tape recorder before he answered, and he went off the record—very unusual for him. I found his off-the-record story difficult to believe, but my skepticism was based mainly on other information I also had received off the record, and it too had been difficult to swallow.

It was known that Cindy was living most of the time with her mother, Mrs. Frieda Sanders, and her two young children in a certain apartment in south Kansas City, but she was seldom seen outside. There had been reports of Minutemen lurking near this apartment complex, keeping her under surveillance, but they had not been con-

---

* Among his conclusions: "At this time it appears that the growth of the Minutemen is almost certain."

firmed. Cindy's mother had been at the trial in November as one of
the most attentive spectators, but Cindy had not attended. Was the
young woman, by then twenty-one, ready to testify for the government
or for DePugh? Had she finally abandoned the Minutemen and the national coordinator whom she had served so faithfully as confidential
secretary, cryptographer, chauffeur, and as Frank Belecky could testify,
bodyguard? Was the government holding the federal indictment against
her over her head? Or did she intend to help DePugh despite the indictment facing her?

I had heard many stories, nearly all of them in conflict with one
another. Since Mary Tollerton's knock on Cindy's apartment door that
night in July, 1965, Cindy had kept her distance from me and my
questions. And now DePugh was refusing to discuss her openly. Very
strange. Most unusual.

By the time a bus had deposited us in Joplin, the show was over.
Joe Henderson, the *Star's* federal courthouse reporter, filled me in on
what had happened. A fifty-five-member jury panel had been assembled
from eight southwest Missouri counties and Judge Hunter was preparing to begin questioning them when defense attorneys Gilwee and
Costello approached the bench and informed the judge that DePugh
had just changed his mind. He would plead *nolo contendere,* meaning
"no contest," almost the same as a guilty plea, but not quite.

Judge Hunter instructed Millin to tell DePugh what the maximum
penalty was if this plea were accepted. Millin obliged. The maximum
penalty could be five years.

Startled, DePugh replied: "I'd rather stand trial."

So Judge Hunter began questioning prospective jurors.

Soon Gilwee was back before the bench. DePugh had changed his
mind again, he said. The plea would be *nolo contendere.* Judge Hunter
asked DePugh for confirmation. DePugh confirmed.

Judge Hunter thereupon sentenced DePugh to one year in prison,
the sentence to run concurrently with part of the four-year sentence
he had been given earlier that month. The Judge also told DePugh
the sentence would not start until his appeal of the other conviction
had been settled.

Millin then asked permission to read a statement of facts about the
charge into the record.

"The facts are," he began, and recited that DePugh had purchased
eight revolvers from a Mr. Russell Levine, a gun dealer in Des Moines,

Iowa, on July 23, 1966. DePugh had used the name "Wayne Morris" and the address of 3435 Euclid, Kansas City, Missouri, which happened to be the real address of Wayne Morse, M-O-R-S-E, the picket.

Although under a state indictment at that time, Millin continued, DePugh was found with one of the eight revolvers on August 20 when arrested in Kansas City on a federal indictment. The revolver was fully loaded, he added.

"Why did he plead *nolo contendere?*" was the natural question. First we asked Costello and Gilwee.

It was because of Cindy, we were told. Cindy had been present when DePugh was arrested and the pistol found in the car. And Cindy was still under federal grand jury indictment for having assaulted Frank Belecky, of the ATTU. Now Cindy was in Joplin ready to testify *against* DePugh, the lawyers said. So why fight it?

This was discussed further in DePugh's presence as Costello drove Gilwee, DePugh, Ken and me to DePugh's motel. DePugh said nothing to contradict the lawyers in the car.

However, once we had left the lawyers, and were preparing to drive back to Kansas City, at DePugh's suggestion in DePugh's car, the former national coordinator of the Minutemen offered a different explanation in a roundabout, typically mysterious way.

Ken and I were standing by DePugh's car waiting for him to gather up his belongings in the motel when he appeared in the doorway and motioned for us to join him.

"Why don't you call Cindy from here," he said. "She's staying in a hotel in town."

"What for?"

"It may be the last chance you'll have to talk with her," he said.

"Last chance?"

"They're probably going to try to get her out of the country."

"Who?"

"The Eye." (Common DePughism for the FBI)

"Out of the country?"

"Well, out of the area."

"Why?"

DePugh continued looking for the telephone number of the hotel.

Ken and I exchanged curious glances waiting for an answer, but it did not come.

"Does this have anything to do with why you changed your plea?"

"Some day the real reason will come out," said DePugh. "I can't tell you now."

I turned down his suggestion.

DePugh seemed disappointed, but did not press the point.

"Maybe one of you had better drive," he said. "I don't have a license, you know."

We had not progressed up U.S. 71 five minutes before DePugh said that we were being followed.

"How do you know?"

"See that car back there?" DePugh said, pointing to the vehicle behind us several hundred feet. "It's a government car."

I could not help commenting a few minutes later that the "government car" had just made a left turn off the highway and was no longer in sight.

DePugh then explained that a government tail from Joplin to Kansas City probably would take at least four cars, one picking us up immediately after the last one pulled away, to avert suspicion.

It took only a few more miles before DePugh was telling us the *real* reason he had pleaded *nolo contendere*, and it hadn't even taken any coaxing.

"This is off the record for the paper," he said, "but you can use it for your book later."

This did not especially put me in the mood to believe what he was about to say, but I listened.

The essence of his story was that he had pleaded *nolo contendere* for Cindy's sake. If she refused to testify against him in Joplin, then the government would go ahead and try her on the assault charge, he said. If she did testify against him, the government would drop the charge against her. Cindy would not testify against him, he said. He was certain of this, he said. She had been loyal to him. Now it was his turn to help her. Thus the plea.

This sounded a lot more gallant than credible. His indecision over what to do in the courtroom weakened the story. So did his attempt to have me call Cindy from his motel room (either an attempt to re-establish communication with her, through me as the dupe, an effort to find out which side she would have testified for, or—but what's the use of speculating?). The explanation his defense attorneys had given me about his reason for the *nolo contendere* plea made a lot more sense.

"I don't know for the life of me why they told you that," DePugh said.

The February "On Target" bade farewell to Cindy as secretary of the Patriotic Party because she soon would be tried "on trumped up charges of assaulting a federal officer."

"Under these circumstances," said the newsletter, "she has had little opportunity to concentrate on the work of the Patriotic Party. It has been necessary therefore, that she resign her position as national secretary.

"Those who had worked with Cindy will always remember her as a real patriot that has given unselfishly of her time and energy for the cause of freedom."

Ken's trip to Joplin apparently whetted his appetite for travel, for a week later he was off to Cheyenne—at Minutemen expense—to testify on behalf of Houghton. With him were Tom Hart, Patriotic Party official, of Milford, Connecticut, and Lester Molyneaux, a party worker. Both of these men had been living at 613 East Alton in January and were also ready to testify that they had seen Houghton in Independence as late as seven-thirty the night of the fifth.

Ken explained his willingness to accompany Hart and Molyneaux to Cheyenne as mainly in the interests of justice. But he also was thinking of doing a master's thesis on the Minutemen once out of the Marines, he said, and besides, he had time to kill. Such a trip might be good for "kicks."

The three witnesses arrived in time for the hearing, but Houghton was an hour late. Despite the distance the witnesses had traveled, the police-court judge forfeited Houghton's $100 bond because of his tardiness.

A furious Houghton managed to talk the judge into a hearing the following day to consider a motion to reopen the case.

As Ken described it afterward, Houghton's appearance at this hearing to argue for himself worked to his decided disadvantage. Characteristically, the California Minuteman talked himself into a hole. The judge overruled the motion.

Ken and his two Minutemen companions returned home without having uttered a word in court. Houghton returned to San Diego having uttered too many. He said later he intended to appeal the matter to a higher court but as of the spring of 1968 had not done so.

Ken Patrick returned home impressed with neither the Minutemen's California coordinator nor Cheyenne justice.

Cindy still bothered me. She knew too much for me not to try once again to interview her. Early in February, DePugh had happened to ask me in the course of a brief conversation:

"Have you talked with Cindy yet?"

On the top of the list of people I would not tell if I had seen Cindy—which I hadn't—was the former national coordinator of the Minutemen. DePugh's efforts to persuade me that she was still a loyal Minutewoman had not convinced me. Did he still hope she would talk with me and I then might reveal to him what she had said? Or was he, by urging me to see her, in effect trying to convince me she would not be worth seeing?

He even went through the motions of starting to give me her unlisted telephone number, but then thought better of it, or pretended to. Instead, he said, he would get word to her that I wanted to talk with her. Wonderful, I thought. Then she would conclude I was helping DePugh. Or was she still really sympathetic to the Minutemen cause, and was DePugh just trying to be helpful?

Without the benefit or handicap of an entree from DePugh, I finally decided to visit Cindy's apartment. Mrs. Sanders, her mother, was home with Cindy's two small children when I arrived. Cindy was not there. Mrs. Sanders opened the door only far enough to peek into the hallway, the chain lock still in place.

She remembered me from nineteen months before, opened the door, suggested we sit at the kitchen table, offered me coffee and told me practically nothing. Cindy, she said, simply had not told her much about the Minutemen.

Mrs. Sanders still seemed to detest DePugh, and spoke briefly of the trouble she had had with Minutemen following her and Cindy, Minutemen keeping their apartment under surveillance, Minutemen telephoning for Cindy and hanging up when Mrs. Sanders answered the phone, or at least she assumed they were Minutemen. She had had to change their unlisted number several times, she said, but the Minutemen kept learning the new number.

Where was Cindy now? "Out." She would not say where.

Would Cindy sit down and talk with me?

Mrs. Sanders said she did not think so, on advice of counsel, that sort of thing. Maybe later, once something was done about the indictment.

I tried to draw her out about DePugh, but she remained vague. At one point she questioned his motives as a Minutemen leader. At another point, she suggested "he may think he's another Abraham Lincoln."

I left my telephone number with Mrs. Sanders. Neither she nor Cindy used it.

One year later—in March, 1968—I made one more stab at solving the mystery of Cindy Melville. The government by then had dismissed its charge against her. Russell Millin had said this was because she had "cooperated with the government."

Both Cindy and her mother were at the apartment this time. My reception was as it had been on previous visits—cautious, but cordial. I was invited inside but not asked to sit down. It was that kind of interview.

Among the questions and answers:

"Did you cooperate with the government, Cindy?"

"Up to a point. . . . I didn't know a whole lot to tell them."

"Are you through with the Minutemen?"

"Oh, yes. I have been for a long time."

"Why?"

"My attorney said that the government would not prosecute me if I quit them, but that if I continued working with them, they'd put me in jail."

Mrs. Sanders interrupted here, pointing out to Cindy that this sounded as though she still wished she were in the Minutemen. She certainly did not want to leave that impression, Mrs. Sanders suggested.

"I'm glad I'm out of it," Cindy said. "I probably would have quit within six months even if nothing had happened."

"Why?"

"Oh, there were a lot of reasons," Cindy said, volunteering none of them.

"She thought DePugh was a kook," Mrs. Sanders said.

"Sometimes he acted sort of like a kook," Cindy agreed without much enthusiasm.

"How do you mean?"

"Oh"—and she groped around for an example—"some of the things he put out to the members were kind of kooky, I guess."

"Cindy feels the same way about DePugh as I do," Mrs. Sanders volunteered, obviously none too pleased with her daughter's answers.

"I've had the impression you detest DePugh," I told Mrs. Sanders.

"That's putting it mildly," Mrs. Sanders replied.

Cindy remained silent, leaving me with the impression that either she did not feel this way herself, or that possibly she was afraid to say how she felt.

"Are you afraid of them?" I asked.

"No," Cindy said, smiling. "If they were going to do anything, they'd have done it by now."

She was attending the University of Missouri at Kansas City, she said, and was engaged to be married.

Before I left, Cindy summed up her status with: "I've started a new life, and I'm much happier now."

As winter passed and the spring of 1967 emerged, Jerry Brooks began to change. Perhaps he missed the excitement of working with the Minutemen, or against them as a federal witness. Possibly he was having second thoughts about the harm he had done the Minutemen in court. He probably also missed the spotlight of public attention.

A few weeks after the trial, DePugh had indicated to me that he did not feel Jerry had hurt the Minutemen much and in fact may have tried to help them.

"All of these people are two-way streets," he said. "Lots of times they go along and provide us information that's of value for a long time and then if they go bad, well, you can't cry too much. I really don't think he's hurt us too bad. No doubt he's given out some information that should have remained confidential. By the same token, I've wondered if he wasn't doing it in a way that would actually help us."

He said he believed the FBI threatened Jerry into testifying against him, warning of legal action against Jerry if he did not cooperate.

"For a fellow who likes his freedom and is the sole supporter of an invalid mother, this is a pretty good talking point," DePugh said. "So I think that Jerry felt that he had to give the FBI the information he did, but I suspect that he colored it up with so much fiction that they didn't know what to believe and what not to. . . ."

Jerry telephoned me from East St. Louis a few days after the trial.

He said he was hiding from the Minutemen at the home of a friend he had known from his underworld days, a man recently released from the state prison in Joliet. He chortled at length over the results of the trial.

In mid-December, I drove to East St. Louis to see Jerry and others connected with the Minutemen in that area. I arrived after dark outside the house in which he was staying, but Jerry was waiting patiently in the bitter cold on the screened front porch.

He ushered me into the house briefly, into an unfurnished living room lighted only by the tiny glare of a television set in the next room. Several youngsters were sprawled around it, presumably members of his host's family.

Jerry immediately handed me two worn, torn cloth-bound books that looked as though they had been dug up from the basement of a used book store—Lenin's *What Is To Be Done* and Marx's *Revolution and Counter-Revolution*.

Then he began fishing into his pockets, retrieving numerous scraps of paper on which he had scribbled reminders of unrelated tidbits he had wanted to pass on to me—the names, addresses and telephone numbers of four Communists in Havana, Cuba; the telephone numbers, he said, of the CIA offices in nineteen United States cities; and the names, addresses and places of employment of thirteen St. Louis residents he had reason to believe were Communists.

We drove to the first motel I could find, where I wanted quiet and no interruptions for taping one more interview with Jerry. We stopped on the way for dinner, but when I urged him to eat well, for I would pay, Jerry ordered only a cheeseburger and a cup of coffee. He drank the latter but nibbled his way through only half the sandwich.

The motel interview was for the purpose of filling in some gaps and seeing how many of his past stories he could recite again without stumbling over essential facts.

"Why did you leave the Minutemen, Jerry?"

"Having been involved with the law in the past," he said, as if in recitation, "I didn't want to be involved in any more activity if it was going to lead to criminal activity or overt acts of violence against the government or any person because I was really trying to straighten up. I thought I was making amends by really going after the Communists, and then I come to find out that I'm in an outfit that advocates exactly the same thing [as the Communists] only I don't know that the Minutemen are subservient to any other nation."

"Well, you knew pretty well from the start that they believed in shooting people, didn't you?"

"Well, I gathered information for myself, and a lot of times I'd give information to the FBI on the Minutemen and then also file it for myself just for future reference. Maybe somebody could use the information, not selling it to them, maybe somebody'd have need for it some time. And so I thought, well, I'll stay in and see what's going on. But when it came down that we're going to take this direct action— let's go down and kill Johnny or Sam—and then my mother, who was paralyzed . . ."

"They were getting to a point they were going to go out and start killing people?"

"They were really gonna go out."

"Did they have a timetable?"

"You name it. 'Let's get going.' I went over and bought ammunition, gunpowder. . . ."

"What set them off?"

"Well, they figured the time was running out. Like DePugh said at the training session, the time for talk, the time for trying to get people elected, those days are over. Now it's the revolutionary catechism. . . ."

Later Jerry tried to explain why he enjoys "agitating" both Communists and Minutemen.

"Let me put it this way," he said. "I like excitement, a little adventure. I don't say all Minutemen are bad. I know a big majority of them that I've met are, especially in the leadership. I've met four hundred, not by name and address, but I know them to talk to them. . . . They were bad and the Communists were bad, so let them fight among themselves. Let's get something stirred up and let 'em have it out. The government can step in and put 'em all in prison."

"You say 'bad.' What do you mean, 'bad'?"

"Well," Jerry replied, "they want to go out and shoot people. People in Washington, congressmen, and senators and ambassadors."

Jerry Brooks was back in Kansas City by February, holed up in a rooming house the address of which again was intended to be a dark secret known only to a privileged few. While in East St. Louis, he told me, the Minutemen had found out where he was and had made life dangerous for him there.

His mother, he said, was now in a nursing home in Springfield, Illinois, in worse shape than she had ever been.

In the course of my cautious but increasingly friendly relationship with Ken Patrick, Ken had indicated an interest in talking with Jerry. Since I enjoyed watching the interplay of personalities among the various persons involved with the Minutemen, I decided (unwisely, as it turned out) to tell Jerry of Ken's interest and let Jerry decide whether he wanted to further the young college graduate's education. I cautioned Jerry that I could not vouch for Ken, that he could be helping DePugh, but Jerry called him anyway and soon Ken was regaling me with accounts of his various surreptitious meetings with him.

One of Ken's accounts intrigued me especially. During a rendezvous with Jerry at the Kansas City public library, Ken said, Jerry had asked Ken to set up a meeting between him and DePugh. "What for?" Well, Ken said, he wasn't exactly sure.

Jerry was telephoning me periodically now, usually to give me a morsel of information about Communists, not Minutemen. He was especially interested now with news of the James Garrison investigation into the Kennedy assassination that was breaking in New Orleans. He kept supplying me the names of Cubans whom I could expect to see mentioned in this probe before long. Names, addresses, the works.

Soon after Ken had told me of the proposed Brooks-DePugh meeting, Jerry called with more gossip about Cuba and New Orleans. When I happened to ask him why he had asked Ken Patrick to put him in touch with DePugh, Jerry promptly hung up without a goodbye.

I paid less attention to this than I should have, and in later calls from Jerry neglected to pursue the matter. The last thing I recall saying to Ken about it was that if I were he, I would not have anything to do with such a meeting, no matter at whose behest. There was such a thing as tampering with a government witness, and I would have hated to see Ken become an accessory in such a charge. If Jerry wished to talk with DePugh so much, it seemed to me, he could always use the telephone.

Jerry's last visit to the *Star* office that winter was made on March 4, a Saturday. He wandered in silently as usual, an oversized overcoat engulfing him. He seemed particularly depressed. He was tired of the "Feds," for some reason, unspecified. He was thinking more about how maybe the Minutemen had the right idea after all. He also mentioned, in a roundabout way, that he might decide to shoot himself. I frankly could not understand what he was driving at, if anything. And he wandered off as abruptly as he had appeared.

Four days later he called with the last names of three men in New York who he said had intended to kill Robert Kennedy when Jimmy Hoffa went to prison.

"You got a pencil? Write these names down."

He gave me the names and hung up.

At noon the following day, Ken called me at the *Star*.

"I think I may have done it this time," he said, and he sounded worried.

"What happened?"

"I'm down at Katz drugstore at Twelfth and McGee with Mr. DePugh," Ken said, and he told me his story.

Ken said he had finally agreed to set up a meeting between DePugh and Jerry Brooks, scheduling it for that morning at the Union Station in Kansas City but not telling Jerry where it was to be until after picking him up in his car.

The rendezvous was at a restaurant in the Union Station. DePugh's wife, his oldest son, Ralph, fresh from Marine Corps duty in Vietnam, and Ralph's wife were there too.

With Robert and Ralph DePugh, Jerry, and Ken sitting together at a table, Jerry told DePugh he was ready to give him information that would "blow the government's case against him out of the water," Ken said.

"That's why I'd set up the meeting," Ken added. "I figured maybe there's been a miscarriage of justice."

More specifically, Ken continued, Jerry told DePugh that federal agents had threatened him with prosecution if he did not testify against DePugh at the trial the previous November. Even more specifically, Ken said, Jerry told DePugh that the agents had "told him what to say" on the witness stand.

"Did he say he had actually perjured himself?" I asked Ken, and later I asked DePugh.

"No," Ken said, "but he sort of implied it."

"No," said DePugh, "but this was the implication."

DePugh and Jerry then took a walk together alone through the Union Station to talk more privately. This walk ended abruptly when Jerry spotted two ATTU agents watching them. They separated with the intention of meeting again in a few minutes at a lawyer's office in downtown Kansas City where Jerry would give and sign an affidavit. Ken drove Jerry to the new meeting place.

As Ken was about to turn his car into a parking lot on Twelfth Street, he noticed to his horror that Frank Belecky had just pulled up on the other side of the street and was motioning to Jerry.

Jerry hopped from Ken's car, crossed the street, and talked with Belecky. He then turned and shouted to Ken that he was leaving with the ATTU supervisor. The DePughs had arrived by then and Mrs. DePugh approached Belecky and Jerry to begin something of an oral tug-of-war with Jerry as the prize. Belecky won.

I found Jerry and Ken an hour later on the fifth floor of the federal courthouse building—the floor on which the district attorney's office and the grand jury room are located. Both had been served grand-jury subpoenas. Jerry was seated in the law library of the D.A.'s office with an ATTU agent who told me Jerry could not talk with me at that moment. Ken emerged from the grand jury witness room briefly, showed me his subpoena and smiled weakly.

"Is Patrick a Minuteman?" I asked Belecky as Ken walked back to the witness room.

"That's what I was going to ask you," he replied.

Both Ken and Jerry signed statements for the ATTU about what had happened, but I was shown neither of them. As far as I could determine, neither Jerry nor Ken was taken before the grand jury that day, or subsequently. DePugh was not charged with tampering with a witness.

Jerry was entirely too erratic for me to spend much time wondering whether he actually had been threatened with prosecution or "told what to say" at the trial by any federal agents. Very likely he had been instructed not to ramble over the entire history of the Minutemen when he took the stand, and just answer the questions asked him. What intrigued me about the affair most was how had the ATTU found out about the secret meeting in advance?

I drove to Jerry's rooming house that night, asking Ken if he wanted to accompany me. Jerry would more likely be truthful with me, I reasoned, if Ken, who also had been at the reunion, were present.

The interview, conducted through a locked door, went like this:
"Jerry?"

"Seven o'clock, Ninth and Main," in a low near-whisper.

"What?"

"Seven o'clock. Ninth and Main."

"Seven o'clock in the morning?"

"Right."

"What about right now?"

"Seven o'clock. Ninth and Main. I've got a subpoena."

At seven o'clock the following morning, at Ninth and Main streets, Jerry Brooks was nowhere to be found.

What in the world had prompted this new intrigue I could not imagine. I suspected that it had been he, rather than Patrick, who had tipped off the ATTU about the meeting in the Union Station restaurant. It would have been simple for agents to follow the two of them from their meeting place to the nearby rendezvous with De-Pugh. But why would he tell them?

I was even more puzzled by this question two months later when I next saw Jerry. He was holding a press conference on television. But to that later.

May 7, 1967, boasted a sunny, warm afternoon that was pleasant enough, with the help of Robert DePugh, to lure 125 men and women from their homes in the Greater Kansas City area to hear a speech by a man whom few had ever heard of before. The speech was scheduled for three o'clock this Sunday afternoon in the Coronation Room of the Pickwick Motor Inn. Knowing the nature of the meeting, many present were not surprised soon after their arrival to be listening to a baritone voice singing these lyrics over a phonograph.

> Let's fight and fight
> Knock out the parasites.
> Let's set our sights,
> Vote, out the parasites.
> That's right, let's fight,
> And fight and fight
> The par—a—sites.

Wayne Morse, the picket who by now was able to boast that he had run for the city council of Kansas City in the general election and polled 2000 of 9000 votes cast in his district, had walked to the speaker's rostrum and placed a portable record player he had brought with him on a folding chair nearby. He then had put a 45 rpm record on the machine, announcing that this was his own, original composition, titled "Don't Tread On Me."

> . . . March on, march on,
> Keep us forever free . . .

Morse stood beside the record player watching the reaction of the audience, which included many who already had heard his song before. Most of the crowd continued talking in hushed tones, assuming an attitude of amused or condescending tolerance for the entertainment.

> . . . Fight on, fight on,
> And keep our nation free.
> And let them see our motto be,
> "Don't Tread On Me."

Several familiar faces were in the crowd, persons I had seen either at Reverend LeRoy's January "Faith and Freedom Rally" or at the Kansas City, Kansas, Patriotic Party meeting the previous September —all sitting silently or whispering to one another more as they would in church than at a "patriotic" meeting.

After Morse had unplugged his record player and left, DePugh walked to the rostrum and opened the meeting officially with a twenty-minute introduction of the featured speaker. The crowd had been attracted to the Pickwick that afternoon with a leaflet which on one side promised "a personal account of the techniques of Communist brainwashing used on political prisoners—here! In these United States—today! in the so-called 'mental hospital' at Springfield, Missouri."

"Fred Seelig, was, for many years, a respected newspaper reporter," the leaflet continued. "Then he attempted to expose the Communist infiltration into the California political machine. Seized illegally by federal agents he was moved from one jail to another for many months, not even permitted to contact his own family.

"Then comes an incredible nineteen months of brutal torture designed to deliberately drive him insane.

"This is a story that must be told!

"The American people must learn the facts—before it is too late for all the rest of us.

"Be sure to come!

"Introduction and commentary by Bob DePugh.

"Sponsored by Patriots' Legal Defense Committee, P. O. Box 1195, Kansas City, Missouri."

On the reverse side was an advertisement for "Destroy the Accuser," a 192-page, paperbound book by Frederick Seelig with a foreword by Westbrook Pegler and "commentary" by Dr. Revilo P. Oliver, a former John Birch Society council member. The cover boasted: "Federal Homo Power Exposed," and the flyer explained this meant "federal homosexual power" was exposed. For Frederick Seelig not only saw Communists under every bed, he saw a homosexual under each bed with him.

". . . Fiendish authorities told him that papers were all made out in advance to commit him in an insane asylum should he tell his story," the leaflet warned, "but then, they laughed, he wouldn't live long enough after what they'd done to him.

"Mr. Seelig for nearly two years was a political prisoner of the late President John F. Kennedy and his Attorney General brother, Robert Kennedy. In this incredible story the author relives the horrors of stacked political Federal Courts, hell-hole Missouri Federal Penitentiary, doctors trained in Kremlin psychiatric torture atrocities. Incapacitated by diabolical torture, he wrote, 'Destroy the Accuser' in segments and in pain. . . ."

DePugh's introduction of Seelig dwelt first on the Communist menace generally, but soon he was discussing psychiatry and "psycopolitics" as taught in Russia, and finally he was declaring that the Communists had made a concentrated effort to control psychiatry in the United States, that this field was "the ultimate in capturing minds."

It was almost a miracle that Seelig had survived his ordeal, DePugh said—"and they'd still like to see Mr. Seelig dead."

Seelig sat beside DePugh at the speaker's table during the introduction. He was a short, middle-aged man, stocky with a perceptible paunch, his dark gray hair in a neat crew cut. As DePugh spoke, Seelig displayed the unconscious habit of puffing his lips forward and filling the space between his teeth and lips with air every several seconds. It gave him the appearance of a friendly bullfrog.

Curiously—although I attached no significance to it until seeing what was to happen later—DePugh asked some young ladies in the audience to pass around collection plates before Seelig even began speaking. The money would go to Mr. Seelig, he said. Several green bills were pulled from wallets, but the sound of coins being plunked into the plates seemed to predominate.

It became quickly clear, as Seelig began speaking, that this was no confidence man, but rather a pathetic figure, deadly earnest in his desire to make others believe the story he resolutely regarded as truth.

"I've been a newspaperman all my life," he began, and he told of having worked on newspapers in Detroit, New York City, Los Angeles, San Francisco, Albany, Boston, Chicago and most recently, in 1960, in Baltimore.

He told of some of his "big stories," his "exclusives," and he did so with a clear ring of authenticity, just as I had heard many a retired old-timer from the newspaper business as he reminisced about his career. Suddenly I liked Frederick Seelig. He rang true.

This was his first speech, he said. He wasn't used to public speaking. Nor was his speech a speech. He talked as he would have alone to one person, or to himself. He had no notes. Occasionally he would forget someone's name, search for it in his mind and apologize when he could not remember. At times he picked up his book to read from it, again apologizing while he put on his spectacles.

But then he was talking about "the fairies, the queers, the people we now call homosexuals," and about the "Communists" with whom he had come into contact while a newspaperman.

His book, if still in print, is available from the Freedom Press Publishing Company in Miami for those who wish to form their own opinion on it. Pegler, Dr. Oliver, DePugh and many in the audience that day to the contrary, the book and Seelig's speech were pitifully unbelievable—pitifully, because the book apparently had been written as the leaflet had said, "in pain."

He accused various persons, both the famous and little known, of being homosexuals, of being Communists, or of being crooks. The psychiatrist who had judged him to be insane, Seelig said, was insane himself.

"Every method of psychiatry is destructive," he told the audience. "They cannot bring forth anyone who has been cured of insanity."

Seelig had been indicted by a federal grand jury for sending libelous material in the U.S. mail—accusations that various California officials were homosexuals, etc.—but before he was tried in court, he was judged insane and therefore incapable of standing trial. He was committed to the U. S. Medical Center in Springfield, Missouri, in April, 1961, and remained there until October, 1962, when he was found sane, freed and the case against him dropped.

The U. S. Medical Center in Springfield holds hundreds of persons committed there for psychiatric treatment, as well as other prisoners who need medical care or who have been convicted of non-violent crimes such as tax evasion and sentenced to brief prison terms.

While in the medical center, Seelig said, he spent four months in a "nerve-breaking cell" presided over by a psychiatrist (and he provided a name) whose specialty was "destroying the nervous systems of prisoners." It took six months to destroy nervous systems under this plan, Seelig said, and he had been there only four months. He did not explain why the early release, but did state that he had suffered brain damage, resulting in his inability to remember many names he once could have recalled quickly. Nine of the other months at the medical center, he said, were spent naked in a bare, "drain-hole cell." Russian psychiatric techniques were used in an attempt to destroy his mind, he said.

Near the end of his hour-long speech, three young Minutemen began quietly selling copies of Seelig's book in the audience. (One man bought three.) It seemed an odd thing to do, selling the books while the man was still speaking, just as it had seemed odd that DePugh would have passed the plate for Seelig before Seelig had even spoken a word. The reason soon became apparent. Whether Seelig knew it or not, a hurried, melodramatic exit was planned for him. Fund-raising afterward would have been anticlimactic and probably not very financially rewarding.

Seelig ended his speech with:

"I was warned not to come to Kansas City. I was told I'd never get out, that I'd get a subpoena to go before a federal grand jury. Well, we're prepared for it. . . . We have a staff of seven attorneys ready if I'm not given a full public hearing."

Seelig then left the rostrum and DePugh rose to approach the microphone. Suddenly Seelig was back at the mike.

"I've just been handed a note that two federal agents are waiting in the lobby for me," he said, and muffled gasps could be heard from a few of the women in the audience. "I'll tell you where they'll send me—back to Springfield, with no federal hearing."

With this, Seelig walked quickly to a side door in the Coronation Room. With precision that suggested they might even have rehearsed the scene, the three young men who had been selling Seelig's book gathered tightly around the speaker.

As the audience craned their necks to watch this dramatic conclusion to his speech, DePugh was telling them calmly that Mr. Seelig would be escorted out the back way to help him avoid trouble.

The three escorts formed a triangular bodyguard shield around Seelig as soon as they were out of the room. They hastened past several television newsmen who had gathered there hoping for an interview, down a flight of stairs, through the hotel lobby and out onto the sidewalk through a side entrance. I had to run to catch them.

"Are you sure they were federal agents?" I asked.

"They were either agents or queers," Roy Branson, Jr., one of the bodyguards snarled over his shoulder, not slowing his pace in the slightest.

"Queers?"

Now I had become part of a rectangular shield guarding the strange little man from sniper bullets, bombs, federal subpoenas, psychiatrists, homosexual assassins or whatever else might be lurking in the afternoon shadows.

I saw it was going to be useless trying to ask him many questions about his book or his ordeal. Seelig looked every bit the hunted fugitive. We walked a block and a half to a car bearing a Florida license plate and all four men quickly began to climb inside it.

"Where are you going now?"

"Los Angeles," Seelig said. "My book's in its second printing and there's going to be a rally out there."

His manner toward me was disarming. I was a reporter. He had been a reporter. We had a bond. All the things he imagined, it therefore followed, I naturally knew were so. The editors who take out certain key facts from stories. The publishers who dictate the Communist line to the editors. When Seelig failed to answer some of my questions, he did so with a shrug of the shoulders, a wrinkle of his brow, a smile or a wink, telling me with his face, "You know I can't answer that. I'm sorry. But you know why. You're a reporter, just like me. You know the ropes."

And they were gone.

On the way back to the Pickwick I encountered a plump, middle-aged woman with wide eyes and a "Wallace in '68" button on her coat. She had just left the meeting.

"Isn't it terrible the things the government does?" she asked in horrified sincerity.

"Did you see any federal agents?"

"Well, there was a man in a kind of uniform in the lobby," she said excitedly, "and there were two other men in regular suits, big men, and one of them went over to the desk and told the telephone operator, 'Get us a cab. We've got to get out of here fast!'"

The telephone operator denied receiving such a request from anyone.

Back upstairs, most of the crowd had left.

"Where do you find people like that?" I asked DePugh.

"I'm just like a magnet," he laughed. "They just are drawn to me."

"Who saw the federal agents?"

"Roy, but he's gone now. He called me out of the meeting and we went downstairs and saw two men. Roy said he's seen one of them over at the courthouse outside the grand jury room before."

Roy Branson had returned by now and was sitting in a chair looking angry.

"Did you see federal agents downstairs?"

"I don't know. I've seen one of them before," Branson said.

"You don't know who they were?"

"They were federal agents or queers."

The Seelig affair seemed decidedly strange to me. It was not really typical of DePugh to try to foist such a story off on his followers in this fashion. What could he have had in mind? Just six days later I found out—or I *think* I found out—what kind of rabbit he was preparing to pull from his hat.

That rabbit was named Jerry Brooks. Happily, Ken Patrick had enlisted in the Marines by this time and was not playing magician's assistant. In his place was pretty Mary Tollerton, fresh from her arrest in West Palm Beach, Florida, on a charge of carrying a concealed weapon.

Shortly after six o'clock, Saturday evening, May 11, I received a telephone call from DePugh.

"Did you see Jerry on television?" he asked me.

"No? When?"

"He was just on," he said, feigning surprise, and then explained that Jerry Brooks had just publicly repudiated his testimony at the November trial, saying that he had perjured himself out of fear of prosecution and incarceration in a prison or mental institution.

I will admit to being surprised. Not flabbergasted, mind you, but surprised.

"I didn't think he was going to do that," DePugh said, "although I've had his affidavit for a couple of weeks."

"Can I see it?"

"I'll run it down to you right now."

In less than a half hour, DePugh was in the office with a copy of an approximately 1700-word notarized statement signed by Jerry.

"My name is Jerry Milton Brooks," the statement began. "I am thirty-seven years of age. I live at 3021 McGee Street, Kansas City, Missouri. . . ."

First he briefly traced his association with the Minutemen from 1961 until December, 1965. While in Norborne in late 1965, he said, his mother was with him living "in a comfortable environment conducive to the improvement of her health." But . . .

"In early December, 1965, my mother and I were taken from our home in Norborne by a police officer. The trip from Norborne to Kansas City was very hazardous for my mother and she became very sick. We went to Kansas City where we took up residence. . . ."

He had told me earlier that he had asked Sheriff Paul Johnson of Carroll County, Missouri, that he be taken from Norborne under police protection, that he had been threatened that his mother would be strangled with piano wire.

Next, he continued in the affidavit, he was contacted by an FBI agent and told that "he wanted to find out about the Minutemen and he said if I did not cooperate, I would be in some kind of trouble."

"I told him that my work with the organization was such that I did not know much about the organization," the statement said. "My mother was also questioned and harassed on several different occasions by federal agents which undoubtedly contributed to her subsequent death. . . ."

In December, 1966, in the interview in East St. Louis, Jerry had told me his mother, already an invalid, had recently been injured in a traffic accident while riding in an ambulance and consequently had been taken to a nursing home in Springfield, Illinois. Never had he mentioned any agents even talking to his mother, let alone bothering her.

Jerry's statement then told of threats and coercion by agents of the ATTU. ". . . They threatened me again and again with criminal prosecution," and later still, an ATTU agent gave him a statement to sign. "A great part of that statement was false," he said, "and I was forced to perjure myself when I signed this statement."

He then listed various parts of this statement, which he said falsely incriminated DePugh, Peyson, Cannon and Houghton. Everything he had said that had gotten any of those men in trouble was now denied.

His reason for lying, he said, was that ATTU agents had threatened that he would be prosecuted along with DePugh and Peyson if he did not cooperate with them, and he was promised immunity from prosecution if he cooperated.

". . . In addition to threatening me with criminal prosecution," his statement continued, "they also threatened me with being put in a mental institution and that they would put me away and I would be subject to very severe, harsh treatment if I did not cooperate and do what I was told by them. They said that I could expect to spend from ten years to life in the penitentiary or mental institution. . . ."

I could not help but wonder, at this point in the statement, whether Frederick Seelig's unusual appearance in Kansas City the week before had been intended to prepare DePugh's sympathizers for this statement.

But Jerry was not through. There was still the problem of Ray Husted, a far more damning witness against DePugh and Peyson than Jerry had been.

"When I saw Raithby Husted at the Federal Building shortly after the grand jury testimony in the summer of 1966," his statement continued, "he told me that he had been threatened and coerced into making a statement that was false, and that some federal agents had drugged him and he had been physically mistreated, including a beating, and made to sign a statement.

"I saw agents beating Raithby Husted in the Federal Building in Kansas City the day he returned from giving a sworn statement to Mr. DePugh and shortly before he was to testify before the grand jury. . . . He said also that he was told to perjure himself and was told the precise testimony to give before the grand jury."

Attempts to find Jerry that night were in vain. We were told that at least one TV station had been called that afternoon by someone identifying himself as DePugh saying that Jerry would be in a room at the Howard Johnson motor lodge in Independence at four o'clock for a news conference. Present with Jerry was a young lady named Mary Tollerton.

We caught the ten o'clock news on KMBC-TV and there was the inimitable Jerry, the television camera zeroing in as close to his face as the lens would permit, repeating parts of his statement almost word for word.

At ten-thirty that night, I received a special delivery letter. It was from Jerry.

"Harry, I must state here and now Robert Bolivar DePugh, Walter Patrick Peyson, Dennis Patrick Mower, James Tollerton, Troy Houghton are not guilty as charged," it began. "I was forced to testify for the government, I lied through the whole trial, and grand jury in K.C., Mo., in 1966. . . ."

Only a few lines in the letter added to the affidavit DePugh had brought me earlier:

"I could not continue living a lie having help [sic] railroad men who are good, brave Americans fighting to preserve America's freedom from Communist takeover.

"Harry, sorry I occupied much of your time with all the false image that was portrayed by me concerning Minutemen.

"I can truly say I thank God I had the chance to speak up for DePugh, Peyson, Tollerton, Houghton, Mower. . . . (They) aren't guilty to the best of my knowledge."

At first blush, the sudden turn in events made me laugh. But I had grown to like Jerry personally, and soon I felt saddened at this apparent change. Why in the world had he done it? When had he been telling the truth and when had he not? What did his meeting with DePugh and Ken Patrick at the Union Station two months before then have to do with this new development? What wild plot or counterplot was now under way, and by whom—Jerry or the Minutemen or both? Poor, kooky little guy with bad teeth, a rotten police record, little money and an overactive sense of pandemonium. What would happen to him now?

CHAPTER 20

JOIN THE MINUTEMEN

For the past seven years the Minutemen organization has grown steadily. We have withstood the worst attacks and fought the hardest battles of any group in the conservative movement. Today, the Minutemen organization is larger, better trained and better equipped than ever before. . . .

From June 5, 1967, notice to members from Robert DePugh.

DePugh had made it clear in *Blueprint for Victory* that the Patriotic Party and the Minutemen's underground organization were parts of what he called a "resistance movement," but the phrase had not captured my imagination much, and I simply had categorized it in my mental Minutemen file as another catch phrase DePugh used to add glamour to his organization.

"Ultimately, I think one of two things will happen," he had said in early 1967 during a long, taped interview. "Either there'll be a dictatorship take over this country, either Fascist or Communist, or a middle-of-the-road kind of dictatorship, and when things get so bad that people will no longer stand for it, then a *resistance movement* will develop that has sufficient ability to speed the collapse of the dictatorship."

Shortly after that interview, DePugh had announced both his "resignation" as national coordinator of the Minutemen and the planned reorganization of the group along more secretive and, it seemed, even more irresponsible lines. It eventually became evident that the Minutemen also were being pushed into a more violent frame of mind.

With the "Executive Council" now supposedly in charge, letters went out to all members early in 1967 from this mysterious group of shadowy figures, telling how the Minutemen were reorganizing.

The Minutemen were to be broken into "resistance networks,"

announced the letter, to achieve greater dispersion and security. Each network would be led by a network director appointed by the "executive council." Each director would be assigned a few other Minutemen members as his assistants. And in each letter was the paragraph:

"By means of this bulletin you are hereby assigned Network No. ——."

Under the new network plan, members were instructed to establish contacts with friends, relatives, other conservative organizations and business associates whom they could use as sources of valuable information, skills and supplies.

In discussing the value of different types of non-members to a resistance network, it was observed: ". . . A wholesaler of explosives might be hesitant to sell dynamite to a member of the Minutemen but would gladly pass a few sticks on to a fellow lodge member who ran into some rock while digging a septic tank."

While members were waiting to be contacted by a network director or his courier, they were urged to continue "working steadily to build your own subnetwork and make other preparations." Among those recommended preparations:

"Make certain that your own weapons, ammunition, files and similar material are safely hidden. . . .

"Make a continuous effort to learn the identity of Communists and Communist sympathizers in your area. . . .

"Obtain and stockpile types of material needed in resistance warfare. . . .

"Select a 'specialty' in keeping with your own talents that would be of value to a resistance movement—first aid, electronics, surveillance, lock-picking, interrogation, photography, explosives, gunsmithing, etc. —and become as expert as possible. . . .

"Prepare the nucleus of an escape and evasion team with the assistance of personal friends you can count on. Arrange alternate hideouts for yourself and your supplies. . . ."

Members also were warned:

". . . We will depend on every member to do his part in support of the organization and its objectives. Proper security is the duty of every member and the time is past when treason or disloyalty will go unpunished."

Another Minutemen document shed further light. Titled "Development of Resistance Networks," it made it clear that network directors would be assigned objectives and projects by the national organization.

"How he gets the job done is up to him," this pamphlet said. "The one requirement is that each mission assigned to his network is properly completed."

And what of "special circumstances that occur on a local or temporary basis?" The instructions said that these "may be acted on without the usual time delay in national communications."

A new sense of urgency, a more fearful anticipation of The Day's arrival seemed now to prevail.

"The Communist-Socialist clique now has firm control of the central government," this pamphlet declared, as DePugh had declared after being sentenced to four years in prison.

The objectives of the resistance networks? They were spelled out too. Ultimately, they were similar to those in *Blueprint for Victory*, it said. Among the more immediate objectives:

"To develop a 'network alert' system so that a maximum number of local patriots can be contacted in the shortest possible time in case of emergencies or important developments. . . .

"Special studies should be made on the use of *terrorism, sabotage* and *assassination* as instruments of psychological warfare." [My italics]

And eight others, a bit less sinister.

Yet another Minutemen document released at about this time was titled "Communications Techniques in a Resistance Movement." This was well-written and full of bright ideas on techniques of spying. Minutemen all over the nation, after pulling their shades and reading this thirteen-page, single-spaced document, must have marveled to themselves over the brilliance of the Minutemen leader—perhaps De-Pugh, perhaps some master of intrigue on the Executive Council—who had written this—unless those Minutemen also had happened to read *The Penkovskiy Papers*, by Oleg Penkovskiy, a master Russian spy. The Minutemen's "Communications Techniques in a Resistance Movement" was an artless steal from that book. Only a few words had been changed—"agent" was replaced with "member," for instance, "resistance officer" for "intelligence officer."

I did not obtain copies of these documents until late in March, after having been informed of the existence of "resistance networks" by an unusual young man whom I had met in a most unusual manner. He had placed a telephone call to a call-in "talk show" on radio station

KUDL in the Kansas City area one day during a discussion of income taxes. The caller, not identifying himself by name over the air, said he wanted advice on a special tax problem.

It seemed as if his two employers in 1966 had been the Federal Bureau of Investigation and the Ku Klux Klan. He seemed to feel this created something of a tax problem. Should he declare income from both?

The moderator naturally tried to draw him out for further details. The caller explained that he had worked for the FBI as an undercover source of information on cases involving the Klan and the Minutemen. Now, he said, he was planning to write a book about it.

Two friends told me they had heard this call. I checked with the radio station. With the caller's permission, the moderator gave me his name and telephone number.

By now I trusted no one. Was DePugh being subsidized by the CIA? Was Ken Patrick a secret agent for *Ramparts* magazine? Was Frank Belecky of the ATTU a member of the Minutemen's executive council? Did Robert Welch really exist? And what about my wife? Sometimes she seemed *too* interested in what I was writing about the Minutemen.

As for Michael Desmond Sadewhite, the young man who had telephoned KUDL, I figured he could be anything up to and including a member of the Martian Secret Service.

He received me cordially at his home, sat me down at the kitchen table, pulled out numerous credentials and a fat scrap book filled with news clippings. He had called KUDL, he said, in hope of attracting its attention sufficiently to obtain an announcer's job with the station.

The documents he showed me verified that he had been a King Kleagle in the Klan in Delaware and Pennsylvania and that he also had had something to do with Klansmen in Virginia. The clippings quoted him under the name of Michael Desmond at Klan rallies. News photos showed both him and his wife at these rallies. His stories of intrigue inside the Klan—rising to positions of leadership in two of the three states, agitating within their ranks in order to start internal feuds —were fascinating. All the while, he said, the FBI had subsidized his activities, not as heavily as he would have liked, naturally, but sufficiently to keep him active for almost two years. The Klan had paid him too, of course. But that is another story.

Sadewhite was twenty-five years old, an inch or two under the average height of U.S. males, solidly built, head of thick, black hair, extraordinarily self-confident and aggressive. He spoke with so resonant a voice that it was easy to understand why he had been attracted to commercial radio work. Nor was it a problem to understand upon talking with him how he had been able to rise to the rank of King Kleagle of two state Klans. He had simply talked his way to the top.

After Sadewhite, alias Desmond, had shifted from the Delaware to the Pennsylvania Klan, he found himself amid men who not only enjoyed the childishness of wearing hoods and burning crosses but who also held certain affections for the swastika and Minutemen weapons caches buried in the wilderness.

After meeting Roy Frankhouser, the Grand Dragon of the Pennsylvania Klan in Reading, Pennsylvania, Sadewhite asked him why he had so many pistols, rifles and ammunition lying about. Why, because the Grand Dragon was also a coordinator for the Minutemen, said the Grand Dragon. Sadewhite expressed an interest in becoming a Minuteman too, and voilà, the Grand Dragon made him a member. Or so Sadewhite thought, at any rate.

Membership in the Minutemen in Pennsylvania at this time—early 1966—was incidental to the Klan membership of Sadewhite, Frankhouser and others in the Grand Dragon's immediate lair of friends. The extent of their Minutemen activities, Sadewhite recalled, was to go out most Sundays into the rural areas of Pennsylvania and bury weapons and ammunition.

On two or three occasions, Sadewhite said, he talked with DePugh by telephone, relaying messages to Frankhouser for him. The messages were usually in code, he said—"like, 'The blue boy has swallowed the red ball,' that type of message."

Once he had successfully undermined the Pennsylvania Klan to his satisfaction, Sadewhite said, he moved his activities to Virginia where he finally tired of his spy role. He didn't feel the FBI was paying him enough considering the risks he took, he said, and he had reason to believe the Klan was finally aware of his unreliability. He moved to the Greater Kansas City area, his original home, in early 1967 and resumed his true identity, Michael Desmond Sadewhite, a man in search of a job in radio.

Before settling down completely, he said, he checked in at the

Kansas City FBI office and identified himself. He urged agents in Kansas City to confirm the role he had played back East, he said, and was thereupon asked to carry out one more assignment for the FBI— this time as a Klansman who wished to become more active in the Minutemen.

Sadewhite agreed. He had not landed a radio job yet and needed the money.

The following is Sadewhite's account of what he did and learned:

> In late January, 1967—about a week after DePugh had announced his Minutemen resignation—Sadewhite telephoned DePugh at 613 East Alton, identified himself as "a friend from Virginia" and said he wished to meet with him. DePugh obliged and a time and a place in Independence were agreed upon.
>
> A snow storm the night before their meeting prevented DePugh from keeping the appointment, so Sadewhite telephoned him in Norborne, lied that he had to return to Virginia the next day and asked if it would be all right if he drove up to Norborne to see him. DePugh agreed.
>
> Sadewhite arrived late in the afternoon and immediately called DePugh at Biolab. DePugh told him to meet him at a restaurant in town.
>
> "He came in alone," Sadewhite said. "He was cagey. I could tell he didn't trust me."
>
> Sadewhite tossed out the names of various Klansmen-Minutemen in the East, told him they were "burying stuff" but that the organization was very weak in the Pennsylvania-Virginia area. As Sadewhite discussed details about Frankhouser he said, DePugh seemed to gain confidence in this "friend from Virginia."
>
> Sadewhite showed DePugh his United Klans of America credentials but was unable to find his Minutemen identification card—he said it was still packed in one of his suitcases.
>
> "I talked of my dissatisfaction with the Klan, that it wasn't active enough in the right ways, that it was taking people's money," Sadewhite said.
>
> He also told DePugh that he had had a run-in with the top Klansman in Virginia, thinking that DePugh, if he checked, would find this out anyway.

"I said I wanted to get involved with the right organization," he continued, "and from what I'd seen and heard, the Minutemen were just that. I said we've got to prepare to fight right here, just as the colonials did. He was lapping it up all the way by now.

"I said, 'What can I do?' He said, 'It's up to you. You can come here and work if you want, or you can go back to Virginia and form a resistance network.'"

Sadewhite said he told DePugh he had to return to Virginia. The Minutemen chieftain told him, "Okay, I'll get you some of our literature."

But first, DePugh wanted to see if Sadewhite was being followed. He told Sadewhite to sit in the restaurant five minutes after he left, then get up, walk around the block, and if he were being followed, two men would pick him up in a car. If not being tailed, he was to drive to another restaurant where they would resume their conversation.

Sadewhite walked around the block, climbed into his car, drove around Norborne for about fifteen minutes to see if he was being followed by the Minutemen—not that it mattered much whether he was—and then proceeded to the second restaurant.

In about five minutes, DePugh and a slender, young, dark-haired, dark-complexioned man drove up in a Volkswagen. The young man was introduced to him as "George" and Sadewhite was introduced to "George" as "Bob," which inadvertently was later changed to "Jim." "George" was Wally Peyson.

DePugh became specific at the second restaurant—in a general sort of way—about what the head of a Minutemen "resistance network" was supposed to do, Sadewhite said.

"I was supposed to go back to Virginia," he said, "and set up a resistance network to actively begin fighting. The new strategy was to involve isolated acts of violence, starting around September and timed to appear as a reaction to the rioting he expected this summer.

"The decision on what to do and exactly when to do it was fairly well left up to the individual leaders. He talked about things like planting bombs in police stations, city halls, state

buildings, sniper activity—although he didn't say against who—
even a bank robbery."

"A bank robbery?"

"That's what he said. I know it's crazy. He said they could
stage a bank robbery and when all the police got there—kill
them. We'd have a machine gun on the roof top, plant bombs
and set them off by remote control."

"Why?"

"He said this would incite the people to fight the police, who
were the enemy of the people. This would show the people it
could be done."

(At this point I reasoned that either Sadewhite was pulling my
leg, or DePugh had pulled his.)

Sadewhite said DePugh told him the Minutemen already had
run through a simulated bank robbery in Kansas City, taking all
the necessary steps up to turning in a false alarm but not including the actual killing, obviously.

"I just took it in stride," Sadewhite said. "I showed no surprise or apprehension or anything. Nor did I act enthusiastic
about anything."

He also quoted DePugh as saying that political assassinations
would be necessary, mentioning Hubert Humphrey, Arthur
Goldberg, Earl Warren and Robert Kennedy, for instance, but
not President Johnson.

Sadewhite also told of DePugh's outline of how critical points
of communications and power around the country could be
seized or disrupted.

"He said we'd have to overthrow the present government
and install our own political arm," Sadewhite said.

As for DePugh's future, Sadewhite said that the Minutemen
leader had told him that he did not plan to serve time in prison
if his appeal failed. DePugh had an "escape route" worked out
and several false identities ready to establish for himself, he said.

DePugh gave Sadewhite half of a dollar bill—serial number
J56077322A—and told him a courier would use the other half
to identify himself to him when he arrived some time in the
future with instructions.

He was to stay in Virginia only as long as it took to set up a network of from fifteen to twenty people, Sadewhite said, and then move to Kansas City where he would continue to run the network through an assistant, the only member of the network who would know his true identity.

When he returned to Kansas City, he said, he was to insert a Help Wanted ad in the *Star* for several days. This would be his signal to the Minutemen he was back in town.

Sadewhite said it was suggested that he move into a certain apartment complex in south Kansas City, taking a particular apartment that would enable him to keep a parking lot under surveillance.

(The apartment complex was the one in which Mrs. Sanders, Cindy Melville and her two children lived.)

As far as Sadewhite knew, DePugh still thought he was setting up a resistance network in Virginia, and someone in the Minutemen was reading the Help Wanted column in the *Star* every day to see when "Michael Desmond" had returned to Kansas City.

"What do you think of DePugh?" I asked him.

"I think he's serious, and I don't think he's crazy," Sadewhite said. "He's probably an egotist, like many of that type. He believes he is accomplishing something."

By late April, DePugh had returned from a long trip over the country during which he had spoken at Patriotic Party gatherings here and there, wherever he could summon members and collect funds for his court appeal.

I telephoned him and we arranged to meet at Winstead's drive-in off Kansas City's fashionable Country Club Plaza.

"What's this resistance network business?" I tried, after the usual amenities.

I had no illusions that he would be surprised that I knew of this new line of Minutemen thought. And he wasn't, or at least did not seem to be. We were playing games again.

Yes, the resistance networks were part of the Minutemen's reorganization, he said.

"What is a resistance network?"

"A network is one real good member," said DePugh. "He may be given three to ten or fifteen ordinary members to work with him. They in turn are put in contact with others—call them sympathizers—to recruit, but not into the organization as such, to add to the influence of the organization."

"How many networks are there?"

"There are more than a thousand networks. I don't know the number. Virtually every good member has been made a network director."

"What do they do?"

"They maintain security, gather information, spread propaganda, recruit, stockpile and train," he said, ticking them off on his fingers.

"How do you happen to know all this?" I asked. "Have you 'returned' to the leadership of the Minutemen?"

"I'm still a member of the Executive Council," he said, after a thoughtful pause.

"As of when?"

"Oh, about two weeks ago."

"Why did you return?"

"Oh, internal dissension. Besides, I'm not entirely comfortable in the Patriotic Party. I never had a lot of faith in it. Still, we're going to try. We'll have a Patriotic Party convention July 2, 3 and 4."

I showed DePugh a copy of the special bulletin on resistance networks and asked him if it was a bona fide Minutemen bulletin. He glanced through it and confirmed that it was.

"It was put out about the time I resigned," he said. "So was a pamphlet on resistance networks and how they work."

"How much more independent are the networks going to be from the national organization now? Isn't there a danger one of them will fly off half-cocked and embarrass the organization?"

"I've always had the theory," DePugh said, "that if you take ten chessboards, put them in ten rooms and arrange the chessmen exactly the same on each, then send ten chess experts into these rooms, the chances are that nine of the ten will make exactly the same move."

He led me off onto another subject before I could ask him about the danger that the tenth "expert" might decide to blow up the Golden Gate Bridge instead of winning the chess game.

Remembering Sadewhite's story of how the resistance networks might strike in reaction to summer rioting, I asked him what their reaction to another Watts riot would be.

"We'd stay absolutely clear of it," he said, "because, assuming it was not spontaneous, the purpose of it would be to turn one American against another."

In California, Troy Houghton, writing still under the pen name of "930," meanwhile seemed to have adjusted to the new militancy of the "Executive Council."

His March, 1967, bulletin carried a menacing little line that presumably was intended to frighten Russell Millin, and maybe all the government witnesses who had testified against the Minutemen leaders the previous November.

"Bobby Kennedy and other key figures in the Hoffa case were placed under police protection when it appeared certain that Hoffa would be imprisoned," said the bulletin. "It would be worth speculating as to whether or not the key figures in the trial of the Minutemen leaders will also be placed under police guard at the time those men begin to serve their sentences."

And California members also received a questionnaire they were urged to fill out and return "in order to complete the new outlines for the underground aspects of the organization." Among the numerous questions asked were:

Are you known as a member of this organization? By whom? FBI? ATTU? Police? Other government agency? (explain) . . .

"Have you infiltrated any leftist or Communist organizations? Which ones? To what extent or in what capacity? . . .

"Do you feel that you could successfully infiltrate other patriotic organizations for the purpose of recruiting support for our own organization? . . .

"Do you feel 'prepared' as a potential underground fighter? 100%? 75%? 50%? 25%? Not at all? . . ."

Further evidence of the Minutemen's new militancy came in the form of two letters, one for network directors, the other for regular members, each signed, "For the Executive Council, Bob DePugh," and each dated June 5, 1967. Both were sprinkled with items difficult to believe, yet taken together, they seemed to say a great deal about the Minutemen of 1967.

They reflected weak organization, a lack of cooperation from many of the network directors, shaky security and, as I read them, evidence of far greater independence of action for individual networks and members.

The letter to network directors began with a reminder that network directors are of "great importance . . . in our present organization." Hard-core members, dedicated to the cause of the Minutemen, would need no such reminder.

Evidence of internal difficulties came in other segments in this letter.

•"I know that members of our National Staff were often brought to the point of tears after working to the point of exhaustion and still being criticized by our general membership for not answering our mail promptly. Some of our Directors are now finding out for themselves how much work is involved in contacting only a few people. If nothing else I hope that this will give you a better appreciation of the problems we face."

It had the ring less of a nationwide underground resistance movement and more of a garden-club president trying to spur her busy committee chairman to greater heights of performance.

•"We are now in the process of sending out a bulletin to our general membership including the regular members of your network. I am sorry to report that the main reason we are forced to send out this bulletin direct is that so many of the Network Directors have failed to forward past bulletins to their members promptly."

Come on, girls, let's get those patios in shape for Garden Week.

•"Each Network Director must realize that he is a key member of this organization. Without cooperation and hard work from all our Directors the entire system will break down and many good members will be left stranded without any contact at all."

This, to men preparing for World War III in their own back yards? Now, about our rose program this year . . .

Both letters demonstrated that awesome communications problems were also confronting the Minutemen. Security leaks were greatly feared, with justification.

"We still have the enormous job of maintaining contact with approximately 1500 different Network Directors," DePugh wrote the directors. "We have said that we hope to do this by courier and it is still our intention to do so whenever possible. Unfortunately our couriers are also parttime workers with limited time and money and we must avoid asking them to run errands of a routine nature."

One of the final items in the bulletin to the general membership was headed "Machine Gun Plans Available." It reminded members that in the DePugh-Houghton-Peyson trial the previous November, it had been brought out that the Minutemen were planning to distribute plans to members on how to make one's own submachine gun. Well, wrote DePugh, that's true. The complete construction plans for an unusually lightweight, efficient and easily made submachine gun were now available.

But he added a paragraph of curious content, leaving at least two key phrases carefully undefined.

"It has never been our intention that these guns should be manufactured illegally in time of peace," he wrote without saying what "time of peace" meant or specifying who it was who would declare "war," LBJ, Nasser, Castro, Kosygin, Ky, Ho, Mao or Robert DePugh. "It is our hope that as many of our members as possible will have a set of these plans hidden out so that these easily manufactured guns can be made by future resistance groups that may need them for the defense of our constitutional republic."

"Defense of our constitutional republic" was also left hanging without elaboration. Defense against whom? Ho, Kosygin, Mao, Nasser, or LBJ and Robert McNamara?

The plans were not being offered free of charge this time. Rather, it would cost a member $20 to obtain them—$20 donated to the "Patriots Legal Defense Fund."

When I tried to contact DePugh to verify that he had actually written this, I found him to be traveling in the East. Wally Peyson was at 613 East Alton, however, and he readily confirmed that such plans were available at that price.

"Isn't this kind of an unusual way to raise money to finance your appeal on a conviction for a crime that involved processing unregistered submachine guns?"

"It's poetic justice," replied Peyson.

Shortly afterward, Wally handed me a pack of 100 gummed stickers the Minutemen were mailing out in quantity to members. They were "for your liberal friends," he laughed. A Minutemen letter had identified these stickers as for use in "Part II of Psy-War Project No. 32," which had been started, DePugh had written, to establish the cross-hairs symbol as a trade mark of the Minutemen. Borrowing from their notorious March 15, 1963, "On Target," the Minutemen now were offering 3-inch by 3½-inch stickers reading:

TRAITORS BEWARE

See the old man at the corner where you buy your papers? He may have a silencer equipped pistol under his coat. That extra fountain pen in the pocket of the insurance salesman who called on you might be a cyanide gas gun. What about your milkman? Arsenic works slow but sure. Your auto mechanic may stay up nights studying booby traps. These patriots are not going to let you take their freedom away from them. They have learned the silent knife, the strangler's cord, the target rifle that hits sparrows at 200 yards. Traitors beware. Even now the cross hairs are on the back of your necks.

MINUTEMEN

CHAPTER 21

JOIN THE MINUTEMEN

. . . Of all these [essential functions of an underground], intelligence is most important. Let's consider one example. Suppose you picked up a telephone book, opened it up to any page at random, closed your eyes and put your finger on one name. Now suppose you read that name for the first time and said to yourself, "Sometime in the next thirty days I'm going to kill this man."

Consider the situation—one man, picked at random, is marked for death. He might be the most powerful, the wealthiest, the most influential man in that city but none of these things would help him in the least. He would be defenseless. Why? Because you would have one thing that he did not have—intelligence. You would know his identity and he would not know yours. So long as that condition continued there would be no possible way in which he could arrange an adequate defense against you.

Exactly the same situation exists between ourselves and our Communist-Socialist enemies. Our success will be directly proportionate to their knowledge of us. . . .

From a pamphlet, "Minutemen Training Program"—1961.

. . . Our strike teams are standing at the ready, and their targets have already been picked, and if I'm killed, my death is going to be avenged very quickly and very efficiently.

From a tape-recorded speech by Robert B. DePugh, sent to regional Patriotic Party meetings—September, 1967.

So, what next, Minutemen? What in the world was "Psy-War Project No. 32"? More Minutemen gobbledegook? Or did DePugh have something concrete in mind, something that should be taken seriously?

As August, 1967, neared an end and I thought I had finally found a point at which I possibly could conclude the chronicling of Minutemen affairs and attitudes, a series of events began to occur at various points over the country—the Rocky Mountains, New York City, New Orleans, Oklahoma City, Denver and Independence, among them. Some of these events were solid and tangible. Others were the product of DePugh's opportunistic hunger for publicity. And some were simply puzzling.

DePugh's quest for notoriety seemed to become so intense at this time that I began to suspect nearly every occurrence that was even remotely connected with the Minutemen somehow to have come about by the design of the Minutemen themselves. Not that they were all pre-arranged for publicity, of course, but when one starts studying the conspiratorial mind, one sometimes begins to develop such a mind of his own.

Evaluating the events was a particular problem for me because of my sensitivity to the fact that DePugh delighted in "using" the news media—myself very much included—to gain publicity for himself and his ploys. This was part of the long, cat-and-mouse game we had played since 1964, but its pace was now accelerating. Each of us was trying to "use" the other, so to speak, he for publicity, I for the close-up view of DePugh and his Minutemen I gained by retaining communications with them—no matter how misleading they tried to be. DePugh undoubtedly would recite a different version of how we played this unusual game, but as I saw it—I hope accurately—my hand was heavy with trump cards.

For one thing, he failed far more often than he succeeded in his attempts at becoming the subject of news stories, critical or otherwise. I tried neither to overplay nor underplay the Minutemen in the *Star*, but striking a fair balance on such an erratic subject was often difficult. Sometimes, I'm sure, DePugh chortled over having suckered me into something. But more often he met with failure in this respect and was either ignored or relegated to the inside pages and left unobserved by the wire services. Ignoring the Minutemen too often would have been a gross case of ostrich journalism, and a breach of trust with our readers, for this was not the sort of organization, in my judgment, that would die on the vine for lack of publicity.

In fact, attempting to muzzle DePugh with the silent treatment would have enabled him to quietly build his organization to a larger size than it has achieved. With so much Minutemen activity being clandestine in nature anyway, DePugh would have been smarter, I think, to have limited his publicity stunts to a minimum after making his first big splash at Shiloh in 1961.

DePugh reasoned that he needed publicity to build the Minutemen, however. Its relatively small size, after seven years, is evidence of the fallacy of this theory, I think, for his goals for membership were staggering when he began. But DePugh also had his ego to contend with, and this was a bigger handicap than was his misjudgment regarding the need for publicity. He had surrounded himself with followers of like mind so completely that he seemed to begin to view the world somewhat through them and their adulation. In so doing, he gained a hopelessly twisted conception of what the great mass of Americans thought and felt. He realized, without question, that the majority would scorn some of his wilder pronouncements, but he seemed to think that these statements would lure into the Minutemen a larger percentage of the minority than it did.

DePugh also was able to build for himself a psychological immunity from criticism. Those who were critical of him, he told his followers, either were members of the Communist-Socialist conspiracy, or were victims brainwashed by those in the conspiracy. And I rather think that he believed a good deal of what he told his followers. Not everything, to be sure, but quite a bit.

At any rate, DePugh viewed news reports about him as helpful to him, and he apparently viewed this book, while in preparation, the same way. And so he not only continued to return my calls, but to call me on his own with regularity, even after some of my feeble attempts to argue him into a non-violent posture of what I lamely labeled "moderate conservatism."*

No efforts were made by the Minutemen through most of the summer of 1967 to capture any headlines, but a few isolated events did occur prior to the sudden spate of developments in late August.

Dennis Mower was found guilty of a firearms-law violation in May and was sentenced to a year in federal prison. He is appealing the conviction at this writing. The government dismissed its charge against Cindy. Troy Houghton seemed to vanish from sight in late May. By August, Bettie, his wife, had filed missing persons reports on him with

---

* I should add that he also called me, and allowed some other Minutemen to talk with me because he seemed to think I had information that might be of some value to him. My questions at times undoubtedly did reveal to him how much I knew. This was unavoidable. But he was mislead many times by jumping to conclusions based on his faulty evaluation of those questions, I am sure. DePugh also thought I had a much clearer pipeline into and out of the federal investigative agencies than I did. When events became too cloak-and-daggerish, I admit I was strongly tempted to throw the man some wild questions based entirely on fantasy, but usually held myself in check. The Minutemen were having enough trouble figuring out what was going on in the world around them without my intentionally adding to their frustrations.

the police departments of several cities. DePugh tried to attract national attention with accusations that Minutemen had infiltrated the Job Corps and had found riot-training, graft and prostitution. His attempt failed miserably. Michael Desmond Sadewhite signed a statement for me detailing his work for the FBI and his meeting in January with DePugh. He did not balk at having it notarized and in mid-July was subpoenaed before a federal grand jury in Kansas City. And I went to DePugh, with Sadewhite's permission, to confront him with the Sadewhite statement.

I took the statement, minus only his true name, address and FBI connection, to 613 East Alton in July. DePugh and Wally Peyson were both there. First I inquired generally about "Desmond." They remembered meeting with him in Norborne and seemed surprised that I knew of it. I had expected DePugh to say he had known all along that Desmond was an FBI plant and had made those rash statements to the man just to confuse "The Eye." But he tried no such ploy. Then I read most of the statement to them. When I reached the violent part, about halfway through the text, DePugh and Peyson laughed. They especially laughed at the bank-robbery story. By the time I had finished reading, however, they had grown serious again, possibly because I had maintained a grim attitude in my recitation, or perhaps because the statement ended with Sadewhite-Desmond's account of how DePugh allegedly intended to avoid imprisonment and had an "escape route."

Yes, they had met him. There was no denying this now. Yes, they had switched restaurants during their conversation more or less as described. And yes, DePugh even acknowledged having given Sadewhite-Desmond half of a dollar bill for future identification purposes. But making him a resistance network director? No. And talk of violence? No! No! No bombings, no assassinations, no robberies. And very, very much, "No," to the escape route story. "I hope Judge Hunter doesn't get nervous over that," DePugh added.

Apparently not knowing of any FBI connection then, DePugh tried to explain away the accusations by saying that Sadewhite sought revenge because DePugh had refused to give him money he had requested at this meeting. Or perhaps the man was in quest of publicity for himself, DePugh suggested. He tried to find out how I had come into contact with this new informant, probably thinking of a leak in one of the federal agencies. I replied, truthfully, that my own

spy network had found Sadewhite all by itself, with no help from the
FBI, ATTU or the Communist-Socialist conspiracy (my "spies" being
two ladies who liked to listen to daytime radio "talk shows"). Soon
DePugh had changed the subject by showing me his new parabolic
microphone for long-distance electronic eavesdropping. He even invited
me to put on the earphones.

The June 5 Minutemen bulletin to members had mentioned that
summer training sessions would be held in three undisclosed locations
and members were urged to attend as either students or instructors.
I initially chalked this off as more wild-eyed fantasy, but eventually
learned that at least two—if not more—were indeed held, in Pennsylvania and Colorado.

A few of the Minutemen planning to attend the Colorado session
had begun setting up camp high in the Rockies when the strange
sequence of events referred to earlier began to occur. A thumbnail
log of these events is as follows:

August 16—Jerry Brooks suddenly confronted the Jefferson County,
Colorado, sheriff's office in Golden with the story that he had been
spirited into Colorado against his will by the Minutemen and needed
protection. He was kept in protective custody overnight, talked with
the FBI and then left. He was seen briefly in Kansas City about a
week later, walking down the street, but he then seemed to disappear
again.

August 23—Four men identified with both the Minutemen and
other rightist groups were arrested in the Bronx, New York, and
charged with the attempted bomb-murder of Herbert Aptheker, the
Communist theoretician. The alleged plot had failed, said the police,
because the bomb had gone off two days late (prompting one assistant D.A. to quip that while the men contended they were Minutemen, actually they were "forty-eight-hour men"). In raids of
about a dozen places involved in the police arrests of these men,
250,000 rounds of ammunition were confiscated, according to the
police inventory, as well as an anti-tank gun, a submachine gun,
seven shotguns, 45 rifles, three hand grenades, 18 sticks of dynamite,
103 blasting caps, two 50-pound cans of explosive powder, a plastic
bomb, 14 pistols, several hunting knives and a machete.

August 25—A sniper assassinated George Lincoln Rockwell, leader
of the American Nazi Party, as he was starting to drive away from a

laundromat in an Arlington, Virginia, shopping-center parking lot. A former high-ranking follower of Rockwell's was charged with the murder.

August 26—DePugh telephoned me from Denver—at least he said he was in Denver—and told me that he had learned through a source high in "government intelligence" that he and Rockwell were two of four right-wing leaders in the United States who had been marked for assassination. The assassination orders, he said, had originated in Havana, Cuba. Had he told me this the day *before* Rockwell's death, I might at least have considered believing such a story. As it was . . .

August 30—Sadewhite, now news director at radio station KUDL, said he finally was ready to make the contents of his statement about his infiltration of the Klan and Minutemen for the FBI public. I suggested Sunday, September 3, as a good date for publication. It would give me time to write the article and get pictures of him. He agreed, adding this also would give him time to arm himself properly. He said he expected retaliation.

August 31—An explosion shook the headquarters of the Patriotic Party headquarters at 613 East Alton in Independence at about two-thirty in the morning. Robert Gourley, a shy, middle-aged Patriotic Party worker who had been living there about a month, his wife and two children were asleep in the building at the time but escaped injury. The bomb blew a hole in an outside wall near the front of the old building and shattered the plate-glass windows in front. Gourley interpreted it initially as a warning to DePugh, tied in with the alleged assassination plot, but some policemen expressed skepticism, suggesting that the explosion may well have been self-inflicted for publicity purposes. The front of the building had been doomed anyway. East Alton Avenue, at that point, was about to be widened, the front of the building to be condemned.

September 2—DePugh called again from Denver and said he had learned that Robert Welch of the Birch society and Robert Shelton of the United Klans of America were the other two right-wingers on the Havana assassination list. He also said he was sending me a tape recording of his voice, duplicates of which would be played the next day at three regional meetings of the Patriotic Party in Dearborn, Michigan (near Detroit), King of Prussia, Pennsylvania (near Philadelphia), and Hot Springs, Arkansas. On the tape, he said, he would denounce William Penn Patrick (Chapter 16). I mentioned to him that the Sade-white article would be in the morning paper. Any further comment? More denials. Wally Peyson dropped the tape off at the airport a few hours later. He gave it to his fiancée and she delivered it to me dutifully. Wally proceeded by airliner to Detroit.

September 3—As Kansas Citians read of Michael Desmond Sade-white's account of Minutemen plans to begin "isolated acts of violence," possibly that month, Patriotic Party members and some Minutemen in the vicinities of Detroit, Philadelphia and Hot Springs heard from their leader by tape recording.

DePughisms abounded on the tape, his views on the Communist conspiracy, his urgent concept of patriotism, his own self-proclaimed selflessness in The Struggle. He seemed either to view himself as a martyr and Messiah, or thought he could con others into thinking so.

At one point he became nostalgic over the little cabin high in the Rocky Mountains from which he said he was making this tape recording, a place where he had gone to find "the quiet and solitude that was necessary not only to make the tapes but to try to find a few answers to the problems that are pressing in upon us."

And he asked: "Who will save America? Who will save this great land? Who will save our freedom?"

Robert Bolivar DePugh, maybe? No, he wasn't ready to say quite that.

William Penn Patrick isn't going to save the country. DePugh made that clear. And maybe not George Wallace either, although DePugh wasn't quite ready to actually denounce him yet. It was just that "liberal" influences were bearing down on Wallace now. Like they did on Goldwater in '64.

He spoke of the explosion at 613 East Alton—"We aren't going to be intimidated by such events as this. In fact, we're not even going to be indignant over it. It's just going to make us a little madder and it's just going to make us work a little harder. . . ."

It was fortunate, really, that the explosion—if it had to occur—occurred the very morning he was preparing to make the tapes, considering that no one was hurt and the damage was slight. It fit well into the speech.

"This situation is grave," he continued. "Our nation is in imminent peril. We don't have time to waste on wishful thinking. . . ." But this was nothing new. We'd been in imminent peril for seven years according to the Minutemen. Surely, he'd have something stronger. . . .

"A few days ago I received a preliminary report from one of our contacts very high up in one of the government intelligence services to the effect that that service had monitored a message from Havana to the Communist assassination teams in this country that four right-wing leaders were to be executed as soon as possible. At the time, I didn't know who the four were. Since then I have been able to personally check with this contact. . . ."

But this was not new either. Surely . . .

". . . Well, it's one down [Rockwell] and three to go."

Surely . . .

". . . Of the four conservative leaders that our Communist adversaries have marked for assassination"—and he was speaking more slowly now—"I don't know what the members of the Klan are going to do if and when Bob Shelton is assassinated"—and he was choosing his words with deliberateness—"and I don't know what the members of the Birch society are going to do if and when Robert Welch is assassinated"—and with determination—"but I do know what the members of the Minutemen are going to do when Robert B. DePugh is assassinated. . . ."

At last!

". . . We know, day by day and hour by hour the location and habits of twenty-five top Communist leaders and traitors in this country. And when I'm assassinated, those twenty-five men had better make sure that they're paid up on their life-insurance premiums. Because our strike teams are standing at the ready . . ."

Strike teams?

". . . and their targets have been picked . . . and if I'm killed, my death is going to be avenged very quickly and very efficiently."

September 3, later—I telephoned 613 East Alton to obtain the exact locations of the regional meetings and found myself talking to a strangely worried Robert Courley, the man who had been asleep in the headquarters when the bomb had exploded three and a half days earlier.

"If there's anything you know about it that I don't know, I surely would appreciate knowing, person to person," he said.

"Frankly, I think the Minutemen did it themselves," I replied, not caring to whom he would repeat the remark. "Who else benefited from it?"

"Well, I kinda think I'm getting caught in the middle of this thing," said the nervous Gourley.

September 6—I decided to visit Gourley at 613 East Alton. He had left. In his place were two men in their twenties who said they had been sent there from the Minutemen training session in Colorado to guard the headquarters against future bombing attacks. I laughed. They didn't. Then they told me the headquarters was under heavy police surveillance at the moment. Three unmarked police cars were parked nearby, they said, and two others were patrolling back and forth. After leaving, I checked and found this to be true.

I returned later in the afternoon with Bob Phillips of the *Star's* Independence office to chat at greater length with the two Minutemen.

An old car with "Support Your Local Police" pasted on the rear bumper was parked in front of the headquarters as we entered. It belonged to the third man now in the building, Wayne Morse, the Kansas City picket and right-wing gadfly.

"You son-of-a-bitch, get out of here," Morse shouted at me as one of the Minutemen opened the screen door for us.

Usually Morse and I could coexist peacefully while conversing. He would call me a Communist and jokingly say the Minutemen planned to shoot me between the eyes instead of having their cross hairs on the back of my neck, and I would call him a bigot and that would be that. But he was in a mean mood this day, possibly upset at my having found him there and unquestionably irritated over his experience that morning in Kansas City Municipal Court. One of his picketing efforts had gone awry again and someone had had him arrested. The police, as usual, had perjured themselves against him, he said ("those dirty, rotten, lying, —— police," his bumper sticker notwithstanding). He told of how he had dragged his Russian flag from police headquarters to the county courthouse in protest over the developments in court. I smiled, Phillips smiled. The two Minutemen smiled.

Eventually Morse cooled down and played his phonograph record, "Don't Tread On Me," for the enrichment of those who had not heard it before. As he was starting to leave, standing by the screen door enlightening us more fully with some of his observations on the world around us, a passing car backfired with unusual gusto, making all of us jump (the bomb hole was only a few feet from us, after all) and causing Morse to feign a gunshot wound in his mid-section like a little boy. Everyone laughed and he left.

The smaller of the two Minutemen identified himself as Robert Bagwell after we had all sat down for conversation, but the other one kept his identity to himself. Bagwell called him "Vinnie," and "Vinnie" called Bagwell "Jim," since "Jim Peters" was Bagwell's Minutemen pseudonym for the moment.

Bagwell was one of the twenty New Yorkers arrested in the raids the previous October. He said he had spent forty-five days in jail, unable to make bond, but had been one of four not indicted later. Therefore he could talk about the New York case while most of the others were forced to remain silent until they had gone on trial.

A gardener from Roosevelt, Long Island, Bagwell was a bitter, soft-spoken, slow-speaking Southerner. He had joined the Ku Klux Klan in Tennessee at the age of fourteen, then had drifted into the National States Rights Party (and bore a large tattoo on one arm with "N.S.R.P." printed beneath an elaborately designed skull). Vinnie's background remained a mystery.

"You the guy who wrote the story about the one who works on the radio station?" Vinnie asked, referring to Sadewhite. "He doesn't work there any more, does he?"

"As far as I know," I replied. "Why?"

"Well, I just wouldn't think he would," said Vinnie with a non-committal smile. "His life isn't worth much any more, is it?"

Before Bagwell could go into much detail about the Queens raids, the telephone rang in the kitchen. Vinnie answered it and returned soon afterward with news that we should leave.

"I never kicked anybody out of any place before," he said, "but that was Security on the phone. [*Security?*] They saw you guys come in and say you gotta leave."

We left.

September 12—"Mr. Robert Bagwell is back in town," the note from the *Star* telephone operator read. "He wants you to go and see him and take your tape recorder." Bagwell had seemed to be angling for publicity on our earlier meeting. Now it was obvious he was. Undoubtedly, DePugh had so instructed him. Still, I was interested

in what he would have to say. I called. We arranged to meet at eight
o'clock at 613. Another Minuteman would be there too, Roy Frank-
houser, the Klan Grand Dragon for Pennsylvania, through whom
Sadewhite had said he had joined the Minutemen originally. I asked
Tom Eblen, assistant city editor of the *Star*, if he wanted to go with
me, since Tom has an unusual interest in the ideologically macabre.
He consented. It was not every day a fellow could meet a real, live
Grand Dragon.

Bagwell and Vinnie were there when we arrived. Thin, wiry, dead-
pan, Bagwell wore thick glasses, a crew cut. He talked with the
same distinctive vocal inflections as DePugh, but with a Southern
rather than Missouri drawl. His manner was of one who felt he had
profound, native wisdom at his command deep inside him as well
as knowledge of many dark secrets and subterfuges that he would
die before revealing.

Before we could proceed with the tape-recorded interview very far,
Ralph DePugh, the Minutemen leader's father, emerged from the
back room, on his way home. Cordial greeting. He told a few jokes
about politics and left.

Bagwell talked in detail about his arrest and stay in jail in New
York. Two 30.06 rifles and a crossbow were found in his cellar. When
first questioned, he said, he was viewed through a two-way mirror
by two informants; he tried to slug both of them, but was restrained.

He said that most of the New York Minutemen who had been
arrested had planned to go on mountain climbing "maneuvers" that
day but had not intended to blow up any camps. The bombs found
in the trunk of one of the leader's cars had been for practice det-
onation in the mountains, he said. As for the three left-wing camps,
the Minutemen had, indeed, staked them out for eventual destruction,
but had had no immediate plans for such acts. I asked when, then?

"When we got in the field and were fighting against the Communists to take back our government," he said. "Then the camps
woulda been blown up, plus some other ones we know about."

"What Communists are you talking about?"

"I'm talking about when the United Nations sends troops in here
to control America."

"Are those the only conditions that you would regard as an armed
Communist attack?"

"Well, when they do that," drawled Bagwell, "they'll have a Communist in as President."

"Such as?"

"Well, Lyndon Baines Johnson would be a damned good start. And McNamara. . . ."

About this time a smallish man with a thin mustache and a glass eye entered and sat down without speaking. He was dressed in a white shirt, tie and suit. It was just about the first time I could recall seeing anyone so formally attired at 613 East Alton in all my visits there. I assumed correctly that this was Grand Dragon Roy Frankhouser.

"You think Johnson's a Communist?" I continued with Bagwell.

"Yes, I do. That's my own personal opinion," he replied.

"Think McNamara's a Communist?"

"Yes, I do."

"Who else?"

"Secretary of State Dean Rusk."

"Anybody else?"

"Well, approximately 150,000 other people who work for the Communists are in the government."

". . . When do you think Johnson became a Communist?"

"Well, President Johnson stated that himself. Exactly thirty years ago."

I inexcusably neglected to ask him when it was that President Johnson had identified himself publicly as a Communist, perhaps because I was so fascinated by Bagwell's sense of history.

"You think Roosevelt was a Communist?" I asked.

"Is this the same Roosevelt that, uh . . . ?"

"Franklin."

"Yeah. That had the treaty signed with Russia. What was the name of that agreement?"

"Yalta agreement?"

"Yalta. Yeah. Is that the one you're talking about?"

"I'm not talking about Teddy."

"Teddy's the one that signed the Yalta agreement?" asked Bagwell.

"No. Teddy's been dead a long time. Franklin was President from 1932 to 1946," I said, showing off, and missing his death by a year.

"Oh, yeah, that's the same one I was thinking of," said Bagwell. "No, I don't think Franklin was a pro-Communist, but he damned sure leaned toward the Communists. . . . He [Johnson] became a card-carrying member of the Communist Party, but I couldn't prove it worth a damn. That's just my personal opinion."

"You think he takes orders from some foreign Communist?"

"Yes, I do. Directly from Russia. He's selling the country right down the drain as fast as he can do it. Him and McNamara and Rusk. They're doing a beautiful damned job of being traitors to this country."

Then we turned to the Colorado training session the previous month.

"What did you do up in Colorado?"

"We trained."

"What'd you train in?"

"Guerrilla warfare."

"Guerrilla warfare? Explosions? Shooting? All that sort of thing?"

"Well, there was no explosions, but there was training in it."

"How to use it?"

"Yeah."

"How to make it?"

"Well, anybody can make it from picking up a book in the library."

"So you didn't have to teach that?"

"No."

"Target practice?"

"Target practice."

"What with?"

"Rifles and pistols."

"Anything else?"

"No, it's against the law to shoot a machine gun."

"Oh. That's right."

"I couldn't put that on tape," Bagwell said, smiling.

"What about mortars, that sort of thing?"

"Noooo," he answered, laughing again. "I'm afraid we didn't use any mortars either. Not that we didn't want to."

He went on to say that the training session had lasted two weeks somewhere in the Colorado mountains and that about 130 Minutemen attended. I later learned the total count was little more than twenty.

"Besides guerrilla warfare, what else did you practice?"

"Well, how to survive in the streets."

"How'd you learn that in the mountains?"

"Well, it's not too hard if you've got a good imagination."

"Well, the Minutemen have a good imagination."

"We really do," said Bagwell. "We had literature on it."

The tape was running out. I wanted to learn about the anti-assassination plans of the Minutemen "strike teams."

"Are you on a strike team?"

"Well, whether I am or not, I'm going to do everything in my power to help raise that number above twenty-five."

". . . Who decides the names of the 'Communists' to be killed? You or DePugh?"

"The council does."

"They put out a list of names, right?"

"They will. They've got a list now. If DePugh is killed, then we'll act upon it."

". . . If the council sends out a list of twenty-five and you say you're going to try to raise that number, does that mean you're going to act on your own?"

"And I imagine there'll be a great deal many other Minutemen who'll do the same thing," Bagwell replied.

"What'll you do if DePugh just disappears instead of just becoming the victim, like Rockwell was, of a known assassin?"

"It'll be up to the council to decide that."

"How do you know that they'll be able to decide accurately?"

"Because I have faith in them."

"Why do you have faith in them? You don't even know who they are."

"Well, that's one of the reasons why I have faith in them. Because I don't know who they are, but they know me."

"So, if they have faith in you, you have faith in them?"

"Right. Like I said, if they know where I'm at and know the code name that I'll be going under at the time and know the number and everything else that goes along with it, then there'll be no doubt in my mind that they are who they are."

"All you know about the council is what DePugh told you about the council, right?"

"That's right."

"That means you have to have an awful lot of faith in DePugh's judgment."

"That's right."

Vinnie interrupted at this point with: "We never met Jesus Christ either, but we believe in him, even though we never seen him."

"That's a good point," said Bagwell.

Vinnie then talked of priests, rabbis and pastors who talk of the existence of Christ, then corrected himself and limited it to priests and pastors.

"You believe in DePugh as much as any priest who told you there's a Christ?" I asked.

"Right," said Bagwell.

"Uhhh, not on the same level," said Vinnie. "I don't consider Bob a real Christ."

"No, Bob DePugh isn't on the same level as Christ would be," agreed Bagwell in deadly earnest, "but I'd believe Bob as much as I would the priest or the preacher."

"Why?" I asked. "What is it about DePugh that gives you this faith in his judgment?"

"Past experiences," said Bagwell.

"You think he's demonstrated good judgment the last six years as leader of the Minutemen?"

"Damn good."

"Why does he face a four-year prison term?"

"Because," said Bagwell, with seeming conviction, "he was framed. . . ."

Soon the tape had run out. That was enough of Bagwell. Next up, Roy Frankhouser.* He talked much more rapidly than Bagwell had. He was obviously used to long, windy discussions of his beliefs. Smiles came infrequently. I sensed a lack of sincerity, yet could not define in my own mind as he talked exactly what impression he wished to leave. He described himself as a "supporter" of the American Nazi Party, said he had picketed with Rockwell at times, acknowledged membership in the NSRP and, of course, the Grand Dragonship of Pennsylvania's Klan. He left his role in the Minutemen as undefined,

---

* Frankhouser figured prominently in *One More Victim* by A. M. Rosenthal and Arthur Gelb (New American Library, 1967), a book about the life and death of Dan Burros, an anti-Semitic Jew who belonged to the American Nazi Party and the Ku Klux Klan. Frankhouser was with Burros in Reading, Pennsylvania, when Burros committed suicide after his Jewish origin had been exposed. Rosenthal and Gelb wrote that while the two men were hiding from subpoenas in Reading shortly before Burros' suicide, Frankhouser tried to calm the nervous Burros with the suggestion that they "go up to the hills where, he said, the Minute Men had caches of guns, and shoot some bazookas, for relaxation."

but was clear enough about the role the Minutemen played in society. He called it a "terrorist organization."

First the Grand Dragon wanted to establish Sadewhite as a scoundrel. The Minutemen were preparing a file on Sadewhite, he said, and would release it soon. Eight months later—still no "file" has been released.) They were going to "take care of" Sadewhite, he said. I asked what he meant by that.

"Well, when I said that, I meant within the law," he replied.

"You're not going to shoot him?" I asked.

"Oh, no, no," the Grand Dragon said. "Heavens no. Heaven help us if we'd do a thing like that. . . ."

He acknowledged knowing Sadewhite well from their Klan days together in and around Reading, Pennsylvania. He recalled having made Sadewhite think that he had enlisted him into the Minutemen, but that this had been a ruse. He said Sadewhite owed him and the Klan money and added that he wanted to see Sadewhite. He asked me not to tell Sadewhite that he was in the area, but I told him I could not agree to withhold such information from Sadewhite and that he had no business asking me to do so. He seemed irked by this, but finally accepted it without even administering a karate chop.

I asked the Grand Dragon four times in the next hour how he happened to join the Minutemen, but he never got around to answering the question. The first time I tried, his answer started off like this:

"Well, I belong to almost every right-wing organization that I know of. If I don't have a paid membership, I have an honorary membership. . . . I have my definite heroes in the right wing—Robert Shelton, Bob DePugh; for personal reasons and the certain satisfaction that I get, I liked to watch Rockwell in action, mainly because of his ability to fight his way out of court. . . ."

I asked the Grand Dragon if he aspired to the role of someone else's right-wing idol.

"No, I don't want to," he said. "If I wanted to, it probably wouldn't be too hard to go out and speak. I have a fair command of the English language and I have been able to take crowds and hold them quite well."

But he said he did not wish to make the personal sacrifices necessary to become as famous as his idols. Not that he had not made plenty of sacrifices in the past—one of them being an eye, which he said he lost when beaten by hoodlums hired by Reading politicians who had been angered by his activities. As for other sacrifices:

"I did [make the sacrifices] in the past when I began some tremendous public speaking crusades as I did through New Jersey, New York, Pennsylvania and the South. I was in demand. Still am. I could speak on any platform of any Klan, any Citizens Council or anything else in the country probably. But at the present time I'm more interested in engineering—engineering the movements toward a general goal, unification, if possible, unification at least of aims and ideas . . . to defeat Communism. . . ."

"How did you happen to join the Minutemen?" I tried again.

"I *did* join the Minutemen," Frankhouser said. "There's no question about that. Or, let's say, I *might* have joined the Minutemen. Well, I might as well tell you, I did. Basically. It's difficult. You run into policies. Policy No. 1 is to say you're not a member. Policy No. 2, is, well, if you're going to admit it, well, you might as well."

We turned to the inevitable subject of when it would be decided by the Minutemen, as a group or on an individual basis, that the time had come to start shooting "the enemy."

"Well," Frankhouser said, "where are you going to draw the line?"

"Where will *you* draw the line?"

"I would say the individual Minuteman has to, to a degree," he said. "If the individual Minuteman wants to go out and pull the trigger, that's his business. If he doesn't, that's perfectly all right. If he wants to wait until such time—the thing is—each man has a thin line where he's drawn the line in his own mind, you understand what I mean, and once that line is past, he springs into action automatically and doesn't need any general orders."

"Have any sprung yet?"

"Some of them might. I don't know. I don't know of any that haven't. Who knows? There's embassies that went up. Who knows that the Yugoslavians blasted them or we blasted them or who blasted them. The beauty of the thing is not to be caught, as far as I can see."

"You think this is right, creating an organization with these individual human time bombs all over the nation?"

"Let's put it like this. As a reasonably sane man, this probably just isn't right, in a way . . ."

And he then went into a long discussion of the evil methods of Communists, trying to justify similar methods by anti-Communists.

"Then you're a revolutionary," I suggested.

"Yeah," Frankhouser replied. "I'm a revolutionary. I believe I would qualify as a revolutionary. Some papers refer to me as 'Riot Roy.'"

"Why?"

"Well, seems as if I have been involved in a few riots."

In response to a question about whom he pictured eventually shooting after a Communist take-over, Frankhouser replied:

"Well, I don't know. Some of my best friends, I'm afraid, will be on the other end of the rifle because I have many friends in the liberal movement."

"You mean you're going to be shooting liberals?"

"Well, let's put it this way. When the lines are drawn, everybody'll know when the lines are drawn. They'll be on one side or the other. The people that are sitting on the fence will find that the fence has been burned down around them and there is no fence any more. And slowly but surely the sides will line up, like in the Spanish Civil War, and bang, some incident will start it and it may end up with a worldwide revolution. There'll be one thing—we'll either take over with a right-wing government and be the anti-guerrillas hunting down the guerrillas in the hills, or we'll be the guerrillas when the enemy takes over."

"When?"

Frankhouser paused, then replied, "I'm honestly puzzled by that question."

And so we turned to the counterassassination "strike teams" DePugh had said were at the ready.

"I'll tell you," Frankhouser said. "It will be done. I know men who will shoot, men whose targets are already drawn up, who are polishing the scope and waiting for the time. If DePugh is killed violently, I'll guarantee you, regardless of whether it's right or wrong, somebody's going to die too. It's going to be tragic but . . ."

"Even if the wrong man did it?" I interrupted.

"It wouldn't matter. I'm afraid the wheels wouldn't take that long to say, well, hold it boys, let's take it easy."

"Your strike teams are ready to kill immediately, no matter who kills DePugh?" I asked.

"If one of our people kills DePugh," Vinnie interrupted from the far couch, next to the bomb hole, "he's gotta be working for someone else."

"Let's put it this way," said Frankhouser, ignoring Vinnie. "I'm afraid that DePugh has reached the point that regardless of whether the rules are right or wrong, that's what's gonna happen."

". . . How do you know?"

"I *know*," said Frankhouser, looking now off into the distance. "I'll just tell you that. I know."

"Have you talked to members of a strike team?"

"I don't know about that. I just *know*. I know that strike teams exist. I know. I guarantee it. . . . It's a tragedy, but it's true. It's reality. I hate to say that. . . . The unbelievable thing to me is the restraint this organization has held its members in check with. I've been in organizations in the Klan that you don't hold them in check. Every so often they go off and do something silly. You know what I mean. It's a miracle. It's Bob's personal personality that holds these people in check."

Then he began a rather good imitation of DePugh talking to other Minutemen:

"Now, hold it. Now that's not the time, boys. Now, let's take our time and think it over. Let's make a little more elaborate plans. And if it does come to that, then we'll do it, but not until we have to. There's no need to start something if it's not necessary. Besides, there may be another way of doing it. I'm not saying you shouldn't, but if you value my opinion, I'd hold off, and if there's no other way, then maybe you'll have to do it."

Frankhouser's admiration for DePugh was now beginning to show through convincingly.

"That little talk will tone them down for maybe a month or two," he said. "He's not irreplaceable. He's not infallible. But he's one of the greatest leaders I've ever met, and one of the few men that can keep up a pace which would overwhelm and morally destroy anyone else. I don't know how he does it."

Earlier in the interview, Frankhouser had been asked to compare DePugh and Rockwell, who I had suggested could have talked rings around DePugh in a debate.

"To a degree, Rockwell was a product of the East," he said. "Fast talking and so forth and so on, with the ability to project himself and so forth, but Robert DePugh is, in my mind—there's a greater depth to the man in the soul. The man is part of the folk legend of—he'd make a Jesse James any day of the week, I guarantee. He'd make a folk legend, a mountaineering kind."

"You think he'll be a folk hero in a hundred years?" I asked a bit taken aback by the emulation at this point.

"Oh, I guarantee it," Frankhouser replied. "They'll sing folk songs about him if we win. If we don't of course, they'll write other things. He comes from America's—the deep roots of Missouri, Southern, well, there's tremendous possibilities. If I was a press agent ready to build an image, I could build it quite easily. No question about that."

As we parted—it was close to midnight—I assured Frankhouser that I had an obligation to tell Sadewhite he was in the area. Frankhouser told me to tell Sadewhite that he had already been out to the radio station once to find him and that if Sadewhite were wise, he should change cars in the next week. He tried to sound as menacing as possible without making an outright threat of violence. I cautioned Sadewhite the next morning without trying to alarm him, feeling a little foolish at becoming involved in what I felt was probably a game, but never certain.

A breathing spell of two days followed, with nothing from Minutemen, anti-Minutemen, defectors, infiltrators, anyone. Tranquillity prevailed.

September 15—Suddenly Minutemen were being accused of having been in on a plot—*the* plot, it was alleged—to assassinate President John F. Kennedy. Their accuser—James Garrison, district attorney of New Orleans parish. The world had first been jolted by the tall, talkative D.A.'s investigation of the assassination in February, 1967, but it was not until now that the Minutemen had received anything more than passing notice. William E. Turner had mentioned them briefly in an article on the Garrison probe in the June 1967 issue of *Ramparts* magazine, but now, in the October issue of *Playboy*, just out, Garrison told writer Eric Norden, who interviewed him at great length, that unnamed Minutemen and/or ex-Minutemen of a Nazi persuasion had been involved. And he elaborated on this to radio station KNEW in Oakland, California, this time mentioning unnamed Dallas and California Minutemen. I immediately began efforts to obtain an interview with Garrison. Because he was busy, and because I did not try as hard as I might have—my skepticism bolstering my apathy—it was nearly six months before I finally talked with Garrison, and then only briefly, by telephone.

It was the Nazi element in the CIA, he said, and some of those persons had once been in the Minutemen. But the Minutemen organization, as such, was *not* involved in the assassination, he said. Tom Bethel, one of his assistants, elaborated on this. Any Minuteman's or ex-Minuteman's involvement in the assassination, he said, was neither sponsored by DePugh nor even known by DePugh.

So much for Garrison. Time will have to tell what that is all about.

September 16—As Wally Peyson, speaking for DePugh, was busy denying the Garrison accusations at 613 East Alton, a new Minutemen defector happened onto the scene. At least he seemed like a defector. Certainly he knew the Minutemen, and some of his information checked out.

This was Ed Bumgardner of Erie, Illinois, a smallish, sallow-complexioned ex-convict in his late twenties. He had joined the Minutemen in 1966 through the Reverend Johnny Bob Harrell, with whom he had served time in the federal prison at Terre Haute. Shortly before I met him, Bumgardner had already led Bob Whearley, night city editor and parttime investigative reporter for the Denver *Post*, to a Minutemen cache of weapons, explosives and "survival" gear in a mountainous area of Summit County, Colorado.*

He had no such tangible evidence for me, but he did have plenty to say in our many meetings and telephone conversations the rest of that year.

Bumgardner had been at the Minutemen training session in Colorado that August and had been made a member of a four-man "strike team" while there, he said. The "strike team's" first assignment, he said, had been to go to the home of a wealthy Illinois coin collector and steal his coin collection. A man in Independence already had arranged to fence the coins, he said. Bumgardner even admitted having suggested the coin collector as their first victim. Proceeds from the burglary, he assured me, were to have been put to patriotic use.

The burglary was not committed, however, and Bumgardner claimed

---

* The upshot of the *Post's* discovery of the weapons and ammunition cache—including an illegal sawed-off shotgun—was an exposé by Whearley of Minutemen in Colorado and a charge of trespassing pressed against Whearley by the Summit County prosecuting attorney. Whearley pleaded *nolo contendere* and the *Post* paid his fine of $150 and $5 court costs for him.

that this was because his conscience had started to bother him and he persuaded his strike teammates to abandon the idea.

Everything that Michael Sadewhite had said about the Minutemen plans, as reported in the *Star*, had been "right on the button," Bumgardner volunteered.

Assassinations? Bank robberies? Bombings?

"Everything he said was what I'd heard," Bumgardner said, "only I heard it later."

Bumgardner had set to work trying to woo the pretty Mary Tollerton away from the Minutemen organization. They had met at the Colorado training session and at the time of our first encounter both of them were hiding from DePugh and his cronies. Bumgardner, in fact, claimed to be carrying a pistol several of the times I saw him. He said the pistol contained dum-dum bullets.

I am happy to report that Mary did, in fact, abandon the Minutemen eventually. She also abandoned Bumgardner.

As the two of them were zipping back and forth between Kansas City and Denver that fall on mysterious missions, it came to my attention that DePugh seemed highly interested in their whereabouts. From what I could gather, DePugh placed considerable value on Mary's membership in the Minutemen, for she had been involved in numerous intrigues by then and knew enough about the organization to be, in his terms, a security risk.

Eventually I managed to talk with Mary about her defection. She explained that she was disenchanted with DePugh, but was still in favor of "militant anti-Communism." She was through with the Minutemen as long as DePugh ran it, she said. What about the Executive Council? There is no such thing, she replied.

"What do you think of all the Minutemen talk of violence, assassinations, 'strike teams,' that sort of thing?" I asked.

"Not at this time," she replied. "It would just lead to chaos. That's only for when the country is in the grips of a revolution."

"Do you think that DePugh thinks he's already in the grips of a revolution?"

"Yes, I do."

"You think he's sincere about this?"

"I don't know."

In early March, 1968, I talked with Mary again, just to be certain she had not changed her mind and returned to the Minutemen fold.

"No," she said. "I don't have anything to do with them."

She offered an additional reason for her disenchantment this time: "There seemed to be more Nazis in it, Nazis and ex-Nazis, and I hate Nazis as much as I do Communists."

One of the more disturbing aspects of the Minutemen, to me, had been the way DePugh had been able to lure young people who otherwise seemed to be perfectly nice individuals into thinking the way he did. It was refreshing to see Cindy and now Mary provide me with something of a happy ending for this book.

One night, late in our acquaintance, Bumgardner telephoned me at home seeking information. Where could he find Cindy? Where was Jerry Brooks hiding out? That sort of thing. By this time my patience was nearing the breaking point. I refused to tell him. "Maybe you're a Minuteman," he suggested, among other things and our conversation ended unharmoniously. Later that evening he telephoned George Arnett of the FBI with, apparently, much the same approach.

Two or three days later DePugh called.

"Heard from Eddie lately?" he asked.

"Yes," I said without elaboration.

"You know where he called you from?" DePugh asked.

"No," I replied, waiting.

"He was out at 613," DePugh said, mischief audible in his voice. "I was listening in on the extension."

"Oh?"

"I thought I'd better tell you," he added, laughing. "If you found out about it from someone else eventually, I didn't want you to think I was sneaky. . . . He called Arnett, too, and Mary."

The national coordinator went on to relate how Bumgardner had done this to demonstrate to DePugh how he was able to "con" the likes of me and others.

A few days later Bumgardner called again.

"Sorry about the way I was last time I called," he began. "DePugh was listening in on the extension."

"Oh?"

"I was trying to get in good with them again," he said, "to get some more information."

"I see."

"I guess it's too late to say I'm sorry, so I won't. . . ."

Then he turned to more important matters.

"They're looking for me now," he said. "They're plannin' to knock me off. . . ."

So long, Eddie.

September 20—Seven Oklahomans, some of them identified as members of the Minutemen, were arrested in Oklahoma City by ATTU agents and local law-enforcement officers who said they confiscated more than 100 weapons, some of them possessed illegally, thousands of rounds of ammunition, Nazi decals, and other equipment.

September 24—Suddenly Jerry Brooks was back, after an absence of four months, and as always, he was full of news.

We started where we had left off—at the meeting of DePugh, young Ken Patrick and Jerry at Kansas City's Union Station back in March. Jerry said he had tipped off the ATTU himself about the meeting, and had intended to set up DePugh on another "gun rap" with the ATTU watching. At the meeting, he said, DePugh failed to bring a pistol Jerry had expected being supplied. Instead, he said, DePugh asked him to change his testimony at the trial.

He met with DePugh and other Minutemen twice after that in Kansas City, he said, and then was forced under threat of death to sign an affidavit claiming he had perjured himself at the trial. But the affidavit "was all lies," he now said.

"The truth is, I told the truth before the grand jury," he said. "I told the truth at the trial of DePugh, Walter Peyson and Troy Houghton."

That actual threats of death were used to persuade him to sign the affidavit seemed hard to believe, Jerry being Jerry. His mood in my presence shortly before his return into the arms of the Minutemen that spring had suggested simply a change of heart, a fresh confusion. Still, this was what he was now saying. It was no wilder than what he had said in the affidavit, and at his television "press conference" in May.

The Minutemen had flown him to Spokane, Washington, after his television debut, he said, and had paid for his room in a comfortable hotel there. They also paid for the extraction of all his teeth by a dentist who was a Minuteman, he said.

"He was real friendly and pulled my teeth and said come in and I'll fix you some plates," Jerry related.

"Why didn't you get some plates?"

"Because I needed the money to get the plates."

"They wouldn't pay for the plates?"

"No. They never did send $400 for the teeth."

And, indeed, Jerry gummed every word of that story.

From Spokane, Jerry said, he traveled by bus to Denver where a Minuteman named "Vinnie" met him. He fled the state a few weeks later, just before the secret training session was to begin in the mountains. The members with whom he was mingling talked too much about revolution and assassinations, Jerry said.

"They were talking all the time about they were gonna shoot somebody," Jerry said. "Could have been just talk or maybe they really have plans, but I know they have a place up in the hills, the fourteen thousand-foot level, in Colorado, and maybe eighty miles out of Denver, and it's well stocked with food, and they have a radio up there, five hundred-watt transmitter, lots of food, plenty of guns, and it's to be run as the national headquarters of the Minutemen—to be run with approximately 50 people there."

At this location, Jerry said, the Minutemen plan to make "their last stand."

September 25—Rich Lauchli, the Collinsville, Illinois, mechanic who by now was serving a two-and-a-half-year sentence in the federal prison at Terre Haute, Indiana, received eighteen additional months to his prison term. This followed a conviction on yet another federal firearms act violation—this one involving the sale of a .50-caliber machine gun to a man posing as a Minutemen leader in Joplin, Missouri.

September 26—Frederick Seelig, the poor, haunted ex-newspaperman whom DePugh had brought to Kansas City for a speech about Communist psychiatry in the United States the previous spring, telephoned the Valparaiso (Indiana) *Vidette-Messenger* and asked that a reporter be sent to his motel room to interview him. The newspaper was later to report that Seelig had told the reporter he was going to destroy his book, *Destroy the Accuser*, because "certain parts are libelous. . . . People have used the book to exploit me." But he also talked of his "two years of torture" and "ultra sound torture. . . . They thought they were destroying my brain."

A few hours later, Frederick Seelig was dead. Suicide was thought to be the cause until an autopsy was held. The coroner's ruling, however: coronary thrombosis.

And just as suddenly as it had begun, the six weeks of rapid-fire Minutemen activity and counteractivity seemed to end.

Somehow, I felt, there would be other periods of time like that. Totally unpredictable. And either grotesque, tragic, ridiculous, laughable or just plain goofy.

The year 1967 ended calmly as far as DePugh's organization was concerned, as best as I could determine. Jerry Brooks went to Anchorage, Alaska, vowing he was starting a new life. Bettie Houghton was by now convinced, she said, that Troy was dead, while others, myself included, guessed he had simply "gone underground," as the Minutemen would call it.

"Are you going underground?" I asked DePugh at one point that fall.

"If I do, I'll do it publicly," he said, "and you'll be the first to know."

"Does that mean you are?"

"I said, 'If.'"

New bulletins and newsletters from the Minutemen and new Patriotic Party literature rolled off the press, which had been moved from 613 to Norborne.

Winter training sessions in 20-to-30-below-zero weather were promised. Bumgardner, identified in the literature only as the Denver *Post's* informant, was warned that he "will certainly be rewarded for his betrayal when the proper time comes."

And DePugh announced he was resuming the duties of "national coordinator" of the Minutemen, stressing how self-sacrificing a move this was. He warned members that the Minutemen soon may be facing "a combat situation" and "some of us must expect to give our lives for the cause of freedom."

It sounded silly at the time, but then I could not guess as I read such language what drama 1968 held for the Minutemen.

CHAPTER 22

JOIN THE MINUTEMEN

Prepare the nucleus of an escape and evasion team with the assistance of personal friends you can count on. Arrange alternate hideouts for yourself and your supplies. Locate people who have never been openly anti-Communist that might offer their homes, cars, etc. for such use on an emergency basis.

From a "Special Bulletin" to Minutemen in 1967 from the "Executive Council."

The year 1968 promised to be too tempestuous for the Minutemen or any other organization that thrives so well on dissent and divisiveness to lie dormant. The Vietnam war was still in progress and the object of increasingly bitter debate. Negro rioting in the cities was all but assured. The presidential election campaign seemed certain to be emotional and frenzied, especially with George Wallace looming so ominously in the wings.

By the end of 1967, I had grown uneasy over having written a word about Mike Sadewhite's infiltration of the Minutemen. I felt I had taken every available precaution, short of putting him on a polygraph, but still there was an outside chance that he had elaborated somewhat on the truth—especially concerning bank robberies and bombings. Or had DePugh been putting him on during their meetings in the Norborne cafés?

Ed Bumgardner's confirmation of the Sadewhite story had not been entirely reassuring. He simply had been too devious. Besides, such anticipated Minutemen activity as these two informants had warned us to expect was supposed to have begun by then. Yet all seemed calm.

Then along came Henry Floyd Brown, a thirty-nine-year-old ex-convict who had spent a total of less than one year of his adult life outside of prison.

In a sense, the Minutemen are as much a radical thought process as they are an organization. Whether the ideas advanced by DePugh and others in his organization had any influence on Henry Floyd Brown may never be known for certain. From my vantage point, it appears that they did. If nothing more, these ideas, reaching Brown in prison as he was becoming a self-educated man, provided him with some sort of weird rationalization for his conduct.

Brown spent time as an inmate at the Oregon State penitentiary and at the federal penitentiary at Leavenworth, Kansas. He claims to have known some Minutemen and he apparently thinks a good deal as a Minuteman is supposed to think. But he insists he is not a member of the organization and persons who feel they know him report that this is probably so. For one thing, Brown is too intent on being a leader himself to ever have allowed himself to become someone's follower—DePugh included.

I wondered briefly whether Brown might be a Minuteman even before I knew his name. This was because I was judging him solely on the events of one hour of his life—his spectacular robbery of the Metcalf State Bank in Overland Park, Kansas, a suburb of Kansas City, early the afternoon of January 19, 1968, and its violent aftermath.

A bomb had exploded outside the Overland Park City Hall and police headquarters first, diverting the attention of the police almost long enough for Brown and another man to hold up the bank a few blocks away and escape with about $13,000.

As can be said of most everything else Brown has tried in his lifetime, this failed too. A police chase ensued. Brown found himself trapped in his apartment. He took several scraps of notebook paper on which some names, addresses and telephone numbers had been written, tried to burn them, then tossed them into the toilet bowl. Neglecting to flush them down the drain, Brown then began a desperate battle with dozens of policemen and FBI agents. He shot one Kansas state trooper, Sergeant Eldon K. Miller, in the head, killing him. He lit the fuse and tossed a dynamite bomb at the officers, but the fuse burned out too soon. Finally he was shot and captured outside his apartment.

A search of the apartment revealed an arsenal of weapons, ammunition, and explosives that would have warmed the heart of the staunchest Minuteman.

Had Sadewhite's and Bumgardner's warnings at last been proven valid? Had DePugh's polemics about how "some of us may expect to give our lives for the cause of freedom" a month before taken on new meaning?

Quickly Brown's criminal record was examined. It was so atrocious as to virtually rule out the theory that this had been a "patriotic," Minutemen-inspired bank robbery. Brown had been out of the Leavenworth prison only since November, 1967. This, it seemed so clear, had been a bank robbery for personal profit, nothing more.

Within twenty-four hours, warrants were issued by the FBI for the arrest of three others involved in the robbery—Andrew Evan Gipson, a thirty-one-year-old former cellmate of Brown's at Leavenworth who had been sent there in 1963 for bank robbery, and their two current girl friends, Mrs. Bonnie Sue Wilane, a twenty-two-year-old beautician and wig stylist, and Mrs. Karen Sue Goetz, a twenty-four-year-old waitress, both quite pretty.

On the second night following the robbery, Bonnie Wilane shot herself three times in the abdomen with a pistol as FBI agents approached her in Cedar Rapids, Iowa, to take her into custody. Gipson and Karen Goetz had slipped out of Kansas City on a commercial flight for California the night of the robbery, but surrendered to Johnson County, Kansas, authorities peacefully by the end of the month.

During the week following the robbery, while Brown was a patient at the Shawnee Mission hospital in Overland Park, word reached the police that an escape might be attempted. Rumors that some unidentified outsiders might try to storm the hospital and rescue Brown were received. This was taken so seriously by the Overland Park police department that officers guarding Brown were armed with automatic Thompson sub-machine guns. No escape was attempted, however.

Brown and Bonnie survived their bullet wounds and all four entered pleas of guilty to state charges. They are now serving their sentences at Lansing. Case closed? From a legal standpoint, apparently. But from an ideological point of view, not quite. Henry Floyd Brown, mastermind of the abortive bank robbery, was a more complex individual than it had at first seemed.

Before I was to have more than a vague inkling of this, my attention was diverted to some startling events in Redmond, Washington, a suburb of Seattle, exactly one week after the Metcalf State

Bank robbery. An eight-column banner headline across the top of the Seattle *Times* of January 26 summed it up this way:

"FBI SEIZES SEVEN IN PLOT TO BLOW UP REDMOND POLICE STATION, ROB FOUR BANKS."

The Associated Press and United Press-International picked it up at once, prompting such headlines as:

"RIGHTISTS SEIZED IN A ROBBERY PLOT" (New York *Times*)

"MINUTEMEN ARRESTED IN BIZARRE PLOT" (Dallas *Morning News*)

"SEVEN CAUGHT IN PLOT TO BLOW UP TOWN—MINUTEMEN CALLED CHIEF CONSPIRATOR" (Boston *Globe*)

"001-007 ARRESTED AT SEATTLE IN PLOT TO BLOW UP CITY HALL, ROB FOUR BANKS" (Arkansas *Gazette*)

Redmond, Washington, is a suburban community west of Seattle with a police force of eleven men and five women, including Chief Robert A. Sollitto. The story that led to these headlines began, as far as Chief Sollitto is concerned, on December 19, 1967, when the FBI informed him that perhaps as many as nine men in the Seattle area were planning to toss a hand grenade into the Redmond City Hall, in which the police headquarters is located, blow up a nearby power plant, and then proceed to rob three Redmond banks and perhaps a fourth bank in nearby Des Moines, Washington. The exact date of this was not yet known for certain, he was told.

The managers of the banks also were informed of these plans. Both the bank executives and police officers were instructed not to tell anyone in their families. Strict security was important.

Since a trial is pending in the case, details about what happened next are somewhat fragmentary. From news accounts out of Seattle and an interview with Chief Sollitto, however, this much is known:

An informant was involved. Whether he was a government infiltrator or a disenchanted member of the group is not known. Through the informant, authorities were kept apprised regularly of the changes that were frequently made in the alleged plans.

Twice they were told the action would begin on dates that were later changed.

On at least five occasions, including Christmas Day, one or more members of the group were followed around Redmond by policemen or FBI agents as they appeared to be making dry runs on City Hall, the banks, and the power plant.

Since the exact timing on the proposed activity was uncertain until the final days, police officers and bank executives alike suffered through many understandably nervous days.

Permission was sought from Ramsey Clark, U. S. Attorney General, to authorize the planting of an electronic listening device on the informant. Permission was granted. On the night of January 25, the informant attended a meeting of the group in a bowling alley in the Seattle area and obtained a recording of the step-by-step details of the activities that were scheduled to begin at ten-thirty the following morning.

Chief Sollitto was ready for them. He already had arranged with Washington state troopers to handle all traffic in Redmond that day and with the King County sheriff's office to take care of all other crimes, some of which, he reasoned, could be planned without his knowledge as diversionary in nature. This freed his small police force to man critical points in Redmond—the three banks, the City Hall (which was evacuated that day except for police personnel), and the power plant.

The police chief said that plans to throw a hand grenade into City Hall were abandoned at the last minute and instead the group had intended to set fire to a barn on the outskirts of town and blow up a power substation that was centrally located in the triangle formed by the banks.

At ten o'clock on the morning of January 26, the men—now down to seven in number—were located in two cars, one in a parking lot in Belleview, next to Redmond; the other in a parking lot in Lake City, a few miles from Redmond.

Chief Sollitto said their plan was to hit two of the Redmond banks simultaneously. The group that finished first was prepared to then rob the third bank there. Whether they actually had decided to proceed to Des Moines for a fourth bank robbery in one day is not known for certain, the chief said.

But before either car could leave the parking lot, FBI agents arrested the men inside them. Ranging in age from twenty to fifty-seven, they were identified by occupation as a longshoreman, a grocery clerk, a church maintenance man, a ship's oiler, a civilian driver for an Army base in Tacoma, a draftsman, and a thirty-five-year-old man identified as a full-time employee of the Minutemen organization.

Some of the other six, the FBI announced, also were members of the Minutemen. Each had a code number for the operation—001 through (yep) 007.

Inside the cars carrying these seven men were found numerous items that helped substantiate the charge of conspiracy to rob banks that was leveled against them:

Floor plans of City Hall and the banks, maps of the area, face masks and rubber gloves, sun glasses, a nylon stocking, cord, camouflage clothing, brass knuckles, a carbine, 10 Molotov cocktails, 9 sticks of dynamite, blasting caps, 400 rounds of ammunition.

Could the Minutemen affiliation of some of these Seattle area men have been incidental to their alleged plans for January 26? Or was this a new way to raise funds for the "counterrevolution"?

The Seattle newspapers had telephoned DePugh in Norborne about the case and had been told he had never heard of six of the men. As for the thirty-five-year-old man identified as a full-time Minutemen employee, DePugh said the man had been dropped from the Minutemen a year previous to then for nonpayment of dues.

When I talked with DePugh a few days later, he had changed his recollection of the thirty-five-year-old's history with the Minutemen. The Seattle press had remembered that this man had identified himself publicly as Washington state chairman of the Patriotic Party at a regional meeting of the party in Seattle in September, 1966. DePugh had appeared on the speaker's platform with him at the meeting.

DePugh told me the man had attended the party's first national convention in Kansas City in July, 1966, had then left the Minutemen to become state chairman of the party, but a few months ago had left the party.

"Could any of the other six be Minutemen without your knowing it?"

"It's possible."

DePugh also surprised me with the information that he had been in contact with an attorney for some of the men in trouble in Seattle in recent days.

"Why?" I asked.

"I'll probably be subpoenaed to appear before the federal grand jury up there," he replied. "It convenes February twentieth."

But he wasn't subpoenaed.

Instead, the grand jury indicted both DePugh and Wally Peyson, in addition to five of the seven men who originally had been arrested. The charge—conspiracy to rob banks.

As conspiracy indictments go, this one was unusually brief. Nowhere in it did the government reveal the kind of evidence it had to link DePugh or Peyson to the alleged conspiracy. Only one clue was offered. This was the date on which the conspiracy was alleged to have begun—August 20, 1967. At that time DePugh had been running the secret Minutemen training session in the Colorado mountains. Whether any of the Seattle area men also had been in Colorado then remained to be seen. Wally had been there at about that time.

A few days before the indictment was returned in Seattle, DePugh bade his wife goodbye at Kansas City's Municipal Air Terminal and flew west. He was seen in Seattle a day or two later by James Caplinger, attorney for one of the Seattle area men who had been arrested outside Redmond on January 26. As Caplinger later was to recall their conversation, he told DePugh he had a feeling DePugh would be needing a lawyer in Seattle soon. He said DePugh indicated he would want Caplinger to represent him if he were indicted and then left Caplinger's office.

As soon as the indictment was returned, the FBI set out quietly to look for both DePugh and Peyson. They could find neither. The indictment was kept secret for two weeks in an effort to make it easier to find the two men. Once it had become evident that both Minutemen knew they were wanted, it was made public and the search intensified.

Mrs. DePugh sounded worried when I telephoned her in Norborne on March 4, the day the indictment was made public. She had not heard from her husband since they parted at the airport, she said.

That night the Reverend LeRoy telephoned my home and left a message for me with my wife. He said he wished to be quoted to the effect that he could not believe that a "great American" such as Robert DePugh was guilty of such a crime.

Jerry Brooks telephoned from Spokane, Washington, the next day (collect, of course). He had tired of the quiet life in Anchorage, he said, and wanted to be back where the action was. Ostensible reason for his call: He said he thought he had seen DePugh a few days before then, eating in a skid row restaurant in Spokane. He had already notified George Arnett of the FBI, he said.

Caplinger, the Seattle attorney, expressed the belief that DePugh would surrender voluntarily once he had "put his house in order."

Mrs. DePugh wasn't so sure.

"I couldn't blame him if he just took out," she said. "He could think it was a plot rigged to get him."

On the same day that DePugh's and Peyson's indictments were made public, Ray Morgan, the *Star*'s Kansas correspondent, surprised me with the news that one of the reasons DePugh was being sought so strenuously was that authorities wanted to question him about Henry Brown and the Metcalf State Bank robbery. He suggested I sound out the Overland Park police department and the Johnson County attorney's office. I did, and was amazed at the results. It was all hearsay, of course, but still, there was a consistency to the bits and pieces that began to accumulate.

Item: According to James Bouska, the Johnson County attorney, Bonnie Wilane told Henry Brown's mother in Cedar Rapids on the day after the robbery that proceeds from the robbery had been intended for use in "recruiting an army to fight Communists." Mrs. Brown had told this to investigators on January 23, Bouska added. This tended to rule out the possibility that the Seattle affair, which occurred on January 26, might have given her the idea.

Item: Lieutenant John Patton of the Overland Park police department elaborated on Mrs. Brown's story of what Bonnie was supposed to have said the day after the robbery. While driving Mrs. Brown from Overland Park to Lansing to see her son, she had told him that Bonnie had told her the "army" Brown had planned to recruit was to have "run the Communists out of the United States and stopped the war in Vietnam." It seemed doubtful that Bonnie could have been frivolous in this story, since she tried to kill herself a few hours after supposedly telling it to Mrs. Brown.

Item: Lieutenant Patton also told of conversations he had had with Brown after the robbery. He said Brown had spoken at length about his desire to "fight the Socialists."

Item: The reader simply will have to take my word for this, because my two sources insist on remaining anonymous. A friend of Bonnie's who is afraid harm might come to her if her identity is made known, told me that before the robbery, Bonnie had told her that her new boy friend, Henry Brown, was a Minuteman.

This had come up in conversation, she said, when Bonnie showed her a pistol Brown had given her. Bonnie told her friend that he had taken her to a pistol range to teach her how to use it.

"I'd never heard of the Minutemen before," her friend said, "so I asked her what it was. She said it was a very patriotic, political organization that believed Americans ought to arm themselves against the Communists."

The other acquaintance who insists on anonymity quoted Bonnie after the robbery to the effect that there was nothing wrong with bank robberies because banks are federally insured and the federal government is run by Communists. Therefore, robbing a bank was the same as stealing from the Communists.

Item: Bouska also told of an interview authorities had had with a confederate of Brown and Gipson from Los Angeles. Interrogated after the Overland Park robbery, this Californian said Brown had sent him $1500 in December to use to purchase hand grenades for use in future bank robberies.

The Californian is now charged in a federal grand jury indictment along with Brown and Gipson for the Tower State Bank robbery in Kansas City, Kansas, on December 22, 1967. Over $15,000 was taken in that robbery.

Bouska quoted the Californian as also saying that Brown and some of his associates had planned to take advantage of racial disturbances and violence in large cities this coming summer.

"He said they had discussed waiting in a city while violence or demonstrations were in progress," Bouska said. "Then they would bomb the local police department, making it appear that the department was bombed by the demonstrators, and during the confusion, commit a bank robbery."

I immediately began efforts to interview Bonnie Wilane and Henry Brown at Lansing. Overland Park Police Captain Myron Scafe and Lieutenant Patton, knowing of my interest, decided they should go see Brown first. They returned from Lansing with the news that Brown had told them that "he was supposed to have met DePugh after the robbery," noting that they had received the impression that this meeting was to have occurred a few days afterward, not on the same day as the robbery. It was impossible to tell from Brown's story whether DePugh himself had known such a meeting was "supposed" to have taken place. But this wasn't all.

"Brown said he was going to discuss the political situation with DePugh," Captain Scafe said, "and if they couldn't get together and DePugh wouldn't go along with what he wanted, he'd have had DePugh killed, and take over the Minutemen organization himself."

The police officers said Brown had told them he was not a member of the Minutemen but was personally acquainted with "quite a few" persons who were.

The two police officers also had asked Brown about the scraps of paper he had tried to burn and flush down the toilet immediately before the gun battle. They wanted to know who the men were whose names, addresses and telephone numbers had been written on the paper, and why he had been so desperate to destroy the names.

"He said he couldn't talk about them," Captain Scafe said. "We asked him if they were right-wingers, and he replied that they were."

In the meantime, I had obtained these names and asked James Flansburg of the Des Moines (Iowa) *Register and Tribune* whether he would have time to check out those who were from Iowa to see if they had anything in common.

He reported back that one of the Iowans had run for Congress in a Republican primary many years ago, but that other than that, he had been able to find no right-wing connections. He had found a common denominator for ten of the eleven, however, indicating that the men might have been enemies rather than friends of Brown.

Of these ten Iowans, five were businessmen, three were lawyers and two were accountants. The five businessmen had been stockholders in a company headed by a relative of Brown. The company suddenly ran out of money and the five stockholders filed suit to force the company into receivership and Brown's relative into resigning as president. The three lawyers had been involved in this suit and the two accountants had given testimony supporting the charges against Brown's relative.

All of which, while still mysterious, shot holes in my tentative theory that these men might have been backers of Brown in some wild, right-wing plot.

I went to Lansing in April to talk with Bonnie Wilane, but she refused even to see me. Meanwhile, Brown had sent word back to me through his attorney that he would not talk with me either. He did grant an interview, however, to Tom Leathers, editor and publisher of the Squire Publishers, Inc., which puts out several well-written weeklies in suburban Kansas City.

Leathers had been a defense witness at a hearing prior to Brown's sentencing because of some photographs he had taken outside Brown's apartment during the gun battle. He had been able to show that Brown apparently had been firing at random out his apartment window rather than at any specific person when one of his bullets struck Sergeant Eldon Miller. Since this testimony helped save Brown from Kansas' hangman, Brown felt indebted to Leathers.

Leathers' interview was as his headline described it, "startling."

"First off, I'm not a part of the Minutemen," Brown told Leathers. "Apparently someone's trying to tie me in with them because that big Seattle bank robbery happened just after mine. And both jobs looked alike. I understand they're after Robert DePugh for the Seattle one—but I don't know DePugh or anyone else connected with the Seattle bank hold-up. DePugh and I think a lot alike, but that's as far as it goes."

Leathers reported in his copyright article that Brown had known several Minutemen when he was a prisoner at Leavenworth.*

"Captain Myron Scafe and another Overland Park policeman were up here the other day trying to get me to talk about the Minutemen—but I didn't have anything to tell," Brown continued.

The interview went deeply into Brown's professed desire to start his own revolution that would bring a new government to the United States. George Wallace appeared to him to be "probably the best" of the politicians he had seen who might lead this new government he sought, although Brown added, "but he's quite radical, and I'm not a racist."

Leathers wrote that Brown spoke of "a lot of businessmen" who would have supported him if he could have gotten an organization started. The organization he envisioned would have consisted of twenty

---

* My query to the warden at Leavenworth as to whether Brown might have been recruited into the Minutemen sometime while an inmate there between 1958 until 1967 brought assurances that the Minutemen were not recruiting any convicts at Leavenworth. Asked specifically about the Rev. Johnny Bob Harrell, who had been transferred from Terre Haute to Leavenworth after recruiting Ed Bumgardner into the Minutemen, according to Bumgardner, the warden said that Harrell kept to himself, was very religious and was recruiting no one.

or twenty-five persons working in small cells in various cities, able to cause "havoc in the U.S.," he said.

"I didn't figure it was wrong to commit a bank robbery because bank funds are insured by the national government," he was also quoted as saying. "No little man's going to get hurt by it—only the federal government, and that doesn't count."

Because Brown has paid few if any taxes in his life, he may have been unaware how the government obtains the money it uses to pay back losses from bank robberies.

Although Brown had quite a bit to say about international affairs, it was his view of domestic issues that were the most astonishing. Said the convict who had been living off the government in prison nearly all his adult life, and who had lived primarily off stolen money in the brief periods he had been free:

"I feel people should earn what they get. I don't believe in the socialistic programs we've been following. The government has no right to give away everything. Free enterprise made us great and it must continue to do so if we are to remain strong."

Leathers also reported that Brown had hoped for a bloodless revolution but that his "partners," whoever they might be, had told him someone would have to die.

"I know it sounds a lot like the Minutemen," he said, "but we're not quite as radical and don't go to the extremes that they do. We (we?) believe in the rights of the individual—whether he's white or black. . . ."

Such as the right to rob banks with your girl friend and kill Kansas state troopers, apparently. Ah, patriotism.

Robert Bolivar DePugh, meanwhile, had vanished. So had Wally Peyson. Henry Floyd Brown, if he had ever been of any concern to DePugh, was hardly worth his worrying about now.

I remembered DePugh's seemingly facetious promise that if he ever "went underground," he would do so publicly and that I would be the first to know.

On March 18, nearly a month since he had last been seen by anyone who would admit it, DePugh proved to be a man of his word. I was at least among the first to know.

An envelope mailed in Kansas City arrived for me that day bearing a brief, personal letter and a new Minutemen "bulletin." The note appeared to be in DePugh's handwriting.

"I don't suggest you wait till they catch me to get your book on the market. Better make this letter the beginning of volume two."

It was signed: "Yours for the revolution, Bob DePugh."

The letterhead on the stationery bore a drawing of a musket-carrying Minuteman from Revolutionary War days and the words: "Minutemen Underground Headquarters."

The bulletin, which I later learned had been mailed to other news media and numerous Minutemen members from various cities over the country, was titled "Underground News Bulletin No. 1." It too apparently had been prepared by DePugh.

"For the past month," it began, "Walter Peyson and I have been hunted by the Federal Bureau of Investigation. The supposedly legal government of the United States has declared that we are fugitives from justice. The fact is that we are fugitives from injustice.

"We are fugitives, not because we made machine guns, or robbed banks or kidnaped little girls. We are fugitives because we dared openly to oppose those traitors in our government who have destroyed our constitutional Republic and are rapidly replacing it with a bureaucratic dictatorship. We are not criminals—we are political refugees in our own land. . . ."

After professing his and Wally's innocence of the bank robbery conspiracy charge, the bulletin continued:

"There is a point beyond which no man can be pushed and still maintain self-respect. Walter Peyson and I have reached that point. We no longer choose to submit docilely to this kind of legal persecution. Neither do we intend to crawl into some hole and hide. We will defend ourselves and what we believe in by other tactics. . . .

"Unlike our soldiers in Vietnam, the Minutemen are not shackled by the government's 'no-win' policy. We have our own strategy—our 'Blueprint for Victory' . . ."

You damn fool, DePugh, I wanted to tell him, but could not. Whether he honestly did feel some "plot" had been devised to put him behind bars, or whether this was part of some long-range plan of continuing melodrama (the "principle of provocation" maybe?) DePugh was now playing an exceedingly dangerous game.

Soon "WANTED BY THE FBI" circulars were sent out to law-enforcement agencies and post offices all over the country with De-

Pugh's and Peyson's pictures, fingerprints, and physical descriptions on them. DePugh's circular unexplainably contained no mention of the Minutemen, listing his occupation instead as "chemist, draftsman." It did offer this warning, however:

"CAUTION: DePugh reportedly carries a pistol and has access to other types of weapons, including hand grenades. Considered extremely dangerous."

EPILOGUE

"When are you going to start shooting?" I asked Troy Houghton, half seriously, as we sipped coffee in a Springfield, Missouri, restaurant in May, 1967, a few days before his "disappearance."

"If Bob goes to jail," Houghton replied, drawing a line across the table top with his right forefinger, "there's people who say *that's* the line."

"Who's going to get shot?" I asked, having no idea whether he was in earnest.

"I've assigned names of certain people to certain people."

"How many to how many?"

"A medium, three-figure amount."

"And who are the intended victims?"

"All have admitted being Communists or have been identified as Communists by the government."

"The names you've assigned people—is this for killing, assassination?"

The California Minutemen leader pondered this for a few moments, then replied emphatically:

"For execution—in the event of a Communist overthrow of our government."

Whether I was supposed to equate his concept of a Communist "overthrow" of the government with DePugh's possible imprisonment was left to my conjecture.

How should one evaluate such talk? And is that all it is—talk? Is DePugh "brilliant . . . dedicated," as his wife told me in March, 1968, after more than seven years of living and breathing Minutemen while trying to raise six children and help run the Biolab Corporation simultaneously? Are the Minutemen members of a "terrorist organization," as Roy Frankhouser said? Are Minutemen "strike teams" at the ready now, waiting to avenge the assassination of their leader? Are they now taking up bank robberies, as a federal grand jury seems to think? Was Jerry Brooks right when he told of a heavily armed camp high in the Rockies from which the Minutemen will make their "last stand"? Should liberals really beware for fear of a Minuteman's cross hairs on the backs of their necks?

American history is filled with examples of small, militant, off-beat organizations. Most of them existed only briefly, becoming merely footnotes to the history of their times. A few have become movements and grew to great size and influence.

The Minutemen are more a frame of mind than an organization or movement. They also are a microcosm of a fearful and fatalistic attitude that finds nourishment in ultraconservative thought. This frame of mind enables them to put faith in nothing but their own conviction that disaster is virtually inevitable, that America is being led irreversibly into totalitarian, Communist control. Angered and bewildered, they blame everything—including their own personal inadequacies—on evil, outside forces. Frantically seeking some recourse, some avenue of escape, they twist their frustrations into the shape of what they feel is a virile, hairy-chested patriotism, violent anti-Communism and, in some cases, racial bigotry and anti-Semitism.

Their penchant for violent answers to troublesome questions is by no means peculiar to the Minutemen. It can be found in varied forms among other "extremist" groups of today. Equally self-debilitating idiosyncrasies are present in some of the violence-bent Far Left and riot-prone Negro organizations that have formed with a fresh sense of militancy in the last few years. The Minutemen have no monopoly on delusions, nor are they unique in their inclination to act out their hostilities in bizarre and destructive ways.

Some of the dangers to American society that the Minutemen and others of the Far Right fear are real enough, to be sure. Those who would close their eyes to the ambitions and evils of Communism are recklessly naïve. Yet anti-Communism can take many forms, some of them foolish, some realistic and worthwhile. The Minutemen and their ideological allies sneer at the fight for domestic progress and reform in such fields as poverty and civil rights, branding them "Socialistic" or "Communistic." Arming themselves against those who would push for such reform, they unwittingly align themselves with the Communists, who know that they can make little headway internally against a nation if it has earned the right to boast it has eliminated poverty and inequality among the races.

The reader has seen in these pages how the Minutemen as a frame of mind function and what some of the manifestations of their thinking have been to date. Being a secret organization, it has been impossible to learn yet all there is to know about it and its members. Probably some serious gaps exist in this book. Certainly, the Minutemen story is incomplete as of this writing. Members in the states of New York and Washington may still be awaiting trial as this is read. The whereabouts of DePugh, Peyson, and Houghton are, at this writing, unknown to me and apparently just about everyone else, including their families. The U. S. Court of Appeals in St. Louis upheld DePugh's conviction in Joplin, Missouri, in April 1968, and may have decided on the firearms-act convictions in Kansas City before this is in print, but too late for the decision to be included. And a few of the persons mentioned in these pages as dedicated members of the organization may have left it before the year is over.

Most aggravating is the very real possibility that some Minuteman, somewhere in the country, may soon wake up one depressingly overcast day, emerge from the wrong side of the bed in which he has tossed all night and decide, finally, that today is The Day.

Once having reached this decision, it is entirely possible that he will proceed to take a pot shot at someone or blow up a building or bridge or whatever else strikes his fancy—all in behalf of God, Country, and the Minutemen, "America's last line of defense."

Considering the inflammatory line fed members and the lack of discretion that Minutemen leaders have displayed in allowing unstable activists into the organization, it is surprising that such a tragedy has not already occurred. Conceivably it already has occurred, and we have not yet learned of the fact. The Minutemen's leadership has been toying irresponsibly with the high-strung emotions of its followers for several years now. It will be almost a miracle if this does not have tragic consequences to someone, somewhere, before the Minutemen become a footnote—or a chapter—in a history of this nervous decade.

As this book goes to press, the accused assassin of Dr. Martin Luther King is being brought back to the U.S. for trial. Two weeks after the assassination, the U. S. Attorney's office for western Missouri, in a motion to have DePugh's and Peyson's appeal removed from the court of appeals docket in St. Louis because they were fugitives, quoted an informant of "apparent reliability" to the effect that DePugh had issued orders to other Minutemen some time ago that if he went to jail, certain persons were to be assassinated. Among those on the assassination list, the D.A.'s office said, had been Dr. Martin Luther King.

Certainly, Minutemen rhetoric automatically places them on the suspect list for that crime, just as one might speculate that the Klan, some black activist group, or the Communists were behind it. Each group could well have felt a benefit from his death and the riots it sparked.

Probably a good-sized majority of those who have been attracted to the Minutemen never would go beyond the worry-and-talk stage of activism unless the President should do something like give Mississippi to Cuba, or if the Communists actually did storm our beaches or drop out of the skies on us. Even in the aftermath of nuclear attack, I imagine that this same majority of Minutemen would attempt to be helpful in restoring order among the survivors, no matter how ineptly they might go about it.

Still there are others who would not be willing to wait that long. And to distinguish the doers from the worriers among the Minutemen is a job that should be of concern to all levels of law enforcement that have reason to believe Minutemen are in their jurisdiction.

The Minutemen, at this writing, may not have yet reached the point at which they warrant outlawing as a group. Such repressive action—or declaring them subversive, as has been suggested by some —could do more harm than good. They do justify a stepped-up watchfulness by law enforcement, however. As good a job as the FBI and ATTU appear to have done so far in keeping tabs on the organization, the Minutemen are erratic, unpredictable and devious. By watchfulness, it should be added, I do not mean harassment. Not that the Minutemen would admit to recognizing the difference, but the police do.

The general public, meanwhile (if I may presume to advise) should take care neither to laugh off the Minutemen nor to overreact to them. Patience is required. And under the right set of circumstances, patience could have the most worthwhile effect.

I do not feel it naïve to think that a great many of those who today call themselves faithful, die-hard Minutemen will eventually realize that the course they are now taking is unrealistic, irresponsible, and self-defeating. With some, it will simply be a matter of maturing. With others, there may come a time sooner or later when they finally realize that rather than effectively fighting or holding back Communism, they are instead sowing seeds of distrust, fear and hate that weakens the United States against all of its enemies—Communism included.

I even hold out the faint hope that Robert DePugh eventually could emerge from the never-never land he has created for himself and redirect his energies and skills to help his country rather than undermine it. I cannot bring myself to look upon most of the Minutemen I have met—DePugh included—as evil men. DePugh's and Peyson's disappearances in open defiance of the federal charge against them—whether valid or not—was melodramatic, foolish, and extremely dangerous for both of them. But even that leaves me more with a feeling of sadness than anger.

Perhaps before the end of this decade, the Minutemen will have faded away, and I hope with apologies to one and all as they do. It is in a way remarkable that they have lasted this long, everything considered. But the Minutemen as a frame of mind, as a state of distrustful nervousness and misdirected, trigger-happy patriotism, will not fade so quickly. Not until we are a far more emotionally stable and wiser nation than we now are.

INDEX